How has light influenced the staging of theatre throughout history?

How does it make meaning?

This diverse collection explores the creative potential of light in the theatre. Through a range of extracts from historical accounts, new research and rare documents, Scott Palmer provides new ways of thinking about lighting as a creative performance practice. Focusing on elements such as

- the emergence of lighting design in the theatre
- equipment and techniques
- the dramaturgy of light
- its impact on actor, audience and playhouse
- the semiotics and phenomenology of light in performance

the book reveals why light has such a profound effect on the audience's experience of a theatrical event.

SCOTT PALMER is Lecturer in Scenography and Deputy Head of the School of Performance and Cultural Industries at the University of Leeds, UK. He is an executive member of the Association of Lighting Designers.

READINGS IN THEATRE PRACTICE

Series Editor: Simon Shepherd

At the heart of every performance lies a tension, a tension between the material object and the magical transformation of theatre. Taking elements of theatre such as sound, puppetry and directing, the series explores this relationship, offering both the vocabulary and the historical context for critical discussion and creative practice.

Published:

Ross Brown: Sound

Jon Davison: Clown

Penny Francis: Puppetry

Scott Palmer: Light

Simon Shepherd: Direction

Forthcoming:

Jane Boston: Voice

Alison Maclaurin and Aoife Monks: Costume

Joslin McKinney: Construction

Readings in Theatre Practice
Series Standing Order
ISBN 978–0230–53717–0 hardcover
ISBN 978–0230–53718–7 paperback
(*outside North America only*)

You can receive future titles in this series as they are published by placing a standing order. Please contact your bookseller or, in case of difficulty, write to us at the address below with your name and address, the title of the series and the ISBN quoted above.

Customer Services Department, Macmillan Distribution Ltd
Houndmills, Basingstoke, Hampshire RG21 6XS, England

Light

Readings in Theatre Practice

Scott Palmer

First published 2013 by
PALGRAVE MACMILLAN

Palgrave Macmillan in the UK is an imprint of Macmillan Publishers Limited,
registered in England, company number 785998, of Houndmills, Basingstoke,
Hampshire RG21 6XS.

Palgrave Macmillan in the US is a division of St Martin's Press LLC,
175 Fifth Avenue, New York, NY 10010.

Palgrave Macmillan is the global academic imprint of the above companies
and has companies and representatives throughout the world.

Palgrave® and Macmillan® are registered trademarks in the United States,
the United Kingdom, Europe and other countries.

ISBN 978–0–230–55189–3 hardback
ISBN 978–0–230–55190–9 paperback

This book is printed on paper suitable for recycling and made from fully
managed and sustained forest sources. Logging, pulping and manufacturing
processes are expected to conform to the environmental regulations of the
country of origin.

A catalogue record for this book is available from the British Library.

Library of Congress Cataloging-in-Publication Data
Palmer, Scott.
    Light / Scott Palmer.
        p.   cm. — (Readings in theatre practice)
    Includes bibliographical references and index.
    ISBN 978–0–230–55190–9
    1. Stage lighting—History.   2. Theaters—Lighting.   I. Title.
    PN2091.E4P355 2013
    792.02′5—dc23   2012032195

This book is dedicated to Tanya, Alexander, Max, Oliver and Eliza – as is its author.

Contents

Illustrations

Acknowledgements

I would like to thank all of my colleagues in the School of Performance & Cultural Industries at the University of Leeds who have supported me throughout the considerable period of researching and writing this book. I am particularly indebted to Sita Popat, Joslin McKinney, Christopher Baugh and colleagues in the Performance Technologies Research group at Leeds for their unstinting encouragement throughout this process.

I am grateful to Simon Shepherd for his insight, feedback and guidance, and to Kate Haines, Felicity Noble and Jenni Burnell at Palgrave for their trust and patience.

I would like to thank the following for their assistance in producing this volume: Alan Clarke, Stephen Di Benedetto, Melissa Trimingham, Chris van Goethem, Rick Fisher, Paule Constable, John Steele, Graeme Gooday, Susan Daniels, Mick Wallis, David Shearing, George Rodosthenous, Rachel Hann, Dorita Hannah, Quentin Scott, Kate Boothby and Simone Gfeller from the Swiss Theatre Collection Berne.

I would like also to acknowledge members of the international scenography research community, creative collaborators, lighting educators, fellow practitioners in the Association of Lighting Designers, and past and present students who have contributed immeasurably to my evolving understanding of performance lighting practices. Finally I also need to thank my family for their understanding and tolerance during the writing of this volume, and my parents, David and Pat, for supporting me through my education and early interest in stage lighting.

The authors and publishers wish to thank the following for permission to use copyright material:

Cambridge University Press and Arthur Holmberg for extracts from Holmberg: *The Theatre of Robert Wilson*, © 1996. Reproduced by permission of Cambridge University Press; David Higham Associates Ltd for extracts from Meyer (trans.): *Strindberg Plays 1*, © 1980, Bloomsbury; Edinburgh University Press for extracts from Mumford: 'Lighting Dance', from *The Journal of the Society for Dance Research*, 3(2) (summer 1985); Indiana University Press for extracts from Fischer-Lichte: *The Semiotics of Theater*, translated by Jeremy Gaines and Doris L. Jones, © 1992. Reproduced by permission of Indiana University Press; Mark Henderson for edited extracts from an interview with the author in 2000; Nick Hunt for 'The Virtuosity of the Lighting Artist: Designer or Performer?', © Nick Hunt; Orion Books for extracts from Stern: *My Life My Stage*, © 1951, Victor Gollancz Ltd; Paula Constable and

Nick Hunt for edited extracts from an interview with Nick Hunt in 2008; Pickering & Chatto Publishers for extracts from Gooday: *Domesticating Electricity: Technology, Uncertainty and Gender 1880–1914*, © 2008. Reproduced by permission of Pickering & Chatto; ProQuest Historical Newspapers *The New York Times* (1851–2006) for review of 'La Loie and Her Dances' in *The New York Times* (1896); Randall Bytwerk for the extract from 'The Oath Under the Cathedral of Light at the 1936 Nuremberg Party Rally', R. Bytwerk (trans.), from http://www.calvin.edu/academic/cas/gpa/pt36dom.htm; Rick Fisher for edited extracts from interviews with Nick Hunt in 2007 and further conversations with the author in 2009; Taylor & Francis for extracts from Patterson: *The Revolution in German Theatre*, © 1981, Routledge & Kegan Paul. Reproduced by permission of Taylor & Francis Books UK; The University of Michigan Press for extracts from Pavis: *Analyzing Performance: Theater, Dance and Film*, David Williams (trans.), © 2003, The University of Michigan Press; University of Miami Press and Copyright Clearance Center Inc. for extracts from Hewitt: *The Renaissance Stage: Documents of Serlio, Sabbattini and Furttenbach*, © 1958, University of Miami Press; The Swiss Theatre Collection Berne for 'Walkyrie 1892 Act III' and 'Orpheus and Euridike, 1926' by Adolphe Appia; Sarka Hejnova for 'Hamlet', 1959 'The Owner of the Keys', 1962, 'Oedipus', 1963 and 'Tristan & Isolde', 1967 (Designs by Josef Svoboda); The Victoria and Albert Museum for 'How the Stage is Lighted' by Louis Gunnis, 1896; Christopher Megginson for 'McCandless' Acting Area diagram' 2012; Georges Bacoust for 'A Midsummer Night's Dream' 2007; Robert Day for 'An Inspector Calls' 2009.

Every effort has been made to trace the copyright holders but, if any have been inadvertently overlooked, the authors and publishers will be pleased to make the necessary arrangements at the first opportunity.

Series Preface

This series aims to gather together both key historical texts and contemporary ways of thinking about the material crafts and practices of theatre.

These crafts work with the physical materials of theatre – sound, objects, light, paint, fabric, and – yes – physical bodies. Out of these materials the theatre event is created.

In gathering the key texts of a craft it becomes very obvious that the craft is not simply a handling of materials, however skilful. It is also a way of thinking about both the materials and their processes of handling. Work with sound and objects, for example, involves – always, at some level – concepts of what sound is and does, what an object is and does . . . what a body is.

For many areas of theatre practice there are the sorts of 'how to do it' books that have been published for at least a century. These range widely in quality and interest but next to none of them is able to, or wants to, position the *doing* in relation to the *thinking about doing* or the thinking about the material being used.

This series of books aims to promote both thinking about doing and thinking about materials. Its authors are specialists in their field of practice and they are charged to reflect on their specialism and its history in order, often for the first time, to model concepts and provide the tools not just for the doing but for thinking about theatre practice.

The series title 'Readings in Theatre Practice' uses the word 'reading' in the sense both of a simple understanding or interpretation and of an authoritative explication, an exegesis as it were. Thus, the books first gather together people's opinions about, their understanding of, what they think they are making. These opinions are then framed within a broader narrative which offers an explanatory overview of the practice under investigation.

So, although the books comprise many different voices, there is a dominant authorial voice organising the material and articulating overarching arguments. By way of promoting a further level of critique and reflection, however, authors are asked to include a few lengthy sections, in the form of interviews or essays or both, in order to make space for other voices to develop their own overviews. These may sit in tension, or indeed in harmony, with the dominant narratives.

Authors are encouraged to be sceptical about normative assumptions and canonical orthodoxy. They are asked not to ignore practices and thinking that might question dominant views; they are invited to speculate as to how canons and norms come into being and what effects they have.

We hope the shape provides a dynamic tension in which the different activities of 'reading' both assist and resist each other. The details of the lived practices refuse to fit tidily into the straitjacket of a general argument, but the dominant overview also refuses to allow itself to fragment into local prejudice and anecdote. And it's that restless play between assistance and resistance that mirrors the character of the practices themselves.

At the heart of each craft is a tense relationship. On the one hand there is the basic raw material that is worked – the wood, the light, the paint, the musculature. These have their own given identity – their weight, mechanical logics, smell, particle formation, feel. In short, the texture of the stuff. And on the other hand there is theatre, wanting its effects and illusions, its distortions and impossibilities. The raw material resists the theatre as much as yields to it, the theatre both develops the material and learns from it. The stuff and the magic. This relationship is perhaps what defines the very activity of theatre itself.

It is this relationship, the thing which defines the practice of theatre, which lies at the heart of each book in this series.

Simon Shepherd

Introduction: Light and Performance

This book is about the relationship between light and performance. It focuses on the way in which light is used as a fundamental aspect of dramatic presentation and attempts to provide new perspectives in thinking about lighting as a creative performance practice.

In order to examine the phenomenal impact of light on performance (in all senses of this word), this collection draws together historical writings, eyewitness accounts and contemporary commentaries from key practitioners and academics to chart the emergence of light as a creative element in the theatrical event. The selection of this material, including writing never before published in the English language, positions this text apart from other books concerned with lighting in performance, the majority of which focus primarily on the practical and technical aspects of using light and the range of equipment and methodologies for arranging light for the stage.[1] This volume seeks to explore ways of thinking about light in performance and to focus on ways in which light has been employed as a dynamic force in a variety of Western performance practices since the Renaissance.

This reader addresses a range of perspectives on light in performance, from the variety of techniques that have been employed and how these directly affected the audience experience, to how light might contribute dramaturgically and how it can be read and understood by an audience. It traces a series of lineages that link together a number of key practitioners who have explored ideas relating to the creative realisation of light in performance. It is not therefore a text that focuses on the technical methods of how light should be created for the stage and neither does it attempt to provide a chronological account of the history of stage lighting. For this, readers are advised to consult Gösta Bergman's seminal *Lighting in the Theatre*.

Light in this text refers to the material substance harnessed for dramatic use, enabling visibility in the stage space and contributing to an audience's experience of the event. Light raises issues not only of what is seen but also how we look:

> Light shapes what we see, it directs our attention, determining what is noticeable and what is hidden. It offers a simple way of making both large, dramatic changes, and small subtle changes in a performance landscape. The play of light

---

[1] Many of these key handbooks are discussed in Chapter 10.

can emphasise form or dissolve shape and solidity, creating ambiguities of depth and scale.

(Tufnell and Crickmay, 1990: 170)

The term 'lighting', in contrast, refers to the technical systems and processes employed to create light on the stage. Lighting is the culmination of those processes and techniques, experienced by the audience as a series of lighting 'states' or cues. Indeed, it is often the lighting that establishes the beginning of the performance, marks its divisions and frequently signals its conclusion through the convention of a fade-down, blackout and/or the switching on of auditorium house lights, for example.

The awareness and acknowledgement of light as a contributing and creative element in the theatre led to the evolution and emergence in the twentieth century of the specialist position of the lighting designer, although it should be noted that in many parts of the world the role is still emerging and not defined in this way. The lighting designer is responsible for shaping and controlling the light and therefore determining what we see in performance and how we see it. This book attempts to investigate the ways in which light contributes to the creation, perception and overall experience of the theatrical event.

In examining historical experimentations with light in performance, this volume examines lighting practices prior to the formalisation of the role of the lighting designer, where the control of light was often undertaken by unnamed individuals contributing as part of a technical or design team and working to the instructions of a director or producer. It is important to acknowledge the contribution of these many, often unrecorded and therefore unknown, technicians whose work and innovations are usually attributed to the director of the production (and the role's historical antecedents). This book engages with, for example, Henry Irving's use of light and Max Reinhardt's lighting techniques, but without always being able to acknowledge the contribution of the individual technicians whose creative work allowed the lighting innovations and ideas to be developed and realised in performance. It is therefore important here to formally acknowledge the unheralded but essential contribution of the lighting technician to the evolution of both the craft and the art of lighting for the stage.

Bergman argues that 'Theatre history research has so far paid only casual attention to the problem of light, [...] and the co-creative, artistic part played by light in the performances' (1977:11). This reader attempts to redress this imbalance through its selection of historical evidence and contemporary reflections on light – this ephemeral, seemingly intangible substance that we do not yet fully understand in scientific terms, but which affects our perception of the performance event so fundamentally.

However, unlike the playwright's script and other aspects of theatrical production, the lighting design is lost forever as soon as the performance is over. Whilst the impossibility of capturing the nature of theatrical lighting in a static image has long been recognised, it is important to reflect on the paucity of visual documentation that provides even basic evidence of the lighting designer's creative contribution to performance. This is not only a historical matter but continues to be an issue in contemporary practice where production photographs are primarily for publicity purposes and focus almost exclusively on the performers in close-up. The longstanding absence of appropriate visual evidence therefore has undoubtedly contributed to the recognition and current status of the lighting designer's role in professional practice and acknowledgement within academic discourse.

Writing about light is in itself problematic and may explain the relative lack of published material that focuses specifically on light as a creative element of performance. How can we make sense of the way light works and describe the impression it makes on us through its temporal transitions? How can we convey the fleeting theatrical moment or describe the phenomenological impact that light has on its audience? And how can we hope to capture this essence on the page?

It is hoped that this book will begin to provide some answers to these questions and, through focusing on specific practices, provide a valuable resource to a range of scholars and professional practitioners concerned with light, lighting education and the broader study of theatre and performance.

Chapter 1

The Evolution of Lighting Design

This chapter looks at the innovations in the use of light in performance during the Renaissance period. What is significant about this period is that it is possible to identify it as the first time when light was used coherently as an integral aspect of the staging of performance events and that the creative potential of light to performance was acknowledged for the first time.

Significant evidence is provided through contemporary accounts from audience members who witnessed performances and detailed written documentation that describe the first systematic approaches to lighting the stage.

Many of these accounts are by architects who were responsible for designing and coordinating these events. The complexities inherent in staging lavish performance spectacles, and the way in which light was used as an integral aspect of Renaissance scenography in Italy, are fundamental to the development of all future performance lighting design principles and practice. For this reason it is important to understand both the way in which light was used in performance by a number of early lighting designers and the way in which this use of light contributed directly to the evolution of the art form itself.

This chapter describes the work of these key figures and give examples of some of the staged events in which lighting played an essential part. These first-hand accounts explain the techniques and principles of early lighting practice and record the discoveries made in using light in performance. These treatises, by artists who were seeking to solve the staging issues arising from a new style of performance, form the first known documents that focus on lighting design for performance. They provide substantial evidence to suggest that Italy is the birthplace of creative lighting for the stage.

LIGHT IN THE ITALIAN COURT THEATRE

This section concentrates on the developments of the Italian playhouse, its perspective settings and the methods suggested for lighting these scenes. It focuses on the work of key architects who designed both the new theatre spaces and the performances staged within them. Their writings reveal how key lighting principles for performance were established and detail the first instruments developed specifically for lighting the stage. Methods of lighting are proposed for both the newly developed scenic stage and for illuminating performers. Lighting positions within the theatre are discussed, and the first accounts of the darkening of the auditorium and the dimming of stage lights during the performance are revealed.

THE PERSPECTIVE SCENE

In order to understand the way in which light was used on the Renaissance stage, it is important to understand the scenic conventions that were established during this period. Theatrical presentation and performance design underwent radical change in the period following the discovery of linear perspective and the rediscovery of the classic text *De architectura*, written by the Roman architect Vitruvius. The link between fine art and architecture was to have a profound influence on the development of the scenic stage. In the fifteenth and sixteenth centuries, artists were employed by Italian courts to produce paintings and sculpture. Following in the footsteps of Brunelleschi, (see Chapter 2) many of these master painters were also commissioned as architects as they had acquired a sophisticated range of skills encompassing engineering and geometry. Their achievements in the design and construction of buildings, often with overtly theatrical facades, led logically to these architects and artists also being employed as theatrical designers. They were commissioned not only to create a theatrical space and auditorium, often within an existing room at court, but also to design the stage environment and the conditions for viewing it. Architects understood that light was not only important to the way a building was perceived but also an essential component in the way that performance was experienced.

During the early sixteenth century the link between perspective painting and the theatrical backdrop was firmly established and was exemplified in the work of designers such as Pellegrino, Genga and Peruzzi, who provided the catalyst for the evolution of a new theatrical form that employed semi-permanent, three-dimensional perspective scenes. These scenic stages, constructed in relief, required new approaches to lighting in order to complete the visual illusion. A number of these architects therefore sought to quantify the theories and practices of this new staging by publishing rules for the design, construction and lighting of these new perspective scenes.

Pellegrino da San Daniele[1] (1467–1547), a master painter and architect, was employed by the court at Ferrara in the role of theatre designer. He is credited with the first perspectival backdrop for a performance of Ariosto's *La Cassaria* in 1508 and although there appears to be no evidence for how this may have been lit, this new approach to scenic design seems to have inspired

---

[1] Also known as Martino of Udine.

Girolamo Genga's (1476–1551) production of Bibbiena's *La Calandria* in Urbino[2]. The city setting is described in a letter by Baldassarre Castiglione as being lit by chandeliers and including a richly coloured eight-sided temple adorned with precious glass jewels. This effect would seem to indicate the backlighting of a built set piece rather than a painted representation and would probably have used coloured glass and *bozze* to create the jewelled lighting effect.[3] There are no surviving drawings of Genga's work, and he is therefore rarely referred to in the evolution of theatrical practice, but his contribution may have been significant because both the opulence of his settings and his great skill as a theatrical designer were praised prominently by both Serlio and Vasari in their writings.

Giorgio Vasari's *Lives of the Artists* is the most important source in describing sixteenth-century theatrical activity in Florence and provides a historical overview and account of earlier spectacles and celebrations. It is from these descriptions that the significance of both Genga and Peruzzi to the evolution of stage and lighting design practices can be ascertained, as lighting effects were clearly integral to the visual impact of their stagecraft. **Baldassare Peruzzi's** (1481–1536) stage design for *La Calandria* introduced the built perspective scene to Rome when it was staged in the Vatican in 1514. Vasari records the importance of the inner light within the scene itself (rather than external illumination) to enhancing the illusion of perspective:

> Nor is it possible to imagine how he found room, in a space so limited, for so many streets, so many palaces, and so many bizarre temples [...] all so well executed that it seemed that they were not counterfeited, but absolutely real, and that the piazza was not a little thing, and merely painted, but real and very large. He designed also, the chandeliers and the lights within that illuminated scene, and all the other things that were necessary, with much judgment [...] This kind of spectacle, in my belief, when it has all its accessories, surpasses any other kind, however sumptuous and magnificent.
>
> (Vasari, Vol. 1. 1912: 814)

Bastiano da Sangallo (1481–1551) trained as a painter of frescoes but specialised as a theatre designer for the Medici dukes in Florence. For Landi's play *Commodo* in 1539 he drew inspiration from Peruzzi's stage design work in Rome by also creating a 'solar light' that travelled against a blue 'sky'. This representation of the sun was created by filling a large crystal sphere with water, and lighting it from behind with candles. The moving light source travelled above the rear of the perspective scene, appearing to rise at the beginning of the play, move across the sky and then set at the ending of the drama.[4]

---

[2] Performed on 6 February 1513.
[3] This technique is described later by both Serlio and Vasari.
[4] See Zorzi and Sperenzi (2001: 145).

The most important contribution to Renaissance staging practice and the first discussion of lighting techniques for the theatre was published in 1545 by a pupil of Peruzzi, **Sebastiano Serlio** (1475–1554). His *Libri d'architettura* established a personal discourse on architectural practice and in the second book he discusses the requirements for the staging of performances in terms of the theatre building, the scenic stage and the necessary lighting techniques, to which he devotes an entire chapter. Serlio developed Peruzzi's ideas in relation to his own practical experience of building theatres and staging drama in Vicenza during the 1530s. Book II of *De Architettura* marks the first extensive account of theatrical techniques since Vitruvius, whose theories Serlio marries with his own staging practice to create a clear manifesto of design for the stage. The publication in Paris in both Italian and French was followed by many translations into other European languages, which ensured a widespread dissemination of the lighting design techniques that had been forged in Italian city-states at this time.[5]

Although Serlio's text borrows heavily on the theories and practices of earlier architects and designers, this publication cannot be underestimated in terms of the impact that it had on the evolution of staging practices and the development of lighting design. The perspective scene was to dominate theatre practice until the twentieth century, and this text marks the first attempt to produce a detailed methodology for the lighting of the stage.

Following Vitruvius' ideals, Serlio advocates three settings for performance, one each for comedy, tragedy and satirical plays. However, these were designed as separate generic perspective scenes – a single constructed pictorial backdrop for the *whole* action of the play. These scenic views were built on a raked picture stage and situated behind a wide, flat forestage. The performers used only the narrow, wide forestage and did not enter this rear scenic stage. To enhance the illusion of perspective, these settings were designed and painted with shadows to look as if they were lit from one direction only. Serlio was aware of the contradiction between this effect and the general frontal illumination that he describes in detail.

Serlio suggests that general light in the form of a central chandelier is provided for the illumination of the entire stage picture, whilst to supplement this 'a large number of candles are placed at the front of the scene'. This suggestion of an overhead fill light coupled with early footlights indicates that a technique has already been established that was to dominate theatre lighting for the next 400 years.

In addition to the general light from the front and above, Serlio suggests that visual interest in the scenic stage itself should be achieved through decorative lighting from behind the scenic pieces:

---

[5] There were nearly 60 editions in seven languages by 1619. First published in both Italian and French in Paris (1545), translated into Flemish (1553), Dutch (1606), German (1608) and English from an inaccurate Dutch translation in 1611.The English edition cited below was published in 1657 and was also translated from a Dutch version.

Among all the things that may be made by mens hands, thereby to yield admiration, pleasure to sight, and to content the fantasies of man; I think is placing
of a Scene, as it is shewed to your sight, where a man in a small place may see
[...] a thousand faire things and Buildings, adorned with innumerable lights great,
middle sort, and small, [...] which are so cunningly set out, that they shew forth
and represent a number of the brightest stones, as Diamonds, Rubies, Saphirs,
Smaragdes, Jacinths, and such like. There you may see the bright shining Moon
ascending onely with her hornes, and already risen up, before the Spectators are
aware of, or once saw it ascend. In some other Scenes you may see the rising of
the Sun with his course about the world, and at the ending of the Comedy, you
may see it goe down most artificially, whereat many beholders have been abasht.[6]

(Serlio [1545] 1657: 23)

This is the first reference we have to back and side-lighting, although these
angles of light are suggested for the lighting of the setting rather than for the
performers.

Serlio identifies a third category of lighting which he terms 'mobile light'
and represents the visible point source on stage – the physical simulation
of celestial objects moving across the sky, in the way that Brunelleschi and
Peruzzi had employed earlier. The passing of the sun or moon was important
for delineating the passage of time within the drama, and the creation of
an 'artificial day' was often essential to preserve the dramatic and temporal
unity.

We understand the way in which lighting techniques had evolved during the Renaissance period because Serlio describes where to place lighting
instruments and how to create specific effects such as lightning. The *bozze*
that Serlio identifies were glass vessels in both concave and convex forms that
could be used to hold oil and a wick to provide a lighting source, or alternatively were filled with coloured liquid and used in front of light sources fixed
on boards behind the perspective scene to create coloured light. In this passage, Serlio notes the practical concerns about fixing these properly so that
they are not dislodged by the dancers.

Serlio also describes the placing of a polished barber's basin to act as
a reflector behind the glass sphere which, in turn, becomes a crude lens.
Together these materials created an early prototype of the spotlight and
particularly interesting is that this instrument was used to create a type of
keylight – 'a great light to shew more than the rest' – and this is the first indication of the artistic need for a differentiation of intensity between lighting
sources.

The *bozze* were the first dedicated theatre lighting instruments and Serlio
provides recipes for tinting liquids to achieve specific colours, although it

---

[6] A modern translation of the last section of this text might read: The horned moon rises slowly –
so slowly that the spectators have not been aware of any movement. In other scenes the sun
rises, moves on its course, and at the end of the play is made to set with such skill that many
spectators remain lost in wonder.

was discovered that this technique reduced the intensity of the light and therefore tended to be reserved for special scenic effects, such as creating the jewelled windows of street scenes. For pastoral scenes (where there were no windows on stage), coloured silks were backlit instead to create variations in coloured light. Bergman (1977: 59–60) argues that these decorative lighting techniques that created a gleaming, jewelled stage were a natural development of mediaeval traditions of using precious stones, and the effect was a theatrical equivalent of the stained glass window.

Serlio – Of the Artificiall Lighting of the Scene (1545)

I Promised in the Treatise of Scenes to set down the manner of how to make these lights shining through, of divers colours [. . .]

The manner to set these shining colours in their places is thus, Behind the painted house wherein these painted colours shall stand, you must set a thin board cut out in the same manner that these lights shall be placed, whether it be round or square, cornered or ovale, like an Egge; and behinde the same board there shall be another stronger board lay flat behind them, for the bottles and other manner of glasses with these waters to stand in, must be placed against the holes, as it shall necessarily fall out, but they must be set fast, lest they fall with leaping and dancing of the Moriscoes. And behind the glasses you must set great Lamps, that the light may also be stedfast; and if the bottels or other vessels of glasse on the side where the light stands were flat or rather hollow, it would rather shew the clearer, and the colours most excellent and faire; the like must be done with the holes on the shortning side: But if you need a great light to shew more then the rest, then set a torch behind, and behind the torch a bright Bason, the brightnesse whereof will shew like the beams of the Sun. You may also make glasse of all colours and formes, some fouresquare, some with crosses, and any other forme with their light behind them. Now all the lights serving for the colours, shall not be the same which must light the Scene, for you must have a great number of torches before the Scene. You may also place certaine candlesticks above the Scene with great Candles therein, and above the Candlesticks you may place some vessells with water, wherein you may put a piece of Camphir, which burning will shew a very good light and smell well. Sometime it may chance that you must make something or other which should seem to burn, which you must wet thoroughly with excellent good Aquavite and setting it on fire with a Candle it will burn all over: and although I could speak more of these fires, yet this shall suffice for this time.

(Serlio [1545] 1657: 28–29)

ARCHITECTS OF LIGHT

As the perspective scene began to become a part of the acting space rather than simply an architectural backdrop to the performance, a number of architect-designers began to develop lighting techniques for different styles of performance.

Leone di Somi (1527–1592) is important to the development of stage lighting because he was the first to identify the shifts of perception created through changing levels of illumination. He considered light as both an expressive and a symbolic element, and he articulated these thoughts in his 1556[7] treatise on the art of theatre. This writing, which ranges from acting techniques and costume design to stage setting, is presented as a series of dialogues between three noblemen who discuss key dramaturgical issues relating to the staging of drama. The fourth dialogue deals with stage lighting and, like Serlio's publication of 20 years earlier, reflects both historic practice and his own innovations. It provides us with a valuable insight into stage lighting techniques of the Italian court theatre and reveals that di Somi is using light as both an expressive and a symbolic element of the drama. Lights are placed within the scene purely to induce gaiety, and changing levels of illumination are used both to create atmosphere and to induce a reaction in the audience. Modern lighting designers learn the age-old mantra of 'bright lights for comedy, darker lighting for tragedy', and this relationship seems first to have been defined by di Somi. The darkening and extinguishing of lights for tragic effect is the first record of the dimming of light during a performance. It is probable that this technique was borrowed from Tenebrae religious services where candles are extinguished one by one to create a solemn, sombre mood as the church gradually darkens.

Di Somi also provides explanations of ways in which indirect illumination can be created, and his experiments with offstage mirrors and colour side-lighting demonstrate both a development of earlier traditions and a new codification of techniques that use light sources that need to remain invisible to an audience. Importantly, di Somi is the first to identify the shift in perception generated when a spectator is placed in shadow, and this concern with controlling levels of illumination throughout the performance establishes conventions that are still in use today. His innovation in darkening the auditorium in relation to the scene was critical in emphasising changes in the levels of light throughout the dramatic action, and eventually became accepted as the standard convention for indoor theatrical (and cinematic) presentations.

THE DIALOGUES OF LEONE DI SOMI (C. 1561)

I believe that these four Dialogues – which truly were composed more for my own personal convenience than from any desire of securing fame – may be of use to others and myself as a set of rules, or at least as a record of what must be done in writing or in producing any dramatic poem; otherwise, I have no doubt, they would prove but useless and ill-pleasing. [...]

---

[7] Nicholl (1948: 237–238) observes that this was probably written in 1561 and that the first publication was mistakenly dated by the copyist and should actually read 1565.

Fourth Dialogue

Interlocutors; Verdico, Santino, and Massimiano

Santino. [...] I want you to tell me one thing, Veridico. Here on your stage are many lighted lamps, giving ample illumination and· making a most lovely show; what, then, is the use of and how originated those many lamps burning on the roofs of the stage-houses? They do not seem to me to aid the perspective, and for ordinary purposes of illumination there are torches enough.

Veridico. I think I have said more than once that plays are produced for the purpose of providing pleasant instruction and of alleviating noyance of mind. Whence I declared, and again I repeat it, the actor should above all other things endeavour to enunciate his lines in a bright and joyous manner. Such, granted that the author provides us with a pleasant, charming plot and that the actor gives to this a vivid interpretation, surely it is equally essential that the architect should represent gladness and joy on the stage. Now it has been a custom, both in ancient and modern times, to light bonfires and torches in the streets, on the housetops, and on towers, as a sign of joy; and hence arises this theatrical convention-the imitating of such festive occasions. The lights are put there for no other purpose but to imitate, in the very first scene, this mood of gaiety.

Santino. I suppose, then, that these lights would not appear in a tragedy.

Veridico. Perhaps they would not be so wholly out of place even in such a play. Quite apart from the fact that there are tragedies with happy endings, we note that nearly all tragedies open in a happy strain; and consequently it will not be unfitting to arouse the mind, so far as we may, to this happiness, although disasters and deaths are to ensue later. I remember once I had to produce a tragedy of this kind. During all the time when the episodes were happy in mood I had the stage brightly illuminated, but so soon as the first unhappy incident, occurred-the unexpected death of a queen-while the chorus was engaged in lamenting that the sun could bear to look down on such evil, I contrived (by prearrangement, of course) that at that very instant most of the stage lights not used for the perspective were darkened or extinguished. This created a profound impression of horror among the spectators and won universal praise.

Santino. It could not have called forth anything but praise.

Massimiano. Will you now please tell us why most of your lights have in front of them transparent or coloured glasses?

Veridico. This was invented by some men who realized a little-appreciated fact-that a brilliant light striking directly upon the eye for any length of time becomes exceedingly irritating. Since, then, the spectator must keep his eyes fixed on the stage, watching the actions proceeding now on this side, now on that, the shading of the lights was devised to minimize the annoyance.

Massimiano. I should be willing to bet that not ten persons out of a hundred who make use of these shades appreciate their object.

Veridico. They would at any rate say that the shades were used to produce a more beautiful effect, and in so doing they would be enunciating part of the whole. Not by my own theorizing, certainly, but from long practice and experience I have made observation of these things and have tried to get at their origins. I have found that it was the ancients who, as the saying goes, snatched them from obscurity. While we are dealing with this subject I should like to point out also that the small mirrors which some managers set at appropriate places in the perspective settings and the far sides of the wings are very effective. They reflect those concealed lights which the architects cleverly place behind columns and in the openings between the wings, thus serving to make the set more gay and bright. Not only can these reflections give no annoyance to the eyes; they have the further advantage that here we obtain light without smoke-a great consideration. I may take this occasion to remark that the producer who does not take care to have a number of holes made behind the scenes so that the smoke from the lamps may have a means of escape will land himself in serious difficulties, for otherwise this smoke, gradually increasing and becoming thicker, will produce so effective a screen that before the second act be done the actors will seem to be not men but shadows, while the spectators, as if blinded, will, without realizing the cause, get the impression that they are losing their sight. Great care ought to be taken of this, though it is a matter to which few pay sufficient attention. So far as my experience goes, there is no real difficulty provided adequate pains are taken beforehand.

Massimiano. Now that you bring these things to my attention I do recall that at the close of plays we have often found our eyes smarting uncomfortably and that we have not been able to see nearly so much as we did at the beginning. I realize that this must have been due to the cause you have referred to.

Veridico. To avoid the smoke screen I have found that the best remedy is to open as many windows as possible under the proscenium, so that the air, entering from below, drives all the smoke through the holes bored in the roof behind the scenery.

Massimiano. That, I believe, would be an excellent device.

Veridico. It is, I assure you.

Santino. I see, Veridico, that on your stage there are many lamps both behind the scenes and in front of them; yet in the auditorium here you have made arrangements for but twelve standing candelabra. The reason I can't imagine; for I have often counted as many as 250 torches in this large hall.

Veridico. It is a natural fact-as no doubt you are aware-that a man who stands in the shade sees much more distinctly an object illuminated from afar; the reason being that the sight proceeds more directly and without any distraction toward this object, or, according to the peripatetic theory, the object impinges itself more directly upon the eye. Wherefore I place only a few lamps in the auditorium, while at the same time I render the stage as bright as I possibly can. Still further, these few auditorium lights I place at the rear of the spectators, because the interposition of such lights would but be dazzling to the eyes. Over them, as you see, I have made small openings so that their smoke can cause no damage.

Santino. By thus introducing only a few lights in the auditorium, then, you obviate the trouble of smoke-fumes and to a certain extent you render the seeing clearer.

Massimiano. There is yet another advantage: he saves the Duke fifty ducats in respect of the torches usually set in the hall.

Veridico. That, I confess, had not come into my mind, nor does his Excellency need to think of such economies, but, as the proverb says, in the end every good proves good.

Santino. Concerning the illumination of the scene you have said, in my opinion, all that can be said.

(trans. Nicholl 1948: 257–262)

Ingegneri – Dramatic Poetry and How to Produce Plays (1598)

The lighting practices described by di Somi were further developed by **Angelo Ingegneri** (1550–1613) who considered lighting to be 'of supreme theatrical importance'. Ingegneri was the first to advocate a fully darkened auditorium with all house lights extinguished once the audience were in their seats, recognising that darkness accentuated the effect of light on the stage. Ingegneri stipulated that lighting instruments should be concealed from the audience's view like other scenic machinery, and this need to mask the sources of the light from the audience was to become a dominant and established convention until the mid-twentieth century.

In addition to the darkened auditorium, Ingegneri also notes the importance of being able to see actors' faces clearly and suggests ways of achieving this through a new lighting position that would be flown out above the front of the stage and masked from the audience's view by a border. This provides the first evidence of directional light for the performers, lighting their faces from above and creating the equivalent of the proscenium arch spotlight bar. Furthermore, this writing provides a clear indication of the challenges of using candles and oil-based equipment at this time and the direct impact of these materials upon the experience of the audience. Ingegneri provides us with a clear methodology for lighting the proscenium stage and its performers, and the conventions that he proposes in 1598 continue to underpin lighting design techniques and performance practices over 400 years later.

There remains […] one matter of supreme importance – the lighting. Lighting in a theatre ought to be pleasing and clear, and the instruments should be so placed that the spectator's view of the stage is not interrupted by hanging chandeliers or lamps; nor should the spectators go in any fear of wax or oil dropping upon them. Moreover, care should be taken to see that there is no bad smell coming from the lamps, and no danger of their causing a fire or of creating disturbance and confusion among the actors behind the scenes. The man that is able to arrange this illumination so that only its splendour is seen, and its effect created without any member of the audience being in a position to say whence or how it is obtained, unquestionably does much to add to the magnificence of a show. Especially is this true if the lights are placed so as to illuminate the faces of the actors. To those who may have charge of theatrical illumination, it may be pointed out that the method of securing this result is by no means difficult, nor does it call for any very great expense. The method, for which I now wish to demonstrate so that it may be of general service in all future productions, consists of hanging up a valance between the stage heavens and the roof of the auditorium, without, of course, bringing it so low as to cut off too much of the set. On the inner side facing the stage it is to be fitted with many lighted lamps, having tinsel reflectors to direct the beams upon the actors. These lamps ought to be firmly fixed at the top and lit before being drawn up to the positions they are to occupy. Naturally, the whole business must be carried out back-stage before the curtain is drawn […] The set will thus glow with light, and yet no one will see the source of that light or at least discern how it has been made so resplendent. Lastly, take care – especially when a valance of this kind cannot be employed – to contrive that the whole of the light falls on the stage, the setting and the proscenium, and does not become diffused over the auditorium. The darker the auditorium is, the brighter the stage will appear; contrariwise, the brighter the auditorium, the more confused will be the spectators' view of the stage, for then that which ought to have been distinctly and easily seen will be rendered obscure and consequently less pleasing. Hence, at the fall of the curtain I recommend that every lamp in the auditorium set there to show the spectators to their seats should be removed. Still further, the less illumination there has been up to that point, the better it will be, for when the curtain falls the light on stage will seem more powerful and accordingly will produce a more lovely effect.

(Ingegneri (1598), trans. Nicholl 1957: 133–134)

The importance of light and shadow, clearly articulated in the chiaroscuro effects of the painters of the period, underpinned the aesthetic of the Renaissance scenic stage, even if the control of the light sources could not have been as accomplished.

Some commentators (e.g. Izenour, 1988) argue that due to the primitive technology available, the lighting of this period can have been little more than illumination. However, there is clear evidence here in the writings of Serlio, di Somi and Ingegneri in particular of a tradition of using light in a creative fashion that went beyond merely illuminating the perspective scene and the performers in front of it.

The contribution of light to the theatrical event was widely acknowledged as an essential component of the performance spectacle. In 1580 the dramatist Giovanni Guarini (like the character Massimiano in di Somi's *Fourth Dialogue*) insists that:

Without artificial lighting, the scene will be deprived of its beauty...Besides expenses will be reduced...for the beauty that can be created by light can be made up only by great expense in adorning devices.

(cited in Pilbrow, 1997: 167)

Whilst it would be inaccurate to argue that there was a unified or standardised approach to stage lighting at this time, the wide experimentation evidenced by these Renaissance designers contributed to the development of a systematic approach to lighting the stage across much of Western Europe during the next century.

ARCHITECTURE, LIGHT AND SPACE

The link between architects, theatrical space and stage lighting was maintained and developed in the seventeenth century. **Vincenzo Scamozzi's** (1548–1616) fascination with light and space is evident in both his widespread architectural work and his detailed theoretical treatise on lighting in his *Idea dell'architettura universale* (1615). This text marks a significant development from the work of earlier Renaissance architects due to his preoccupation with the effects of light on interior spaces. It is important because it reflects a new way of thinking about light, space and form.

Leonardo da Vinci (1452–1519) had already studied and described the effects of light for artists,[8] while Serlio had begun to describe the types of light within the architectural features of classical buildings, such as the Roman Pantheon, suggesting ideal methods for illuminating the statues that were displayed there. Serlio concluded that *il lume di sopra* (lighting from above) was best suited to these spaces. Scamozzi developed Serlio's aesthetically pleasing 'statuary light' in practice and sought to differentiate the lighting of the space with that of the object contained within it. Scamozzi's writings and architectural plans propose a detailed taxonomy of architectural light that identifies six qualities of light within a building that distinguish between trajectories and directions of light, levels of illumination, and diffusion of direct light and indirect lighting. Scamozzi's control of natural light within buildings is cited as being inherently theatrical (Davis, 2002). The altar in the private chapel in the Doge's Palace in Venice, for example, was treated almost as a miniature stage setting. Scamozzi's complex manipulation of natural light sources in this space includes the use of high windows obscured behind columns to create an ethereal glow in the recess, and the altar within this space is illuminated dramatically when it catches flashes of sunlight. This composition using the unseen light source of the sun is redolent of the way that off-stage lighting can create dramatic images through side-lighting.

SCAMOZZI'S TYPOLOGY OF LIGHT

- light of the open, sunlit sky;
- open skylight experienced directly from an aperture in the roof;
- living vertical light (light which is alive, open from heaven, from the summit of the Dome and spreads across the floor of the room);
- levels of illumination (strong, mediocre and weak);
- directions of light (vertical, horizontal and diagonal);
- direct lighting (open, alive) and indirect lighting (secondary light, reflection or refraction) (after Davis, 2002).

Scamozzi's typology demonstrates the way thinking about light was central to the evolution of architectural space and interlinked with theatrical practices of this period. Scamozzi's theatrical influence is marked by his role in completing Palladio's Teatro Olimpico in Vicenza, with its permanent perspective stage setting designed for its first performance of *Oedipus*. Representing seven streets of the city of Thebes, the setting was clearly designed

---

[8] E.g. Da Vinci Notebooks, Vol. 1, *Second Book on Light and Shade*.

and built with its illumination in mind. Scamozzi's influence on theatre architecture and the stage environment is perhaps better evidenced in the theatre he built at Sabionetta, which is regarded by many as the prototype of the modern playhouse. Scamozzi's drawings and writings also influenced Inigo Jones, who brought many of the staging innovations of the Renaissance to Britain, including the hidden sources of light that he had first observed in Italian court theatres.

STAGE LIGHTING DEVELOPMENTS IN SEVENTEENTH-CENTURY EUROPE

Renaissance lighting techniques were refined and adapted during the seventeenth century by key practitioners in the Italian states and beyond. The technical developments in stagecraft and lighting are detailed clearly in the writings of two architects, the Italian **Nicoló Sabbattini** (1574–1654) and the German **Joseph Furttenbach** (1591–1667). Together, their publications provide us with evidence that lighting techniques were becoming more standardised at this time, and they demonstrate clearly how the theories expounded by Serlio nearly 100 years earlier had developed into widespread practice. Their writings provide us with a clear description of staging techniques in the early seventeenth century and indicate the technical sophistication that had evolved. The practical difficulties of creating light on stage with the technology available are clearly evident, as is the need to find ways of masking the lighting equipment to keep it from the audience's view.

Nicoló Sabbattini

Nicoló Sabbattini provides the first account of standardised, functional stage lighting equipment and the first example of a basic dimming mechanism to control the amount of light from individual sources. Like his predecessors, he was an engineer as well as a trained architect and his *Manual for Constructing Theatrical Scenes and Machines* (1637–1638) was dedicated to explaining in practical terms how to set up a theatre and the various methods for creating all of the elaborate effects expected in the court theatre of this period. In terms of lighting, Sabbattini illustrates several types of lights that were already in theatrical use and discusses practical considerations such as how to illuminate the auditorium whilst managing the hazards of dripping hot wax from candles onto the audience. Sabbattini was also concerned about where lighting equipment should be located for specific effects and how these lights could be dimmed.

Developing Scamozzi's theories, the importance of the direction of light is highlighted and the interrelationship of the painted shadows within the perspective scene and the dominant angle of illumination is of particular aesthetic concern. Sabbattini advocates the use of strong directional lighting for maximum visual effect, and this represents the first published example articulating the importance of keylighting on the stage:

16. HOW TO PLACE THE HIGHLIGHTS AND SHADOWS IN PAINTING THE SCENE

If the lighting is thought of as coming from the opposite direction, that is, from behind the scenery, as others devise, the scene will appear so crude and dark that even if a large quantity of lights are placed there, the spectators will experience dissatisfaction since they will always have the impression that they are not seeing clearly, or with pleasure, the various parts of the scenery [...] but if the illumination is set at one side, left or right, the houses, the back shutter, the stage floor, and the whole scene will have a finer appearance than by any of the other methods. It will give complete pleasure to the spectators, for the highlights and the shadows are distributed in the way that will give the greatest beauty [...] [and] the greatest praise will be gained by this method of painting the scene and placing the light.

(Sabbattini, N. trans. McDowell, J. in Hewitt 1958: 59–61)

Sabbattini is perhaps best known in the history of theatre lighting for his description of the first stage lighting dimming mechanism. In Book 2 of his treatise he explains how cylinders of soldered tin are lowered by cords over each lighting source to create a mechanical dimmer: 'in such a manner that by one motion at the side of the stage, the cords with the cylinders descend over the lamps and so darken them' (ibid.: 111–112).

In contrast to di Somi, who advocated lower lighting levels for tragedy, Sabbattini suggests that these devices are to be employed for the *intermezzi*[9] and that (non-dimmable) light sources within the auditorium should be placed away from the stage so as not to interfere with the darkening effect. This was clearly important in achieving specific effects, such as revealing Hell or creating the effect of sunrise: 'for greater illusion and verisimilitude, the entire stage should be darkened' (ibid.: 174).

Although stage lighting techniques were not uniform in Italy, let alone elsewhere in Europe, the pioneers of the Italian court theatres were clearly influential in establishing techniques and conventions that were to dominate staging practice and lighting principles into the twentieth century and beyond.

Travelling groups of players also began to disseminate the new Italian staging methods more widely, whilst translations and publication of books, such as Serlio's *Second Book of Architecture*, were influential in communicating the new staging techniques to a wider audience. Furthermore, artists, scholars and architects who had travelled to Italy as part of their 'Grand Tour'

---

[9] For more detailed discussion on lighting for *intermezzi*, see Chapter 2.

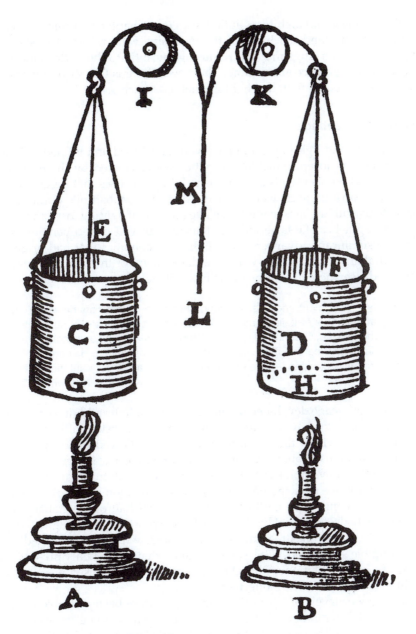

Figure 1 Sabbattini's dimmer mechanism, c.1637

returned to their native countries influenced by what they had experienced. The architects Inigo Jones and Joseph Furttenbach, for example, studied techniques of the Italian stage and were both influenced by accounts of the spectacular production for the Medici wedding festival in Florence in 1608 by the engineer and architect Giulio Parigi (see Chapter 2). Their fascination with the scenes and machines of the *intermezzi* were recorded in sketches, drawings and writings that contribute significantly to the understanding of scenographic practice at this time. Their own designs for performances also helped to disseminate Italian lighting methods further.

Joseph Furttenbach

Italian stage and lighting techniques were developed and refined in Northern Europe by Joseph Furttenbach, who was fascinated by the techniques he observed on his travels and published three treatises that described how specific theatrical effects were created. Alongside Sabbattini's writing, these provide us with the most comprehensive account of lighting instruments and theatrical practice of this period. Furttenbach's private experimentations also led to a significant advancement in lighting techniques that had originated in the Italian court, and his work pre-dates many of the later 'innovations' observed elsewhere in Europe in the next 150 years:

> (I)n the development and specialization of lighting instruments he was far ahead of what we know of Italian practice. As we have no evidence of such interest in instruments elsewhere in the whole century, we may conclude that Furttenbach made important contributions to the development of lighting. He certainly records for us creative thinking far ahead of much of the practice for centuries afterward.
> (Kernodle in Hewitt, 1958: 184)

Furttenbach's stage developed significantly through the addition of a rear pit and, more importantly for future scenic practice, a system of borders overhead, which divided the sky into sections and allowed overhead lighting positions to be used above the stage whilst being concealed from the audience.[10] A key development from Sabbattini is the control that Furttenbach is able to achieve over the on-stage lighting in relation to a darkened auditorium – in contrast to the brilliantly lit festival hall of the Italian courts. Furttenbach also writes of his own practical explorations with light: 'I experimented in a small theatre with a miniature stage which I have erected in my own humble shop' (ibid.: 236) – an innovation that significantly pre-dates the type of experimentation with light in scale model boxes used by scenic and lighting designers in the modern era.

With lower levels of auditorium lighting, Furttenbach was able to create a greater differentiation between light levels to accentuate its overall dramatic effect. In *The Noble Mirror of Art* (1663), Furttenbach emphasises the importance of reducing light levels on stage in combination with sound and scenic elements to create specific theatrical effects: 'whistling wind with the

---

[10] This is described and illustrated by Furttenbach in *Architectura Civilis*, Ulm 1628, 28–30, 52–55 and *Architectura Recreationis*, Augsburg 1640, 59–70.

thunder and lightning, especially if the lights are darkened, will seem like a natural storm' (in Hewitt, 1958: 230). Furttenbach also explains in detail how the on-stage lighting could be dimmed in a similar method to that illustrated by Sabbattini:

HOW TO CHANGE DAY INTO NIGHT

During such a storm the daylight should get dimmer and gradually become dark like night. It could be arranged that the oil lamps and lights behind the scene be put out and later relighted. But that would require time, and extinguished oil lamps produce a bad smell. Hence we have little boxes or covers specially made of black metal that by cords are drawn over and then away from the oil lamps on the floor behind the masking screen, as well as over and away from the oil lamps behind the proscenium. They can be drawn over all of the oil lamps at a time, or only part. They cover the lamps but still permit them to burn, so that it seems night on the stage. The cord from each lamp is led up above the stage and thence to a single handle for all of the cords. When this handle is forward, the lamps shine as for a bright day, but when the handle is drawn back then each cap covers its oil lamp so that not a ray is seen. Thus it was made to grow dark with the thunder and lightning in the scene where Pharaoh grew obdurate, and through the act of Moses it became night for a time in Egypt. This effect for such occasions gives great delight to those who see it.

(ibid.: 230–231)

Furttenbach's Four Methods of Stage Lighting

In *The Noble Mirror of Art*, Furttenbach provides practical details for four distinct methods of lighting the stage, beginning by describing the *bozze*, the standard lighting instrument of the Italian stage:

'First by Oil lamps – For lighting the stage a glass oil lamp of medium size is used [...] just the sort ordinarily used in church' (ibid.: 234), which is placed within an iron ring that is in turn secured to a part of the stage – these are in effect rigging positions:

There should be a number of these rings ready for the lamps at the back of the parapet, back of the side walls of the proscenium, between the sections of the heavens, at the rear pit, and at other places. [...] In practice such an oil lamp has often given a good light for as long as twelve hours with 1/4 pound of olive oil, for water is continually poured in to raise the oil and the floating wick until the last drop of oil is burned and only water is left. This saves considerable trouble and expense. As many as 50 lamps can well be distributed around the stage and up to the heavens to light a scene.

(ibid.: 234–236)

Whilst these observations regarding the lamps and their positioning were not new, Furttenbach's description of specialised reflectors does seem to develop the simple devices such as Serlio's barber's basins and the tinsel reflectors behind the proscenium described by Ingegnieri. In his second method of lighting, *The Mica Reflector*, Furttenbach describes the first lighting units 'with a strong white tin reflector' (ibid.), which seem to be designed specifically for theatrical use and significantly positioned above the stage.

Furttenbach advocates the use of gold tinsel foil scored with a lattice of crossed lines to give a shimmering glow and to which he added a thin layer of mica to improve the quality of the light, noting that 'Experience shows how strong a splendour will be cast by lamps fitted with such reflectors and screwed in the heavens and about the entire scene' (ibid.). This method was also adapted for wax candles, and when the same coating was applied to a wedge-shaped box attached to the wall of the theatre, the effect would be to focus the light. This '*Leaning Light*' was Furttenbach's third method of lighting and he noted that these units 'will cast a strong splendour downward to the floor of the scene as well as upward into the clouds of the heavens'.

The Standing Light Box was the fourth method of lighting the stage. Made from white tin, it had angled sides and floor covered in reflective tinsel to direct light forwards: 'A candle in a *Pfifferling*[11] placed at the centre will send out a splendid glow'. Furttenbach also notes that the light box has other uses: 'It can also be used away from the stage, as for reading, writing, or drawing at night' (ibid.: 238). This innovative device seems to represent the first dedicated theatre lantern and, being portable, enabled a more flexible use of light throughout a performance. The standing light box 'could be placed equally well on the floor or on a table', but its principal use was as a special light within the scenic stage at the rear where it would 'serve to light the royal throne or the sea' (ibid.).

Furttenbach's contribution to the development of stage lighting lies in both the development of these specialised lighting instruments and also in refining the techniques of the Italian theatres. Reflectors added to the multiple oil lamps in the wings and to the continuous run of footlights at the front of the stage prevented the audience from becoming dazzled and significantly improved the overall quality and levels of light. In addition, the creation of new lighting positions concealed by borders above the stage, with reflectors to angle the light downwards, began a technique of lighting that became widely adopted across Europe and beyond, and has remained a central practice ever since.

By the eighteenth century, theatre lighting had evolved from simple illumination into a recognised art form that was capable of making a significant creative contribution to the performance event. However, a plateau had been reached and, as Penzel notes in summarising the achievements of stage lighting in the Renaissance period, technological

---

[11] A metal bracket or supporting ring.

developments would be required before further artistic progress could be made:

> Precedents for most of the major lighting conventions in positioning, coloring, dimming, floodlighting, translucencies, and auditorium darkening were established by the early seventeenth-century. The inspiration and creativity of the Renaissance stage artists is indisputable: the basics of stage lighting were created with only the most rudimentary means. The technology would be two centuries in coming, but the Renaissance genius for viewing in terms of light and perspective would provide the guiding principles.
>
> (Penzel, 1978: 13)

Chapter

2   Light as Spectacle

This chapter is concerned with the overt use of light in performance and its contribution to visual events. It charts the use of light in early religious and festival performances and examines the way spectacular images have been created with light for a wide variety of purposes. Many of the performances in this chapter have been realised outside of the theatre building but have borrowed theatrical techniques or employed lighting techniques that were subsequently adopted in theatre practice.

The spectacular image often incorporates light at its heart. Natural phenomena such as rainbows, shooting stars, solar eclipses and the Aurora Borealis can make a profound impression on us, and these images created by light deeply affect our psyche.

We are naturally drawn towards light; we are biologically programmed by it. Our circadian rhythms are reset each day by the light of the sun and our eyes are unconsciously drawn to observe the brightest object within our field of vision and to focus upon it. This principle, known as *selective visibility*, is invaluable both to the lighting designer and to dramatic art. It allows moments to be foregrounded overtly by directing an audience's attention to a particular area on the stage, but it can also guide attention subliminally. We are subconsciously drawn towards light, we are attracted to the movement of light whether this be from a lighthouse, flickering flames or sparkling water, and we are fascinated by changes in the colour of light such as the light in the sky at sunset. The combination of these qualities is evident in the firework – a technology that has for centuries been central to the creation of the spectacular image in marking important festive and celebratory occasions.

Robert Lepage links our innate relationship with light to the communal experience we engage in through performance:

> We have to remember something very important about what theatre and opera are about: a celebration of light, that's what it is. The only plays in Greece, when there was a lot of light in the middle of the night, were when they could burn these big pieces of wood in pyres so they could illuminate the theatre. People would gather around those bonfires – you know how hypnotic fires are – and there was a communal, collective connection. It was a celebration of the light. In Japan, the first Noh plays were the opportunity to put light in the middle of the night. The idea of theatre is first of all to bring people in a dark room and do the festival of light.

Of course the fire of these theatres was replaced by technology, by electricity, but people still come to the theatre to sit around the fire.

(Lepage in Delgado and Heritage, 1996: 157)

The use of light in performance is a natural extension of our fascination with the effect of light upon our bodies.

Aristotle viewed all of the visual aspects of drama as spectacle ('opsis') and whilst acknowledging its potential, condemned its use in the staging of tragic drama:

The spectacle has, indeed, an emotional attraction of its own, but, of all the parts, it is the least artistic, and connected least with the art of poetry. For the power of tragedy, we may be sure, is felt even apart from representation and actors. Besides, the production of spectacular effects depends more on the art of the stage machinist than on that of the poet.

(Aristotle, *Poetics VI*)

The impact of the word was therefore valued more highly than that of the image, whilst the means of creation was also seen as having little to do with the artistry of the writer – and therefore somehow divorced from the creative process:

Fear and pity may be aroused by spectacular means; but they may also result from the inner structure of the piece, which is the better way, and indicates a superior poet. For the plot ought to be so constructed that, even without the aid of the eye, he who hears the tale told will thrill with horror and melt to pity at what takes place [...] But to produce this effect by the mere spectacle is a less artistic method, and dependent on extraneous aids.

(Aristotle, *Poetics XIV*)

Aristotle's hierarchy of theatrical elements, which is inherent in the distinction between the artistry of the writer and the craft of the artisan, has dominated Western performance practices that have tended to prioritise the importance of the word over the visual image in theatrical presentations. Light is at the heart of this debate since the potential power of the scenographic image is revealed, enhanced and highlighted through it. The contribution that light makes to the theatrical 'spectacle', and the recognition of the creative role of the lighting designer, have only gradually been acknowledged in the twentieth century and many would argue that the role of light in performance still remains to be fully acknowledged.

THE AESTHETICS OF LIGHT

The origins of our fascination with light are outlined in Umberto Eco's essay *The Aesthetics of Light*, which explores the mediaeval response to colour and light and traces the image of God as light from paganism into the Christian tradition through the writings of St Augustine and the metaphysical and aesthetic analyses of Robert Grosseteste and St Bonaventure. This writing assists us in understanding our fascination with light, its deep-rooted metaphysical associations and our responses to its inherent splendour within performance spectacles.

> The most obvious symptom of qualitative aesthetic experience was the medieval love of light and colour. [...] But when it came to their experience of colour - of gems, materials, flowers, light, and so on - the Medievals revealed instead a most lively feeling for the purely sensuous properties of things [...] [and] developed an art form in which, to an unsurpassed degree, the brilliance of simple colours is married to the brilliance of light: the stained glasswork in Gothic cathedrals. [...] Apart from single colours, however, philosophers and mystics alike were enthralled by luminosity in general, and by the sun's light. Medieval literature is filled with joyous acclaim of the effulgence of daylight and of fire. A basic structural principle of Gothic cathedrals was that they should give the effect of light erupting through an open fretwork.
>
> Grosseteste[1] [...] defined light as the greatest and best of all proportions, as proportionate with itself so to speak: 'Light is beautiful in itself, for its nature is simple and all things are like to it. Wherefore it is integrated in the highest degree and most harmoniously proportioned and equal to itself: for beauty is a harmony of proportions'. Thus identity was the proportion par excellence, and was the ground of the indivisible beauty of God, fount of light; [...] to perceive the created world was to perceive its beauty also, whether in its proportions as known to analysis, or in the immediacy of light.
>
> (Eco, 1986: 43–51)

EARLY USE OF LIGHT IN PERFORMANCE

Light has always played a vital role in theatrical performance. In the earliest drama, natural daylight illuminated performances in Ancient Greek theatre staged in the open air and performed throughout the day from first light to sunset. The prevailing light conditions were able to be employed by the playwright as an aesthetic, atmospheric element of the drama and plays were organised to take advantage of specific lighting conditions during the day. Aeschylus' *Agamemnon*, for example, opens with the watchman awaiting a beacon signal on a distant mountain peak to herald the fall of Troy:

> And now, as ever, am I set to mark
> When shall stream up the glow of signal-flame,
> The bale-fire bright, and tell its Trojan tale-
> Troy town is taken:
> And the fire signal is seen reddening the distant sky;
> But now at last fair fall the welcome hour

---

[1] See Robert Grosseteste, *On Light*, translated by C. Riedl (1942).

> That sets me free, whene'er the thick night glow
> With beacon-fire of hope deferred no more.
> All hail!
> Fire of the night that brings my spirit day,
> Shedding on Argos light, and dance, and song,
> Greetings to fortune, hail!

Light provides the visual signal to commence celebrations, but it also creates a central symbol at the beginning of the drama. It operates on several levels. It is probable that the scheduling of the performance in the early morning allowed this lighting effect to be seen by the audience in the landscape beyond the theatre and the illusion of the darkness to be more easily communicated. The fire creates a positive symbol that literally brings forth light from darkness, but in its form of a red warning beacon has more subtle connotations. It both announces the victory over Troy and also the imminent return of Agamemnon, and the Watchman's initial joy at seeing the signal gives way to words of foreboding. Light is therefore used as visual spectacle and as a dramaturgical device in the opening of the drama.

Although light sources were probably used onstage in early performances, they became a requirement as soon as performances moved indoors. Flaming torches, braziers and domestic oil lamps with floating wicks powered by animal or vegetable fat were used both to provide illumination and to denote night when they were brought onto the stage.

MEDIAEVAL FIREWORKS AND FLAMES

From the twelfth century onwards, firework technology began to make an impact on festivities, and the potential of these spectacular lighting effects was recognised and adopted in mediaeval performances. Spectacular fire and smoke images were designed and coordinated by firework masters who might be considered as the very first lighting designers. Butterworth (1998) details ways in which light was used in mediaeval performance practice through the use of fireworks and also from flame, the colour of which was determined by the particular combustible material used as fuel:

> Thrust lynnen rages into oyle of hempseed, and after dippe them in melted tallowe, then putting them into Cressets giu[v]e fire to them, & you shall see that they all burne and giu[v]e a great light.
>
> (Lucar cited in Butterworth, 1998: 60)

Lucar's instructions for creating cresset lights (published in 1588) indicate an ancient way of creating illumination for events after dark that was much brighter than candles or torches. The cresset consisted of an iron basket to hold the fuel and, when employed in outdoor performances, was usually fixed to the end of a pole, handled by an operator and accompanied by an attendant carrying a bag containing spare fuel.

Using ancient Eastern technologies, fireworks were developed in Europe into an art form of their own during the sixteenth and seventeenth centuries. In France, *feux d'artifice* were employed in large-scale theatrical public spectacles and staged using built structures on which the fireworks were installed. Ships, palaces and settings commonly used in mediaeval pageants, such as Hell's Mouth, were presented and the effect of the light was often intensified by placing these structures adjacent to water. The reflection of the light created a mirrored duplicate image, multiplying the light sources and their consequent visual impact.

These events can be seen as equivalent to the experience of the modern fairground or the nightclub, since they offered a temporary escape into a hedonistic world defined through both light and darkness. Bergman suggests that these celebratory feasts of light were:

> the most expressive and sonorous manifestations of the joy of life of the Baroque, the experience of the flying moment, the blazing light in the darkness of impending death.
>
> (1977: 46)

FESTIVALS OF LIGHT

Light as a phenomenon can be seen to be at the centre of the Renaissance world, both literally and metaphorically. The Enlightenment marked a fundamental shift in traditional patterns of thought and behaviour during the fifteenth and sixteenth centuries when the ideas and values of the modern world began to emerge. The combination of economic, social and technological developments led to new scientific and geographical discoveries, a quest for new knowledge and, crucially, the opportunity to disseminate this knowledge widely through the printed text. The potential of the individual was championed and the individual artist was celebrated and encouraged for the first time. In the preceding chapter we have seen the results of this new knowledge, through practitioners who began to use and to write about light in both architecture and the theatre.

To understand the impact of light in the Renaissance period it is necessary to understand the role that darkness played in everyday life – as well as in staged events. In the Italian city states, a particular set of circumstances arose that created the climate for artistic and intellectual pursuit. Buoyed by new-found wealth from trade, the cities began to compete against each other and the promotion of lavish performance spectacles was one way in which this enlightenment was publicly demonstrated. Light was an essential element of these events, which were staged at night-time or in covered interior spaces. At one level, light provided illumination so that the action could be seen, but it also represented a conscious display of opulence that signified the wealth of the patron or city state in which the performance was staged. An overt use of light created an astonishing spectacle that contrasted with the darkness of the world beyond the court and provided a symbolic and temporary respite from the difficulties of everyday life.

Daily life was regulated by the sun. Only the wealthy could afford the candles and oil lamps necessary to alleviate their homes from darkness. Although tallow candles had been created in the late thirteenth century, their supply was heavily regulated and prices fixed.[2] Since candles were a luxury that few could afford and artificial light was used sparingly after dark, the public world could be dangerous after sunset. Hand-held lanterns were necessary to guide travellers after dark and the city streets offered a place where criminals could operate freely. Dekker comments on these dangers in London's dark streets in a number of pamphlets that reveal the safety inherent in portable lights.[3]

At a time of regular outbreaks of plague, the water feasts, firework extravaganzas, courtly processions, *trionfi* and other entertainments staged in Italian cities of this period provided festivals of light that were a celebration of artistic and scientific achievement and, at the same time, a momentary escape from the trials of everyday life. These performances became a visual representation and celebration of the progress of the Renaissance, with light representing a triumph of humanity and life over death and darkness.

Some of the architects responsible for designing and coordinating these spectacles recorded the outcomes of their work and, through describing their discoveries in using light, created the first known documents that focus on lighting design for performance. Eyewitness accounts also provide firsthand corroboration through descriptions from an audience perspective of the spectacular scenic effects and the dazzling worlds created with light.

ILLUMINATED ANGELS

Filippo Brunelleschi (1377–1446)[4] is a seminal figure of the Italian Renaissance, who combined his expertise in architecture, mathematics, clockwork and machinery in designing theatrical settings for biblical performances in churches. These regular festival events employed theatrical devices to

---

[2] By 1709 tallow candles were heavily taxed in Britain. It was not until 1831 that the tax was dropped, allowing more people to be able to afford to have light in their homes after dark.

[3] See Thomas Dekker's *Lanthorne and Candle-light* (1608), *The Belman of London* (1608) and *Villanies Discovered by Lanthorne and Candlelight* (1616).

[4] Brunelleschi is credited with developing one-point linear perspective in a painting of the Florence Baptistry in 1415, which revolutionised the fine arts and subsequently led to the development of the scenic stage.

enable celestial objects and performers dressed as angels to fly through the air amidst brilliant explosions of lights and fireworks. The Russian Bishop Abraham of Suzdal described a number of performances that he witnessed in Florence in 1439 that are amongst the first accounts of lighting in performance.[5] *The Annunciation* at San Felice was one of the most spectacular performances and was described by Vasari (1550),[6] who informs us that Brunelleschi was employed to augment this celebratory performance event which

> was truly something marvelous, demonstrating the genius and the industry of him who was its inventor, for the reason was that there was seen on high a Heaven full of living figures in motion, with an infinity of lights appearing and disappearing almost in a flash.
>
> (Vasari, 1912: 355–356)

Brunelleschi experimented with reflectors, translucent materials and moving light effects, and in this performance lighting was built into scenic items where it could be concealed and then revealed theatrically through spring-loaded mechanisms. The combination of candles, torches and highly polished reflective surfaces, together with the moving scenery, created a spectacular range of effects with light as a central symbolic force.

Vasari describes a large, revolving half-globe that supported 12 boys dressed as angels with golden hair who were surrounded by circles of light:

> above the heads of the angels, were three circles or garlands of lights, contained in certain little lamps that could not be overturned. From the ground these lights appeared like stars, and their brackets, being covered with cotton-wool, appeared like clouds.
>
> (ibid.: 356–357)

From the large orb was lowered another internally lit 'globe', which contained another cluster of eight smaller angels from which the Angel Gabriel then emerged and descended further. The lighting on this final structure dimmed remotely through an ingenious sprung mechanism, as the angel stepped out to speak to the Virgin Mary. As the angel rose back into the air the lights blazed again: 'the lights, which had gone out on his issuing forth, being rekindled' (ibid.: 358). The performance culminated with the angel choir revolving with the scenic machinery around the illuminated 'globe', creating an effect 'with innumerable lights and very sweet music, [which] truly represented Paradise' (ibid.).

---

[5] His enthusiastic accounts are preserved in fragments that remain of his written travelogue and which were copied by Russian monks and later published in German in *Russische Review* (1877).

[6] Vasari drew upon detailed technical information from an earlier account of the performance.

THE MEDICI WEDDING FESTIVITIES (1579)

The scenic techniques that were developed for religious dramas became increasingly elaborate and refined as they were restaged on a regular basis. Importantly, the techniques established for religious festivals were also employed in other performances at this time. Raffaello Gualterotti recorded the lavish lighting of the Medici marriage festival staged in Florence in November 1579, and his vivid description and engravings of the event provide us with a unique insight into the use of light in performance spectacles at this time.

The elaborate festival procession took place in the courtyard of the Palazzo Pitti in Florence, which had been converted into an indoor theatre by stretching sailcloth across the roof of the space. This material both obscured the night sky and reflected light back into the performance space. It is clear that the lighting of this event was a prominent aspect of the performance, which drew heavily on the traditions and techniques of mediaeval fireworks as well as the developing scenic and theatrical lighting practices. Gualterotti emphasises the brilliance of this spectacle, describing an astonishing array of overhead decorations, including 60 suspended angels with candles in their hands. These were supplemented by gilt-burning oval basins and rows of large, white lanterns along the walls and the top gallery of the courtyard. At floor level each pillar held a golden, jewelled royal crown with twin torches; every archway was lit by a pyramid-shaped light source and a multitude of torches and lanterns – some shaped like Grecian urns were placed on pedestals. The use of polished metal basins and ornaments also helped to reflect the light from the many candles and magnified their visual effect.

Around the courtyard a series of loci were arranged in the tradition of mediaeval pageants complete with scenery representing cliffs, caves, mountains and specific locations, such as Apollo's Temple, that were required for the dramatic narrative.

In addition to the spectacular dressing of the courtyard with light, the procession that entered and moved through the space used mobile light sources which augmented the splendour of the courtyard. Fireworks, torches, lanterns and candles were mounted on performers and incorporated into costumes and onto the chariot wagons themselves. A white and gold triumphal chariot headed the parade and was drawn by two elephants complete with torches and candles to highlight the golden carvings and mythological scenes depicted on its sides. The chariot's wheels depicted the moon, the sun and the heavens, and candles built into the wheels ensured that these too sparkled with light as the chariot moved through the courtyard.

The procession continued with further wagons; as observed by Gualterotti, one pulled by two lions, a monster with five fire-spitting heads, a dragon and the Forge of Vulcan belching fire and smoke seemed as if a large mountain of fire was crossing the space. Mars entered on the back of a scorpion with his lance alight, and fireworks were seen to erupt from a golden star on his back. Venus appeared in a golden seashell, encrusted in precious stones and mounted on a silver sea, while escorted by furies breathing fire and smoke and protected within a circle of light by cupids, each holding a burning torch.

The combined effect of the multitude of light sources and their movement, together with the reflections in the shining surfaces and costumes, created an astonishing effect of brilliance. Gualterotti was clearly enraptured by the beauty of these images and overwhelmed by the physical sensations created by the 'wonderous light', which 'out of night [...] created the brightest of days' (Gualterotti 1579: 41).

INTERMEZZI AND THE ROLE OF LIGHT

The spectacular lighting effects that had first been developed for religious and outdoor festivals were incorporated into theatrical performances at court as an integral part of the *intermezzi* – the interludes staged between each act of classical dramas. These popular interludes were highly visual performances that frequently echoed the content of the main play and often took the form of theatrical dances incorporating music and complex scenic effects. Light made an important contribution to these spectacles through highlighting specific scenic items and also adorning the performers. Dancers created moving light effects by manipulating torches rather like sparklers whilst simultaneously balancing burning torches on their heads and even in their mouths!

The *intermezzi* became increasingly sophisticated through the sixteenth century, and began to overshadow the dramatic action amongst which they were interspersed. These elaborate performances are important as they mark the beginning of both opera and ballet as art forms, but their intricate staging is also significant in developing scenic practices and new lighting techniques.

In 1589 **Bernardo Buontalenti** (c.1531–1608) designed a production of Bargagli's comedy *La Pellegrina* for the wedding celebrations of Grand Duke Ferdinand and Christine of Ferrara. The performance took place in the theatre of the Uffizi Palace in Florence, which Buontalenti had designed three years previously for another royal entertainment. The six *intermezzi* for this entertainment provided a lavish musical and visual spectacle and are now regarded as more important than the play in which they appeared since they represent the origin of opera. The setting for the play was the city of Pisa, but the stage itself represented a 'great machine' which could be transformed quickly into seven settings so that the spectators had the effect of every-thing taking place in a dream. Before the play began the stage was masked by a red curtain and all of the torches in the auditorium appeared to ignite by themselves, causing widespread astonishment.[7] Footlights built into the

---

[7] Nagler's main source for this description is Bastiano de'Rossi *Descrizione dell'Apparato, e degl'Inter-medi* (Firenze, 1589). This performance is thought by some scholars to be the first use of red curtains to obscure the stage.

balustrade at the front lit the stage while 16 chandeliers, each with 18 tapers, illuminated the auditorium.

The first *intermezzo*, *Harmony of the Spheres*, was a prelude to *La Pellegrina*. Nagler describes this event using a range of source material from eye-witness accounts:

> Several sunbeams burst forth from behind the cloud [...] and the spectators were at a loss as to how it moved as it gradually floated to the earth, headed toward the temple, and then vanished into it. [...] [Afterwards] the starry heavens appeared, with four clouds rising up. So realistic were these imitations that one might have expected rain at any moment. [...] The celestial background glowed brilliantly [...] in the lower regions its luminescence was dimmed by the colors of the rainbow. Towards the end of the first intermezzo 'the clouds rose from the lower part of the stage, sunlight streamed in, while in the upper regions night was swiftly approaching [...] the seven clouds dispersed, the heavens closed, the stars grew pale, sunlight flooded the sky, and, as if by magic, a view of the city of Pisa appeared on the stage.
>
> (Nagler, 1964: 74–75)

The complexities of this staging were significant and the notes of Girolamo Ser Jacopi, the engineer and technical coordinator entrusted to realise Buontalenti's vision, are informative. Nagler's reading of Ser Jacopi notes that the lighting for the play *La Pellegrina* itself was designed for maximum effect. Stagehands were positioned to watch over the lamps and light them when required and, because of the ever-present danger of fire, they were entreated to exercise the utmost care in both refilling the oil lamps and trimming their wicks.

Buontalenti took every precaution to place the costumes that he had designed in their proper light, while each flying machine contained an abundance of lamps and the stage was illuminated by lights:

> 'fastened to the back walls of the houses in the Pisa setting ("appiccati alle case"); these light sources were moveable ("mobili") and could be rotated ("uoltando")[...] to cast light on the intermezzo wings. The sky was perforated [and] in each of the apertures lamps were concealed, so that the heavens could be made to shine with the brightness of day.
>
> (Nagler in Gassner and Allen, 1992: 255)

The rapid, multi-sensory transformations and spectacular stagings of the six *intermezzi* in this production proved so popular that they were frequently restaged independently from the play in which they had originally appeared.

In France, techniques developed in Italy were also evident in lavish court spectacles that echoed the techniques of the Italian *intermezzi*. The 1581 performance of the *Ballet comique de la Reine* in the great hall of the Petit Palais Bourbon, for example, included clouds that shone gold with lights placed behind them and employed Serlian staging techniques to ensure a glittering occasion with many oil lamps: 'spreading over the garden a hundred thousand colours through the transparent glasses'.[8]

SCENIC EFFECTS – MOOD AND EXPERIMENTS IN LIGHT AND SHADE

The importance of light to the Renaissance stage and the evolution of lighting design methodologies explored in the previous chapter continued to be developed in Italy throughout the seventeenth century as increasingly elaborate staging methods evolved to realise them.[9] Instead of hiding behind a curtain, the scene change became an integral part of the stage action and was undertaken without any significant change in lighting, to the wonder and admiration of the audience.[10]

In Britain, stage lighting practice had not developed significantly beyond simple illumination, even when theatrical performances had moved indoors. **Inigo Jones** (1573–1652), like Furttenbach, was influenced heavily by the staging techniques of Parigi's *intermezzi* that he had observed and admired. Jones was central to the development of lighting techniques in Britain, and he copied the staging and lighting methods that he had witnessed to illuminate the lavish masques for the Stuart court. Jones imported Italian lighting devices in 1607 and used these *bozze* to light the indoor spaces that he had transformed for theatrical use. Jones used concealed lighting in the Serlian tradition in combination with translucent scenic pieces: calico and oiled, covered flats which, when backlit, revealed effects such as stars in the night sky. For the *Entertainment at Theobalds*:

> were placed Diaphanall glasses fill'd with severall waters that shew'd like so many stones of orient and transparent hiewes
>
> (cited in Nicholl, 1957: 135)

These spectacular court masques, heavily influenced by the *intermezzi*, owed their success to the exquisite visual presentation and an overt exploitation of setting, costume, lighting and sound. This style of performance and its power over its audience seemed to bring into question the primacy of the written text. Ben Jonson, who collaborated with Jones on many of the court masques, famously ridiculed the contribution of the new dramaturgy. The poet's anger at the sublimation of his prose to what he regarded as the transitory nature of Jones' visual experience reignited a conflict between the power of the word and that of the image that echoed Aristotle. The prominence and potential power of the scenographic statement continued to be an issue underlying

---

[8] Beauioyeulx, B *Balet Comique de la Royne* [sic] 1582 Torino (1965: 4ff) in Bergman 1977: 118–119.
[9] A mechanised stage was developed from the basic system of grooves and shutters, allowing complex changes of scene to be achieved rapidly in full view of the audience.
[10] E.g. *Il Bellerfonte* Venice, 1641, see Nicholl 1966: 118.

Western theatrical practice and light that, in emphasising the visual, was a key constituent in detracting from the spoken word and the art of the performer.

SERVANDORI AND DE LOUTHERBOURG

The Italian **Giovanni Nicholas Servandori** (1695–1766) also exemplified the new scenic tradition that had emerged from the Italian courts. Working in France, he orchestrated great firework spectaculars for the royal court and designed complex stage compositions for a range of operas. Servandori used combinations of reflective and transparent gauze materials together with imaginary painted light effects. When these were lit by both hidden lights and visible, radiant light sources, he was able to create a startling array of effects including the representation of moving water, such as waterfalls and the dappled light of forests. In the opera *Scaderberg* (1735), he designed the interior of a palace for the final act with columns and arches in which were suspended real, visible lamps as an integral part of the décor. These visible light sources were supplemented by offstage lights that illuminated the stage in the Serlian tradition, creating a jewelled effect through the backlighting of translucent materials. An upstage altar appeared to be adorned by precious stones, and these glittering radiant light sources were a central focus for the scene.

Servandori's scenography developed independently of the musical drama through his *spectacle d'optique*, which first opened in 1738 at the Salle des Machines. Although we do not have information about the precise lighting techniques that were employed on this stage (the largest in Paris at the time), there is evidence that the lighting was an expensive but essential element of these visual performances. Servandori's *spectacle d'optique* represented an opportunity to use emerging technologies to undertake further experimentations with light on a stage, but without the need to prioritise the illumination of the actor. To maximise the visual effect, the audience viewed the stage action from a *darkened* auditorium where chandeliers would be hoisted out of the auditorium prior to the performance in the manner espoused by Ingegneri and widely practiced in Italy.

Servandori's early optical spectacles used light to recreate famous paintings on stage, to present specific locations and mythological stories that were reminiscent of the *intermezzi*. Combinations of painted and live figures and effects such as fire, volcanoes, thunder, lightning and other meteorological elements were central to the visual spectacle. Later performances in the 1750s were more romanticised and concentrated on illusions of nature through an interplay of light that created moonlit shadows, forest scenes with light piercing the foliage, and figures glimpsed in rays of sunshine and then swallowed by mists and darkness. These light shows, which sometimes incorporated marionettes, were important not only because they foreshadowed the work of artist-designers such as Loutherbourg and Daguerre, but also because they provided means for experimentation and the practical development of Servandori's lighting craft. This expertise was to culminate in his design for the opera *Ezio* in Dresden in 1755–1756, in which 8,000 lamps and candles were carried by extras in lavish scenic processions which, despite striking similarities with *intermezzi*, were considered revolutionary by the audiences that witnessed them.

Phillippe-Jacques de Loutherbourg (1740–1812) was responsible for introducing a new scenic aesthetic to British audiences that adopted continental lighting and staging techniques. He may well have been influenced by Servandori's work, since his significant contribution to lighting practice is also distinguished by the spectacular presentation of romantic landscapes and the creation of atmospheric images on the stage.

The control of all of the visual components of the stage that Loutherbourg requested in his famous letter to Garrick (see p. 62) enabled a wide range of spectacular effects to be achieved using combinations of light, paint and scenic materials in a unified manner. Bergman recounts Loutherbourg's innovative use of lighting in Garrick's pantomime *A Christmas Tale* in 1773, which had 11 separate settings:

> in act III the garden was changed so that flowers and trees appeared in red. de Loutherbourg achieved this fairy tale effect by using different coloured filters, described in detail by the author Henry Angelo.[11] Variously coloured silk screens were attached crosswise on a pivot placed before a light source between each wing and border. If one side was turned towards the light source, the whole stage was suffused by one colour, but if the pivot was turned 90° so as to produce a silk screen of another colour, a change of colours was achieved.
>
> (Bergman 1977: 218)

Coloured light created in this way from invisible sources was key to producing the changes in atmosphere and facilitated a range of visual transformations including moonlit scenes, illuminated clouds and 'the sea and a castle at a distance with the sun rising'.

THE EIDOPHUSIKON

Like Servandori in Paris before him, Loutherbourg left the large-scale stage to experiment with light in a more tightly controlled environment. During 1781–2, Loutherbourg presented the results of this work in his Eidophusikon, a miniature theatre with an 8 × 6 foot stage in which the combination of lighting and scenic mechanisms was able to create complex visual effects that could not at this time be achieved at full scale on the Drury Lane stage.

---

[11] See *Reminiscences*, Vol. II London, 1828: 326.

The first exhibition in this experimental theatrical space was held on 26 February 1781 at Loutherbourg's house on Lisle Street near Leicester Square. The scenes presented were

1. AURORA; or the Effects of the Dawn, with a view of London from Greenwich Park.
2. NOON; the Port of Tangier in Africa, with the distant view of the Rock of Gibraltar and Europa Point.
3. SUNSET; a View near Naples
4. MOONLIGHT; A View in the Mediterranean, the Risings of the moon contrasted with the Effects of Fire.
5. The Conclusive Scene, a STORM at Sea, and Shipwreck (in Dobson, 1912: 278)

When viewed from a darkened auditorium and augmented by sound, the combination of mechanised scenic effects, coloured shifts of light and the use of transparent materials and smoke created a unique series of visions that had widespread public appeal. Loutherbourg referred to this multi-media exhibit as his 'movable canvas', and it presented a spectacular theatrical experience of nature's phenomena. Artists such as Gainsborough and Reynolds were fascinated by its effects and visited the Eidophusikon regularly. They studied the landscapes, perspective views and the effect of lighting on these visions and considered it as a major work of art (Baugh 2007: 50).

An account by John Britton[12] suggests that Loutherbourg had availed himself of a new technological invention, the Argand lamp, to achieve his dazzling atmospheric effects, although this was unlikely in the Eidophusikon's first incarnation. Britton recollected that

> The clouds in every scene had a natural motion, and they were painted in semi-transparent colours, so that they not only received light in front, but by a greater intensity of the Argand lamps employed, were susceptible to being illuminated from behind. The linen on which they were painted was stretched on frames of twenty-times the surface of the stage, which rose diagonally by a winding machine. De Loutherbourg excelled in representing the phenomena of clouds. The lamps were above the scene and hidden from the audience, – a far better plan than the "footlights" of a theatre. Before the line of brilliant lamps on the stage of the Eidophusikon were slips of stained glass – yellow, red, green, purple, and blue; thereby representing different times of day, and giving a hue of cheerfulness, sublimity, or gloom, to the various scenes.
> (Britton, *Autobiography I* 1850: 97–101 cited in Penzel, 1978: 23)

---

[12] Britton's account is often cited as a contemporary account, but was actually not published until 1850. Britton would have been nine years old in 1781

The second programme of scenes, presented by Loutherbourg in March 1782, includes similar atmospheric effects to those demonstrated by Servandori in his experimental *spectacle d'optique* over 30 years earlier:

ACT THE FIRST
Scene 1. The SUN RISING in the Fog, Italian Sea Port.
Scene 2. The CATARACT of NIAGRA, in North America
Scene 3. (by particular desire) the Favourite Scene (exhibited 60 Nights last Season) of the STORM and SHIPWRECK.
ACT THE SECOND
1st. The SETTING of the SUN after a RAINY DAY, with a View of the Castle, Town and Cliffs of Dover.
2nd. The RISING of the MOON, with a WATER-SPOUT, exhibiting the effects of Three different Lights, with a view of a Rock Shore on the Coast of Japan.
THE CONCLUSIVE SCENE
SATAN arraying his TROOPS on the BANKS of the FIERY LAKE, with the Raising of the PALACE of PANDEMONIUM, from Milton[13]

The shifts of coloured lighting in the last scene were recalled by W.H. Pyne:

> In this tremendous scene, the effect of coloured glasses before the lamps was fully displayed; which, being hidden from the audience, threw their whole influence upon the scene, as it rapidly changed, now to sulphurous blue, then to a lurid red, and then again to a pale vivid light, and ultimately to a mysterious combination of the glasses such as bright furnace exhibits, in fusing various metals.
>
> (Pyne 1823: 284)

SPECTACLE AND THE NINETEENTH-CENTURY STAGE

Spectacle played a major part in popular entertainment throughout the nineteenth century. Projected light contributed to magic lantern shows and the immersive experience of both panoramas and dioramas. Improvements in lens technology and in the use of gas allowed a new variety of lighting effects to be created for the stage. E.T. Smith of Astley's Theatre reminds us of the importance placed on the visual aspects of performance at this time:

> For a person to bring out merely a talking drama, without any action in it, or sensational effects, is useless; the people will not go to that theatre; they will go where there is scenic effect, and mechanical effects to please the eye.
>
> (Booth, 1981: 2)

---

[13] From the advertisement of Loutherbourg's second programme in *The Morning Herald*, 12 March 1782.

Techniques in gas lighting, limelight and the carbon arc offered new possibilities in tandem with materials such as gauzes and painted scenes, and these developments are explored further in Chapter 9.

Henry Irving's (1838–1905) production of *Faust* (1885–1888) certainly aimed 'to please the eye' and combined the creative possibilities of electricity with advanced techniques of gas lighting. His use of supernatural lighting effects created a visual spectacle that culminated in a scene which

> ended amidst a shower of gold, and the rocks pierced through and through with a brilliancy as of forked lightning, the audience is left breathless with astonishment. Nothing like it has ever been seen on the spectacular stage, and this act alone would be enough to secure the success of the production had it no other merits than the marvellous display.
>
> (Brereton 1886: 76)[14]

The increased importance attached to the visual aspects of staging during the latter half of the nineteenth century ensured that light became an increasingly important dramaturgical component. This can be seen in the work of contemporary dramatists and through practitioners such as Irving, who recognised the creative potential of light and, crucially, the importance of the control of darkness. Irving dimmed stage lighting in order to obscure the scene changes, which were carried out with military precision by up to 100 stagehands, allowing spectacular and astonishingly speedy transformations to be achieved. A review of the first night of Irving's *Henry VIII* noted:

> It would tax the imagination to believe what can be done on the modern stage until this splendid revival has been witnessed. There are fourteen complete scenes, elaborately set, and they change almost without descent of the curtain as if by magic. The lights are turned down; there is momentary darkness, and a gorgeously equipped scene, complete with furniture, is changed to another equally rich, literally in the twinkling of an eye. What would our ancestors not have given for these marvellous mechanical appliances which ... have enabled a capable manager to add beauty to beauty, and to bring the theatre as near to nature as it is conceivably possible to do.
>
> (*Daily Telegraph* 6 January 1892)

The tradition established in the nineteenth century for visual splendour and elaborate staging was developed further in the twentieth century by practitioners such as **Herbert Beerbohm Tree** (1852–1917), who used moving limelight on top of washes of light created by the new electric light source to create stage pictures that rivalled Irving's work. However, this particular aesthetic was soon to be superseded by modernist approaches to performance in which elements of darkness were acknowledged as vital to the performance experience.

---

14 Brereton's original review appeared in *The Stage* 25 December 1885.

REINHARDT'S *THE MIRACLE*

Borrowing heavily on the symbolist movement and influenced by the staging experiments of Lugné-Poë, **Max Reinhardt (1873–1943)** sought to create spectacular theatrical moments using colour, movement and light. These aims were exemplified on an epic scale in Reinhardt's most famous production, *The Miracle*. For the original production created in London in 1911,[15] the giant Olympia exhibition hall was transformed into a cathedral-like space to house the entire performance. This demanded the bold use of light and darkness on a vast scale and the combination of pageantry, music and setting created a spectacular experience – one observer exclaiming: 'those who remember it will remember to the end of our days how it feels to behold a miracle' (cited in Styan, 1981: 71). *The Miracle* demonstrated Reinhardt's ability to coordinate scenographic elements to maximum effect:

> Streams of coloured light, yellow, blue, and white, flaming through the latticed surface of square black boxes or prisms posed on stork like legs. Forty-seven electric fans drove up the yellow silken ribbons upon which the light from the forty arc lamps beat. The shrieks of the revellers filled up the intervals of the fiery effects as they made themselves felt in the conflagration overhead. For some moments we stood in the midst of blinding lights, flashing flames, and crashing winds. Then the bell rang and there was the silence and darkness of death.
>
> (Carter, 1914: 232–233)

Light and its absence became integral to Reinhardt's dramaturgy. MacGowan provides a contemporary account of the rather heavy-handed climax to *Orpheus*, which again relied upon light and darkness to create spectacular moments which, in this instance, did not seem to have been sufficient to redeem the whole drama:

> For the beginning of the descent into Hades, Reinhardt [...] makes the descent of the gods far more memorable than it can have been in any other production. Yet it all seems a trivial and half-hearted effort.
>
> (MacGowan & Jones, 1922: 109–110)

SON ET LUMIÈRE: MASS SPECTACLE AND IMMERSIVE PERFORMANCES

The tradition of the Renaissance spectacular of light in tandem with sound can be traced into the twentieth century through the night-time presentations of *son et lumière* events staged against historic or architectural backgrounds that are transformed and animated through light. In the modern era these

---

[15] It was restaged in New York and performed in major European cities until 1932.

events are linked to ideas relating to colour music (see Chapter 8). Jean Michel Jarre's celebratory millennium night offering, for example, with laser lights, massed performers and electro-pop music presented against the backdrop of the pyramids in Giza, provides a contemporary example of this ancient tradition.

The Storming of the Winter Palace – A Case Study

In Russia in the first decades of the twentieth century, mass public spectacles were frequently staged on public holidays to celebrate historical events. *The Storming of the Winter Palace* was re-created on the same site in St. Petersburg on the third anniversary of the October Revolution.[16] It is perhaps the best-known mass spectacle and can be seen as a twentieth-century expressionistic equivalent of the Renaissance theatrical extravaganzas, albeit created for a very different political and social purpose. Conceived by the director and dramatist **Nikolai Evreinov** (1879–1953), this epic spectacle represented his notion of 'theatre-in-life' in practice. It was staged on an unparalleled scale with the assistance of the military, involved around 10,000 participants and was witnessed by over 100,000 people. Evreinov was interested in the notion of theatre as event and understood that the dramatic power of such mass spectacles should be built on the combination of acoustic and visual effects. The Winter Palace itself would serve as a giant actor that light would bring to life. Evreinov used cinematic techniques to reveal the inner life and historic events within the palace, arguing that 'The director must arrange it so the stones themselves seem to talk' (in Golub 1984: 196).

The production was staged at 10.30 p.m. and used geometric, angular stages which faced the palace across the square and clashed with its ornate architecture. These two platforms for the massed groups of dancers, students, military personnel and government employees represented the opposing forces of good (the Reds) and evil (the Whites). The audience's attention was directed from one stage to another by sudden changes in the lighting designed and created by Professor Majzel. One searchlight was attached to the top of the Aleksandrinskaja Column in the middle of the square, while others 'shot beams of light across the cloudy sky' (Golub 1984: 198). Silhouetted groups of figures in the square were isolated through flashes of light and then quickly disappeared back into the darkness. These lighting shifts worked in combination with the noise to create an intimidating effect on the spectators, who were roped off in a central area of the square and completely surrounded by the action. Cars sped into the arena from the streets beyond with headlights on and horns sounding while the battleship *Aurora* (which had taken part in the original event) was anchored nearby and its guns were used to 'bombard' the palace once again. Coupled

---

[16] On 7 November 1920.

with machine gun fire as the battle raged between the Red and White armies on the bridge, it must have presented a daunting and exhilarating experience.

The action unfolded as the lights within the Winter Palace itself flashed on and off to reveal the developing narrative behind the building's 50 windows, whilst celebratory fireworks completed this spectacle of light and sound as midnight arrived.

THE CATHEDRAL OF LIGHT

While *The Storming of the Winter Palace* could be seen as a forerunner of Artaud's ambition for a 'Theatre of Cruelty' (see below), the military precision needed to orchestrate such an event was a precursor to the mass popular events staged in Germany in the 1930s. The Nuremburg Party Rallies were staged using theatrical techniques on the Zeppelinfeld – an enormous architectural 'stage set' in Nuremburg. For the fourth Nazi Rally held there in 1936,[17] Albert Speer designed a *Lichtdom* or 'Cathedral of Light' to celebrate the arrival of the Führer and the subsequent processions of thousands of flags. The beams of 120 aircraft searchlights were employed to project light into the sky from around the periphery of the Zeppelinfeld. Whilst we should be wary of the overall tone and intention of this anonymous official report, its content matches the impression that this event had on other eyewitnesses and demonstrates the impact of light on those who experienced the event:

Just before 7: 30 when it was nearly dark, a floodlight shoots heavenward. The small spotlight's beam reveals more than 200 enormous swastika flags that fly from 12 metre flagpoles in the evening breeze. Suddenly one realizes the enormous size of the field and drinks in the unforgettable picture. More lights illuminate the flawless white marble platform, an unforgettably beautiful sight. [...]
More lights shoot across the field, revealing the endless brown columns, [of men] showing their movements, until suddenly, at a command, the 90,000 are in place.

A festive mood fills all, as if they knew what an experience awaits them. But what actually happens surpasses all their expectations.

Orders blare from the loudspeakers, hurried automobiles dash here and there. Shortly before 8, the spotlights at the south fade. It is the direction from which the Führer will come. [...] The colonnade slowly circles the field, then suddenly — as the shouts of those on the other side of the platform announce the Führer's arrival — 180,000 people look to the heavens. 150 blue spotlights surge upward hundreds of metres, forming overhead the most powerful cathedral that mortals have ever seen. [...] Several stars shine through the deep blue curtain of the cathedral of light, and the flags of the German nation flutter in the soft wind.

---

[17] 8–14 September 1936, the Cathedral of Light was first created on 16 August for the closing ceremony of the 1936 Berlin Olympics.

Now the flags cascade in, through eight side entrances, with another flood coming in at the wide middle entrance. Spotlights illuminate the flags at the head, casting a silver glow that intensifies as it nears us.

(Anon.,1936: 170–177 trans. Bytwerk)

Artaud, Light and *The Theatre Of Cruelty*

Like Evreinov, **Antonin Artaud** (1896–1948) advocated a new form of theatrical spectacle that would impact directly upon his audiences. He also regarded light as a critical element of his new form of 'total theatre', which he envisaged as a transformative and transcendant experience. Artaud's writings, heavily influenced by the thinking of **Alfred Jarry** (1873–1907), have had a significant influence on a wide range of practitioners and his ideas continue to have currency. *The Theatre of Cruelty: First Manifesto* (1932) argued for performances that would break down perceived barriers between audience and performers in which all elements of the theatre would be used. The qualities of light were to be harnessed in an immersive experience for the audience, who would be seated centrally to allow the dramatic action to envelop them. Artaud tells us that whitewashed walls in the space were 'designed to absorb the light', but the intention was clearly to reflect light and so emphasise its impact on the performance: 'Because of the diffusion of the action over an immense space it will mean that the lighting of a scene and the various lighting effects of a performance will impact on the audience as much as on the actors' (Artaud, 1964: 116). Artaud proposed to return the theatre to a form based on the physical understanding of images and repeatedly compared the power and physical effects of light to that of a storm. In *An End to Masterpieces* (1933), light is emphasised alongside sound as a critical element to create a vibratory sensory experience that can impact like a 'whirlwind' upon the body. Artaud argues that light should not be 'designed merely to colour or to illuminate' but to create violent, physical images which can 'pound and hypnotise the sensibility of the spectator' and through a repetition of light patterns induce trance-like effects on an audience.

These radical propositions suggested complex arrangements of light that echo the ideas of the Futurists (see Chapter 8) but that techniques of the time were unable to create. In this excerpt from *The Theatre of Cruelty*, Artaud envisions what might be possible with more advanced technology. This is a radical manifesto for lighting that makes a phenomenological impact on the audience and therefore has relevance today for our thinking about the role and potential of light in performance:

We have no intention of boring the audience to death with transcendent cosmic preoccupations [...] Every spectacle will contain a physical and objective element perceptible to all. Cries, groans, apparitions, surprises, theatrical tricks of all kinds, the magical beauty of costumes taken from certain ritual models, dazzling lighting effects, the incantatory beauty of voices, the charm of harmony, rare notes of music, the colours of objects, the physical rhythm of movements whose crescendo and descrescendo will blend with the rhythm of movements familiar to everyone, concrete appearances of new and surprising objects, masks, enormous puppets, sudden changes of light, the physical action of light which arouses sensations of heat and cold, etc.

(Artaud, 1964: 111 trans. Palmer)

Artaud argued that all elements of the theatre should be employed in creating this chaotic, multi-sensory experience and a new ideal language of theatre will evolve in which 'even light can have a precise intellectual meaning' (ibid.: 113).

LIGHTS. – LIGHTING. The lighting equipment currently in use in theatres is no longer adequate. In view of the particular action of light upon the mind, the effects of all kinds of luminous vibrations must be investigated, along with new ways of diffusing light in waves, in sheets, or in fusillades of fiery arrows. The colour range of the equipment currently in use must be totally revised. In order to produce particular tonal qualities, one must reintroduce into light an element of thinness, density, opacity with a view to producing heat, cold, anger, fear, etc.

(ibid.: 114)

LIGHT AND TECHNOLOGY – ROCK AND ROLL

The desire for visual spectacle created through the use of light drove a significant number of technological developments within the lighting industry towards the end of the twentieth century. The role of the popular music and event industries was central to this demand, which became commercially driven by product designers and lighting manufacturers rather than as a response to a specific technical or artistic need. A notable exception to this statement includes Svoboda's development of low-voltage contralights and the hazer (see pp. 113–114) – created in response to a specific artistic problem and which coincidentally later impacted directly on large-scale music performances. The haze facilitated visible beams of light in the air above the stage while new lighting sources at a higher colour temperature allowed textured light effects to be created. The stage and its performers were therefore no longer the sole focus of attention as the void above the stage had become the lighting designer's new canvas. The introduction of lasers and remotely controlled moving lights enabled this canvas to be manipulated in a multitude of ever-changing ways.

The visual spectacle demanded by the music industry to augment live music events continues to be driven by market forces and the perceived need to make each event a memorable audience experience that is often bigger and better than the last. Light has been central to realising these aims, and frequently initiated the development of new lighting technologies. In the 1970s, lighting units such as the Par can were developed specifically for the rock industry, allowing the rigging of hundreds of fixtures and enabling spectacular washes of saturated coloured light to be created. These fixtures soon found their way into conventional theatres, where they offered a versatile, high-output, low-cost solution to creating similar effects with strong shafts of light.

In 1980 the lighting rental company for the concert touring industry, Showco, developed the first automated lighting fixture, which allowed the instantaneous change of colour through dichroic filters and, uniquely, the ability to move remotely.[18] This revolution created new creative possibilities for the fluid use of light in performance, since lights no longer had to be focused solely in one place and their parameters, such as the size and shape of the beam, focus, size and colour, could all be changed remotely from the control desk. The complexities of these new technologies demanded an accompanying need for highly specialised technicians to service the lanterns and a new breed of control board operators to programme and operate them (see Chapter 11).

LIGHT AS URBAN SCENOGRAPHY

As we have already seen, the dramatic lighting of the environment dates back at least to the Renaissance light festivals and water feasts, where the active interface between light and darkness represented a triumph of life over death. Festivals of light invariably begin with darkness, into which light encroaches and the power and subtlety of light as a tool for transformation is celebrated in societies all over the world. Our associations with peace, pleasure and safety are deeply embedded in the concept of light within these cultural events.

Temporary and permanent illuminations of buildings fulfil a variety of purposes, from commercial promotion and advertising to creative interventions and celebratory events. On occasions, these objectives might coincide, such as the conspicuous illumination of the Portsmouth Gas Offices undertaken to celebrate the Coronation in 1911, and the measure of its impact can be ascertained through its capture on a postcard of the time (see Figure 2). Light in the form of advertisements dominates and even defines some city locations, such as New York's Times Square and London's Piccadilly Circus, while the seaside town of Blackpool in north-west England has famously engaged in an ostentatious public illumination of its promenade and trams as a commercial venture to extend its holiday season. Singapore has sought to define its city through light and, as host to the inaugural night-time Formula One Grand Prix, has used light to create a spectacle for a worldwide television audience.

---

[18] The prototype was demonstrated to the rock group Genesis, who agreed to invest in the development of the technology resulting in the VARI*LITE®. The opening night of their *Abacab* tour in Barcelona on 25 November 1981 saw the first use of the Series100™ system with 50 VL1™ automated fixtures.

GAS OFFICES ILLUMINATED. CORONATION. 1911. SILK.

Figure 2 Postcard recording the illumination of the Portsmouth Gas Offices for the 1911 Coronation

Lighting of the environment is directly linked to affluence, and the lighting of city buildings and squares has developed in recent years to embrace aesthetic rather than simply practical concerns. Lighting designers have been commissioned to create both temporary and permanent statements in light that can have a major impact on the experience of the city. These interventions can be regarded as urban scenography and, in contrast to theatre lighting, have a permanence and profile through their high visibility. Town planners and arts funders have increasingly come to recognise that light has a transformative impact on the urban environment:

> Today, light is considered by many local authorities to be one of the main components of their policy for urban development and for enhancing their international influence, used to show off all the riches of their heritage and playing an important role in improving the quality of life in the city.
>
> (LUCI Association)

Light is used as a strategic aspect of urban planning and can bring a 'greater comfort and tranquillity to the inhabitants of cities' (ibid.). The French city of Lyon has been at the forefront of the use of light as an integral element of its architecture and city spaces. Light impacts on the way in which its urban environment is experienced and the way the city itself is perceived in national and international terms. For Lyon, light has become an integral aspect of its own self-image and has been used to assert and reveal its identity. The historic and spectacular Festival of Lights[19] held in the city each December has been the catalyst for embracing light as a transformative element. During the festival, residents place lights in their windows and buildings are dressed and adorned with light. As the city in which the Lumière brothers captured light through the medium of film, it is particularly appropriate that Lyon has chosen to define itself through using light to sculpt public space. In addition to the annual festival, therefore, Lyon has sought to re-imagine itself through its 'Light Plan' and has employed lighting designers to transform over two hundred buildings and public areas into permanent nocturnal panoramas. Many other cities worldwide have followed this example in using light as a key material to regenerate the urban environment,[20] while digital technologies have enabled new interactive experiences and street games to be created with light.[21]

---

[19] See www.fetedeslumieres.lyon.fr/.

[20] See http://luciassociation.org/.

[21] See Palmer and Popat (2006) for an account of their work with KMA on *Dancing in the Streets*, an interactive light installation for York.

Chapter

3

Light, the Playhouse and the Scene

This section examines the development of light in performance in relation to the stage setting, the performer and the developing architecture of the theatre space during the seventeenth and eighteenth centuries. Changes in practice came about as a direct result of a changing visual aesthetic and a number of scientific discoveries, such as advances in lenses, reflectors and the light source itself. These impacted on the appearance of the stage and auditorium and made new demands on what was to be illuminated and how it was to be lit. Many of the developments in this period were directly related to the work of the architect-designers of the Italian Renaissance as their practices became disseminated more widely.

HOW TO LIGHT THE STAGE (C. 1637)

In Chapter 1 we explored the impact of Sabbattini on the development of lighting design techniques. His 1637–8 publication *Manual for Constructing Theatrical Scenes and Machines* also discusses the way in which the auditorium should be lit for performance, with lighting concentrated near to the front of the stage to increase overall levels of illumination. His writing gives us a detailed impression of the difficulties of lighting an indoor space with the technology of the day:

38. How to Place the Lights Outside the Stage

The lights in the hall or theatre outside the stage should be of different kinds and in diverse places. Some persons use oil lamps, others torches of white wax. As far as the first are concerned, they are less expensive but do not give that splendour which torches do. However, when the illumination is given by good lamps and these are filled, not with bad, but with the best kind of oil, mixed with some pleasing scent to obviate bad odours, they make no poor showing and the spectators are the better assured that the torch wax will not fall on them.

(Sabbattini in Hewitt 1958: 93)

Sabbattini advises that lights are placed: 'as near to the stage as possible, but so that they do not interfere with the view of the machines which may descend from the heavens during the *intermezzi*. They are accordingly to be placed at the sides leaving the centre space free and open' (ibid.: 95).

There are also some practical considerations for onstage lighting. As Ingegneri had earlier advocated (see p. 10), these light sources were hidden behind the top of the proscenium arch in order to illuminate the painted vaulted sky that ran continuously overhead[1] and sloped down to the backdrop. Lights were also located onstage behind scenery, but needed to be placed with care:

> They must be set so as not to interfere with the changing of scenes and with the machines, and so that, during the dancing, they do not shake and fall down, particularly the oil lamps. This is one of the things that much harms the reputation of a stage director.
>
> (ibid.: 95)

Offstage light sources that could not be seen by the audience were essential in creating the perspective scene, but needed to be complemented by freestanding footlights at stage height which lit both the scenic buildings and the costumes of the performers. These footlights were concealed by a painted parapet at the front of the stage, but Sabbattini notes that there are problems with this technique, including the bad smell arising from the oil lamps in this low position and 'the impediment experienced by actors and dancers because of the glare of these lamps' (ibid.: 96). Issues with the presence of footlights at the front of the stage were to dominate lighting techniques and debates about staging practices until the mid-twentieth century, when a combination of technological advancements and aesthetic concerns finally rendered them obsolete.

Sabbattini provides the first accounts of a standardised functional lighting equipment with footlights, side-lighting and lighting from above the stage concealed from the audience's view. His approach is essentially a practical one, using the upstage surfaces of the proscenium arch as lighting positions and ensuring that the downstage central area was the brightest part of the stage. There is, however, no account of the darkening of the auditorium, and the onstage decorative jewel lights of Serlio's stage seem to have disappeared in favour of pronounced directional lighting within the perspective scene. Bergman notes that: 'Sabbattini is alien to di Somi's and Ingegneri's optical, scientifically founded reasoning' and, although this seems to represent a return to practices of 50 years earlier, 'it reflects conventions which still survived in large parts of Italy' (ibid.: 74).

---

[1] With occasional divisions into lateral sections to allow for moving clouds and other machines to cross the sky.

Sabbattini explains in detail several practical methods of lighting the lamps, with an awareness of the safety of the audience and performers:

> I should remark here that plenty of water should be ready above the beams or the heavens and below the stage [...] for where there are so many lamps, and the other lights that are used in the intermezzi, accidents can occur easily. If there is quick remedy at hand no one will be harmed and there will be little disturbance.
>
> (Sabbattini *41 How To Light The Lamps* in Hewitt, 1958: 98)

THE ELIZABETHAN PLAYHOUSE AND NATURAL LIGHT

In Britain in the same period there is little evidence of a significant development of theatrical lighting beyond the techniques developed in mediaeval pageantry. Elizabethan performances took place either in indoor spaces at court, in public halls or taverns where there was little attempt at any specialised lighting for the stage, or alternatively in purpose-built outdoor theatres, with performances usually played in the afternoons and lit by natural, if subdued, daylight:

> Elizabethan lighting came from all around [the actor]. To the amphitheatre audience, there was no impression of light focusing on the actor, no sense of light exposing him to the interpretive scheme of a lighting designer [...] English Renaissance actors moved in more natural surroundings. They performed in a pleasant ungovernable light that shone on the tiring-house façade and spectators as well as on the actors. Like the bare, open stage, the overall illumination permitted not only flexibility in staging but also a sense of continuity between the stage and the auditorium, between the actors and their background.
>
> (Graves, 1999: 123–124)

The stage itself was shielded from direct sunlight by a permanent canopy, often painted underneath with stars and known as 'the heavens', whilst the orientation of Elizabethan playhouses such as The Globe 'permitted sunlight to play across at least part of the auditorium during the performances, but always kept the stage in shade' (Orrell, 1988: 90). It seems clear therefore that the actors performed in relatively even and diffused lighting conditions, although during winter months and on overcast days the stage must have appeared rather gloomy at times. Webster refers directly to this issue when explaining the lack of success of the first performance of *The White Devil* at the Red Bull in 1612: 'since it was acted, in so dull a time of Winter, presented in so open and blacke a Theater' (cited in Graves, 1980: 239).

The Elizabethan outdoor theatre, performed during daylight hours, had little requirement for stage lighting. The non-localised setting of the stage was augmented through specific stage properties, and mood and locale were largely left to the language and the ability of the actor to stimulate the imagination of the audience. Sir Walter Raleigh observed that

The whole scene is heavy with the sense of night and the darkness of conspiracy, yet the effect is produced by nothing but the spoken words and the gestures of the players.

(cited in Lawrence, 1927: 129)

In Shakespeare's *A Midsummer Night's Dream* the mechanicals grapple with theatrical conventions for denoting 'night' in their 'play within the play' and wonder how to get moonlight into the room in which they hope to perform. Their first solution to this problem in their tragedy of *Pyramus and Thisbe* reflects the practice in early indoor performances of simply opening shutters to allow light into the room through large windows. At night, artificial light from candles and burning sconces attached to walls would have provided illumination. Shakespeare provides us with a deliberately comic representation of the moon by the character Starveling, but the lantern that he holds clearly symbolises the moon. The convention was easily understood by the Elizabethan audience since lanterns and torches carried onstage automatically signified night, while the visual image was often reinforced by accompanying sound effects, such as owls hooting or clocks striking.

WINDOWS AND SHUTTERS

Performances staged indoors drew on traditions of indoor festival practice and relied upon existing lighting implements to illuminate the stage area. Cressets (torches with an open iron cage to hold flammable material), braziers and oil lamps provided portable lighting, while burning sconces attached to walls could also provide general illumination. Branched chandeliers with candles that required constant manual trimming would also have been used when daylight was shut out of the performance space. The closing of shutters on windows was on occasion part of the action, creating a cross-fade from daylight to night – although this process may have been rather clumsy and time consuming. Shutters were closed to prepare the theatre for certain types of drama. Thomas Dekker provides a lively contemporary account of daily life and at one point describes the city of London as shuttered:

like a private playhouse, when the windows are clapt down, as if some Nocturnal or dismal tragedy were presently to be acted.

(Dekker, 1606: 19)

Furttenbach also noted the importance in the theatre space of windows that could be opened to allow additional natural light into both the auditorium and the stage area. This may seem strange from our modern perspective where we attempt to keep any extraneous light from the black box of the theatre space, but it is important to note that this technique of opening and shuttering windows plays an important part in the lighting of the

Figure 3 A 1658 engraving of Schouwburg Theatre, Amsterdam, built in 1638. Note the high-level windows each side of the stage, the central chandelier and the candles on the auditorium walls. A large window behind the audience also allowed daylight into the theatre and provided frontal illumination to the stage

theatre stage at this time. It certainly underpins lighting traditions in France and Britain throughout the seventeenth and eighteenth centuries, providing respite from the heat and fumes of the oil lamps as well as an economic solution to supplement the candles and oil lamps for performances staged during daylight hours.

Engravings of the Schouwberg Theatre, Amsterdam, in 1658 clearly show a large, arched window allowing both auditorium and stage to be flooded with daylight. Since performances began at 4 p.m. the natural light needed to be supplemented in winter and in poor weather by a large copper chandelier that was suspended close to the stage. In the theatre building that replaced it in 1665, windows can also clearly be seen above stage left, allowing light to fall diagonally onto the stage.

Furttenbach also suggested that windows were an important consideration in the building and illumination of theatre spaces:

It is very important that the windows be planned at the right places for the proper lighting and for plenty of air [...] A winged window at the back of the building and another on each side let in light and air for the dressing room. Two more opposite one another on each side of the rear pit let in enough light so that by day no oil lamps will be needed there. Again two at the sides of the scene add more light.

No windows are placed at the sides of the front pit. The walls there are left unbroken so that the spectator will not be blinded, but will sit in darkness and have the greater wonder at the daylight falling on the streets between the houses as well as the light of morning coming from between the clouds. Then the actors appear for the prologue and tell the contents of the play.

It were better if no windows were put at the sides of the audience, so that spectators, left in darkness like night, would turn their attention to the daylight on the stage [...] Then at the sound of the trumpet and drums, before the curtain is let down, the windows of the auditorium can be closed by shutters, or filled with green leafwork so that the air can come in and the room still be darkened.

(Furttenbach, 1640: 59–70 in Hewitt, 1958: 206)

In the 1680s, the Swedish architect **Nicodemus Tessin** the Younger (1654–1728) describes a series of technical innovations observed in the Venetian opera houses. Overhead lighting had not developed here over the full stage as Furttenbach had employed, but instead a mobile batten of light was used in a selected area above the stage to illuminate the tracking overhead scenery, such as chariots and transparent clouds. At stage level in the wings, vertical lighting poles (booms) allowed light sources to be rotated and so the intensity of the side-light could be varied. Footlights could also be raised and lowered in a special trap at the front of the stage, allowing the intensity of the front-light to be controlled.

The evolving dramaturgy used these new lighting methods to instigate sudden scene changes between brilliantly illuminated environments and menacing scenes using dimmed light to suggest dusk or darkness. Bergman (1977: 96) argues that such visible changes, with the curtain up, stretched the lighting techniques of the time to their extremes. Tessin comments on the practicalities of achieving these lighting 'cues' in his notebooks[2] and hints at the difficulties of presenting such elaborate lighting effects in performance:

The illuminated scenes are most easily presented at the end of an opera for then one need not think about changing the lights.

(ibid.: 97)

Tessin also notes the continuation of the Serlian scenic technique of jewelled windows, of scenery covered by oiled paper with lights placed behind. Tessin also recounts the technique of painting light effects and shadows directly onto the scenery – a scenic practice of representing light in two dimensions that continued in European theatre even into the twentieth century.

AUDITORIUM VERSUS STAGE

The balance between the lighting of the stage area and the auditorium became a key issue during the eighteenth century. In France from the 1670s

---

[2] *Unveröffentliches von Nicodemus Tessin d.J* trans. Bergman, 1977: 92–98.

onwards, an increasing distinction was made between the lighting of the performers, the specific lighting of the 'scene' and the lighting of the audience. Drawings and paintings of Covent Garden in the 1760s show that the thrust stage and the auditorium were lit by flown chandeliers outside the proscenium arch that equally lit both the main acting area and the audience area. Further flown chandeliers illuminated the remainder of the house and clearly interfered with sightlines from the balcony. There was therefore little sense in prioritising the stage lighting over that which gave general illumination to the auditorium. Stage and auditorium were illuminated equally throughout the performance in a constant state, and any illusion of darkness was created by 'a contract of imaginations' (White 1998: 149) between actors and audience. However, White makes a persuasive case that dramatists writing for early indoor theatres structured their plays around lighting changes:

> Comparatively significant lighting changes in the illumination levels on a candle-lit stage can be effected through the use of supplementary light brought onto and then removed from the playing area. [...] Rather than reducing the general lighting state, a common technique seems to have been to add lights shortly before a scene intended to be 'dark', so that the removal of these lights would give the impression that the stage had, in fact, been darkened.
>
> (White 1998: 149)

The techniques and conventions established in the Italian court theatres did, however, gradually influence the evolution of new staging practices across Europe in the eighteenth century. Technological developments on the continent continued to make a gradual impact on theatrical practices, although the lighting techniques that played such a major part in the scenic spectacles at court had yet to be adopted by the public playhouses. On the Restoration stage in Britain, staging and lighting techniques were still lagging significantly behind the practices that had been established on the continent of Europe for some time:

> For Scenes and Machines they are no new invention [...] They are excellent helps of imagination, most grateful deceptions of the sight, and graceful and becoming Ornaments of the Stage, transporting you easily without lassitude from one place to another, or rather by a kinde of delightful Magick, whilst you sit still, does bring the place to you. Of this curious Art the *Italians*, this latter age, are the greatest masters, the *French* good proficients, and we in *England* onely Schollars and Learners yet, having proceeded no further than to bare painting, and not arriv'd to the stupendious wonders of your great Ingeniers, especially not knowing yet how to place our Lights, for the more advantage and illuminating of the Scenes.
>
> (Flecknoe [1664] 1908: 96)

The commercial public theatres of this period did not adopt the lavish production styles of the Italian court theatres. Both in France and in Britain, theatre spaces were illuminated primarily by candle-burning chandeliers while the acting area remained a bare 'neutral space' with the apron, as the most important part of this stage, extending beyond the proscenium wall. As the scenic elements became more important and the stage area itself deepened, the issues inherent in illuminating the performers on this larger stage became critical and required a reappraisal of how the stage was lit.

CANDLES AND OIL

Onstage lighting was achieved by battens (rows of candles, lamps or 'floats' – a series of wicks floating in oil) as footlights at the front of the stage. This provided localised light for the performers downstage. This light was augmented by a small number (perhaps three or four) of additional chandeliers that provided light from above the stage to illuminate the 'scene'. These hoops each supported around 12 candles and were in turn supplemented by side-lighting in the wings, invisible to the audience and mounted on vertical battens (booms) or 'scene ladders'. The onstage lighting was predominantly there to illuminate the scenic elements and was not used to light performers in the way that side-light is used today. The scenic stage beyond the proscenium wall was still relatively dim and predominantly used as a backdrop to the action, which was clustered downstage near the footlights.[3]

Oil footlights became more widely adopted as the preferred and most efficient method of lighting the performers. Evidence from the Comédie Française provides us with comprehensive listings of the lighting requirements of the 1719 season.[4] From these detailed financial accounts of the numbers of candles and oil lamps it is clear that there was a concentration of light on the forestage, which was illuminated both from below by footlights and from above by chandeliers. The upstage scenic stage was partially illuminated by lights in the wings and left in semi-darkness unless a special effect was called for. Lighting at the Comédie Française was divided into two types – 'ordinary', denoting standard lighting for the general illumination of both the stage and the auditorium, and 'extraordinary', a term which seems to suggest improvised additional lighting for specific dramatic effects and also required for the illumination of the minor plays staged on the same evening.

By 1757, however, significant staging reforms had taken place. The overall number of chandeliers had been reduced to just four (which were to be

---

[3] The dimly lit scenic stage space comprised a series of stock flats or cloths to suggest a generalised locale for the action. This scenery was generic so that the settings could be used in many different plays. The actors followed a number of rigid conventions, entering the stage through permanent doors built into the walls downstage of the proscenium, always facing the audience when speaking and rarely turning across the stage or upstage.

[4] *'Dépense des Chandelles orders et des Lampions et Chandelles extraordres à commencer aujord'huy'.*

cleaned at the beginning of each month) and only two of these were hung close to the stage.[5] The overall light levels in the auditorium had therefore been reduced while at the same time the level of illumination on the stage had been increased by the use of oil lamp footlights with multiple wicks instead of tallow candles. The actual number of candles used in the wings was also significantly increased and lighting was added from the flies, above the stage area and to the upstage areas, which nonetheless still would have appeared relatively dim in comparison with the main acting area adjacent to the footlights. In 1759, however, stage reforms at the Comédie Française reflected a new approach to the visual arrangement of the stage and the two chandeliers over the forestage were removed completely, finally severing the link between the lighting of the auditorium and that of the stage area.

AUDITORIUM LIGHTING AND SOCIAL CONDITIONS

Bergman (1977: 91) notes that there were social as well as economic reasons for the darkened public auditoria in late seventeenth-century Italian cities, where performances began by the tradition of removing the central chandelier that was suspended above the proscenium. This convention

> surprised foreign visitors as late as the first half of the 19th century. In the Rome theatres darkness became complete. The box owners were forbidden to have light in their boxes to avoid its streaming out into the darkened auditorium.
>
> (ibid.: 92)

Prevailing social conditions were also key to the tradition in Northern European theatres of maintaining an even illumination both onstage and in the rest of the house. There was little sense of any delineation with light, especially as it was commonplace for audience members seated at the sides of the stage to take an active part in the performance. The social event of attending the theatre was not only to see the play but to be seen. When staging reforms in Paris reduced the number of chandeliers hanging over the audience to prioritise light upon the stage, Lavoisier (1781) criticised the result since there was insufficient illumination to be able to recognise other theatre-goers in the auditorium.[6]

In contrast, in London the sconce fixtures on the front edge of the boxes at the sides of the stage would certainly have been a significant visual distraction. Nicoll reminds us of the audience's experience of relative levels of illumination when entering the playhouse auditorium:

---

[5] Jules Bonnassies *La Comédie-Française, Histoire Administrative* (1658–1757) Paris, 1874: 353 cited in Bergman, 1977: 170.

[6] 'et même dans une partie des loges, une obscurité telle qu'on y reconnaît difficilement, à quelque distance, les personnes qui y sont placées' (Lavoisier, [1781] 1865: 92).

if we were suddenly enabled to be present at a performance in Garrick's Drury Lane, our eyes would certainly be continually conscious of and oppressed by its dim outlines. It may, on the other hand, be justifiable to suggest that the contemporary public, on entering the playhouse, must paradoxically have been impressed, and even afflicted, by its glare. After leaving their own inadequately lit houses and walking through the streets in winter's blackness, the sight greeting their eyes must have proved both welcome and attractive – and yet, despite their conditioning, it must be assumed that their eyes also would have been unable to see clearly all parts of the interior: some areas would have appeared to be bright and others obscure [. . .] the scenic area must always have been rather dim and difficult to see - dim, because the candles cannot have illuminated it sufficiently, and difficult to see, because of the distracting glare of the rings above. The main platform, on the other hand, must have been the brightest spot in the playhouse, with its candles overhead, and in the side sconces, with its footlight lamps augmented by radiance from the auditorium.

(Nicholl, 1980: 116)

When Garrick visited the Comédie Française in 1763 he observed that the house appeared to be 'dark and dirty', but he was to soon change his opinion on the lower levels of illumination that he experienced in French theatres and came to realise how the removal of the auditorium chandeliers affected what was seen on stage.

LIGHT AND THE ACTORS – THE PROBLEM OF FOOTLIGHTS

The arrangement of lighting equipment for illumination of the stage had a profound impact on the physical use of the stage space by actors. Where footlights were in use, the greatest illumination of the stage was at the front, with the luminous intensity decreasing towards the back of the stage according to the physical principles of the inverse square law.[7]

The light from footlights, supplemented by overhead chandeliers hanging outside of the stage space, therefore caused difficulties both in seeing the actors if they moved upstage and in the illumination of scenic elements behind the performers. This problem became exacerbated as the Baroque stage spaces grew deeper.

LIGHTING IN THE MANNHEIM COURT THEATRE – A CASE STUDY

In an account of the Mannheim court theatre in Germany, French architect and lighting pioneer **Pierre Patte** (1723–1814) observed the methods

---

[7] As light spreads away from its point source it will illuminate a larger area, but its intensity will be reduced in proportion. At double the distance the light beam will illuminate four times the area but will only be a quarter of the intensity, and at three times the distance the area will be nine times bigger but only a ninth of the original intensity.

Figure 4   Engraving of the Schouwburg Theatre, Amsterdam, in 1768 (rebuilt 1665). It shows oil footlights, auditorium lighting and overhead chandeliers which were typical of continental practice in the eighteenth century

of lighting the opera performances staged in this building designed by Alessandro Galli-Bibiena. Completed in 1741 and responding to Italian scenic innovations, it had a deep scenic stage that was significantly larger than the auditorium, which held 2,000 people. In 1782 Patte critiques the narrow proscenium opening that caused sightline difficulties, and his description of the lighting echoes the practices observed in the Venetian Opera Houses 100 years earlier:

> The ceiling in the auditorium is level and elevated 54 feet above the floor; in the middle there is a trapdoor that can be opened to let down a large candelabrum laden with 18 torches or candlesticks, serving to illuminate the auditorium until the curtain is raised; at that moment it disappears and the auditorium is illuminated only by the mirrored reflection of about 1,200 candles that usually illuminate the theatre.
>
> (trans. Corneilson, 1997: 63)

Patte was to suggest front-lights from the boxes in the auditorium as a partial solution to the issue of how to illuminate the performer, and as a way of counteracting the unnatural angles of light on the face caused by footlights.

Furttenbach had already proposed lighting solutions to these problems of visibility, with lighting instruments hidden in a rear pit to illuminate upstage scenic elements and overhead stage lighting, masked by scenic borders, to provide adequate illumination of the performers. However, these innovations were not widely adopted until the acting area of the stage had retreated behind the proscenium arch.

The problems associated with the adoption of footlights to solve the problems of seeing the actors were also exacerbated by the smoke that they generated. Sabbattini had already noted this, and it was still problematic well into the eighteenth century. Madame Riccoboni's discussion with Diderot in 1750 clearly underlines why the actors were unable to move all over the stage and why it was a technical necessity for them to gather in a semi-circle close to the footlights to deliver their lines:

> Firstly, the actor who turns his face towards the second wing is not heard by more than a quarter of the audience; secondly, in an interesting scene [...] three feet from the footlights the actor no longer has any mimics.
>
> (Diderot, 1875: 306)

The suggestion here is that the performers could not be heard when they could not be seen sufficiently and that if they moved upstage their stylised actions and facial expressions suddenly became invisible. Consequently, any sense of immediacy and rapport with the audience had been lost. Although this observation may have been an exaggeration, the levels of illumination achieved by the combination of the existing technology and the placement of lights clearly dictated where actors could stand and where they could move on the stage. This combination of factors played a significant role in establishing the rather static, mannered style of performing that perplexed Diderot and hindered his desire for a more 'natural' presentation.

Resistance to suggested changes in both lighting methods and technology was also evident from the actors in Paris who, especially at the Comédie Française, consistently delayed the implementation of technological improvements. In 1783 they objected to suggestions that the wax footlights be replaced by oil lamps with multiple wicks, on the grounds that the smoke would adversely affect their chests and throats.[8] This inherent conservatism was also evident in their resistance to gas footlights early in the nineteenth century, which ensured that this particular lighting technology was introduced there only in the 1870s, around 50 years after the other major theatres in Paris had converted to gas.

Writing in 1802, the Architect Louis Catel summed up the problems with footlights:

> Unfortunately, it is almost impossible to invent something better to replace this type of lighting, which lights the actors from below in a most unnatural, even unpleasant way. Attempts have been made to avoid this by using side-lights attached to the walls of the proscenium, but because it is much too wide, not

---

[8] *Délibérations d'assemblée*, 25 avril 1783 Bibliotheque de la Comédie Française, cited in Bergman, 1977: 196–198.

enough light reaches the centre of the stage. If we were to try directing the light down from above, the great distance would also prevent enough light from reaching the actors.

(Catel, 1802 in Schivelbusch, 1995: 195)

LAVOISIER – A REAPPRAISAL OF LIGHTING TECHNIQUES IN THE THEATRE (1781)

At the end of the eighteenth century, methods of lighting the stage had become a significant aesthetic concern. The unsatisfactory impact of lighting on the theatrical event was the focus of a speech made in 1781 by the famous scientist **Antoine Lavoisier** (1743–1794) to the Academy of Sciences in Paris. His 'Paper on how to illuminate the auditoria' (Lavoisier, 1865: 91–101) is highly critical of the indiscriminate methods of illumination in the playhouse and the obstruction to the sightlines caused by the suspended chandeliers, especially for those seated in the balconies and boxes. Lavoisier notes the disturbances caused by the lowering of the chandeliers and constant trimming of the candlewicks. He also acknowledges recent developments in the replacement of oil and tallow candles by wax and the abandonment of some of the auditorium chandeliers, in favour of more delicate constructions centred in the auditorium near the stage. Importantly, Lavoisier notes that the consequences of this change had resulted in an increased reliance on the footlights and an unsatisfactory spill of light onto the walls of the auditorium. He reveals the impact that these lighting changes have made on the gloomy auditoria and to the overall experience of theatre-going, complaining that there is insufficient light to recognise other theatre-goers, to read a text with even a large type and that away from the footlights students cannot see sufficiently to follow the play in their textbooks.

Echoing Ingegneri, Lavoisier laments the problem of dazzling light between the eyes of the audience and the illuminated stage, which distracts and makes it difficult to discern objects and action on stage. Like Furttenbach, Lavoisier calls for a comprehensive solution that included subdued lighting for the house, overhead lighting with parabolic reflectors or *réverbères* above the stage for the scenery and (like Sabbattini and Furttenbach) screened footlights for the actor. Lavoisier advocated lights with reflective mirrors in units similar to those designed earlier by Furttenbach, allowing the candle's light to be intensified and directed forward. These special elliptical lights with reflectors (reverberators) should, he suggested, also be concealed within the ceiling for illuminating the audience but should be brighter in the stalls and decrease in intensity towards the circle.

Lavoisier's suggestion of the addition of a tube to the front of the *réverbères* to direct the elliptical beam, and a yoke that allowed the light source to be swivelled and tilted to direct the light on stage, provides the first primitive focusable lantern for the stage. Lavoisier's work during this age of scientific discovery and endeavour inspired and influenced Aimé Argand, who was to be responsible for the next significant technical development in lighting in the 1780s.

The Paris theatres exploited recent scientific discoveries in optics and took advantage of local experimentation in street lighting technology. A variety of 'reverberator' units, originally developed to improve the brightness of the city lights, are recorded in the documentation of productions. The addition of Lavoisier's parabolic reflectors coupled with the adoption of multiple wicks resulted in a significant improvement to the overall levels of illumination achieved on the stage. This technological advance seems at least partly a direct response to the growing levels of ambient light outside of the theatre and a consequent shift in public expectation of how interior spaces might be illuminated. However, it is worth emphasising that the onstage lighting behind the proscenium is still at this point essentially for the illumination of the scenery and that the footlights and auditorium lighting near the front of the stage remained the primary means of illuminating the performers.

Economic factors also impinged on what was possible. The Paris Opéra in 1783 was largely illuminated by oil lamps, each with eight wicks that created an array of nearly 800 separate flames, with each flame producing about twice as much light as a wax candle. However, evidence suggests that financial concerns meant that rehearsals took place in much lower lighting conditions and it was not until the final dress rehearsals that performances took place under full stage lighting. Even then, this full lighting may only have been used for the first few performances before a cheaper, subdued and perfunctory alternative was used. Evidence for this is provided in correspondence between the Italian designer Ferdinando Quaglio and the Comédie Française at the beginning of the nineteenth century, where Quaglio is clearly seeking to ensure the quality of the lighting in his design for a revival of Voltaire's *Semiramis*: 'the illumination should be to my taste and regardless of expenses, particularly during the first two or three nights' (cited in Bergman, 1977: 240). However, the theatre's unsympathetic response indicates that light was still regarded as functional and Quaglio was told firmly that the theatre would organise the lighting since they did not consider this aspect to be the responsibility of the scene-designer.

LIGHT AS SIGN – *CHIAROSCURO* AND PAINTED SHADOWS

During the Baroque period it was changing aesthetic taste rather than technological developments that affected how light was actually used on the stage, and the organisation of light was an uneasy relationship between that of the wax and oil fixtures and the *painted* light of the settings. Complex oblique perspective scenes had evolved through designers such as Andrea Pozzo and through successive dynasties of scenographers who were employed widely in theatres across Europe.[9] These grander, non-symmetrical perspective settings, with their painted shadows, initiated a new form of composition for the entire stage, not simply as graphic backdrops. Complex combinations of perspective painting and stage constructions provided audiences with a rich visual feast and a romanticised view of the world in monumental and atmospherically charged stage pictures created by the layering of scenic elements and a light that was primarily signalled through the medium of paint.

The style is perhaps best exemplified by the 'theatrical' designs of the artist **Gianbattista Piranesi** (1720–1778), whose paintings were influenced by the scenic techniques of the time. The subsequent widespread publication of prints of his paintings in turn influenced stage designs. Piranesi used directional lighting to evoke images such as dark prison cells, sunlit courtyards and Roman ruins. When these settings were recreated on the stage, however, the *chiaroscuro* effect (an Italian term meaning 'clear–dark'; see below) was still achieved largely by paint. Shadows were painted on canvas and other scenery whilst the stage remained illuminated mainly from the front by a general wash of stage lighting, accentuated on occasion by directional lighting from the wings through methods that had been developed a century earlier. These scenic practices had spread widely throughout Western Europe by the eighteenth century and continued to inspire – and at the same time to be influenced by – the work of other fine artists.

Other commentators, like Servandori and the Venetian philosopher and writer Count **Francesco Algarotti** (1712–1764), were beginning to question the visual aesthetic being employed on the stage. Algarotti criticised the staging practice of opera and advocated a new style of performance where all elements of the music, including the singing, should be subordinated to a unifying poetic vision in which lighting should play a vital part. In *Saggio sopra l'opera in musica* (1755) he observed:

> Another thing which is very important to observe and which it would be a great mistake to neglect, is the lighting of the sceneries. One does not know at all how to distribute it evenly and with economy. The elements are poorly illuminated and always with insensitive shades, which do not make them stand out. What wonderful thing might be created if they learnt the art of distributing the light – if it were to be concentrated *en masse* on some parts of the stage, excluding others, wouldn't it then bring to the stage the power and vivacity of the chiaroscuro that Rembrandt succeeded in putting into his painting? It might even be possible to create that delightful interplay of light and shade that you will find in Giorgione's and Titian's paintings?
>
> (Algarotti, 1773: 81)

Algarotti was fascinated by light and having studied Newton's theories of light, colour and optics, he suggested techniques using filtered lighting

---

[9] E.g. Bibienas 1680s–1787, Galliaris 1700s–1823, Mauros 1680s–1820, Quaglios 1630s–1942.

through oiled paper to produce soft tones of vaporous light. Algarotti envisaged a stage of greater illusion and argued against the uniform, even illumination of the scenic stage in favour of heavy accents of light and shade
through directional lighting. *Chiaroscuro* relates to the technique of defining
areas of light and shade as a way of revealing three-dimensional form. It was
adopted as a term initially in fine art to describe any significant contrasts
between light and darkness and, as Brockett suggests, this aesthetic was to
underpin reforms in scenic practice:

> Perhaps the most important innovation of the late eighteenth century was the
> introduction of 'mood' into design. Before the late eighteenth century, settings
> were for the most part painted so that every detail was depicted clearly. Now
> designers began to emphasize the atmospheric values of light and shadow [...]
> Scenic designers began to depict picturesque places as seen by moonlight or
> interiors illuminated by a few shafts of light. Color played only a minor role in this
> trend, for the palette was limited. Settings were painted in sepia or pastel shades
> of green, yellow and lavender. Mood, therefore, was achieved primarily through
> the juxtaposition of masses of light and shadow.
>
> (Brockett 1991: 317)

Writings of the time, however, show that there were contradictions between
the illusionary painted scenery, with its two-dimensional evocation of light
and dark, and the actual practical lighting of the stage. The inconsistency of
the visual image presented to the audience is remarked on in this review of
a 1760 revival of Rameau's *Dardanus* at the Paris Opéra. Designed by Pierre
Antoine de Machy (1723–1807), a pupil of Servandoni, the set of a prison
was presented in imitation of the *chiaroscuro* effects in Piranesi's *Carceri
d'Invenzione*:

> The scenery [...] is one of the most beautiful examples of perspective that we have
> seen on the stage. This prison is taken from the engravings of the celebrated
> Piranesi, the Venetian architect [...] At last we see a scene stripped of boring
> monotony and cold symmetry but which is ingeniously conceived and tending
> towards the grandiose, whose ground plan and angular arrangement allows one
> to catch a glimpse of beautiful vanishing points, and whose effect of light and
> shade is caused by two lamps.
>
> It is painted freehand and rendered with the intelligence which controls the
> Piranesi engraving. One can nevertheless, reproach the painter for not having kept
> his foregrounds strong enough in order to make the background recede; for hav-
> ing over-lighted the lower portion of the ceiling from the fifth wing on, and for
> having kept the first flat too dull, which naturally ought to be all the more lighted,
> because it is placed beneath the lamp. Moreover, as it is supposed that the prison
> is lighted only by two lamps, it was noticed that, in general, the scene was too
> uniformly lighted. It would have been more appropriate to make total night with
> the wings, as has been done with the footlights, in order to concentrate all the
> light on the place where Dardanus is seated, which, if it had not been lighted by
> an inappropriate light, would have given greater illusion and would have caused

the terror which the sight of such objects should naturally inspire. This darkness would have made a still more striking contrast with the brilliant clouds which come down into the prison in order to beautify it with light.

(*L'Avant-Coureur* describes the scene, 21 April 1760 in Nagler, 1952: 319–320)

NOVERRE AND THE *BALLET D'ACTION* (1760)

In the same year, the dancer and choreographer **Jean Georges Noverre** (1727–1810) envisaged a form of dance that could be staged discretely as a performance in its own right, not simply as an interlude within a performance of an opera. Noverre saw the ballet as a unified work of art in which technical display for its own sake should be discouraged and which would require the musician, designer and choreographer to collaborate closely to achieve artistic unity. He was critical of the *vraiement* of Servandori's experimental stages and conceived the '*Ballet d'action*' as a living picture, or rather a series of moving painterly images of colour, patterns and tone that linked to a central narrative. Lighting was a key aspect of Noverre's new dance form and, in his 1760 treatise, he outlined practical measures to achieve a unified style of presentation that would achieve a balance between painted light and stage light:

> It is not the great number of lamps, used at haphazard or applied symmetrically that gives good light on the stage. The difficult thing is to be able to distribute the light unevenly ('par parties ou par *masses* inégales') so as to set off the parts that need strong light, to tone down where necessary and to put wholly in shadow where no light is needed. In the same way as the painter provides shades and degradations in his pictures for the sake of perspective, the person setting the light should consult him, so that the same shades and degradations can be seen in the lighting. There is nothing so ugly as a scenery painted in the same hue and without shades. 'Lointain' [remoteness or distance] and perspective are lacking there. In the same way: if the different parts of the painting which, together, form the whole, are illuminated with the same intensity, there will be no united effect, no contrasts, and the painting will be without effect.
>
> (Noverre, 1760: 18 trans. Bergman, 1977: 180)

Issues arising from the painted scene and the intensity of light were to become even more prominent during the next century, when the painting of shadows on scenery could no longer be sustained aesthetically.

LIGHTING DEVELOPMENTS IN LONDON – GARRICK AND DE LOUTHERBOURG

The 1760s marked an important shift in lighting practices. Influenced by techniques observed on the continent, **David Garrick** (1717–1779) at the Drury

Lane Theatre sought to achieve a new truth or *vraisemblance* on the stage. This demanded a new approach to lighting and in 1765, with the assistance of Jean Monnet, director of the Paris Opéra, Garrick imported lighting equipment and techniques that he had admired there. The new equipment led to a reform of staging practice in Britain and resulted in the removal at Drury Lane of all overhead chandelier lighting, the installation of footlights and the increased prominence of light sources behind the proscenium, including the addition of vertical battens of lamps which were hung behind wing shutters. The *Universal Museum* noted in September 1765:

> The public were agreeably surprised at the opening of Drury Lane-theatre, to see the stage illuminated with a strong and clear light, and the rings removed that used to supply it, though to the great annoyance of many of the audience, and frequently the actors themselves.
>
> (cited in Bergman, 1977: 216)

The loss of the chandeliers was especially welcomed since it removed the threat of hot dripping wax from above and reduced the frequent interruptions from the candlesnuffers. The adoption of continental practices shifted the lighting emphasis from the auditorium to sources behind the proscenium and above the apron, although in many ways these changes further emphasised the role of the footlights.[10]

Garrick introduced a new form of footlight to the British stage. This 'float' consisted of a long metal trough set into the front of the stage and which held rectangular metal saucers each containing two wicks and floating on oil. The entire trough was counterweighted so that it could be lowered below the stage floor by the prompter, through a series of ropes and pulleys. This allowed for a primitive dimming of the front-light, while the increased lighting from concealed sources in the wings created 'a perfect Meridian of Wax'[11] and a new visual experience for Garrick's audience.

The adoption of continental lighting techniques represented an improvement in the types, numbers and positions of light sources on the London stage which, in combination with the introduction of reflectors, allowed light output to be maximised. The importance of light as an integral aspect of Garrick's staging can be seen both in the rapidly rising lighting expenses at Drury Lane[12] and his later employment of Loutherbourg.

The influence and working methods of Strasbourg-born painter and scenographer **Phillippe-Jacques de Loutherbourg** (1740–1812) were a major influence on British staging practice. Loutherbourg's control and mastery

---

[10] Penzel notes that footlights had been used in Britain since at least 1670 and that therefore the notion that Garrick brought the footlight over from France is clearly erroneous (1978: 21).

[11] *The Public Advertiser* 25 September 1765 in *Drury Lane Calendar* 1938 xvii (Nicholl, 1980: 117).

[12] These rose steeply from around £400 per annum in 1747 to £1,200 in 1766 and £2,000 by Garrick's retirement in 1776 (Stone, 1962, IV, I ccxxxiv–v).

over all of the visual aspects of performance, including a detailed concern with light, established the role of the designer as central to the theatrical process. His pre-employment letter to Garrick, probably written in March 1772, demonstrates the importance that Loutherbourg placed on the control of lighting as an integral aspect of the visual experience for the audience as well as a new hierarchy in working practice to serve the creation of a unified visual image:

> I do not want to do for you a commonplace thing such as has already been done in some other places, but really something which will do me honour, and profit you and me.

> In order to achieve this, I must invent scenery which will have the effect of creating a new sensation upon the public. To this end, I must change the method of lighting the stage so as to serve the effects of the painting. [. . .] Furthermore, I must make a small model of the settings and everything which is required, to scale, painted and detailed so as to put the working painters and machinists and others on the right track by being able to faithfully copy my models, and if I deem it necessary to retouch something in the final display, to enhance the effect, then I must do so. I shall draw in colour the costumes for the actors and the dancers. I must res*f*onne [discuss] my work with the composer and the ballet-master. In this way, you may see that I will spare nothing for the success of a project to which I have committed my reputation. If you were to give me full authority over all of your workers, I would use this trust as an honest man and would treat your interests as my own. You will bear the necessary charges for all the materials for this work . . .

> (cited in Baugh, 1987: 127–128)

Loutherbourg was employed specifically to design elaborate spectacles, fairytales and pantomimes at Drury Lane, and his work there was heavily influenced by the Italian staging techniques which he had observed first hand in Paris. Loutherbourg's vision had the effect of drawing the performers from the neutral playing space of the apron into the scenic stage and, by doing so, instigated a new style of performance for British audiences. The critical response to Loutherbourg's designs for *The Runaway* at Drury Lane, in the *Morning Chronicle* of 16 February 1776, neatly summarises the impact of his achievements claiming that he was:

> The first artist who showed our theatre directors that by a just disposition of light and shade, and a critical preservation of perspective, the eye of a specta-tor might be so effectually [sic] deceived in a playhouse, as to be induced to take the produce of art for real nature.

> (cited in Thomas, 1944: 68)

Loutherbourg's experimental work (see pp. 30–32), together with his painstaking organisation of the main stage at Drury Lane, had a significant influence on future staging practice. His use of cut cloths with perspective vistas transformed the way in which the entire stage space was organised and illuminated, and supports the view that he has a right to be considered as the first modern scenographer.

The interrelationship of paint and light remains central to the dramaturgy of this period. Light was clearly acknowledged as critical to the way in which painted scenes were experienced and, in order to create 'new sensations upon the public', light for Loutherbourg became more important than simply working sympathetically to 'serve the effects of the painting'.

The new prominence of scenery within the theatrical event was to dominate future staging practices, and by the first decade of the nineteenth century the neutral stage space had disappeared. In order to accommodate the new scenography, the plain apron stage along with its auditorium doors vanished behind a proscenium arch and was replaced by a new space of performance. This pictorial stage instigated a fundamental change in the relationship between the audience and the stage, since the theatrical event was now viewed entirely through the proscenium frame.

TECHNOLOGICAL DEVELOPMENTS IN THE EIGHTEENTH CENTURY

A series of technological advances in lighting technology occurred within a short period in the latter half of the eighteenth century. We have already noted the scientific experimentations with lenses and the mirrored metal reflectors or *réverbères* which, with their multiple wicks, had made an impact in the streets and then the theatres of Paris. Throughout the seventeenth and eighteenth centuries the levels of illumination of the stage had very gradually increased, but the naked flame and the various methods of reflecting this light towards the stage had reached their peak. In the mid-1770s, oil lamps were made more efficient by Léger's development of a twisted, ribbon-like flat wick to replace the single-stranded one, and in 1820 Cambacérès invented the plaited or braided wick which was self-trimming and for the first time negated the need for a candle snuffer. Although these two important developments were critical for developing candle technology, a more significant invention, as far as lighting the stage was concerned, was made by the Swiss chemist **Francois Pierre Ami Argand** (c. 1750–1803) who, between 1780 and 1784, developed and patented the Argand burner. This innovation provided a substantial increase in the levels of illumination available from a single flame whilst also using less oil than conventional oil lamps. Its tubular wick allowed air to pass through the flame and a hollow cylinder placed over the wick created an updraft that intensified the flame and multiplied the light output:

> A lamp so constructed as to produce neither smoak (sic) nor smell and to give considerably more light than any lamp hitherto known, by converting the smoak into flame, by causing a current of air to pass through the inside of air on the outside of the wick by means of a chimney.
>
> (*Patent 1425*, 1784 in Penzel, 1978: 24)

Further improvements, including the use of a glass chimney (Quinquet and Lange) and locating the reservoir for the oil beneath the lamp (to avoid obstructing the light in one direction), improved the overall light output to around ten times that of a wax candle. The Argand burner had a major impact on lighting levels in the public sphere, and the substantial multiplication of the brightness not only improved overall levels of visibility on the stage but enabled atmospheric directional light and shadow effects to be achieved much more easily. The improvement in the level and quality of light when good oil was used explains the relatively rapid adoption of this new technology in the theatre.

The first performance of Beaumarchais' *The Marriage of Figaro* by the Comédie Française on 27 April 1784 employed Argand lamps in the newly opened Odéon, where a number of lighting experiments had taken place prior to its opening:

> They have used an invention by MM Lange and Quinquet. This lamp, which is of a very superior kind, though it still leaves a lot to be desired, was judged to be the best they had tested. It is live, soft and neat without the least smoke and not very expensive.
>
> (L.P. de Bachaumont, *Mémoires secrets*, vol. XXX, London 1786: 260 cited in Bergman, 1977: 200)

Argand lamps, or quinquets as they were known in France, made an immediate impact in the public sphere and began to be used for the lighting of streets, buildings and wealthier private homes. Later developments of circular wicks, double cylindrical tubes and the use of good-quality spermaceti oil enabled a whiter light to be produced that was measured to be the equivalent of 8–12 ordinary wax candles. The quality of the oil was an essential element that determined the type of light and the amount of smoke given off. There were problems, however, and their uptake in theatres was not universal but rather a gradual process from the 1780s. Dripping oil from auditorium lights and the shattering of the early glass chimneys from the effects of the heat were frequent problems, but despite this the Argand lamp revolutionised stage lighting at the turn of the nineteenth century:

> We can now, by means of this [lamp], illuminate with a small number of flames and need not fear to put out or dim the other lamps by the heat and vapour from one lamp. One now illumines the largest stages up to the middle agreeably and, without any great difficulty, even brilliantly.
>
> (C.G. Langhans[13] trans. Bergman, 1977: 202).

The improvement in the quality and colour of the light was significant, but the tenfold increase in the level of illumination from the Argand lamp enabled a more flexible use of the stage. Langhans' observation is important

---

[13] *Über Theater und Bemerkungen über Katakustik in Beziehung auf Theater* (Berlin, 1810: 29).

as it suggests that for the first time performers could move upstage away from the footlights without worrying that they wouldn't be seen. A larger area of the stage was therefore available for dramatic action to take place, and the increase in lighting levels instigated by the Argand burner (and accelerated by the subsequent advent of gaslight) also promoted a gradual toning down of the declamatory acting styles towards a less heightened style of presentation. Traditions relating to facial expressions and the application of make-up were also gradually revised, while a move towards a 'correctness' of historical costume styles in combination with the increased light levels allowed for darker colours to be used rather than the lustrous materials in which performers had hitherto been dressed in order to reflect what available light there was on the stage.

Baugh observes that 'Argand lamp technology provided sufficient illumination to introduce the possibility of projecting special effects' (2007: 52) and cites Elliston's production of *King Lear* at Drury Lane in April 1820, which was described in the diary of its stage manager James Winston as being lit 'by a new process from the top of the stage' (Nelson and Cross, 1974: 8).

This 'new process' relates specifically to a projection used in the storm scene and was even advertised in advance on the playbill as 'After the manner of *Loutherburg's* [sic] *Eidophusikon'*:

> [o]verhead were revolving prismatic coloured transparencies, to emit a continuously changing supernatural tint, and add[ing] to the unearthly character of the scene, King Lear would one instant appear a beautiful pea-green and the next sky-blue, and, in the event of a momentary cessation of the rotary motion of the magic lantern, his head would be purple and his legs Dutch-pink.
>
> (Cowell, 1844: 47)

The brighter light of the Argand burner had opened up new opportunities in both lighting the stage and in scenic projection techniques which, as a result, were to proliferate in exhibitions, fairgrounds and theatres throughout the next century. This invention had maximised the light available from the oil lamp, which was now a highly portable and relatively efficient light source. As well as encouraging a new visual aesthetic on the stage, the brighter light had liberated the performers from the tyranny of the footlights and the constant need to position themselves downstage. However, despite the new technologies, the actual techniques for lighting the stage had not changed significantly since the Renaissance period. Experiments with keylighting and colour to establish both mood and atmosphere were an important development, but the actual lighting equipment and its positioning within the stage area and front of house had not fundamentally altered. It would take the arrival of a new technology, that of gaslight, to provide new artistic possibilities which would be created from a further increase in the intensity of light and, for the first time, the opportunity for remote control over the light sources on the stage.

Chapter

4   Light and the Audience

This chapter concentrates on the impact of light upon viewers of performance. It includes essays by academic commentators seeking to understand the function of lighting on the stage, and how we might decode light signs on the stage in an attempt to explain how lighting makes meaning and is felt by an audience in performance.

Academics in the twentieth century repeatedly sought to explain the way in which events on stage can be decoded and understood: 'The art of lighting, which claims to be a visual art, is obviously not only a spatial but also a temporal art' (Jan Mukařovský 1976: 229).

One of the key models for doing so was offered through semiotic analyses that attempted to provide a systematic explanation of theatrical performance. Building on the work of Otakar Zich in *Esthetics of Dramatic Art* (1931) and the work of Prague School scholars such as Petr Bogatyrev, Jindřich Honzl and Jan Mukařovský, a number of academics have addressed the stage event from an explicitly structuralist approach. For Jiří Veltruský, 'as soon as an act by itself [on the stage] attracts the attention of the perceiver, its properties become signs. It then enters the consciousness by means of signs and becomes meaning' (Veltruský, 1964: 84). Although the limitations of this method of analysis have increasingly been acknowledged, important observations relating to how light can make meaning on the stage have been articulated through the use of semiotic analysis (see Pavis, Esslin and Fischer-Lichte, below).

One of the primary alternatives to semiotics is found in phenomenological analysis. Bert States, a leading exponent of this method, acknowledges the complexities of signs on stage:

we tend generally to undervalue the elementary fact that theater—unlike fiction, painting, sculpture and film—is really a language whose words consist to an unusual degree of things that *are* what they seem to be. In theater, image and object, pretense and pretender, sign-vehicle and content, draw unusually close. Or, as Peter Handke more interestingly puts it, in the theater light is brightness pretending to be other brightness, a chair is a chair pretending to be another chair, and so on.[1]

(States, 1985: 20, italics in original)

Light on the stage rarely draws attention to itself or asks to be understood by the audience as 'theatrical light'. However, in a sequence from Cirque de Soleil's performance of *Varekai* (2002), a performer attempts to escape the attentions of a single follow-spot on an otherwise dark stage. In this rare instance the light itself becomes the central focus of a comic scene as the onstage figure attempts to hide in the darkness from the constantly searching, playful light. The audience's attention is thereby drawn to the physical manipulation of the light from above the stage space and the comedy stems from an implicit knowledge of the conventions and function of the follow-spot. In this example the light represents a particular type of theatrical light of the most identifiable and prominent sort, but more usually light in the stage space is intended to represent the light found outside the theatre.

In forms of performance rooted in realism, which attempt to create a recognisable representation of the world, stage lighting frequently attempts to replicate sunlight – either directly or indirectly (e.g. as if reflected from the moon). In interior settings, stage lighting may instead attempt to mimic the effect of light from a candle or a lamp. Motivating light sources, which are visible to the audience and dictate the composition of a scene (e.g. lamp, candle, chandelier), are rarely bright enough on their own to achieve sufficient visibility, so a theatrical 'cheat' is often employed by the lighting designer through the use of offstage light sources to allow the scene to appear to be illuminated by the visible source. Motivated light from offstage, where the source is not visible to an audience, is typical in performances that are rooted in any form of realistic representation and may therefore provide the main compositional element on stage. Theatrical moonlight streaming into the stage space through a window, for example, may provide the main key-lighting for a scene, even though the moon itself is not visible. The stage lighting signifies moonlight – it is, in Handke's words, 'brightness pretending to be other brightness'.

In other instances, the relationship is more transparent:

In Act 2 of *Waiting for Godot*, Beckett's stage direction (1965: 52) signals a key moment in the play as the stage is suddenly transformed into night and requires the moon itself to become the motivating light source. The uncanny way in which the light appears to 'fail' and the moon rises not only foregrounds the temporal aspects of the play but also emphasises the uncertain nature of the environment in which the characters find themselves. In this example the light is an object which signifies the moon and that also draws attention to itself through a deliberate theatricality in its sudden

---

[1] States refers here to Peter Handke's *Kaspar and Other Plays*, trans. Roloff et al., 1969: 10.

appearance on stage. This in turn conditions, shapes and reinforces how the entire landscape of the play is perceived by the audience.

Although stage light is able to signify meaning through pretending to be 'sunrise' or 'sunlight through trees', the precise way in which it acts upon the audience in a theatrical performance is complex. Although the patterns, colours and structures of light may provide a dynamic articulation of space, they rarely bear any relation to the creation of a realistic representation of the external world at all. In contemporary dance performances, for example, light is rarely pretending to be 'other brightness' but is an integral material element of the overall composition and creates a dynamic virtual architecture of the performance space.

While light is recognised by many commentators as a fundamental creative element in theatrical performance and its direct impact on an audience's reception acknowledged, few have sought to attempt a detailed analysis of this relationship. Patrice Pavis provides a possible explanation of why academics have tended to shy away from attempting to deal with this subject: 'The stage event is not always easy to describe, because signs in current performance practice are often tiny, almost imperceptible, and invariably ambiguous, if not unreadable' (Pavis, 2003: 24). Light, as the most ephemeral of these 'signs', is perhaps the most difficult to quantify through language in this way.

In *Theatre Audiences*, Susan Bennett acknowledges the role of the *mise en scène* in the signifying process, but largely ignores the direct impact of light on the audience experience, despite observing in a description of lighting moments from Beckett's *Play* that the audience need to be able to decode the blackouts (Bennett, 1997: 150–151). Hans-Thies Lehmann writes of the development of 'A *theatre of scenography*' and argues that meaning is communicated in post-dramatic theatre through 'visual dramaturgy' (Lehmann, 2006: 93) but ignores the specific role that light performs.

Martin Esslin, in *The Field of Drama*, also notes the importance of visual signs in dramatic performance and argues that they have been overlooked by scholars in favour of the tangible evidence of what remains after the performance – the word on the printed page. Esslin specifically acknowledges the role of light in creating meaning:

> The use of light plays an ever increasing role among the visual signifying systems of drama. It has an obvious iconic function indicating day and night, sunny and gloomy conditions, etc. and also displays equally obvious symbolic aspects. [...] But the most important function of light in dramatic performance is deictic.[2] It is the lighting that can direct attention to the focal points of the action, almost literally an 'index' finger pointed at the area of maximum interest. A spotlight may draw attention to the leading character and follow his movements. It may highlight an important object. This is equally true of the stage and of the cinematic media.

---

[2] 'Deictic' is a semiological term for the function of indicating.

Indeed, in the cinema the 'lighting cameraman' is one of the dominant creative personalities. On the stage the emergence of sophisticated lighting apparatus nowadays electronically pre-programmable, has led to more and more intricate nuances of lighting in complex and subtle lighting plots, and to the emergence of the 'lighting designer' as one of the principal creative artists contributing to the performance.

The style and detail of the lighting may – both in the theatre and in the cinematic media – determine the whole 'texture' of the performance, it may keep the action in a chiaroscuro throughout, or, as in the style advocated by Brecht, plunge it into unvarying and glaring clarity (even in scenes taking place at night, when that fact will have to be indicated by properties such as lamps or candles), with all the innumerable variations that lie between these two extremes.

(Esslin, 1987: 76–77)

Pavis, in *Analyzing Performance*, notes the recent technical developments and growing importance of lighting to the reception of performance, 'No other stage system has made as much technical progress in recent years as lighting has' (2003: 191), and argues that in order fully to appreciate performance, spectators need to be 'sensitized to the dramaturgy of light' (ibid.: 192).

DRAMATURGY OF LIGHT

When one attends a performance, one can always try to understand the lighting design as system, that is, the *mise-en-scène* of light, the production's particular way of bringing light and shadows to bear within the performance.

The type of light used needs to be established: whether it be natural sunlight or moonlight, or artificial light (currently capable of recreating the conditions of natural light).

One should signal the moments at which light intervenes in the performance as it unfolds, and with what kinds of effect.

The kinds of phenomena, whether fleeting or ongoing, that light has enabled us to perceive should also be evaluated: isolated effects or continuous changes of atmosphere, revelation of a feeling or overshadowing of an action, and so on.

One should ask oneself what the light illuminates as well as what it conceals, whether the *mise-en-scène* established light in order to place itself in the shadows or vice versa.

Light facilitates understanding. If a lit object is well contrasted, it will be clearly recognized. Light is responsible for the degree of comfort and discomfort in the act of listening, the more or less rational understanding of an event. When the bright, open wash of a Brecht or Jean Vilar production is replaced by the twilight stage of a Patrice Chéreau or André Engel production, it is as if the vision of the world has darkened. When Giorgio Strehler (and his lighting designer Guido Baroni) successfully reconcile the white Brechtian light of a dramaturgy that has nothing to

hide with the sensual, southern European light of an Italian Renaissance painting, lighting achieves a unique compromise between rationality and subjectivity. [...]
An appreciation of lighting entails an understanding of the ways in which light impacts upon the other components of the performance. [...]
Every aspect of the actor is sometimes affected by light: his energy is either heightened or muted. An actor's relationship with the spectators is transparent, particularly with the lights on full, or disrupted if he is blinded by a shaft of light or reduced to a voice in the shadowy gloom. If an actor needs lighting in the same way that a plant needs water (as Chéreau suggests), sometimes they can be victims of lighting that is violent, antagonistic toward them, as if it set out to destabilize or assault them. An experienced external eye will be able to distinguish between an aggression effected with the actors' 'agreement', and an untimely intervention by a lighting designer who has failed to consult either the director or the actor.

In short, lighting allows the dramaturgy of a performance to be guided and inscribed in time, particularly in terms of the temporal and narrative articulation of the action.

(Pavis, 2003: 191–195)

SEMIOTICS OF LIGHT

The German scholar Erika Fischer-Lichte examines the variety of ways in which light makes meaning in *The Semiotics of Theater*. In this important text she moves from the practical and functional role of light, such as its ability to create space on the stage, to an analysis of the way in which light signifies meaning. She develops Handke's observation as to how light in the theatre is used to signify light itself, but moves beyond this assertion to examine the codes and conventions of light. In acknowledging the potential of light in performance through the technological developments of the twentieth century, Fischer-Lichte explores the complexity of the range of meanings that may be created with light within specific cultural contexts:

Lighting

We have listed lighting as the third category of signs which are capable of adding to the possible significations of the stage space. Since 'lighting' can refer both to the technical installations which produce certain kinds of light on the stage and the quality of light itself, we will in the following, for the sake of clarity, use the term 'light' when referring to light in the sense of a specific sign system, and the term 'lighting' for the technical facilities which serve to generate these signs in the theater.

Both natural and artificially produced light – like natural and artificially created spaces – can be interpreted in terms of their practical and symbolic functions. Making a space visible is, generally speaking, a practical function of light. Illumination of the space is what first allows the latter to become evident and to look like a room.

In addition to this basic, practical function – and usually as a consequence of it – light can assume a wide variety of symbolic functions that are developed, fixed, and regulated in the widest variety of cultural codes – such as religion, poetry, painting, astronomy, meteorology. Nearly every culture not only has learned to interpret light as a sign in relation to the time of day and season of the year, but has also developed a rich store of light symbolism which, in its earliest origins, can probably be traced back to the juxtaposition of day and night, light and shadow.

In the theater light can be employed both in its practical function and as a sign for its symbolic functions.[i] It did not come to be used as a system which generates meaning until a relatively late date – in the case of Western theater since the seventeenth-century – when the time of day at which theater performances were held was changed from the afternoon to the evening, and the location moved from open squares to an enclosed room. The introduction of light as a theatrical system that generates meaning did not, however, coincide with this change. For, to the extent that light was merely used in its practical function[ii] – namely, in order to render the stage space and action on the stage visible – it was not possible to define it and understand it as a theatrical sign. It was not until the constant, unchanging lighting on the stage had been abandoned and the transition to more differentiated lighting had been accomplished – regardless of how this was done – that it became possible to assess and interpret the light on the stage as a theatrical sign.

In its quality as a sign employed in a given culture as well as in theater, light functions on the basis of the unities of (1) intensity, (2) color, (3) distribution, and (4) movement. If one of these factors charges, the meaning of the light can also change. Thus, for example, intensive yellow light on the stage may signify noon-day sunshine, dim yellow light afternoon sunshine, dim bluish light moonlight. Light distributed flooding the entire area can indicate an open space outdoors and light falling in rays, a forest. Light coming from the left may refer to the morning, and moving farther toward the back of the stage and from there to the right, the course of the day through midday to evening.

One of the fundamental sign-functions of light on the stage is to signify *light*: sunlight, moonlight, torchlight, candlelight, the light of a rainbow, neon light, and many others. By fulfilling this function, it can perform other functions at the same time that are related to the respective kind of light. For the light in each case has to be produced as concrete light that, for its part, may refer to meanings which have been developed in the widest variety of cultural – often poetic or iconographic – codes. Sunlight, for example, can be signified by bright yellow, muddy yellow, golden, or reddish yellow light, etc. This procedure may, depending on what is appropriate, define the sun as a ball of fire, an egg yoke, hair of the gods, or something of that nature; moonlight, as silver, bluish, greenish, or reddish light, depending on whether the moon is to be apostrophized as a silver ship crossing the heavens, the pallor of death, a drowned body, or a blood-red dagger. The particular way in which the light constitutes the meaning of "sunlight" or "moonlight" thus already implies and suggests the various possible symbolic meanings which are to be assigned to sunlight or moonlight in the context of a given performance.

In denoting "light," light can also connote a large number of other meanings. In view of these possible meanings, we shall distinguish between sign functions of the light that can only be performed in relation to other theatrical signs such as mimicry, gesture, external appearance, decoration, or props, and independent sign functions, which are related to categories such as place, time, characters, etc.

The technology which has been developed to date permits effects to be achieved with lighting on the stage which were neither possible nor conceivable for hundreds of years in the theater. The film camera can focus on isolated individual aspects of the actor – such as his mimicry in close-ups, a particular movement of the arm in a waist shot, parts of the costume such as the hat or boots – or of the decoration and individual props and present them to the audience. However, on the stage the actor is always present in life-size, and the arrangement of set elements and props constitute a complex which can only be changed by the actor in the course of his actions or by the stage hands during scene changes. Lighting makes it possible to take such signs out of this complex and isolate them. The light can fall solely on the actor's face or his moving hand, or illuminate a single element of the set or a prop, and its position in the room can at the same time change. In film a close-up both declares the isolated element temporarily as the sole agent of meaning, and magnifies its dimensions, thus offering it to the audience with a special emphasis on its function as a sign to be interpreted. In theater, on the other hand, the stage space remains present in its entirety – albeit as a large black hole – regardless of which elements are isolated by the light, and the individual elements such as the face, hand, the cross on the wall, or the rose retain their original dimensions. The use of light to isolate elements of the stage space thus results in a modification of the signifying quality of the elements thus isolated. The nature of this modification cannot be defined in generalized terms, but rather has to be investigated on a case-by-case basis. It can be said, however, that isolation based on the use of light frequently actualizes possible symbolic meanings. The light thus becomes fused with the sign it isolates, which we can qualify in a certain way as a specific sign that is capable of generating new meanings not previously thought of. In other words, the light transforms the sign of a sign system into a different sign of this sign system and creates new possible meanings to be actualized by it. It brings about a change in the possible meanings provided for in the repertoire of the respective sign systems, without itself functioning as a distinct sign with its own meanings.[iii]

If, on the other hand, light is employed as an independent sign, it can for its part constitute a multitude of different meanings. The light can signify the place at which X finds himself. Appia, for example, created the forest through which Siegfried goes with nothing other than a movement of light and shadow. Gründgens created Faust's grave with an oblong beam of light on an empty stage. Thus, light can signify a room or a hut, the inside of a cathedral or a cave, and any number of other things, and can even completely replace set decoration.

Light can be used to indicate the *time of day and season of the year*. If the light denotes sunlight, for example, it connotes daytime – and, in addition, the kind of light often indicates whether it is morning, noontime, afternoon, twilight – and moonlight connotes nighttime. It can signify a hot summer day or a gloomy winter afternoon, rainy or sunny weather. Moreover, it is able to indicate not only meteorological processes, but also both other natural courses of events and events in human society – in other words, *situations* and *actions*. This function is usually fulfilled by light in connection with nonverbal, acoustic signs, especially with sounds. In this way it can indicate conflagrations and storms, volcanic eruptions and meteors speeding through the heavens, trips in outer space and battles. Light can, in cooperation with sound, even temporarily replace the actor: Flashes of light and battle sounds can, for example, create the impression of a battle in which enemy soldiers are attacking each other, without a single actor having to be present on the stage.

The light can furthermore constitute meanings that are related to the personalities of the *characters*. It can identify a character as a saint or other luminous figure or signify that a character is lonely by isolating the entire character on stage, to name but two of them. When employed in connection with a character, light is primarily used as a sign that is capable of constituting meanings on the subject level. It primarily serves to make statements about their special status and their particular constitution. It was widely used in this function in baroque theater, especially in the apotheoses at the ends of the plays.

Light is one of the most important media for creating a particular *atmosphere*. In order to perform this function, it will usually be necessary to go back to cultural codes other than that of the theater, especially since one has to assume that specific light codes are developed in the culture in question and function accordingly. In our culture, for example, bright warm light is generally interpreted in relation to a quiet, warm, friendly atmosphere, whereas cloudy or cold light is as a whole understood in relation to an apprehensive atmosphere that provokes anxiety or sadness. A certain kind of moonlight is felt to be romantic, a specific kind of brightness – such as that of neon lamps – as obliterating feelings. If light in the theater is to constitute a certain atmosphere as meaning, it will therefore be necessary to go back to the corresponding light codes which function in our culture.

These light codes, however, are related not only to moods, but also to ideas. Thus, for example, darkness connotes the realm of the evil, the demonic, whereas brightness connotes that of the good, the divine. If light in the theater is used in a way that permits it to be related to such ideas, the light is also capable of signifying *ideas*. For example, a stage flooded with light at the end of a performance can point to the victory of the divine; if it sinks completely into darkness, the dissolution of the world in chaos. Such meanings can, of course, only be constituted from the context of a certain performance or by laying the groundwork of a corresponding valid theatrical norm.

Since it was first introduced, light as a system which generates meaning in theater has been employed in a wide variety of ways and with various objectives in mind. Whereas in baroque theater it was used primarily for the portrayal of natural catastrophes and apotheoses in order to signify the association between immanence and transcendence, its primary function in Romantic theater was to create atmosphere. In the realist and naturalist theaters, on the other hand, the objective was primarily to utilize light in its basic function – namely, to signify light – in a way that would create the illusion of a real room for the audience. In this case, light was supposed to be as "natural" as possible.

It was not possible to exploit the full range of meanings which light can have in theater until the twentieth century, by which time the necessary technical prerequisites had been created. However, even in our century the various theatrical norms diverge considerably from one another in terms of their use of light. Whereas Appia declared it the dominant sign in his theatrical code and developed its utilization accordingly, Brecht was determined to remove the sign system of light altogether from his theatrical code. Light was to be used merely in its practical function and to illuminate the stage space completely and evenly. When light was eliminated as a system that generates meaning, the fact of its elimination advanced to the status of a sign which was capable of signifying in a special way Brecht's rejection of atmospheric bourgeois theater.[3]

(Fischer-Lichte, 1992: 110–114)

Selected notes to pages 110–114

i. The practical function was fulfilled by natural light until the use of artificial lighting/daylight made the stage visible. If light is used on stage as a sign for its practical function, e.g., a candle is lit in order to show that the room is illuminated, then this always functions simultaneously as the sign for its symbolic functions. Here, these would be, for example, the onset of dusk, character X's fear of the dark, X's intention of giving a signal, or showing the way by means of the light of the candle, which she has set on the window sill, etc. Light is thus used in theater either in its practical function or as a sign for its possible symbolic meanings.

ii. If, for example, the stage servant in Kabuki theater approaches the actor and holds his candle up to the latter's face, then the candle exclusively fulfills a practical function: it is intended to make the actor's mimic gestures all the more visible. The issue whether light is used in a practical function or as a sign for its symbolic functions is something that can only be decided on the basis of the respective theatrical code.

iii. To my mind, Tairov was the first to use light in this function in individual scenes in various productions: the magic of the objects which moved through space without any visible cause was thus lent immediate expression. This type of use of light was later expanded further and perfected by the Black Theater in Prague and, in its train, numerous puppet and pantomime stages.

THE EXPERIENCE OF LIGHT

Barbara Bolt, an Australian artist and academic, is concerned with both the processes of making art and the way in which art makes meaning. In *Art Beyond Representation* she challenges existing Western approaches

---

[3] For alternative perspectives on Brecht's use of lighting as signification, see Chapter 6.

to understanding how we see and respond to works of art. The role of light is fundamental to the processes of both making and receiving creative work, but Bolt critiques prevalent Western approaches that are dominated by thinking rooted in the Enlightenment.

In a wide-ranging chapter, 'Shedding Light on the Matter', Bolt focuses on the thinking of the German philosopher Heidegger, 'whose experience of the world was predicated on the assumed illuminating quality of European light' (Bolt, 2004: 123), and examines alternative approaches to our understanding of the meaning of light. Citing the work of three contemporary philosophers, Merleau-Ponty, Levinas and Irigaray, she explains how they have been critically engaged in rethinking the relationship between light and matter, and that 'All three are in agreement that the relationship between vision and embodiment forms the nexus of signification' (ibid.: 127). She uses her own experience as a fine artist creating work in the unrelenting glare of light in the Australian outback to question our received notions of light and its impact on human creativity, asking: 'What if there is *too much* light? What if in the glare of the midday sun nothing is revealed?' (ibid.: 124).

Light, Bolt argues, should not be assumed to be a neutral medium but regarded as an active substance. Of particular interest to performance practitioners is the way in which this physical experience of light might help us to understand not only its physiological impact, and the way in which it affects the creative process, but also the way in which it conditions the actual reception of images.

THE PHENOMENOLOGICAL IMPACT OF LIGHT

Artaud acknowledged that light also affects audiences at a phenomenological level, evoking feelings and making a direct visceral impact that conditions our response. (see pp. 39–40). This important aspect of performance research has until recently been largely neglected by scholars, but our understanding of how light makes us 'feel' is an integral aspect of how it makes meaning. Stephen Di Benedetto (2010) has written about the physiological impact of light on the audience and, using Robert Wilson's work in particular, explores how light stimulates our brains and makes us feel in performance. (ibid.: 31–68). Melissa Trimingham in analysing Oskar Schlemmer's theatrical practice has drawn on the work of Gibson (1983) and Merleau-Ponty (1964) to explore the physical reception of light, our experience of light as audience members and our 'situatedness' as 'see-ers' in visual space.

In tracing the limits of semiotic analysis in relation to understanding performance, McKinney and Butterworth (2010) also focus on the experience and reception of the scenographic event, which offers 'a phenomenological encounter for the audience that stimulates embodied understandings of the physical and material world. Light fading to black on stage can evoke feelings in the pit of one's stomach' (ibid.: 184). Acknowledging the way in which we respond to light and the primary role that it plays in the visceral experience of being *in* an audience is essential to our understanding of performance. The phenomenological impact of light therefore needs to be recognised as central to the formation of theatrical meaning and our embodied responses to light acknowledged alongside potential semiotic readings on stage.

Chapter

5   Light and Space

This chapter investigates the origins of the use of light as an expressive material in defining, shaping and creating stage space. It focuses on the first modern theorisations of light as a designed element in performance and a legacy that extends throughout the twentieth century into modern lighting design practice, where the expressive qualities of light, its power of suggestion and its potential contribution to performance practice are often taken for granted.

The origins of contemporary thinking about light in performance can be attributed to the thinking and writing of two outstanding theatrical visionaries, Adolphe Appia (1862–1928) and Edward Gordon Craig (1872–1966). Their separate publications around the turn of the twentieth century revolutionised the way in which we think about light within the stage space. Both advocated a new role for light, not simply as an illuminating force but rather as a force to create aesthetic darkness. Light was recognised as a central and essential component of live performance – as an agency in its own right and not dependent on other elements on stage. In this respect, Appia and Craig's contributions mark the origins of modern lighting design in performance and have had a profound influence on all subsequent theatrical practice in the West. Their radical proposals foreground the idea that light itself could, on occasions, even become the dominant and most important element on the stage.

For the first time in these writings, light was considered as a temporal art, giving life to the stage through both defining and animating the space. Both Appia and Craig recognised the fluidity of light and its potential creative contribution to the development of dramatic art. Both practitioners made the link between light, space and music and what they advocated was in direct opposition to the outmoded staging practices of the time which, they argued, negated the creative potential that was inherent in the use of light and shadow.

Particularly in the decade from 1895, Appia and Craig marked a synchronous response to the complex forces of a 'new creative Zeitgeist' (MacGowan 1921: 78) – a key moment in time which many commentators have compared to the major changes of the Renaissance and where 'deep-seated shifts of sensibility inevitably bring about a change in man's way of seeing and looking' (Bablet 1982: 10). This transformation at the end of the nineteenth century was especially evident in the fine arts, in architecture and in the theatre, where Appia and Craig laid the foundations of modern performance practice and inspired future generations of directors and designers. Appia's 1897 treatise, *La musique et la mise en scène* (translated into German and widely circulated as *Die Musik und die Inscenierung*, Munich 1899), was the first widespread publication of his work, and it communicated for the first time the idea that light on the stage can affect our emotions directly and instantaneously, just like music does. These detailed written scenarios and sketches suggested ways in which light and space ought to be employed to evoke an emotional response in the audience. Appia's writing was revolutionary, and his proposal to place light as the central force of the drama was regarded by many of his contemporaries as largely incomprehensible (MacGowan 1921: 81–82).

Appia and Craig's approaches to the role of light originated not only at a time of ideological change but also on the cusp of a technological revolution. Their ideas were in part inspired by recent advances in technology but, importantly, they also anticipated future technical solutions to lighting the stage which became available as the twentieth century progressed and which were ultimately necessary to implement their respective visions in full.

The adoption of electricity in the theatre created the catalyst for the new approaches to stagecraft. On a practical level, its harsher light exposed the artificiality of the painted scene flat, demanding a new stage aesthetic. Electricity also offered a conscious and conspicuous control over a natural element in such a way as to almost denaturalise it. This technical and artistic freedom allowed an unparalleled opportunity to transform the way in which light might be employed on the modern stage – resolving the relative difficulties of creating and controlling light and unleashing a new potential for a fluid, dynamic approach to creating light and space in the theatre for the first time.

APPIA – LIGHT AND MUSIC

Adolphe Appia's impact on the thinking and practice of theatre production in the twentieth century stemmed from his vision for a new art form and was coupled with a dissatisfaction with contemporary staging techniques, which he regarded as fundamentally unsuited to the artistic intentions of the work. This disjunction was particularly heightened in opera productions, where the staging, he observed, failed entirely to meet the expressive heights demanded by the music. He demanded the abolition of flat, painted scenery in favour of a living, sculptural and 'plastic' stage space.

The inspiration for Appia's ideas relating to light and space came directly from Richard Wagner's music, and his first studies (1892–1894) were created in direct response to Wagner's libretto and musical score for *Das Ring*

Des Nieberlungen.[1] Wagner had advocated the idea of the *Gesamtkunstwerk* or 'total art form' in his essay *The Art-Work of the Future* (1849), and Appia's writings and detailed scenarios can be seen as a unique and logical reaction to Wagner's call for a synthesis of all of the artistic elements on the stage.

Das Ring Des Nieberlungen exemplified Wagner's ideas for a new artwork and, in this epic opera or *Worttondrama* (literally 'word, tone-drama'), words, music and movement were composed to work together in a new synthesis. The singing voice was presented as a form of heightened speech, and this was enriched by musical themes or leitmotifs from the orchestra. These recurring musical symbols were designed to register in the audience's memory and to provide a subconscious stimulus amidst a continual flow of dramatic action. Appia understood the emotive and symbolic power of these musical 'motifs of memory' on the audience. They work on multiple levels in the opera, not only to foreshadow the future but also to imbue the dramatic present with a heightened richness through an evocation of the past. Appia's musical training enabled him to make connections between the temporal aspects of this new form of drama through recurring musical leitmotifs and the way the stage environment itself might also be able to respond to the complex harmonic variations that were designed to convey powerful emotions.

Appia recognised the need for a scenographic solution to match the composer's ambition for a fluid theatrical form and that light would be central to achieving this. In 1882 he had witnessed a performance of Wagner's *Parsifal* at Bayreuth and could not reconcile the intense disappointment of this experience with the expressive nature of Wagner's music. Although Appia was impressed with the Bayreuth Festspielhaus itself, which placed the audience in darkness, hid the orchestra and attempted to create an equality between spectators, he was appalled at the visual quality of the staging, observing in 1925 that 'if everything in the auditorium at Bayreuth expresses his [Wagner's] genius, on the other side of the footlights everything contradicts it' (cited in Bablet 1982: 68).

By 1888, Appia had made a conscious decision to attempt to resolve the problems he had witnessed in the staging of opera performances across Europe and to seek to reform existing theatrical practices. Between 1889 and 1890 he studied the technical realisation of performance lighting through voluntary work at theatres in Dresden and Vienna (see pp. 87–88). This period provided a crucial grounding in the processes and practicalities of staging performances, and Appia's understanding of the existing production techniques both enabled and inspired him to create his own solutions, which were first published in *The Staging of Wagnerian Drama* in 1895.

---

[1] *The Ring of the Nibelungs* – Wagner's cycle of four operas written between 1848 and 1874 and often referred to as the *Ring Cycle*. They comprise *Das Rheingold, Die Walküre, Siegfried* and *Götterdämmerung*.

Light offered the key to this solution and Appia was later to make this explicit, arguing that light's relationship to the drama equated to that of music to the score. In 1908 he presented his ideas expressing the link between light and music in *Comments on the Theatre*:

> There is a mysterious relationship between music and light: 'Apollo was not only the god of song but also of light'. Let us no longer separate what he has divinely united, let us try to obey him...Sound and light! two elements which, from an aesthetic viewpoint, defy analysis.
>
> 'Where other arts say: 'That *means*', music says, 'That *is*' (Richard Wagner)
>
> Where form and colour try to express something, light says: 'I *am*; forms and colours will only exist through me'.
>
> How are we to approach these all-powerful elements; Who will help us to join them in an indissoluble union?
>
> Some great musicians have never even [...] taken any notice of light; great painters and sculptors have never taken notice of music. But what does that matter to us in the theatre? Since we ourselves possess the necessary technical means.
>
> However, it seems to me, on the contrary, that we too are guilty of similar indifference, and that it is important to make light visible to the inattentive eye of the musician and to make music more accessible to the often recalcitrant ear of the visual artist. Only then can we begin our conquest of the *mise en scène*.
>
> [...] Rhythm intimately unites the life of sound with the movements of our body. Here we already have a beacon, an important transposition. On the other hand, plastic forms are indispensable for the light to be expressive. There remains the task of uniting the movements transmitted by rhythm to our body, which are the essence of music flung into space, with plastic forms revealed through light, which are the essence of light.
>
> The centre where sound waves, on the one hand (through rhythm), and light beams, on the other (through plasticity), converge, is the human body. This is the meaning of the term conciliatory, the temporary incarnation of the god of song and light.
>
> With one hand Apollo assembles sound waves, with the other, light beams; then irresistibly he brings both hands, both these elements, together-bestowing upon them the full authority for their mutual interdependence.
>
> The new scenic order will be based on the presence of the human body, of the plastic and moving body. Everything will be subordinated to it.
>
> (Appia, 1908 in Volbach, 1989: 177–178)

Appia argued that only light and music can express the inner poetic nature of the drama and, through his detailed staging synopses, the musicality of light was expressed in both word and image. These documents are now regarded as the first lighting scores.

Appia recognised that the creative function and expressive possibilities of light are possible through the control of its volume (the size and shape of the beam), its intensity and colour and, critically, its direction (the location of light sources around the stage was consequently of fundamental importance). The musicality of light could therefore be achieved through a consideration of the way in which these properties of light might allow a fluidity and plasticity of the stage space. The tones and rhythm of music could be matched by the levels and direction of light, and Appia was to argue that, for the dramatic presentation of Wagner's operas, shadows and light should have the same importance as the music itself.

MUSIC, SPACE, LIGHT – APPIA'S VISION FOR WAGNER'S *RING*

The combination of Appia's musical background and scenographic sensibility ensured that the relationship between music, light and space was central to his unique creative response. Working directly from the music, his preliminary ideas for an idealised production of Wagner's *Ring Cycle* explored a revolutionary scenographic approach based on the expressive use of light and space. Appia advocated a malleable, shifting stage space articulated through light, and this 'plasticity' was envisioned in temporal terms rather than as a series of static images against which the actor would perform. The resulting vision is described and located precisely in relation to pages and bars in the score, in turn creating a lighting score that is linked directly to the music and evolves over time.

Appia's unique vision is exemplified in this scene for Act III of *The Walkyrie*, which is expressed through an introductory commentary, a written scenario and a series of expressive sketches. This study marks a watershed in thinking about the dramatic potential of light on the stage and, in the first paragraph of this excerpt on 'Lighting', the key concepts of active and passive light are introduced.

The scene is envisioned with diffuse general lighting, principally from overhead, and a series of expressive lighting moments created through a combination of directional 'active' light (such as the red light for Wotan), and a third type of light which Appia defines as 'projected light' that would be responsible for creating the clouds on the backdrop, and special effects such as the Magic Fire.

These selected excerpts from the scenario show in considerable detail how Appia was thinking about the overall composition and development of the drama. This can be seen through the way in which it was envisaged that the space was to be used by the performers and how specific lighting moments would work in conjunction with the music and their movement. Appia describes the key components of the setting that was also to be used for *Siegfried* and *Götterdämmerung* – a rocky mountain summit that ought to appear lifelike should be made up of 'practicables' but yet not appear like a staircase. The formation of rocks creates a natural overhang which, when lit from above with ambient passive light, creates a natural darkness for the cave entrance below. The overall effect Appia contends should be of subtle shadows and patches of light. The backcloth shows nothing but sky and becomes a key expressive element when illuminated, throwing the foreground into sharp silhouette against the bright sky. One or two fir tree branches extend over the scene, leaving the sky completely open. No trunks are visible, for 'if the entire tree were shown the living impression (of the summit setting) would be destroyed'.[2] None of the scenic elements should be considered in isolation but instead should work together to form a coherent image that is animated by light.[3]

ADOLPHE APPIA – *THE WALKYRIE*: COMMENTARY AND SCENARIO FOR ACT III (1892)

Lighting

Two essential elements: movement and repose. In the first the role of lighting is active, in the second it is of a passive calmness with slight and imperceptible variations, only interrupted by the episode of the Magic Fire, which, because of its magic, has nothing in common with the ambient light.

The sky provides the visual interest until the arrival of Brünnhilde. Then the focus of the drama sets the place of action in the sky that previously served only as a kind of commentary, but now remains, to the end, a living thing. One must therefore treat it as such and consider the projections and the other elements as *actors* whose tasks when taken together have all the importance of an acting *role*.

The act begins during the day; it is the storm which darkens the atmosphere; the sky to the rear must remain clear, the rocky mass of the setting should always remain in silhouette, the foreground dark with shadows diminishing imperceptibly up to the crest.

After the departure of the Walkyrie, all becomes calm, and everything should serve to create the most limpid sky possible. The projectors have nothing further to do except prepare for the Magic Fire.

Almost without noticing, the sun sets, its light slowly diffusing and disappearing. The thin crescent of the moon must merge into the surrounding landscape.

---

[2] Appia in note on original sketch – 'si l'on representait le sapin entier, cette impression serait aneantie: c'est pourquoi la presence de l'arbre n'est qu'indiquee'.

[3] It is interesting to note here that there appears to be a contradiction – Appia has clearly expressed the need for a three-dimensional setting that replicates a mountain peak, but he has yet to completely renounce the use of painted scenic items with the shadowy fir trees. 'The branches of the fir trees throw a light shadow over all of the setting to the right; this painted shadow must become *real* for Act III of *Siegfried*'.

Depending upon the arrangement of the projectors, of which there should be a great many, it may be necessary to divide them into two categories: those providing the backdrop with the vague movement of clouds with slow modulations and streaks of clear blue sky and those responsible for the movement of individual clouds in the sky and against the rocks, for lightning flashes, for apparitions (the Walkyrie) and for the Magic Fire. It is absolutely essential to leave as little to chance as possible.

The delicate question will be the arrangement of the lighting itself to preserve the scenic harmony between the state of the sky and that of the setting. Two aspects must be kept separate: the darkness should be deep enough to create the silhouette of the setting and the performers (with the exception of pp. 210–214) yet the light should never be so strong as to make the facial expressions visible.

A pool of diffused light coming from above strikes the slope in the foreground. Natural shadows created by the construction of the setting, cannot be controlled in this chiaroscuro and they therefore contribute a chaotic effect to the first half of the act. Perhaps towards the end, in order to emphasise the calmness and serenity of the atmosphere, one should spread a little diffused light over the scene. The comer of the cave remains completely dark and the shadow of the fir trees on the right, which is a painted shadow, may be perceived as *real* because of the diffused lighting.

THE RIDE OF THE WALKYRIE

Until electric photography is introduced into the theatre, which would create a series of movements through quasi-simultaneous projections, the scene of the Walkyrie will remain incomplete [...]. A realistic image will always be ridiculous because of the spectators' literal-mindedness; and no matter what projection is shown, it will always be imperfect in a drama of this type. The alternative adopted in the scenario remains the only alternative solution. It goes without saying that an artist of the first order should be commissioned to create these apparitions.

Magic Fire (*Feuerzaube*)

This is not a decorative but a *mimetic* effect. It is a magic act, completely independent of the surrounding natural environment, totally in the service of Wotan's will and created through his gestures. The scenario describes the evolution of this effect.

Projection will be essential. Very little steam and *without noise or violent movement* (it is not a volcano!). Perhaps a number of small fireworks thrown by hand and integrated with the core of the flame might be a convenient method. In any case, part of the floor of the lower platform will be specifically constructed for this effect, and in the composition of the rocks of the upper platform one must remember that channels will be necessary for the passage of the fire.

The light that ushers in Wotan is *blood-red* without variation; the Magic Fire is *fire*.

Appia continues with a detailed scenario with page and bar references. This is in effect the first lighting score and it is important to note that he is describing the scene as if the audience are looking at it. The fir trees on the right are therefore stage-left.

Scenario

171/2 Curtain: The set in silhouette. The eye only perceives bit by bit those parts of the terrain not set against the sky. The foreground is dark. The sky is bright, a rainy grey with an increasing veil of indistinct and ever-shifting clouds. A few isolated clouds move from left to right near the mountain summit, chasing and criss-crossing the sky. Everything is in crescendo until 210 when the projections merge into the setting itself. […]

172/5: In a violent lightning flash *emerging from the cloud*, we perceive a vague colourless form, that can be distinguished only by a cloak, a mane of hair flowing in the wind, a spear, a reflection of armour, all shrouded in clouds. A second into 173 we see a similar apparition coming closer. The two figures are only visible by the lightning, which silhouettes them so fleetingly that one can only sense their immobility, and this effect is further heightened by the fast movement of the clouds.

173/5–6: Waltraute and Schwertleite descend to the upper platform; Ortlinde does the same but stops somewhat higher. 174/1: All three are seen in right profile by the audience. The cloud reaches the fir tree. Several brilliant *white* lightning flashes outline the branches, and then the sky returns to its appearance at the beginning of the scene and gradually the number of clouds increases.

Later in the scene, Appia describes the contrast between the figures on stage and the light behind them:

During 207/8–9; the Walkyrie circle around the ridge … while the storm gathers force. Imperceptibly the clouds have changed direction since Brünhilde's entrance and are now chasing from left to right in a vortex, ever-darkening but not obscuring the [outline of the] rocks. The eye becomes accustomed to the lack of light and the scene on the lower platform can be clearly followed due to the white costumes. The foreground remains dark and Brünnhilde and Sieglinde indistinct. The sky remains as clear as possible to maintain the silhouette of the setting at all costs.

and as Wotan approaches there is a further dramatic shift in the lighting:

210: Clouds invade the summit and the ridge (perhaps a gauze in front of the summit). A soft, continuous wind sound can be heard from the right. Incessant lightning from the bottom right [upstage left against the backcloth] make the Walkyrie suddenly visible and then plunge them into darkness; distant rolls of thunder. A blood-red light grows in intensity to the right which is clearly distinct from the rest of the lighting. All that can be done with projections must be used to make the sky terrifying whilst also emphasising the right side. […]

Figure 5 Appia's 1892 drawing of 272/1. As Wotan departs he creates 'a strong silhouette against the light' as Brünnhilde sleeps in the shadows (Swiss Theatre Collection, Bern)

> The darkness obscures everything except the broad mass of movement [of the Walkyrie]; these images run beneath it. The light increases without illuminating the Walkyrie. The wind and thunder grow incessantly as if a cataclysm is approaching. Lightning flashes blend constantly with the light. The sky is a whirlwind from left to right; the summit is lost beneath clouds. [...]

> 213: The entire scene is like a whirlwind and the Walkyrie can only be sensed through their singing. 214/1: the wind and thunder are at full crescendo having reached peak volume. They *stop dead* on a great lightning flash without thunder. The blood-red light pierces the trees against a puff of smoke, illuminating the ridge and the clouds. The light increases until 214/2, when in a great burst of smoke, Wotan appears. The light dies out at once. The sky lightens bit by bit, just enough to make the figures distinct. The clouds desert the ridge but still obscure the summit. The foreground remains dark.

Later in the scene as Wotan and Brünnhilde embrace, 'a vague silvery light spreads across the sky' (264/1) and as he places her to sleep under the tree

> the thin crescent moon casts a silvery glow, through the branches which are seen in relief. This is not a *lighting effect*; everything is perfectly calm and clear.

The final section of the scene does involve a lighting effect that Appia envisages would be created through pyrotechnics.

MAGIC FIRE

269/1: One flame then two, three, four, etc., emerging from the same point (from the metal spear), form a beam of light *without steam*. 269/3: The beam of light, without diminishing, seems to divide itself into a dancing, shimmering multitude, but yet remains compact. 270/2: The central glow of flame spreads into a large semicircle, sparkling and dancing; a little steam. All is now focused on these beams that spread out, licking the rocks, intertwining and climbing rapidly. 270/3: Wotan traces at his feet with the point of his spear as if to mark a path which turns to his (the actor's) right. He climbs back onto the rocks, and with a sweeping gesture indicates the summit, the spear always held upright. The fire follows his movement *exactly*; the brightest nucleus of light corresponds with the tip of his spear, followed by the sparkling and the wild dance of the flames. The steam, very light, quietly follows the movement in the wake of the light. The projections spread over everything. 270/5: The flames reach the edge of the precipice and spread out mainly behind the ridge; descend and disappear *quickly*. There remains nothing but a *glow*, which becomes still. The ridge and summit are encircled in steam, which rises slowly, lit from *below* with a red light and high up in the clear, bright sky a crescent moon and a few faint stars.

Wotan watches the path of his spear and the fire. 271/1: He reaches the steps leading to the upper platform, his head held very high, facing Brünnhilde. 271/5: He ascends as far as the upper level. 272/1: On the platform above the steps, a strong *silhouette* against the light, his spear raised high at an angle in Brünnhilde's direction, his arm fully extended. 273/1: Second measure: he lowers his spear, leaning against it, remaining still, his chest extended towards Brünnhilde. 273/5: He turns slowly to the left, crosses the upper platform, climbing. 274/3: He arrives on the overhang and turns back. 274/5: He disappears behind the rock into the light [see Figure 5].

THE FINAL IMPRESSION OF GREAT STILLNESS

That Wotan should exit from the same place he entered would be an unfortunate effect.

The magic fire, being *pantomimic*, requires mathematical precision in relation to the music.

> (Appia, trans. Palmer, *Oeuvres Complètes* Vol. 1, 1880–1894: 124–168)

ACTIVE LIGHT

Appia's distinction between active and passive light is central to his creative vision and it is necessary here to discuss these ideas, which have frequently been misinterpreted in English language translations and commentaries on his work (see also pp. 144–149)

The passive or diffused light ('éclairage passif', 'lumière diffuse' or 'Helligkeit') refers to the general light of the stage area usually from footlights and border lights, which were common to existing stage practices at the end of the nineteenth century and were principally concerned with the widespread illumination of the stage space. In contrast, active light (*lumière actif* or *Gestaltendes Licht* and sometimes referred to in English translation as 'living light' or 'formative light') refers to intense, focused light that crucially allows distinct shadows to be created. 'Active light' therefore not only offers specific visual effects but could also provide a subtle, versatile source with expressive potential. By creating shadow, 'active light' could transform the stage environment, reveal three-dimensional form and, in varying its intensity, colour and beam quality, light could become a co-player in the drama – a poetic and active agent to animate the stage space and bring the drama to life. This articulation of the function of shadow and its manipulation through light represents a paradigmatic shift in theatre practice. In previous eras, shadows were a necessary by-product of light that needed to be accommodated. Appia's vision placed light and shadow, and its movement over time, as central to the dramatic experience.

Active light has sometimes been misconstrued as 'mobile' or 'moving light', and the term has been widely misunderstood. It is important to note that Appia didn't know the precise theatrical terminology in French for the lighting techniques and equipment which he had witnessed first hand in Dresden, Leipzig and Vienna.[4] He therefore uses the term *rampe mobile* to denote lights that were temporary and not fixed in position. The permanent lighting adjacent to the stage consisted of the footlights, border lights above and groundrows positioned upstage to backlight translucent scenery and to light scenic backdrops. These installations were non-movable fixtures restricted to their gas power source to which they were permanently connected in series and which gave out a 'passive', flat and even light. Mobile lights in contrast were flexible, individual units rigged and positioned specifically to achieve directional light. The term *rampe mobile* therefore refers to light sources employed behind the proscenium, predominantly positioned in the wings or on bars above the stage and which offered *independent focusable sources* able to create the directional 'active' light with distinct shadows. Typical examples of movable units would have been gas standards or bunchlights, but Appia was primarily referring to the newer focusable 'spot-light' lanterns with lenses that offered a quality of light that differed significantly from the more general 'flood-lights'. Crucially for Appia, the portable electric carbon arcs derived from Dobosq (see pp. 183–185) and developed in Germany by Hugo Bähr were central to his vision of flexible, movable and defined light sources, and also for the creation of active, projected imagery, such as clouds.

Appia was not simply a theorist as many have labelled him. He was clearly inspired by working with Bähr at Dresden's Hoftheater in 1889–90, and his

---

[4] See Bablet-Hahn, M.L., 1992: 373 notes in Appendix.

future thinking about light on the stage derives directly from this experience as a *practitioner*. His philosophical vision of 'active light' therefore draws heavily upon this practical knowledge of lighting techniques with gas and electric carbon-arc sources for focusable lighting from offstage as well as for projectors. It is also interesting to note that Appia's description of lightning, Magic Fire and the effect of Wotan's illuminated spear can also be traced back directly to Bähr's own lighting work and his commercial catalogue of effects.

Appia's 'active light' was therefore to be created and manipulated by non-permanent light sources that could be arranged around the edges of the stage space to offer a new fluidity and flexibility through the creation of shadow. These units were to be rigged for specific effects and then, as in contemporary practice, returned to the lighting store after the production. In this way they are mobile lights since they are not permanently fixed to their supply. Appia was not therefore advocating light sources that moved during the actual performance to create 'active light', as has previously been interpreted – or indeed 'moving lights' as we currently understand the term in modern stage lighting practice.

However, many of the independent mobile sources used to create 'active light' would have been powered at the end of the nineteenth century by the electric carbon-arc, and each of these would have needed its own human operator (see pp. 180–186, 226). In this sense, these portable, specialist lights were truly moving lights, just like a follow spot, and although *rampe mobile* refers simply to the portability of directional lights, today's light sources that move physically during the performance could be seen as a logical extension of Appia's vision and lighting theory.

LIGHT, PROJECTION AND THE CHOREOGRAPHY OF SPACE

Appia's writing prefigures later technological developments in electric lighting, focusable sources and projection technologies. In the opening to his 1891–1892 essay *Comments on the Staging of The Ring of the Nibelungs*, which preceded the pictorial designs and lighting score, he acknowledges that his proposal for a new 'active' role for light was prevented by the nature of the existing staging practices. This writing provides an insight into the practical difficulties of the prevailing staging conditions and clearly expresses the disjunction between light and painted scenery. In advocating a new holistic approach to design for the stage, Appia's ideas demanded a revolution in staging practice – what he terms a new 'choreography' of production elements and in which light needs to play a central role:

> The art [scenography] is still in its infancy, not [...] because of the means available but because the manner in which they are used. [...] The realization of the drama on the stage, difficult to begin with because of the numerous media required at present, is completely thwarted by the impossibility of bringing these diverse

efforts together with even relative precision. [...] The intentions concerning the *mise-en-scène* (choreography in the full sense of the word) are inferior to those which motivate the creation of the lyric drama itself. [...] just as conventional signs regulate the requirements of the music, so a method must be discovered to determine the choreography. The other representational elements, being inanimate, are completely manageable; and although they are at present still left in the hands of the ignorant or foolish, they will in the future obviously become an integral part of the score.

So defined the scenic conception will work hand in hand with the very composition of the drama. The two will be united if not always in one person, at least in the most intimate unity of purpose.

(trans. Volbach, 1989: 89–90)

Although this particular text was not published in full until 1954, it is an important document as it demonstrates Appia's revolutionary thinking about how light and space could contribute to performance and how all elements on stage need to be choreographed. The thoughts set out here represent the first articulation of Appia's ideas, which were to be revisited in all of his major writings in the succeeding 30 years (see pp. 144–149) and which were to have such a major impact on future theatrical practice. His scenographic vision for Wagner's operas was in direct opposition to what he termed the illusionistic theatre and was predicated on three key elements: stage space, painting and lighting – or form, colour and light.

Appia's critique suggests that the uniform over-lighting of the stage space results in nothing truly being 'seen'. The modernist tendency to make all visible was aided by the new electrical technologies, but the quality and glare of the new light created a number of aesthetic difficulties on the stage. Appia notes the perceived hierarchy of production elements and lack of communication between technicians, and proposes solutions to lighting exterior and interior scenes from above the stage.

This text concludes with a vision for the future use of projected light as a scenographic element. Traditional stage lighting combined with textured light employed through scenic projectors is offered as a solution to the 'lifeless' nature of contemporary painted staging. Appia foregrounds the importance of the power of suggestion and acknowledges that through the use of light and, crucially, shadow, 'anything is possible in the theatre'.

APPIA – COMMENTS ON THE STAGING OF *THE RING* OF THE NIBELUNGS, 1891–1892

First published in *Revue d'histoire du théâtre* (1954a), 1–2 (trans. Volbach)

Lighting

In a drama such as the author of the *Ring* has given us, the expressive means are apparently exhausted: the music drives to the limit the suggestion and development of the most subtle nuances furnished by the libretto. Under favourable conditions, acting shows us this passionate world in a frame suited to increasing its significance. What then causes that extreme weariness, that disappointing void, in spite of all the indispensable and honest efforts of the imagination as regards the scenic part of the performance, the part which is the author's only indirectly? Why does the throughgoing spectator, who is enraptured in this marvellous world, which the music suggests to him and the libretto substantiates, feel the need to complete his aesthetic satisfaction? Why this weariness of expectation rendered unbearable by the drama's persistence in its course? Because a living element, vibrant with excessive life, is offered him in a lifeless atmosphere. Because, as previously stated, on the one hand, the expressive means are wantonly exhausted and, on the other, the preeminent medium is missing, namely, *lighting*, without which plasticity and mimetic expression are inconceivable. The drama, all shadow and highlight, sharp contrasts and infinite nuances, is projected on a uniform surface all parts of which are monotonously clear. That this monstrous incongruity affects our receptive organs is not astonishing. Unfortunately, the drama itself is affected by it – primarily in its musical phase, whose effects are enriched or impoverished in direct relation to the lack of corresponding light effects (a light effect is not an isolated factor; the entire production is affected by it).

This persistent flaw is sanctioned by the audience-at-large, whose need for expression in the performance consists in the desire 'to see' as much as possible, to have the best possible view, to miss no facial expression, none of the smallest gestures, no detail of a costume, of brush strokes, or parts of a setting. Accordingly, a night scene calls for blue light less bright than day light but, just the same, permitting the audience 'to see' everything. In an interior setting, a room, one must be able to probe the tiniest recesses; the same room at night lighted by the glimmer of a weak lamp must still be sufficiently illuminated lest the least detail of living persons and lifeless objects be lost, etc. The result is-and let no one accuse me of exaggerating-that nothing is *seen* at all. An object lit from three or four directions throws no shadow and, from a theatrical viewpoint, does not exist. Today's staging, almost without exception, is merely a collection of such non-existing objects, the characters included. The drama, trying desperately to manifest itself, uses for this end only abstractions less alive than the pages in the score where it waits to be born.

Scenic painting (spatial arrangement included) developed independently of lighting, leaving the latter behind to make the modem inventions serve its own convenience; consequently the artist does not consider the lighting offered him equal to his scenic ideas and counts on it only in the most general way. He sees himself thus obliged to create, through deceptive painting, the effects denied him through actual light and shadow. Those charged with lighting very beautifully painted drops naturally have no other worry than to make the picture visible lest any detail be lost. Variations in the ground plan have induced these technicians to employ more or less ingenious devices, but solely to illuminate the painting; they have gone a long way towards perfection in the field of special effects (moon, water, clouds, etc.) always however applied separately to each of these phenomena, with little concern for the scenic painter and without regard for the consequences which the success of any one of those special effects is bound to provoke.

At present, conditions are such that, if the question of stage lighting is raised, one is answered with the supposedly unsolvable problem of the painted shadows. And indeed the two suppliers of decorative elements, the scenic painter and the electrician (I limit myself to these two in order to simplify the explanation-the technician serves both) are so far apart that it is difficult to imagine their collaboration in creating a harmonious agreement regarding the setting. Before his canvas pieces the painter believes he has complete freedom, and rightly so since he knows his picture will be illuminated so that not one of his ideas is lost; and this is his aim. The electrician asks few questions about the setting-in-preparation; he knows that the painter is acquainted with the electrical equipment and its recognised possibilities for light changes. So he leaves the field to the painter, ready, when the goods are delivered, to manipulate with inconceivable indolence the wonderful media at his disposal. The requirements of the characters are taken care of, almost all of them, at the last minute, and in the same old way, with which the painter has nothing to do and in which the living drama merely has to assist . . .

The more restricted the setting (painting and spatial arrangement), the more independent and flexible is the lighting. One may even assert that, through light, anything is possible in the theatre, for it suggests unmistakably, and *suggestion* is the only basis on which the art of staging can expand without encountering any obstacles; material *realisation* is of secondary importance.

The increase and perfection of the lighting equipment presents no real difficulties under the extraordinary conditions of a festival, but the manner of utilising it cannot be determined by any rule. This remains flexible, dependent on a thousand esthetic problems. Based on experience, a list might perhaps be compiled on which the painter could rely; yet by the same token, experience turns into routine and if the aims are foolish the routine will be foolish too. It is therefore necessary not to confuse the artist who gives the order with the technician (electrician) who will always search for new and better ways to satisfy the artist's demands. Between the two no absolute understanding is possible; each of them needs to be entirely independent, they will meet always in agreement.

One reason for the current childish settings undoubtedly is that the scenic artist and the technician believe they are mutually dependent and thus paralyze their efforts. It is evident that the construction of the contemporary stage, which serves the sole purpose of facilitating the practice of established conventions, cannot admit as complete a reform as would be desirable, but light in its superb flexibility somehow adjusts itself to everything and thus lessens the difficulties that the setting, itself, could not overcome alone.

The worse way to illuminate the contemporary setting (without taking into account concessions that an attempt at reform would bring about) is first to light *naturally* as for the place indicated by scenery (exterior, interior, etc.), then to add *artificially* what is needed to modify the natural lighting to the quality of the picture and the requirements of the ground plan. It is obvious that the setting must be brought to life by the characters for whom it is built and that these characters must be considered an *important part* of it.

Yet, it is evident that if faces, gestures, groups and the entire pattern of movement are to have life, they must be given *shadow*. Therefore the current use of fixed footlights must be irrevocably done away with and replaced by portable strip lights completely subordinated to lighting from above with the single aim of creating artificially the *diffused light* of day. With more freedom, border lights will serve the same purpose.

Light, in the precise sense of the word, will invariably be furnished by means of movable instruments. There are two distinct methods: one for exteriors, another for interiors. For exterior settings, the light will *always* come *from above* save for some few exceptions; the height of the characters is taken as the maximum angle and all comes from the same direction. For the interior setting the light will enter very obviously through the openings (never horizontally) reinforced extremely subtly by footlights or by special instruments to provide diffused light.

Since the action of the *Ring* occurs outdoors almost entirely, the former lighting method will prevail.

Projection, which has reached such marvelous perfection, although it is employed merely in isolated cases for special effects (fire, clouds, water, etc.) is indisputably one of the most powerful scenic devices; as a connecting link between lighting and setting it dematerialises everything it touches. Easy to handle, it lends itself to all kinds of effects.

This should not make us satisfied with just any, more or less improved, magic lanterns; rather, the numerous instruments must satisfy the same standard as portable lighting equipment; the functioning of projectors must be the best possible today, the choice of lens satisfactory and the specific effects required for each production executed by an artist of the first rank.

Projection thus prepared takes an *active* role on the stage-it must now and then even supersede the part played by the characters (see the sky in act 3 of *The Walkyrie*). It is rarely absent and when its purpose is not definitive, at least it supports lighting in the creation of a variable atmosphere for the entire setting. Moving gauze (simulating clouds, fog, et al.) will never be obtained without projection, whose use conceals the unnatural crudeness of this device. It must include the whole gamut from a vague, hardly noticeable motion to the most striking images.

When electric projections become a regular device for the stage they will deserve the epithet all-powerful as there will be few assignments they will be unable to fulfill.

For the time being the following plan requires merely a larger number of machines (and stagehands) and more versatile equipment for shifting. It gives projection a truly active part, sometimes even a *role* that the diverse machines will share but that will nevertheless be guided by a single purpose.

(in Volbach, 1989: 91–95)

RHYTHMIC SPACE

Appia also developed a number of abstract stage settings that explored the interrelationship between light and space. These 'rhythmic spaces' envisioned environments for dramatic work that would become active with the

Figure 6 Appia's drawing for *Orpheus & Eurydice* (Act II Hell – the entrance to the underworld) realised in 1912 in the 'light-producing space' of Hellerau Festspielhaus (Swiss Theatre Collection, Bern)

introduction of the performer's body. The opposition established between the angular geometric forms and the malleable human form could assist in conveying psychological and emotional states when unified through light. Appia was able to realise these ideas in practice when he was invited to work with Jacques Dalcroze at the Hellerau Festspielhaus near Dresden in 1912–1913. The public presentation of work at two festivals promoted their explorations of eurythmics, and the combination of light, space and movement astonished contemporary audiences and altered the future direction of performance in Europe forever.

The Festspielhaus had been designed by Heinrich Tessenow and, working alongside the artist Alexander von Saltzmann, Appia created an unprecedented lighting installation in which over 7,000 lamps were employed, some hidden behind calico walls. This enabled light to be reflected from the white walls and diffused through the fabric to create a light box of limitless infinity:

> Instead of a lighted space, we have a light-producing space. Light is conveyed through the space itself, and the linking of visible light sources is done away with.
>
> (von Salzmann, cited in Beacham, 1994: 94)

Whilst these lights created diffused light, movable spotlights from behind panels in the ceiling of the hall were able to provide the 'active light' that

Appia demanded. The installation was controlled by a light organ that enabled a single operator to choreograph light in response to the music and movement within the space.

LIGHT, SPACE AND MOOD – EDWARD GORDON CRAIG

At roughly the same time as Appia's works were first published, the English director and designer Edward Gordon Craig was also recognising the need to re-evaluate and reform staging conditions. Craig, like Appia, was to be inspired by the relationship of light and music but had already experienced the theatrical use of light first hand. As an eight-year-old, he had been awestruck by the experience of seeing how the lighting and theatrical illusions of Irving's production of *The Corsican Brothers* had been created. In 1889, at the same time as Appia was learning about lighting practice with Bähr in Dresden, Craig was working as a young actor in Irving's company at the Lyceum and witnessing his innovative use of gas lighting at first hand (pp. 188–197). This connection with Irving was as influential for Craig as that of Bähr for Appia: 'To begin with, I acknowledge my debts to the limelight men of the Lyceum and to Rembrandt' (Craig, E.G., 1913: xi) and, although he was to reject the overt pictorialism of Irving's approach, this formative experience was to provide the grounding for his future scenographic thinking and practice.

A more profound influence, however, was a lecture-demonstration by the artist Hubert von Herkomer which Craig attended in 1892 in London. Von Herkomer undertook experiments with light in his own private theatre studio and amazed his audiences with electric light and gauzes, just as de Loutherbourg had over a century earlier (see pp. 30–32). In his lecture, von Herkomer argued passionately against the use of footlights, attacked the lack of expression on the stage and demonstrated a range of atmospheric effects with light, scenery and lantern slides: 'It is through the management of light that we touch the real magic of art', von Herkomer proclaimed – a mantra that unconsciously echoed Appia, and might also neatly summarise Craig's own later thoughts on the role of light in modern drama (Bergman, 1977: 333).

Von Herkomer was the chief influence on Craig's most influential early production – a staging of Purcell's opera *Dido and Aeneas* that used coloured lighting to transform a single stage setting and to create rhythmic movement through painting with light rather than pigment. In recalling the impact of von Herkomer's performances, Craig's son observed that

> Because of the absence of footlights the actors had looked less artificial. Herkomer's side-lit gauzes, placed six feet or more in front of his backcloths, had achieved a depth of colour such as he [Craig] had never seen before – he

only knew of the painted gauzes used in pantomime scenes. He decided that whatever happened he would have gauzes too, and side-light them with different colours, the rest of his lighting coming from *above* the proscenium.

(Craig, E., 1968: 119–120)

Edward Gordon Craig, like Appia, was inspired by the potential of light to transform the stage space and recognised the need to change existing production practices, from the shape of the theatre building itself to the role of the director who, he argued, should have an all-encompassing eye. He also rejected the realistic approach of existing performance practices (such as those at the Lyceum) for a theatre that was instead based on the art of suggestion in which the expressive potential of light and its ability to transform space would assume primary importance.

Dido and Aeneas at the Hampstead Conservatoire in May 1900 provided the first opportunity for Craig to explore his scenographic vision with light and, to achieve it, he needed to build a special lighting bridge inside a false proscenium in order to accommodate six limelights and their operators. These instruments with interchangeable gelatines in blue, amber and green ensured that the main lighting was, in the style of von Herkomer, to come from above the stage. The creation of a specialist lighting bridge was a key innovation which pre-dates those later used in Germany and elsewhere. Less powerful electric lights, also with changeable gelatines, were positioned to the sides and two projector spotlights provided front-light from the back of the auditorium in the absence of footlights. Although he didn't know it, Craig had thereby created a direct equivalent of Appia's moving lights and likewise employed them to create 'active light'. A contemporary critic observed that

the real triumph of the setting was, however, in the use of light and shade; it was as carefully considered as in a wood engraving, and added immeasurably to the tragic simplicity of the whole performance.

(*The Review of the Week* 11 August 1900, cited in Craig, E.,1968: 123)

Craig's use of vibrant colour combinations produced deliberate clashes in stark contrast to contemporary staging practices. Using variations in coloured light from above the stage and against the gauzes, he was able to achieve subtle shifts of light that were perceived differently by the audience depending on from where they were viewed, but created an astonishing and seemingly infinite perspective. In the last act, Craig used yellow light from above to create a beautiful tragic finale: 'Under the play of this light the background becomes a deep shimmering blue, apparently almost translucent, upon which the green and purple make a harmony of great richness ... '.[5]

---

[5] Mabel Cox's review in *The Artist, an Illustrated Monthly Record of Arts, Crafts and Industries*, July 1900: 131, cited in Bablet, 1966: 41–42.

Like Appia's designs for 'rhythmic space', Craig's evolving notions for a theatre of the future rested on architectonic scenes which responded to changing light and which, when combined with movement, created a visual, music-like counterpoint.

The ability of light to evoke different moods became central to his scenographic practice. In 1902 Craig became entranced by the way in which natural light could influence the way architectural space was perceived. He regularly encountered the Duke of York's steps near The Mall in London and was fascinated by the way the space changed character from the early morning light until night-time. He would stand and watch the steps in the changing evening light, asking his muse, Elena Meos, to act as a figure whilst he sketched the scene and made notes:

> Elena would be the figure that moved up and down or across the steps – some-times quickly, other times majestically. Occasionally a group of children would accidentally give the necessary patterns he sought, and one night, when the road cleaners were using hoses and the jets of water were back-lit by the street-lamps, Ted was overcome with joy.
>
> (Craig, E., 1968: 161)

This experience formed the basis of Craig's later theoretical explorations of light and space, which demonstrate the potential for light to alter the per-ception of space through a series of imagined scenarios. Craig's *The Steps*, created in 1905 but not published until 1913, contains four scenes, each based on a separate mood, and demonstrates how a single architectural, stage-like space might convey meaning through sound, movement and, in particular, the way in which it is lit. He explains his fascination with architectural space and the way in which the steps are able to create a 'drama of silence' through four distinct lighting states. Each mood is accompanied by a written synop-sis, but it is the images themselves that are the most expressive element and provide a lighting storyboard that has remarkable similarities with Appia's work of the same period. *The Steps* communicates on a level beyond the text itself; it has a clear temporal aspect, and the organisation of human figures and the manipulation of light suggest a kind of poetic vision of a life journey. The space, and the way it is perceived through changes in the quality and direction of light, becomes the main character in this drama.

EDWARD GORDON CRAIG'S *THE STEPS*

FIRST MOOD

> I think it is Maeterlinck who pointed out to us that drama is not only that part of life which is concerned with the good and bad feelings of individuals, and that there is much drama in life without the assistance of murder, jealousy, and the other first passions. He then leads us up to a fountain or into a wood, or brings

a stream upon us, makes a cock crow, and shows us how dramatic these things are. Of course, Shakespeare showed us all that a few centuries earlier, but there is much good and no harm in having repeated it. Still I think that he might have told us that there are two kinds of drama, and that they are very sharply divided. These two I would call the drama of speech and the drama of silence, and I think that his trees, his fountains, his streams, and the rest come under the heading of the drama of silence -that is to say, dramas where speech becomes paltry and inadequate. Very well, then, if we pursue this thought further, we find that there are many things other than works of nature which enter into this drama of silence, and a very grand note in this drama is struck by that noblest of all men's work, architecture. There is something so human and so poignant to me in a great city at a time of the night when there are no people about and no sounds. It is dreadfully sad until you walk till six o'clock in the morning. Then it is very exciting. And among all the dreams that the architect has laid upon the earth, I know of no more lovely things than his flights of steps leading up and leading down, and of this feeling about architecture in my art I have often thought how one could give life (not a voice) to these places, using them to a dramatic end. When this desire came to me I was continually designing dramas wherein the place was architectural and lent itself to my desire. And so I began with a drama called 'The Steps'.

This is the first design, and there are three others. In each design, I show the same place, but the people who are cradled in it belong to each of its different moods. In the first it is light and gay, and three children are playing on it as you see the birds do on the back of a large hippopotamus lying asleep in an African river. What the children do I cannot tell you, although I have it written down somewhere. It is simply technical, and until seen it is valueless. But if you can hear in your mind's ear the little stamping sound which rabbits make, and can hear a rustle of tiny silver bells, you will have a glimpse of what I mean, and will be able to picture to yourself the queer quick little movements. Now on to the next one.

SECOND MOOD

You see that the steps have not changed, but they are, as it were, going to sleep, and at the very top of a flat and deep terrace we see many girls and boys jumping about like fireflies. And in the foreground, and farthest from them, I have made the earth respond to their movements.

The earth is made to dance.

THIRD MOOD

Something a little older has come upon the steps. It is very late evening with them. The movement commences with the passing of a single figure – a man. He begins to trace his way through the maze which is defined upon the floor. He fails to reach the centre. Another figure appears at the top of the steps – a woman. He moves no longer, and she descends the steps slowly to join him. It does not seem to me very clear whether she ever does join him, but when designing it I had hoped that she might. Together they might once more commence to thread the maze. But although the man and woman interest me to some extent, it is the steps on which they move which move me. The figures dominate the steps for a time, but

Figure 7a Craig's *The Steps*, c.1905: first mood

Figure 7b Second mood

Figure 7c Third mood

Figure 7d Fourth mood

the steps are for all time. I believe that some day I shall get nearer to the secret of these things, and I may tell you that it is very exciting approaching such mysteries. If they were dead, how dull they would be, but they are trembling with a great life, more so than that of man – than that of woman.

FOURTH MOOD

The steps this time have to bear more weight. It is full night, and to commence with, I want you to cover with your hand the carved marks on the floor and to shut out from your eyes the curved fountains at the top of the steps. Imagine also the figure which is leaning there, placed over on the other side of the steps – that is to say, in the shadow. He is heavy with some unnecessary sorrow, for sorrow is always unnecessary, and you see him moving hither and thither upon this highway of the world. Soon he passes on to the position in which I have placed him. When he arrives there, his head is sunk upon his breast, and he remains immobile. Then things commence to stir; at first ever so slowly, and then with increasing rapidity. Up above him you see the crest of a fountain rising like the rising moon when it is heavy in autumn. It rises and rises, now and then in a great throe, but more often regularly. Then a second fountain appears. Together they pour out their natures in silence. When these streams have risen to their full height, the last movement commences. Upon the ground is outlined in warm light the carved shapes of two large windows, and in the centre of one of these is the shadow of a man and a woman. The figure on the steps raises his head. The drama is finished.

(Craig, E.G., 1913: 41–47)

LIGHT AND THE SCENE – CRAIG'S 'A THOUSAND SCENES IN ONE SCENE'

'I believe in the time when we shall be able to create works of art in the Theatre without the written play, without the use of actors' (Craig, E.G., 1912: 53).

Craig aimed to create a new and simplified dramatic form in which 'things played their parts as well as people' (1923: 15), and he experimented with ways of simplifying the elements of stage setting to architectonic forms that could offer infinite expressive possibilities when articulated with light. The painter Piot commented: 'Craig wants his scenery to move like sound, to refine certain moments in the play just as music follows and heightens all its movements; *he wants it to advance with the play*' (cited in Bablet, D., 1966: 122–123).

Craig suggested that one way of achieving this new form of drama could be through the use of solid three-dimensional units that would adapt to the actor's movements. These 'Screens', envisioned in 1907 and patented in 1910, offered 'A Thousand Scenes in One Scene' since they could be manipulated in space and with lighting to create a multitude of settings. Craig experimented with the effects of light on the screens in a miniature modelbox, exploring ways in which the scene could be animated and transformed by shifting light.

He compared the relationship of light and setting to the union between two dancers or singers who are interdependent but yet in perfect accord: 'The relation of light to this scene is akin to that of the bow to the violin, or of the pen to the paper' (Craig, E.G., 1923: 25).

The playwright W.B. Yeats made a similar analogy when working with Craig's model in 1910, and was astonished by the transformations that could be achieved under lighting:

> Henceforth, I can all but produce my play as I write it, moving hither and thither little figures of cardboard through gay or solemn light and shade, allowing the scene to give the words and the words the scene. I am very grateful, for he [Craig] has banished a whole world that wearied me and was undignified and given me forms and lights upon which I can play as upon a stringed instrument.
>
> (Yeats, 1910: 81)

Subsequently the screens were employed in a series of performances at the Abbey Theatre in Dublin, designed by Craig, and this new mode of scenographic presentation was to have a significant impact on Yeats' future writing for the stage. Following a performance of *The Hour Glass* in January 1911, he makes observations about Craig's practice which echo the key concerns of Appia:

> The primary value of Mr Craig's invention is that it enables one to use light in a more natural and more beautiful way than ever before. We get rid of all the top hamper of the stage, all the hanging ropes and scenes which prevent the free play of light. It is now possible to substitute in the shading of one scene real light and shadow for painted light and shadow. Continually in the contemporary theatre, the painted shadow is out of relation to the direction of the light, and what is more to the point, one loses the extraordinary beauty of delicate light and shade. This means, however, an abolition of realism, for it makes scene-painting which is, of course, a matter of light and shade, impossible. One enters into a world of decorative effect which gives the actor a renewed importance. There is less to compete against him, for there is less detail, though there is more beauty.
>
> (Yeats, 1911)

The screens were also (and most famously) employed in Stanislavski and Craig's 1911–1912 production of *Hamlet* at the Moscow Art Theatre, where the role of light was not to create an illusion of reality but rather an expressive force to heighten the tragic atmosphere. Craig again employed diffused light predominantly from above the scene but also from the wings. More importantly, moving sources of light were used to create angular shadows, selective pools of light and animated, projected effects which deliberately jarred and created a visual underscore to the play. This use of portable fixtures echoed Appia's use of mobile light and emerged from Craig's exploration with light on the miniature modelbox stage. The model stage allowed Craig to experiment with the combined possibilities of light, space and scenic objects, and to communicate his lighting intentions for *Hamlet* in advance, as well as pre-senting a range of other possible scenarios. Craig developed an extraordinary ability to present these transformations in miniature performances, and this technique was to be embraced later by other pioneers of the art of light-ing design, and certainly influenced the evolution and establishment of the career of Michael Northen, who in 1950 became the first officially accredited British lighting designer.[6]

A Florentine architect's response to Craig's model theatre was published in *The Mask*:

> And the elements of which Craig makes use for his creations are nothing or almost nothing: some screens and some electric lights. He sets upon the stage of his little theatre (no bigger than a child's marionette theatre) his tiny screens, and while you look on, with a rapid movement of the hands, arranges them in a certain way: a ray of electric light comes to strike between those simple rectangles of cardboard, and the miracle is accomplished; you behold a majestic scene: the sense of the small disappears absolutely: you forget the dimensions of the theatre, such is the scrupulous equilibrium of the lights and of the lines which Craig knows how to give the scenes. Another slight movement of the screens (always before your eyes) and the scene changes and then changes again, without the lines and the light effects ever recalling to you that which you have already seen. And thus one passes from the vision of a piazza, a street, an imposing portico to that of an audience chamber, a prison or a subterranean dungeon.
>
> Craig is a great painter, a great architect, a great poet. He paints with light, he constructs a few rectangles of cardboard, and with the harmony of his colours and of his lines he creates profound sensations, as only the fathers of poetry know how to create. [...]
>
> We are far, very far, from the usual scenographic resources, be they even the best that can be remembered.
>
> (Craig, E.G., 1915: 159–160)

Craig's influence in Europe spread quickly from the publication and trans-lations of *On The Art of The Theatre* (1912). In conjunction with the growing understanding of the ideas of Appia, the two practitioners became responsi-ble for a major re-evaluation of staging practices and a heightened awareness of the dramatic application of light in performance. Through their prac-tice and theorisations, both Craig and Appia demonstrated the expressive potential of lighting and the suggestive power of light, space and colour. In Germany, for example, their influence is directly acknowledged in the work of Brahm, Jessner and Reinhardt; in France with Jouvet and Copeau, and the widespread experiments with Fortuny's lighting system (see pp. 126, 207–210). In Eastern Europe the legacy of Appia and Craig can be seen in the early work of Meyerhold and in the scenography of Josef Svoboda

---

[6] Northen (1997: 64–76) provides a fascinating account of the creation and use of 'The Model Stage'.

(see pp. 108–114), whilst in the United States this new thinking heavily influenced the work of Robert Edmond Jones and the adoption of new stagecraft techniques. In contemporary practice the work of Robert Wilson (see pp. 115–117), which embraces the interplay of space and light, can also be seen as a direct legacy of the work of Appia and Craig.

LIGHT AND SHADOW IN THE THEATRE – ROBERT EDMOND JONES

Robert Edmond Jones (1887–1954) was a scenographer who had a profound influence on the development of American theatre in the twentieth century. He acknowledged the influence of Appia and Craig and his evolving staging style and, especially through productions of the plays of Eugene O'Neill, influenced a wide range of post-war dramatists, directors, designers and cinematographers. His seminal text *The Dramatic Imagination* (1941) drew upon his extensive practical production experience in collaboration with a wide range of theatre workers, and evolved from a passion for theatre to embrace new creative possibilities and thereby to become a rejuvenated art form. This ambition for a new theatre, where 'A good scene should be, not a picture, but an image' (1969 [1941]: 25), consciously echoes the ideas of Appia and Craig. Jones' manifesto acknowledges both the art and the craft of theatre production and, in this important chapter on light, he reflects on his experience of creating light for performance and analyses its creative potential.

In acknowledging the elemental 'livingness' of light, Jones seeks to explain the dramatic importance of light in its animation of the stage space, suggesting that there is a special quality or 'uncommon' light in which the performers are illuminated when they appear onstage. This 'lucid light' enables an audience to see beneath the surface reality and thereby both expose and suggest hidden depths.

This wide-ranging, inspirational discourse on the nature of dramatic light ranges from the essential problematics of lighting the stage to a poetic reflection on the fundamental role that light plays in our imaginations. Jones equates our instinctive responses to light, and importantly also to its absence, shadow, with a more profound symbolic relationship, which hints at the human condition and the journey towards death. In recognising the ability of light to penetrate the subconscious and to communicate to an audience at a profound level, he clearly expresses an ambition for light to animate the stage that still has currency. The final paragraph provides a salutary reminder to all contemporary practitioners of the need to find a balance between the art and the craft of lighting for performance.

Excerpts from Chapter VI 'Light and Shadow in the Theatre'

The Dramatic Imagination, 1941 (1969), Jones, R.E., pp. 111–128

PROFESSOR MAX REINHARDT once said, 'I am told, that the art of lighting a stage consists of putting light where you want it and taking it away where you don't want it.' I have often had occasion to think of this remark-so often, in fact, that with the passage of time it has taken on for me something of the quality of an old proverb. Put light where you want it and take it away where you don't want it. What could be more simple?

But our real problem in the theatre is to know where to put the light and where to take it away. And this, as Professor Reinhardt very well knows, is not so simple. On the contrary, it demands the knowledge and the application of a lifetime.

Future historians will speak of this period in theatrical history as the spotlight era. Spotlights have become a part of the language of the theatre. Indeed, it is hardly too much to say that they have created our contemporary theatre idiom. Once upon a time our stages were lighted by gas-jets and before that by kerosene lamps, and before that by tapers and torches. And in the days to come we may see some kind of ultra-violet radiation in our theatres, some new fluorescence. But today our productions are characterized – conditioned, one might almost say – by conical shafts of colored electric light which beat down upon them from lamps placed in the flies and along the balconies of the theatre. Lighting a play today is a matter of arranging and rearranging these lamps in an infinite variety of combinations. This is an exercise involving great technical skill and ingenuity. The craft of lighting has been developed to a high degree and it is kept to a high standard by rigorous training in schools and colleges. It has become both exacting and incredibly exact. The beam of light strikes with the precision of a *mot juste*. It bites like an etcher's needle or cuts deep like a surgeon's scalpel. Every tendency moves strongly toward creating an efficient engine behind the proscenium arch. Almost without our knowing it this wonderful invention has become a part of the general *expertise* of Broadway show-business. We handle our spotlights and gelatines and dimmers in the theatre with the same delight and the same sense of mastery with which we drive a high-powered automobile or pilot an aeroplane.

But at rare moments, in the long quiet hours of light-rehearsals, a strange thing happens. We are overcome by a realization of the *livingness* of light. As we gradually bring a scene out of the shadows, sending long rays slanting across a column, touching an outline with color, animating the scene moment by moment until it seems to breathe, our work becomes an incantation. We feel the presence of elemental energies.

There is hardly a stage designer who has not experienced at one time or another this overwhelming sense of the livingness of light. I hold these moments to be among the most precious of all experiences the theatre can give us. The true life of the theatre is in them. At such moments our eyes are opened. We catch disturbing glimpses of a theatre not yet created. Our imaginations leap forward.

It is the memory of these rare moments that inspires us and guides us in our work. While we are studying to perfect ourselves in the use of the intricate mechanism of stage lighting we are learning to transcend it. Slowly, slowly, we begin to see lighting in the theatre, not only as an exciting craft but as an art, at once visionary and exact, subtle, powerful, infinitely difficult to learn. We begin to see that a drama is not an engine, running at full speed from the overture to the final curtain, but a living organism. And we see light as a part of that livingness.

Our first duty in the theatre is always to the actors. It is they who interpret the drama. The stage belongs to them and they must dominate it. Surprising as it may seem, actors are sometimes most effective when they are not seen at all. [...] In nine cases out of ten our problem is simply that of making the actors and their environment visible.

Visible, yes. But in a very special way. The life we see on the stage is not the everyday life we know. It is [...] *more so*. The world of the theatre is a world of sharper, clearer, swifter impressions than the world we live in. That is why we go to the theatre, to dwell for an hour in this unusual world and draw new life from it. The actors who reveal the heightened life of the theatre should move in a light that is altogether uncommon. It is not enough for us to make them beautiful, charming, splendid. Our purpose must be to give by means of light an impression of something out of the ordinary, away from the mediocre, to make the performance exist in an ideal world of wisdom and understanding. Emerson speaks of a divine aura that breathes through forms. The true actor-light – the true performance-light – is a radiance, a nimbus, a subtle elixir, wherein the characters of the drama may manifest themselves to their audience in their inmost reality.

Perhaps the word *lucid* best describes this light. A lucid light. I think of the exquisite clarity in the prints of Hiroshige. A light of 'god-like intellection' pervades these scenes. They are held in a shadow-less tranquillity that cannot change. The peace of the first snowfall is in them. Everything is perceived here; everything is understood; everything is known.

Or I might use the word *penetrating*. If we look at a portrait by one-of our fashionable portrait-painters and then at a portrait by Rembrandt, we see that the one is concerned mainly with the recording of immediate surface impressions. His approach is that of a journalist who assembles a number of interesting and arresting facts for his leading article. The other penetrates beneath the surface into the inner life of his subject. In the portrait by Rembrandt we see not only the features but the character of the sitter; not only the character, but the soul. We see a life that is not of this moment but of all moments. We sense 'the ultimate in the immediate.' The portrait of an old man becomes a portrait of old age.

Or I might use the word *aware*. When we see a good play well performed we are brought to the quivering raw edge of experience. We are caught up into the very quick of living. Our senses are dilated and intent. We become preternaturally aware of each instant of time as it passes. In this awareness we see the actors more clearly, more simply, than we have ever seen human beings before. They seem, in some strange way, more *unified*. [...] And we see them in a different light. It is this *different* light that should be given in the theatre.

But more than all these necessary qualities, the lighting of a play should contain an element of surprise, a sense of discovery. It holds the promise of a new and unforgettable experience. [...]

Lighting a scene consists not only in throwing light upon objects but in throwing light upon a subject. We have our choice of lighting a drama from the outside, as a spectator, or from the inside, as a part of the drama's experience. The objects to be lighted are the forms which go to make up the physical body of the drama – the actors, the setting, the furnishings and so forth. But the subject which is to be lighted is the drama itself. We light the actors and the setting, it is true, but we illuminate the drama. We reveal the drama. We use light as we use words, to elucidate ideas and emotions. Light becomes a tool, an instrument of expression, like a paint-brush, or a sculptor's chisel, or a phrase of music. We turn inward and at once we are in the company of the great ones of the theatre. We learn from them to bathe our productions in the light that never was on sea or land. […] I try with all the energy of which I am capable to bring this other light into the theatre. For I know it is the light of the masters.

I find this light of other days in the paintings of Ryder and Redon and Utrillo, in the etchings of Gordon Craig, in Adolphe Appia's drawing of the Elysian Fields from the third act of the *Orpheus* of Gluck. Here it is for everyone to see, achieved once and for all, so clearly stated that no one can escape it. […]

Lucidity, penetration, awareness, discovery, inwardness, wonder […] These are the qualities we should try to achieve in our lighting. And there are other qualities too. There is a quality of luster, a shine and a gleam that befits the exceptional occasion. […] And last of all, there is a quality of security, a bold firm stroke, an authority that puts an audience at its ease, an assurance that nothing in the performance could ever go wrong, a strength, a serenity, Bowing down from some inexhaustible shining spring. Here, in a little circle of clear radiance, the life of the theatre is going on, a life we can see, and know, and learn to love.

But creating an ideal, exalted atmosphere, an 'intenser day' in the theatre is only a part of our task, so small a part that at times it seems hardly to matter at all. However, beautiful or expressive this light may be, it is still not a dramatic light. Rather, it is a lyric light, more suited to feeling than to action. There is no conflict in it: there is only radiance. Great drama is given to us in terms of action, and in illuminating dramatic action we must concern ourselves not only with light, but with shadow.

How shall I convey to you the meaning of shadow in the theatre – the primitive dread, the sense of brooding, of waiting, of fatality, the shrinking, the blackness, the descent into endless night? *The valley of the Shadow … Ye who read are still among the living, but I who write shall have long since gone my way into the region of shadows … Finish, bright lady, the long day is done, and we are for the dark. …* It is morning, the sun shines, the dew is on the grass, and God's in His Heaven. We have just risen from sleep. We are young, the sap runs strong in us, and we stretch ourselves and laugh. Then the sun rises higher, and it is high noon, and the light is clear, and colors are bright, and life shines out in a splendid fullness. Jack has his Jill, and Benedick his Beatrice, and Millamant her Mirabell. But then the sun sinks down, the day draws to its close, the shadows gather, and darkness comes, and voices fall lower, and we hear the whisper, and the stealthy footfall, and we see the light in the cranny of the door, and the low star reflected in the stagnant tarn. A nameless fear descends upon us. Ancient apparitions stir in the shadows. We listen spellbound to the messengers from another world, the unnatural horrors that visit us in the night.

I shall leave the doctors of psychology to explain the connection between this ancient terror and the dread of the unknown darkness in our minds which they have begun to call the subconscious. It is enough for us to know that the connection exists, and that it is the cause of the curious hold which light and shadow can exercise over the imagination of an audience. At heart we are all children afraid of the dark, and our fear goes back to remote beginnings of the human race. See the mood of an audience change, hear them chatter or fall silent, as the lights in the theatre are raised or lowered. See them rush to the nearest exit at the sudden rumor, 'The lights have gone out!' See their instant reassurance as the broken circuit is repaired and the great chandelier blazes once more. It is such instinctive responses that give light its dynamic power in the theatre.

Our greatest dramatists have woven light and shadow into their creations. Dramatic literature is filled with examples. We see Lavinia Mannon as she closes the shutters of the Mannon house, banishing herself forever from the light of day. We see the moon shining fitfully through scudding storm-clouds over the ramparts of Elsinore, where the unquiet ghost of Hamlet's father wanders, [...] We hear the tortured cry of Claudius, 'Give me some light! Away!' The dim shadows of Pelléas and Mélisande embrace one another far away at the end of the garden; [...] Here is the most wonderful example of all, the great classic example of dramatic insight:

Lo, you, here she comes! This is her very guise,
and, upon my life, fast asleep. Observe her: stand close.
How came she by that light?
Why, it stood by her. She has light by her continually, 'Tis her command.
You see, her eyes are open.
Ay, but their sense is shut.
What is it she does now?

Shakespeare animates the scene with his own intense mood. The candle flame lives in the theatre. It becomes a symbol of Lady Macbeth's own life -flickering, burning low, vanishing down into darkness. *Out, Out, brief candle!* ... Where the layman might see nothing more than an actual candle, made of wax, bought for so much, at such and such a place, the dramatist has seen a great revealing image. He has seen deep into the meaning of this terrible moment, and the taper is a part of it, [...] little flame, little breath, little soul, moving before us for the last time ... And the shadow on the wall behind 'that broken lady' becomes an omen, a portent, a presage of her 'sad and solemn slumbers,' a dark companion following her, silent and implacable, as she passes from this to that other world. *She should have died hereafter. Life's but a walking shadow* ... When we think of this scene we remember, not only the dreadful words and the distraught figure, all in white like a shroud; we see vast spaces and enveloping darkness and a tiny trembling light and a great malevolent shadow. The icy fear that grips us is built up out of all these elements. And when we put the scene on the stage we do not serve Shakespeare's drama as we should serve it until we have given each of these elements its full value and its proper emphasis.

As we dwell upon these great examples of the use of light in the theatre we cease to think of harmony and beauty and think instead of energy, contrast, violence,

struggle, shock. We dream of light that is tense and vivid and full of temperament, an impulsive, wayward, capricious light, a light 'haunted with passion,' a
light of flame and tempest, a light which draws its inspiration from the moods of
light in Nature, from the illimitable night sky, the blue dusk, the halcyon light that
broods over the western prairies. [...] Here before us as we dream is the frame
of the proscenium, enclosing a darkness like the darkness that quivers behind
our closed eyelids. And now the dark stage begins to burn and glow under our
fingers, burning like the embers of the forge of Vulcan, and shafts of light stab
through the darkness, and shadows leap and shudder, and we are in the regions
where splendor and terror move. We are practicing an art of light and shadow that
was old before the Pyramids, an art that can shake our dispositions with thoughts
beyond the reaches of our souls.

The creative approach to the problem of stage lighting – the art, in other words, of
knowing where to put light on the stage and where to take it away – is not a matter
of textbooks or precepts. There are no arbitrary rules. There is only a goal and a
promise. We have the mechanism with which to create this ideal, exalted, dramatic
light in the theatre. Whether we can do so or not is a matter of temperament as
well as of technique. The secret lies in our perception of light in the theatre as
something alive.

Does this mean that we are to carry images of poetry and vision and high passion
in our minds while we are shouting out orders to electricians on ladders in light-
rehearsals?

Yes. This is what it means.

JOSEF SVOBODA – LIGHT AND PSYCHO-PLASTIC SPACE

The legacy of Appia and Craig's work is also clearly evident in the work
of Czech scenographer **Josef Svoboda** (1920–2002), whose fascination with
the use of light as a way of defining space characterised his designs for
performance in the second half of the twentieth century.[7] Svoboda demonstrated a remarkable combination of the qualities of an architect, the detailed
technical knowledge of an engineer and a scenographer's artistic sensibili-
ties. Light is often the central defining feature of his scenography as a way of
defining and shaping stage space and in communicating the inner thoughts
and feelings of the characters. He refers to his stages as 'psycho-plastic'
spaces, created through the interplay of light, space and, in his later work,
through the use of complex projection surfaces. 'The psycho-plastic space
is elastic in its scope and alterable in its quality. It is space only when it
needs to be space' (Svoboda in Burian, 1970: 126). The possibilities of textured light and space, using multiple surfaces within the stage environment,

---

[7] Svoboda openly acknowledged his debt to both Appia and especially Craig in his keynote
address at the Theatre Design Conference *Theatre in Britain and Europe – A Visual Dialogue?*
Royal Haymarket Theatre, London, 8 May 1998.

contribute to Svoboda's idea of the 'polyphonic spectacle' – a space that has many contrapuntal sounds and which enables communication with the audience on multiple levels. Light is fundamental to the creation of these psycho-plastic spaces, allowing key ideas of the drama to be elucidated and explored through intangible dynamic forces of time, space and movement. The French academic Denis Bablet analyses Svoboda's use of light in this context and, in foregrounding the possibilities and potential of light, echoes ideas from earlier in the century, such as those of the Futurists (pp. 164–169) and Artaud (see pp. 39–40):

> light has become one of the chief modes of theatrical expression, not only because of the possibilities it offers to illuminate, to imitate natural phenomena, and to underly and suggest the psychological atmosphere of the drama; but even more so, because of is ability to take part in the creation of the scenic universe, or more precisely to become one of its protagonists. Certainly, no one has gone further than Josef Svoboda in the exploration of light's potentials and use. Light: a means of modelling space, of making it burst into being before our very eyes, indeed of creating it. Light: a fluid whose musical nature has become common-place, which can explode and fan out, concentrate itself, vary in intensity and direction, freeze, and then again become extraordinarily agile. Light: gushing from everywhere or from one sole source, direct or reflected. Light: sharp beams or evanescent mist that haloes the characters in a mysterious aura. Light: which can provoke the dramatic event, lull the spectator or assault him with extreme violence. The list of possibilities and functions are virtually endless.
>
> (Bablet in Ursic, 1998: 34)

Svoboda's scenography was also characterised by a ceaseless search for theatrical solutions to specific design problems, which enabled him to put into practice many of the creative ideas that the technologies of the time had prevented both Appia and Craig from pursuing. His work displayed a willingness to employ whatever materials and means were necessary to create and express his scenographic vision, and this entailed dialogue with engineers and scientists. Frequently Svoboda's vision was focused around a single central visual image, such as the staircase for *Oedipus* (1963), the enormous mirror for *La Traviata* (1992) or the famous cylinder of light for the 1967 production of *Tristan and Isolde* (see Figure 7).

In this extract from *The Secret of Theatrical Space*, Svoboda writes about his explorations with light and space in three key productions and explains how experimentation with light and the ability to seize on accidental hap-penings was fundamental to the creative process. In a clear parallel with Appia's thinking, Svoboda discusses the use of three types of light in his production of *Hamlet*, which itself has strong echoes of Craig through both the single flight of steps and the use of movable screens to reflect the light. This production also first established Svoboda's concept and innovative use of *contralight* – a steeply angled backlighting using low-voltage lanterns to

Figure 8 Svoboda's lighting for *The Owner of the Keys*, Prague, 1962

create a bright curtain of light[8] (see pp. 223–4). This writing is important also in its discussion of the way that light and space work together with the ideas of the play, and it is in these productions at Prague's National Theatre in 1959–60 that Svoboda's notion of the stage as flexible, 'psycho-plastic space' first evolved.

Jose Svoboda from *The Secret of Theatrical Space*

Edited and translated by J.M. Burian (1993: 56–60)

The much discussed *Hamlet* of Jaromir Pleskot (1959) has a special position among my works. After all, it's a play that has traditionally been a touchstone for each generation. My scene was created by movable black reflective panels in five lateral rows, with light, and only the most necessary furniture. With concentration on every step, Hamlet ascended the stairs toward the nocturnal panels that bore a projected image of the royal colours. He stopped, because it was here, at this spot, that the Ghost was to speak to him.

But how to present the apparition of a ghost on the modern stage? It had to accord with an unromantic or even anti-romantic interpretation of Hamlet [...] a

---

[8] This concept created a new piece of lighting equipment, 'low-tensile truss-battens', known worldwide as 'Svobodas' and manufactured by ADB. This lighting unit was also the precursor to Pilbrow's Light Curtain and the moving DHA Digital Light Curtain created originally for *Miss Saigon* and used widely today in large-scale musical and opera productions.

sober, reflective person, a noter of facts and curber of fantasies. Hamlet stood before the dark mirror, in which were reflected two spotlights, like eyes, and at that moment we heard the Ghost speaking in Hamlet's own voice.

Originally we counted on a 'natural' ghost, the old, familiar theatrical ghost. The only reason he didn't appear was simply that it was done exactly that way thirty years before! [...] in Hilar's and Hofman's production in 1926. Hofman was also a creator of trick effects and described them in detail: 'The actors wore slippers with sound absorbing felt soles; everything took place in silence, like a dream. The ghost of Hamlet's father had his naked right arm phosphorescently painted, so that it glowed under ultraviolet light even when the figure itself was invisible.'

With the chief electrician at the National Theatre, we speculated and tested ad infinitum. Suddenly a chance movement of lighting instruments on the bridge, the reflection of lights from the semigloss surface of the panels—and the problem of the ghost's apparition was solved. Chance, or sudden impulse? Sometimes I ask myself, couldn't I have perceived the essence of the matter on the very first day? Once we know something, we wonder why we were blind to so many previous hints. Yet we wonder only after we know.

The scene for *Hamlet* was based on the interplay of three types of light, the prototype of which is light and shadow on a stone in nature: an intensely illuminated surface exposed to the sun, under it a deep black shadow, and at one side a half-shadow and softened light reflected from an adjacent stone. It's the prototype of any plastic form created by sharp and diffused light and reflection. Our spotlights were aimed from the front lighting bridge at twelve panels covered by a special black plastic material which had nearly fifty percent of the reflectability of a black mirror. The actors and scenic details, immersed in a uniform level of light, were simultaneously illuminated by direct and reflected light. As a result, the range of shadow values was essentially extended, hard contrasts disappeared, and forms were fuller—in the optical sense, more real. Moreover, light penetrated even to those places otherwise impossible to light.

Without going to blackouts or lowering the curtain, the scene and its lighting pattern changed twenty-four times merely by shifting the reflecting panels. Of course, for more nearly perfect work with light we would have needed more backstage space so that the sources of light could be farther removed from stage objects. Indeed, that's the only way that the geometry of the lighting could have been improved.

The twelve black reflective panels that created the scene for *Hamlet* transformed the actor into a shadowy silhouette [...] The play contains no hidden levels that the spectator is only supposed to uncover gradually; there is no mystery of subtexts. Active participation is expected of the viewer, who may be deliberately led astray in order to be confronted by himself a split second later. But the play must remain an open play, the stage a stage, and its space entirely determined by the dynamic relations of its characters.

The expressive principle of our scene was based on stairs that functioned as a gradually ascending surface interrupted by parallel black strips of shadow, and on mobile panels that could change the place of action in a moment.

Figure 9 Svoboda's lighting for *Hamlet*, Prague National Theatre, 1959

But did the movement of the panels accomplish realistic changes of locale? Of course not. The set fulfilled a different function than the one we usually ascribe to it. It did not conventionally describe the place of action or even create it. It placed the action in absolute space, which can represent any place and any time. That is, the scene did not picture a concrete place. The movement of the abstract panels not only indicated spatial changes but was also a materialization of rhythm, by means of which the action progressed. Similar to the function of a film cut, it evoked the psychic state of the characters.

Of course, conventions of the day affect our perception. The movement of the panels could have been interpreted by some as merely abstract play and an imperfect change of the place of action. But since Shakespeare always counted on the spectator's power of fantasy, why not give it adequate opportunity? If I set out in the opposite direction, I'd end up with a mere illustration of the text. For all the pros and cons, this production of *Hamlet* was an important milestone for me. In addition to everything else, in preparing for it I came up with my principle of contralighting. And so my first encounter with Shakespeare was as it ought to be: full of joy at the discoveries, impatience with my own limitations, and a longing to make further discoveries.

Then in 1960 came the truly risky experiment with contralights from specially designed low voltage instruments in the staging of Chekhov's and Krejca's *The Sea Gull*. If it hadn't worked, there would have been no performance; but there was no way of telling our fate until technical rehearsal.

What is a scenographer to do with Chekhov? If he steps aside and lets only the text speak, something's missing. If he starts to illustrate the plays, there's something in excess.

How to capture the atmosphere in which words mean something different from what they signify anywhere else? How to create a claustrophobic space in which people are far apart? Or the sense of distance in which characters nonetheless feel close to each other?

The Sea Gull, my first Chekhov, was not born without pain. I reduced all scenographic devices to a space covered in black, with one fundamental curtain of light in the proscenium opening (tilted toward the audience and taking the place of a scrim curtain), and ten other, smaller curtains of light distributed in the depth of the stage with specially constructed low-voltage lamps with parabolic reflectors. They were masked by twigs, through which streams of 'sun' light penetrated. The resulting impression of an orchard with its sultry heat and total atmosphere, affected the spectator in a palpably physiological way.

The particular lighting hardware, the ceiling of branches with leaves of nylon netting (which did a good job of both catching the light and letting it through)—all this we conceived and worked out for the first time. Now everything depended on whether our gamble would pay off. We scoured the city for necessary parts and assembled them. Our all-night experiments were confined to the workshops; we had to wait for two days of scheduled lighting rehearsals on stage. We had no other solutions in reserve. I was in agony at the endless waiting. Indeed, from that time on I've always kept some sort of backstop solution in my pocket as an 'anxiety-easer.' The ultimate success of our work was a result of our team's faith in the project; they delivered professional work and, insofar as possible, left nothing to chance. The desire to get to the very essence of Chekhov's text was clearly evident in the actors' work as well. They demonstrated what it means to take off creatively from a thought-out conception of a performance into the realm of a fully realized production.

Seven years later (1967) I used a similar principle of contralighting for a production of Wagner's *Tristan and Isolde* in Wiesbaden, this time confidently, because I had already tested it. But six days before the opening it became clear to me that the principle simply wasn't working. How was it possible? Everything was the same as in Prague, except perhaps that the Germans used latex instead of glue and there

Figure 10   Svoboda's cylinder of light for *Tristan & Isolde*, Wiesbaden, 1967

was less dust on the stage. Should I have blown dust onto the stage? Nonsense. What would the singers say, and what of the authorities overseeing work safety? I tried to thicken the air with normal aerosol sprays. Their effect was temporary at best, while also generating an undesirable smoky fog that drifted about in the upper reaches of the stage. Of course, it also quickly dried out from the heat of the lighting instruments. We tried an apparatus used in factories to reduce dust by forcing water vapor into the work areas. The air did thicken a bit, but again only in the upper reaches of the stage, intermittently and unevenly; I was really desperate. It was a very costly and keenly anticipated production, and my prestige was very much at stake. Finally, an enterprising German engineer understood what I was concerned about. He experimentally loaded the tiny fog droplets with a uniform electrostatic charge so that they were uniformly spread throughout the space. And this water vapor became the equivalent of the dustiness of a Prague stage. When we no longer wanted the fog, we introduced droplets with the opposite electrostatic potential and the droplets would begin to cluster together, fall to the floor, and clear out the space. And so another production was saved by a method intended for another operation entirely.

Theatre, of course, is not always the most ideal place for experiment. It's confined by the straitjacket of the repertoire and fixed limits of time. On paper or in a model, fantastic dreams may be expressed. But only when all the personnel of a theatre want to make this dream their own, can one truly begin. And so in every theatre two groups of people are absolutely essential: those who conceive, and those who actualize. The great challenge is to bring together fellow workers from entirely different professions who speak the same language.

ROBERT WILSON – THEATRE OF LIGHT

Robert Wilson (1941–) is a contemporary artist, director and designer who uses visual and spatial elements as the primary text. Light is fundamental to his theatre and he uses it to activate the stage space, animate objects, guide the audience's gaze and create striking scenographic images. The culmination of *Einstein on the Beach* (1976), for example, featured an extraordinary sequence with an overpowering, frenetic montage of flashing banks of light as the spaceship loses control in a cataclysmic atomic event. In contrast, the first ten minutes of *Monsters of Grace* (1998) simply offered its audience an empty stage as an overture with barely perceptible light shifting against a white cyclorama – a prelude to the consciously technical accomplishments of three-dimensional holographic projections that were to follow. It is light that gives Wilson's productions their distinctive character and, in this next extract, Arthur Holmberg provides a fascinating insight into Wilson's thinking about light and its practical realisation in the theatre. Holmberg's analysis originates from personal conversations with Wilson, observation of his working processes and interviews with contemporary lighting designers, such as Jennifer Tipton, who have collaborated with Wilson. This extract underlines the central importance of light to Wilson's image-based theatre and offers us a unique insight into a contemporary practice that can be seen as a true development of Adolphe Appia and Edward Gordon Craig's ideas of more than a century earlier.

'The deep surface'

Excerpt from *The Theatre of Robert Wilson*, Holmberg (1996: 121–128)

'Light is the most important part of theatre. It brings everything together, and everything depends on it. From the beginning I was concerned with light, how it reveals objects, how objects change when light changes, how light creates space, how space changes when light changes. Light determines what you see and how you see it. If you know how to light, you can make shit look like gold. I paint, I build, I compose with light. Light is a magic wand.'

Wilson's drama is a drama of light, and the director's analogies – painting, building, composing – explain how he uses it. Painting suggests light as a device to organize stage pictures, and light is Wilson's main resource for visual composition. 'A set for Wilson, [...] is a canvas for the light to hit like paint.'[9] Through dominant and subsidiary contrasts, Wilson creates a hierarchical visual structure. [...] [that] enables the eye to perceive the formal elements of composition as a harmonious whole. [...]

---

[9] Interview with Tom Kamm, scenic designer for *the CIVILwarS*, May 1990.

Light constructs our sense of space: [...] 'Theatre doesn't live in words,' Wilson holds. 'It lives in space. A director works with space. Light lets you see the architecture of the space. Other directors pore over the text. I draw space. I always start with light. Without light there is no space. With light you create many different kinds of spaces. A different space is a different reality'.

Composing suggests the rhythmic element in Wilson's lighting. Wilson's lights are fluid, constantly changing and changing constantly our perceptions. The genius of Wilson's lighting [...] can only be understood through time. [...] Wilson's lights cast their spell through subtle shifts. *Quartet,* which ran ninety minutes, had 400 light cues. It is Wilson's ability to *durchkomponieren* – to through-compose a complex structure with lights – that leaves other lighting designers agog. [...]

Wilson's lights give his productions an unmistakable look. The two most characteristic aspects of this look are the dense, palpable textures. One can feel, taste, smell the light in Wilson – and the way people and objects leap out from the background. [...] And unlike most directors, for whom lights are an afterthought tacked on at the end of the creative process, lights are on Wilson's mind from the start. They form an integral part of his original thinking about any work. The first preliminary sketch he makes of the stage space already indicates the source and kind of light he wants. Lights are breathed into the production from its conception. [...]

Although Wilson has worked in many different kinds of spaces [...] he has a penchant for the proscenium arch. His compositions may not stop at the frame, but he uses it as a compositional device to organize the stage picture. 'I prefer a proscenium for many reasons [...] I like the distance it creates between stage and audience. And I like what it lets me do with lights.' The picture-frame stage, by emphasizing the dominant dimensions of width (the horizontal) and height (the vertical), tends to flatten depth. To increase the sense of depth, Wilson not only uses the translucent RP[10] and wings, but also divides the floor into horizontal zones of light parallel to the picture frame. By lighting the zones alternatively with warm (yellow) and cold (blue) light, he increases the sense of depth. Like Cezanne, Wilson sets up tension between depth and flatness. [...]

Spots [of light] on the floor distract from the director's primary compositional focus, and they drive him berserk. [...] Sidelights eliminate this problem [...] [and] enhance the plasticity of the body, especially as it moves through space. Since a Wilson actor frequently speaks with his limbs, not his tongue, sidelight works magic by heightening the dimensional quality of the actors' movements while separating them from the background. [...]

Another device the director uses to make objects jump out from the ground is to play warm (yellow) light off against cold (blue). Color temperature plays a key role in his lighting. Incandescent light turns increasingly yellow as the intensity decreases. To counter this tendency [...] Wilson uses a special blue gel (Lee 201) over the lights he wants cold [...] to direct the gaze where he wants it. Thus, an actor's face or hands (the parts of the body Wilson tends to emphasize with

---

[10] Rear projection screen – allowing Wilson to create a wall of light upstage and to backlight or create silhouettes.

special lights) are hit with a cold light, the body with a warm one. Furthermore, he usually whitens and lightens the face and hands with makeup he calls 'the porcelain look.' Because of the dominant contrast, the eye goes first to the face. If an actor is wearing a white shirt lighter than the face, the director has it tinted down [...] In *Quartet* Wilson at times lit one half of Lucinda Childs's body with warm light, the other half with cold. This chiaroscuro effect sculpted the body; and the actress, detached from the surrounding environment, seemed to float in space. The director uses many tightly focused, bright specials to iris in and highlight a hand, a face, a foot, or an object as the rest of the stage darkens. Wilson calls it a zoom and compares it with a cinematic close-up. [...]

If Wilson works miracles with relatively simple equipment, one thing he does need is time, and plenty of it. [...] He spent two days lighting the prolog [sic] of *Quartet*, which ran fifteen minutes. Easily he can spend three hours lighting one hand gesture. [...] To watch Wilson slave away over lights is to understand the craft, discipline, precision, stamina, and obstinacy needed to create great theatre. [...]

Light in Wilson creates its own formal structure. At times this structure runs parallel to the text without doubling it; at times, it contradicts the text; at rare times it illustrates the text. Lights work subliminally on our feelings. They are one of the theatre's strongest weapons to create emotional climate. Wilson is a master of generating atmosphere through lights [...] [expressing] the unconscious – thoughts and feelings hiding just beneath the skin. These emotions can never be heaved into the mouth; language cannot speak them. Light whispers them. In sum, 'light,' says Wilson, 'is the most important actor on stage'.

Chapter

6   The Dramaturgy of Light

With the development of a central control for gas lighting and mechanisms that allowed a more subtle use of both levels of light and coloured light on the stage, dramatists began to understand how light might be used as an expressive element in their plays. Accordingly, lighting effects became an integral aspect of stage directions, and this chapter concentrates on tracing this heritage from the plays produced at the end of the nineteenth century to practitioners working in the early twentieth century.

Around the beginning of the twentieth century the key concern of playwrights and directors alike was to use lighting primarily to recreate realistic environments on stage. The work of Belasco perhaps best exemplifies this approach (see pp. 230–231), but others had begun to question existing staging practices and to envision a new form of drama in which light might be an integral element of the theatrical experience. Echoing Appia, André Antoine in 1903 advocated that

> light is the life of the theatre, the good fairy of the *décor*, the soul of the staging. Light alone, intelligently handled, gives atmosphere and color to a set, depth and perspective. Light acts physically on the audience: its magic accentuates, underlines, and marvellously accompanies the inner meaning of a dramatist's work. To get excellent results from light, you must not be afraid to use and spread it unevenly.
>
> (Antoine, 1903)

STRINDBERG AND IBSEN – LIGHT IN MODERN PSYCHOLOGICAL DRAMA

August Strindberg, who was inspired by Antoine's productions at Théâtre Libre, wrote a preface to his play *Miss Julie* (1888) which is often regarded as the manifesto for naturalistic theatre. It can be seen as a direct response to Emile Zola's call for a new art form to revive the theatre, and his wish for 'a new drama' goes beyond the strict naturalism advocated by Zola both in terms of the possibilities for the actor and also in terms of what he demanded from the stage setting and lighting. Strindberg champions the importance of the power of suggestion in performance, and there is a hint of the future potential of the new art that would be explored in his later works. The preface is a call for a revolution in staging practices that reveals the playwright's vision for a dramaturgy that requires a holistic approach in which all of the theatrical elements – script, actors and visual elements – combine to communicate layers of meaning and work towards a common artistic goal:

As regards the decor, I have borrowed from the impressionist painters asymmetry and suggestion (i.e., the part rather than the whole), believing that I have thereby helped to further my illusion. The fact that one does not see the whole room and all the furniture leaves room for surmise – in other words, the audience's imagination is set in motion and completes its own picture [...] But when one has only one set, one is entitled to demand that it be realistic – though nothing is more difficult than to make a room which looks like a room, however skilful the artist may be at creating fire-spouting volcanoes and waterfalls. Even if the walls have to be of canvas, it is surely time to stop painting them with shelves and kitchen utensils. We have so many other stage conventions in which we are expected to believe that we may as well avoid overstraining our imagination by asking it to believe in painted saucepans.

[...] Another not perhaps unnecessary innovation would be the removal of the footlights. This illumination from below is said to serve the purpose of making the actors fatter in the face; but I would like to ask: 'Why should all actors be fat in the face?' Does not this bottom-lighting annihilate all subtle expressions in the lower half of the face, particularly around the mouth? Does it not falsify the shape of the nose, and throw shadows up over the eyes? Even if this were not so, one thing is certain: that pain is caused to the actors' eyes, so that any realistic expression is lost. For the footlights strike the retina on parts of it which are normally protected (except among sailors, who see the sun reflected from the water), so that one seldom sees any attempt at ocular expression other than fierce glares either to the side or up towards the gallery, when the whites of the eyes become visible. Perhaps this is also the cause of that tiresome habit, especially among actresses, of fluttering eyelashes. And when anyone on the stage wishes to speak with his eyes, he has no alternative but to look straight at the audience, thereby entering into direct contact with them outside the framework of the play – a bad habit which, rightly or wrongly, is known as 'greeting one's friends'.

Would not side-lights of sufficient power (with reflectors, or some such device) endow the actor with this new resource, enabling him to reinforce his mime with his principal weapon of expression, the movement of his eyes?

[...] In a modern psychological drama, where the subtler reactions should be mirrored in the face rather than in gesture or sound, it would surely be best to experiment with strong side-lights on a small stage and with the actor wearing no make-up, or at best a minimum.

If we could dispense with the visible orchestra with their distracting lampshades and faces turned towards the audience; if we could have the stalls raised so that the spectator's sightline would be above the actors' knees; if we could get rid of the side-boxes (my particular *bête noire*), with their tittering diners and ladies nibbling at cold collations, and have complete darkness in the auditorium during the performance; and, first and foremost, a small stage and a small auditorium-then perhaps a new drama might emerge, and the theatre might once again become a place for educated people. While we await such a theatre, one must write to create a stock of plays in readiness for the repertoire that will, some day, be needed.

I have made an attempt! If it has failed, there will, I hope, be time enough to make another!

(Strindberg, 1888 trans. Meyer, 1980)

In the plays of Strindberg's contemporary Henrik Ibsen, light also becomes a suggestive and expressive dramatic element and is included in the written playscript as an essential component of the drama. Frequently this is in the form of atmospheric weather conditions, such as the mist in *Ghosts*, present metaphorically in the play and literally through a window in the setting. Ibsen's use of light also extends to the practical use of lights on stage as a symbolic signifier. In the opening scene of *The Wild Duck*, for example, the servants are seen lighting lamps but also putting green shades over them, whilst beyond them a brilliantly illuminated dining room is partially glimpsed. The majority of the stage is therefore seen in rather subdued light, which mirrors the world of the play in which truths have been obscured. Daylight and moonlight are also used as revealing forces whilst the lighting of a lamp and the subsequent removal of its shade later in the play mark key turning points in the dramatic action. Ibsen therefore uses light both metaphorically and symbolically as an integral aspect of his dramaturgy, which underscores the entire journey of the play, just as in *Ghosts* where the fading of light mirrors the gradual loss of sight of its main character.

STANISLAVSKI, LIGHT AND CHEKHOV

Senelick acknowledges the importance of Ibsen's writing to the evolution of a new dramatic form and its consequent impact on Anton Chekhov:

The technical innovations of the modern stage, including electric lighting and *mises-en-scène* [sic] intent on reproducing 'real life', required expert handling to blend and harmonise the various elements. Chekhov's development as a playwright from 1888 to 1904 coincides with this move from a stage governed by histrionic and spectacular display to one in which ensemble effect and the creation of 'mood' reigned supreme.

(Senelick, 1997: 3)

In this section we look in some detail at the way in which Nemirovich-Danchenko and Stanislavski planned and implemented the lighting as an integral part of their response to Chekhov's *The Seagull* staged at the Moscow Art Theatre (MAT) in 1898. This production marked an important moment in the history of Russian theatre, and for many represents a watershed in production values and techniques. There is a significant amount of documentation associated with this production, including Stanislavski's detailed plans for the performance, which are recorded in detail through his production score:

'New forms. We must have new forms!', Konstantin demands in his passionate appeal for a future theatre in Act I of *The Seagull*. These words, expressed prior to his abortive attempt at staging his own symbolist play-within-the-play, mirror Strindberg's concerns and can be seen as encapsulating the manifesto for a new form of drama which was realised in the MAT production.

The production of *The Seagull*[1] embraced new possibilities, particularly in the use of lighting and sound to create the atmospheres that were suggested and required by Chekhov's art. The production moved beyond a strictly naturalistic dramatic presentation and focused instead on creating a theatre of mood in an effort to reveal the drama and tragedy beneath the surface of every character. The evocation of atmosphere on stage (created by light and in combination with sound and setting) was seen as conveying the inner feelings of characters, and Stanislavski also noted the phenomenological impact which this had on the actors themselves. The use of light at the MAT therefore made a fundamental contribution to the evolution of his acting 'method'.

Stanislavski's response to the lyricism and atmosphere of the text was carefully plotted in a detailed production score, which became the blueprint for the production:

> I shut myself up in my study, where I wrote a detailed *mise-en-scène* as I felt it and as I saw and heard it with my inner eye and ear. While I was engaged on this work I did not worry about the feelings of the actors!
>
> (Stanislavski, cited in Balukhaty, 1952: 54)

Building on the achievements of the Meiningen Players, Stanislavski's approach mapped out in detail the settings, each character's movements, their location on stage and how they would be seen by the audience. Lighting plays a significant role from the moment the play begins. The convention was for the curtains to open onto a fully lit stage, but *The Seagull* would offer a radical alternative as indicated by the first note of Stanislavski's score:

> The play starts in darkness, an August evening. The dim light of a lantern on top of a lamp-post, [...] distant sounds [...] [including] the slow tolling of a distant church bell – help the audience to get the feel of the sad, monotonous life of the characters. Flashes of lightning, faint rumbling of *thunder* in the distance.
>
> (Balukhaty, 1952: 139)

---

[1] First performed at Moscow Art Theatre 17 December 1898.

It is interesting that the striking visual effects which Stanislavski envisages are rooted and justified in realistic terms, but the overall intent is to create a series of poetic images which move beyond a naturalistic response to the text:

> At this time Nina's shadow can be seen on the curtain of the stage, as she sits down and assumes her pose. Yakov's shadow can also be seen on the curtain as he busies himself behind the scenes. The shadows can be seen because the moon has risen behind the curtain, and the people on stage are between the moon and the curtain. [...]

> They all take their seats. The footlights are to be lowered imperceptibly so as to throw into relief the silhouettes of those sitting on the rocking bench when the curtain rises and the moon lights up from the back of the stage those sitting in front

> (ibid.: 157)

The play-within-the-play at the beginning of *The Seagull* is clearly imagined using light and shadow to create striking visual images, and Stanislavski responds like a lighting designer to Chekhov's stage directions:

Stanislavski's production score, Note 49 (ibid.: 159):

The curtain goes up; the view of the lake is revealed; the moon above the horizon is reflected in the water; NINA, all in white, is sitting on a big stone.

49. On the stage is a table, on it a chair or a stool, all covered with some dark material – and moss. Nina is sitting on the top of it; she is draped in a white sheet, her hair hangs loosely down her back, the sheet, as it falls down her arms, forms something that resembles a pair of wings, through which Nina's bust and arms are faintly outlined. Her face is not visible, as the light is behind her. Only the contours of her figure can be seen, and this lends it a certain transparency. This picture is supplemented by the silhouettes of the figures sitting in the foreground. The lantern, which is alight in front of the stage, will to some extent interfere with the audience's view of Nina, and that, too, should heighten the dramatic effect of the scene.

There are two famous lighting requirements in Act I. In the middle of Nina's soliloquy, at the point where Chekhov indicates that 'the will-o'-the wisps appear on the stage', Stanislavski indicates:

> 50. Several men, hidden in different places in the bushes, are holding bits of lighted material on thin wires which they are waving about in all directions, raising and lowering them all the time.

> (ibid.: 159)

and he also has a practical solution for Satan's blood-red eyes that appear from the lake:

> 52. The two red spots to be made by the symmetrical battery of I. I. Geppert,[2] which he adapted for the owl in *The Sunken Bell*.

(ibid.: 161)

However, it is not the practical solutions that distinguish this production but the overall intent and the coordination of all of the scenographic elements to create the world of *The Seagull*. Lighting was often kept to relatively low levels to establish this atmosphere. For example, at the opening of Act IV:

> When the curtain rises – a pause of between ten and fifteen seconds. Semi-darkness. *One lamp on the wall* is alight. *Both stoves are being heated, and a reddish glow spreads from them through the whole room.* ...Wind. The rain is beating against the windows, sound of rattling window-panes and frames [...] Outside in front of the window, a lantern on top of a lamp-post is alight.[3]

(ibid.: 247)

In performance, however, there were difficulties in realising Stanislavski's original artistic vision as the new lighting aesthetic collided with existing scenic practices. Although the critical response to *The Seagull* was overwhelmingly enthusiastic, the contribution of the lighting did receive adverse comment. *The Courier*[4] acknowledged the suspense that had been created on stage but also criticised the lighting at the beginning of acts I and IV as 'dim and ominous, it made it difficult to see and hear' (ibid.: 76), while the brighter lighting of acts II and III exposed the crude painting and construction of Simov's settings. The journal *Theatre and Art*[5] recognised the innovative contribution of light and acclaimed the production as the 'first serious victory' of the new theatre with its atmosphere of

> blurred half-tones as background, and the foreground covered with a light haze which did not allow any colour to come through clearly [...] and that was why it made such a great impression...(it) was not simply an interpretation of the play, but an embodiment of it.

(ibid.: 78)

Through this production, Stanislavski had established what became widely known as 'Chekhovian mood'. Rather than present a strictly naturalistic

---

[2] Geppert was the stage manager of the MAT.
[3] In the original, the words shown here in italics were underlined in red by Stanislavski.
[4] 19 December 1898.
[5] 10 January 1899.

version of the play, this new dramaturgy involved a careful choreography of both light and sound to create poetic landscapes in which the drama could unfold. Stanislavski experimented with non-conventional ways of using light and was unafraid of using it in a way that was essentially non-naturalistic.[6] The use of darkness, often punctuated by light from natural sources rather than conventional stage lighting, became typical of his approach: 'It was often so dark on stage, that not only the actor's faces, but even their figures could not be seen.'[7] Act II of *Three Sisters* provides a good example of this. It begins with only a single shaft of light visible in the room from Andrei's offstage doorway and 'When Masha and Vershinin conversed, they sat down, stage left, in semi-darkness, and the only source of light was two candles in the dining room, at the rear of the stage.'[8]

While Stanislavski was often criticised for an over-elaborate approach to staging, light became an essential component in communicating both the external truth and the inner feelings of the characters. Stanislavski argued that this 'mood' was more important for the effect that it had on the actors than what was communicated to an audience, allowing performers to become immersed in the world of the drama. The actress Olga Knipper, responding to the atmosphere evoked by light, remarked that the setting for the last act of *The Seagull* felt so cold and dusty that 'you wanted to wrap yourself in a shawl'.[9] The impact of the role of lighting on the actor contributed to the later development and formalisation of Stanislavski's acting technique. Allen, citing Stanislavski's notes directly, argues that

> Without the various lighting and sound effects; 'it would have been difficult to create inner truth on the stage, to create true feelings and emotions among the external, coarse, obtrusive falsehoods of the theatre'. In other words, the 'mood' of the production helped the actors to become absorbed in the 'world' of the play. The 'atmospheric' elements of light and sound acted as a kind of trigger, touching subconscious emotional chords: 'They felt external truth, and intimate memories of their own lives rose again in their souls, enticing from them those feelings which Chekhov was talking about. Then the actor ceased to act, and began to live the life of the play, became the character. ...*It was a creative miracle.*'
>
> (in Allen, 2000: 48 (italics in the original))

---

[6] See production notes for the culmination of Act I and opening of Act II of *The Cherry Orchard* (Allen, 2000: 36–37) where moving, reflected and dazzling light is designed to impact on the audience.

[7] Nemirovich-Danchenko's letter to Chekhov (cited in Allen, 2000: 48).

[8] This description comes from Stanislavski's production plans *Rezhisserskie ekzemplyary K.S. Stanislavskogo* vol. 3, 1983: 132, 145 (cited in Allen, 2000: 238).

[9] See Allen, 2000: 49.

A STAGE GOVERNED THROUGH LIGHT

The Austrian director Max Reinhardt (1873–1943) is an important figure in the development of modern lighting techniques. Heavily influenced by Craig, he was able to take advantage of technological developments and new German lighting equipment to experiment with scenographic elements in search of his own version of Wagner's 'total art work'. Although the actor was always at the centre of his practice, Reinhardt rejected the naturalistic stage in a search for a new form of spectacular theatrical expression in which light was to play a key role. Reinhardt argued that

> There is only one objective for the theatre: the theatre; and I believe in a theatre that belongs to the actor. No longer, as in the previous decades, literary points of view shall be decisive ones . . .
> What I have in mind is a theatre that will again bring joy to people, that leads them out of the grey misery of everyday life . . . I want to show life from another side than that of merely pessimistic negation, yet equally true and genuine in its gaiety, filled with colour and light.
>
> (Esslin, 1977: 9)

Influenced by Craig's theories and the high production values of Otto Brahm, Reinhardt was to move beyond the comparatively tentative uses of light in naturalistic plays and to embrace a radical new performance style in which the stage was governed by light.

Technological developments were central to the development of expressionist drama techniques in Germany in the first decade of the twentieth century. The availability of new lighting equipment and a new awareness of light through photography and the cinema contributed to the evolution of *chiaroscuro* techniques in stage settings that no longer attempted to create a naturalistic environment for the actor to inhabit. Instead, production practices sought to create a more abstract visual representation of the themes of the drama in which the performers were simply just one of the visual components. A contemporary critic responded to the impact of the staging of the 1920 premiere of Kaiser's production *Hölle Weg Erde* (Hell Way Earth), suggesting that 'César Klein's stage sets were illustrations to the text; they did not focus on the actor but on the visual tone of the scene. One did not so much hear as read the play with their help' (Ihering, trans. Patterson, 1981: 69).

Reinhardt aimed to create performances that brought the actor and spectator together. Light became an increasingly important element of his productions, which were planned meticulously and recorded in a *Regiebuch*. This process developed the earlier techniques of Meiningen and Stanislavski in making a detailed record of all of the production's aspects and their timings. Detailed notes on movements, set and costume drawings, lighting direction and the musical score were included alongside Reinhardt's historical research and writings relating to his interpretation. A contemporary reviewer observed that productions were characterised by a

> totality of conception, the fidelity to a single mood of exotic richness; the play is not conceived in one mood, the setting in another, the lighting in another; line and mass blend with colour, colour with lighting, lighting with music, and music with the story, the whole affording a singe sensuous impression.
>
> (Cheney, 1914: 55)

The collaboration with the scenographer Ernst Stern was a key element of Reinhardt's successful staging. When they didn't work together as in *Orpheus* (1921), the results were regarded as less than impressive, but MacGowan and Jones acknowledge that Reinhardt's work, including his experimentation with lighting equipment and scenery, played a major part in establishing the role of the designer in the theatre (1922: 111) and suggested that Reinhardt's artistic success lay principally in the impact of the staging of spectacular theatrical moments (see p. 36).

Reinhardt was concerned with the overall experience of the theatrical event, and both light and movement were key to his art form and underpinned his model of 'aesthetic drama'. In *Salome* (1902) in Berlin, Reinhardt adopted Fortuny's sky dome, a sky-blue silk against a cyclorama lit by Fortuny's indirect lighting and a keyed moonlight effect (see p. 210). Images achieved through collections of shadowy figures in half-light were a typical visual component of Reinhardt's later work (see excerpt on *Danton's Death* below).

LIGHTING 'BEHAVES LIKE THE MIND'

The role of light became more prominent as Reinhardt sought to resolve the staging issues in the much smaller Kammerspiele studio theatre in Berlin. In 1916, Reinhardt rigged a spotlight in the roof over the centre of the stalls and developed a system of rapid scene changes that relied upon this single source of light. This unnatural and rather primitive effect served to destroy any theatrical illusion of reality on the stage – and was used repeatedly, both between scenes and as a recurring production style, which came to typify the expressionistic productions of *Das junge Deutschland*. This distancing effect created by the use of light was a precursor to the techniques later used by both Piscator and Brecht. A contemporary review of Weichart's production of *Der Sohn* in 1918 demonstrates how this technique of directional lighting, emphasising key figures in the drama, was becoming widespread:

Herr Weichert [...] places the Son – as the only truly physical presence – spatially in the centre of the action, a centre that becomes the objectified focus of the play because it is he that gathers the illumination of the spotlight about him.[10]

(Stahl in Patterson, 1981: 101)

Patterson also notes that

With this use of directional spotlighting the director could throw the central figure of the scene into unprecedented prominence, a device particularly appropriate to Expressionistic plays treating of a protagonist moving through the darkness of a dream world about him [sic]. In addition, hard lighting from above cast unreal shadows on the face of the actor, so creating the chiaroscuro effect so beloved of Expressionism and frequently seen in the atmospheric lighting of the early cinema.

(ibid.)

In Reinhardt's production of Sorge's *The Beggar* (1917),[11] light became the dominant design element not simply as a theatrical device but as an integral expressionistic force in the drama:

The lighting apparatus behaves like the mind. It drowns in darkness what it wishes to forget and bathes in light what it wishes to recall. Thus the entire stage becomes a universe of mind, and the individual scenes are not replicas of three-dimensional reality, but visualized stages of thought.

(Sokel, 1959: 41)

Following directions in the text, Reinhardt's lighting for *The Beggar*[12] deliberately emphasised one group of characters or space over another before then shifting in a dreamlike manner to highlight another area of the stage. A moving spotlight picked out the ghostly white faces of individual characters who stepped out of the scene, isolated by light against a black gauze whilst the rest of the stage was in darkness. The shifting light was a visual equivalent of the onstage character of The Poet's stream of consciousness:

When the latent substratum [of the drama] emerges, the centre of the stage is obscured while a particular corner – significantly supplied with couches or benches – is highlighted. When the mind shifts back to the surface plot, the corner sinks into darkness, while the centre is illuminated. The corner scenes, so

---

[10] Stahl, E.L. *Neue Badische Landeszeitung*, Mannheim, 19 January 1918.

[11] Written in 1912 but not staged until 1917.

[12] Patterson argues that this is the first truly expressionistic production and where stage lighting. 'has become an art-form, judged not by verisimilitude but by effectiveness' (1981: 54).

Figure 11 Stern's design for Act II of *Der Bettler* (*The Beggar*), Berlin, 1917, shows that light was integral to the expressionistic staging

> puzzlingly unrelated to the main action centre-stage, can now be seen as only apparently unrelated. These scenes function as symbolically disguised commentary and reflection on the themes discussed in the centre, and in that lies their dreamlike quality.
>
> (Sokel, 1963: xv)

Light in Reinhardt's production is therefore no longer simply a way of illuminating the stage space but a dynamic element that is at times dramaturgically dominant:

> *Der Bettler* is performed on an empty stage. There is no pretence, no construction to reduce the space. The light tears out a piece of the great black space, which, untouched and limitless, seems to be waiting to be filled: the action takes place here. Or a man stands alone, as a patch of light in front of a black surface. In this darkened space a room is defined by a few pieces of furniture, window and door-frames and free hanging pictures; a birch in blue light represents a garden. One is a long way from reality ... At every moment reality is sacrificed for inner truth, most boldly and most successfully, I feel, when a starry sky appears over the heads of the lovers in their room without walls or ceiling.
>
> (Herald, 1918: 30 trans. Patterson, 1981: 55)

LIGHT AS EXPRESSIVE FORCE – FROM MORNING TILL MIDNIGHT

In this extract, Patterson provides an analysis of Kaiser's play *Von Morgens bis Mitternachts*. Written in 1912 (and also produced by Reinhardt), it provides an insight into how light became integral to the expressionist style of dramatic presentation:

(L)ighting is now employed not merely to illuminate the set and actors but as a further means of artistic communication. The first reference to light is in the snowfield scene, where Kaiser prescribes 'Sun casting blue shadows' reinforcing not only the physical coldness of the scene but also suggesting the barren landscape of the Cashier's soul, the *tabula rasa* before he begins his spiritual journey. This requirement could be fulfilled by backlighting the upstage area with a blue 'wash' and projecting strong 'sunlight' from a source at the front. On the appearance of the skeleton, the sun is obscured by clouds, to break through again at the end of the scene as the tree resumes its former shape, an obvious use of atmospheric lighting.

By contrast with the warm interior lighting of the hotel and home scenes, the cycle race is lit by the harsh glare of an arc-light. Although it is not prescribed by Kaiser, it would be appropriate here to use a spotlight to isolate the Cashier in his ecstatic monologues, just as the Lady's appearance in the bank might be accentuated by the use of a follow-spot. Such devices deliberately flout realism and serve to provide a focus.

The night club scene begins in darkness. Music is allowed to establish a mood, until the waiter enters and turns on a red light. While wholly acceptable on a realistic level, the red light in which the scene is played clearly reinforces the erotic ambience. Such colour symbolism was common practice in Expressionist theatre. Already in the stage-directions for *Der brennende Dornbusch* (The Burning Thornbush), written in 1911, Kokoschka required a white light while the male figure spoke, interrupted by red light while the woman replied, and red light was used again by Weichert in his 1918 production of *Der Sohn* for the appearance of the prostitute.

The most startling lighting effects occur at the end of the play, although here again they are acceptable on a realistic level. Following the Policeman's instructions to switch off the light, all the lights on the chandelier go out except one, which lights up the bright wires above the stage in such a way as to create the image of a skeleton. When the lights are turned on again, all the bulbs explode, leaving the dying Cashier in darkness (although presumably a glimmer of light must illuminate him outstretched against the cross). The final stage-direction summarizes the despairing mood of the ending: 'It is quite dark'.

(Patterson, 1981: 69–70)

LIGHT AND DARKNESS – DANTON'S DEATH – A CASE STUDY

For Reinhardt's production of Büchner's *Danton's Death*, 1916–1921, the designer, Ernest Stern (1876–1954), suggested a scenographic concept that dispensed with realistic scenery and instead relied primarily upon the effect of masses of bodies in light. In this extract, Stern recounts his design process and cites Herald's contemporary account of the production:[13]

When I read the play my impression was of dramatic, tragic and fantastic scenes which flamed up for a short space and then disappeared. The chaos of the revolution struck me as a terrible storm to the accompaniment of the constant rolling of thunder, sometimes near, sometimes in the distance, the scene lit up with flashes of lightning, the passionate actors in the drama appearing for a while as though in the spotlight and then fading into the background. In one respect my work on *The Green Flute* helped me here because it struck me forcibly that 'lighting' was the solution for the problem of staging *Danton* just as it had been for the fantastic Chinese fairy tale. The revolving stage was quite out of the question, and fortunately Reinhardt agreed with me that *Danton* required a special system of décor and I was allowed to carry out my own ideas on the subject:

'Reinhardt undertook the daring experiment of producing a famous realistic piece whilst abandoning realism in the scenery and presenting the visual aspect of the great revolutionary drama chiefly as human bodies and lighting effects. [...] The impression of tremendous plenitude and variety of life, the impression of passion-ate movement, was obtained by lighting up only one small part of the stage at a time whilst the rest remained in gloom. Only individuals or small groups were picked out in the spotlight whilst the masses always remained in semi-darkness, or even in complete darkness. But they were always there and they could be heard murmuring, speaking, shouting. Out of the darkness an upraised arm would catch the light, and in this way thousands seemed to be where hundreds were in fact. This principle of the rapid play of light and darkness was maintained throughout. Scenes would flash up for a second or two. Lights would go out, darkness would persist for a fraction, and then lights would go up elsewhere, and this rapid and often abrupt change reinforced the rhythm of the piece. The last words of one scene were still being spoken when the first words of the next would sound and the light change to it. The sound of singing, the whistling of "The Marseillaise," the tramping of many feet, booing, the echo of a speech being delivered somewhere, applause from out of the darkness. A lamp-post lights up and the mob is seen hanging an aristocrat. Half-naked furies in colourful rags dance "La Carmagnole". And already the light turns to a peaceful room in which Danton is resting in the arms of a *grisette*. And because whatever is the important thing for the moment is suddenly illuminated out of the darkness in a fiery or ghostly white light, the pro-ducer is able to stress the main figures of the play and their action to the utmost: Danton, the People's Tribune; the young Desmoulins; the sea-green Robespierre; St Just with the fair-haired, girlish head and the heart of ice – they appear for a

---

[13] Herald's account is from Stern and Herald (1919: 86–91).

moment or two and disappear again. And at the end the slim Lucille who has lost her Desmoulins leans exhausted against the guillotine. A short and deeply moving moment in the cold light of the moon.'

My name is nowhere mentioned in all this, but, in fact, it was I who had tried something completely new, namely, to paint with light, to stress only the essentials. Fortunately, in Germany the scenic artist does the lighting and not the producer as in England, and that is because, after all, it is part and parcel of the scene and can make or mar it.

(Stern, 1951: 161–163)

The technological development of lighting equipment allowed for brighter, whiter and focusable light although a review of the production attributes its success not to the light but to the darkness itself, which 'gives birth to light'.[14]

The use of steeply angled harsh white light on stage was often used to create exaggerated and unnatural shadows that complemented the effects of the distorted stage settings. Light and darkness were therefore able to accentuate the disjointed and nightmarish world in which the protagonist of the drama was frequently immersed. The quality of light and the way it was manipulated were also able to impact directly on the audience, evoking similar feelings of unease and disorientation.

The evolution of light as a designed element in Reinhardt's practice is neatly summarised by his literary adviser, Arthur Kahane:

At the most, scenic decoration can only be frame, not function. The elaboration of details, the emphasizing of nuances disappears; the actor and the actor's voice are truly essential, while lighting becomes the real source of decoration, its single aim to bring the important into the light, and to leave the unimportant in the shadow.

(Carter, 1914: 122–123)

The Tribüne theatre in Berlin was established in 1919 especially to stage the new expressionist plays and with the aim of creating a new relationship between the stage and its audience. Converted from a hall, it was a small 296-seat studio auditorium with none of the features, such as footlights or front curtains, typical of existing theatres. Its co-director, Karl Heinz Martin, suggested that

Such a theatre without any machinery and technical gadgets, without a cyclorama or sky-dome, without revolving or sliding stages can in its immediacy reveal the soul and its message without distraction or limitation.

(Bab, 1928: 178 cited in Patterson, 1981: 99)

---

[14] The phrase originates in Siegfried Jacobsohn's *Max Reinhardt* Berlin (1921: 133).

This theatre space therefore relied upon a dramaturgical intervention through light but, despite the physical nature of the Tribüne, there was still a perceived need to mask the lighting and, in common with Reinhardt's theatres, a light-drum was built above the auditorium to hide the equipment from the audience's view. It would be Piscator and Brecht who would soon challenge these staging practices.

However, the acknowledgement of the particular nature of this theatre space and the concentration on the central idea of the expressionist drama both demanded bold staging and lighting solutions. Martin's scenographer, Robert Neppach, used jagged lines, angular flats and crude paintings of objects such as windows to provide selective fragments of the protagonist's environment that were far removed from a naturalistic approach to setting. The distorted perspective of these elements was often accentuated by light to reflect the anxieties of the drama's central figure, while the absence of a stage curtain at the Tribüne led to Martin's use of the blackout to denote the end of scenes.[15] As well as being a practical solution, this technique served to emphasise the disjointed nature of the protagonist's world and further emphasised the uncomfortable nature of the experience of the audience.

BRECHT, LIGHTING AND *VERFREMDUNGSEFFEKT*

Bertolt Brecht (1898–1956) used light for a very different theatrical purpose in his productions in Europe in the 1930s and 1940s. Borrowing on the techniques he had observed from working alongside Reinhardt and Piscator, Brecht and his collaborators offered a radical alternative to theatre performance practices through stripping away a range of existing theatre conventions. The way in which the stage was lit was integral to Brecht's artistic and political aims for the drama, where the overriding concern was to establish a dialogue between the stage and auditorium in which ideas could be examined critically by an audience. To create this kind of interaction, bright lighting was an essential component:

THE LIGHTING[16]

> Give us some light on the stage, electrician. How can we
> Playwrights and actors put forward
> Our images of the world in half darkness? The dim twilight
> Induces sleep. But we need the audience's

---

[15] Patterson (1981: 102) suggests that this was the first use of the blackout in the German theatre, but it is likely that this device had previously been used by Reinhardt at the Kammerspiele and had already become an accepted convention for denoting scene endings for expressionistic dramas staged in smaller theatre spaces.

[16] *Die Beleuchtung* in *Gedichte aus dem Messingkauf (Wünsche des Stückeschreibers)* in Brecht, (1966: 144).

Wakeful-, even watchfulness. Let them
Do their dreaming in the light. The little bit of night
We now and then require can be
Indicated by moons or lamps, likewise our acting
Can make clear what time of day it is
Whenever needed. The Elizabethan wrote us verses
About a heath at evening
Which no electrician can match, nor even
The heath itself. So light up
What we have laboured over, that the audience
Can see how the outraged peasant woman
Sits down on the Finnish soil[17]
As if it belonged to her.

(Brecht, 1987: 426)

Brecht's use of light, however, went beyond a fundamental concern for levels of illumination, although he was critical of the prevailing conditions for lighting the stage.[18] To analyse the role of light in Brecht's work it is essential to understand his desire to change the nature of the traffic between the stage and the auditorium, and his purpose in staging dramatic work. Brecht had become dissatisfied with the limited ambitions of contemporary theatre in the 1930s, where

> A technical apparatus and a style of acting had been evolved which could do more to stimulate illusions than to give experiences, more to intoxicate than to elevate, more to deceive than to illumine. What was the good of a constructivist stage if it was socially unconstructive; of the finest lighting equipment if it lit nothing but childish and twisted representations of the world; of a suggestive style of acting if it only served to tell us that A was B? What was the use of the whole box of tricks if all it could do was to offer artificial surrogates for real experience?
>
> (Brecht, 1959 in Willett, 1964: 133)

Brecht had developed ideas about the need for a new dramatic form through working alongside Erwin Piscator. This formative experience enabled him to develop his own epic style of theatre production in which a revolutionary approach to stage design emerged in collaboration with scenographer Casper Neher, the stage environment being created through experimentation in rehearsal alongside the playwright and actors.[19]

---

[17] The original refers here to Tavast-land in Finland, suggesting that the poem was written in 1948, and it references the production of Mr Puntila and his Servant Matti, which premiered in Zurich in that year.

[18] 'Thanks to the poverty of our lighting arrangements, the splendour of Neher's sets cannot be photographically reproduced.' Footnote to 'The Fourth Night, The Playwright's Speech about the Theatre of the Stage Designer Caspar Neher', Brecht, c. 1942 *The Messingkauf Dialogues* (2002: 82).

[19] See Baugh, (1994) 'Brecht and Stage Design; the Bühnenbildner and the Bühnenbauer'.

The purpose of Brecht's theatre was to create conditions that would encourage the spectator to adopt an attitude of inquiry and criticism of events portrayed on stage. Borrowing on the distancing and estranging techniques that Piscator employed through the use of film projections, for example, Brecht sought alternative methods of creating *Verfremdung* – a distancing effect which he regarded as essential in countering any suggestion of illusion on the stage. Light could be used to facilitate this ideal and prevent audiences from becoming immersed in the drama:

> In this new method of practising art empathy would lose its dominant role. Against that the Verfremdungseffekt (V-effect)[20] will need to be introduced, which is an artistic effect too and also leads to a theatrical experience. It consists in the reproduction of real-life incidents on the stage in such a way as to underline their causality and bring it to the spectator's attention. This type of art also generates emotions; such performances facilitate the mastering of reality; and this it is that moves the spectator.
>
> (Brecht, 1965: 98–99)

Since the first condition of the distancing effect was to purge the stage of everything that was illusory, this ruled out any attempts to make the stage convey atmosphere or mood, or the flavour of a particular place or time. Night-time scenes were not achieved by the convention of dimming the over-all light levels on the stage, for example, but instead were often represented in the same way as on the Elizabethan stage, with the introduction of stage properties such as lamps, or the appearance of a sickle-shaped moon symbol. In his notes on the 1948 Zurich premiere of *Mr Puntila and his Servant Matti*, Brecht makes important observations about the role and style of light:

> The symbols of the sun, moon and clouds, like the hanging signs for pubs and shops, hung in front of the high broad wall of birch bark which forms the back-ground of the Puntila set. Depending on whether it was day, evening or night the birch wall was lit strongly, weakly or not at all, whilst the acting area was always fully lit. The atmosphere was thus established in the background and divided from the rest of the performance.
>
> No kind of coloured lighting was used. Wherever the lighting rig is efficient enough, the light should be as evenly spread as in our variety theatres where acro-batic arts are shown. Harsh spotlights extinguish the facial features. Darkness,

---

[20] Willett actually translates this as 'Alienation Effect' (A-effect), which is a term that is contested by contemporary Brecht scholars. 'The German for alienation is *Entfremdung* – a passive word meaning 'being made strange', whereas Brecht invented the term *Verfremdung* as an active word meaning 'making strange'. The usual translation nowadays is 'distancing', with the German term *V-Effekt* used for its application (e-mail correspondence with translator Alan Clarke 15 December 2009).

even if relative, diminishes the responses reflected on the faces; lighting that ener-
gises the public is recommended, determined by means of photographs.[21] [...]
The set designer can achieve colour and contrast without the help of coloured
lighting. [...] Every glance at the stage, with regard to meaning and use of space
and colour, can capture a meaningful picture.

(Brecht, 1962: 109–111)

Brecht argued that 'The audience's tendency to plunge into such illusions has
to be checked by specific artistic means' (Willett, 1964: 136), and a very bright
illumination of the stage would help to achieve this. Around 1940, Brecht
observed that

a half-lit stage coupled with a completely darkened auditorium makes the spectator less level-headed by preventing him from observing his neighbour and in turn
hiding from his neighbour's eyes.

(Brecht, 1951: Appendix note)

Bright, uncoloured[22] lighting therefore predominated on Brecht's stage since
it enabled the distinction between empathy and detachment to be more
clearly delineated in performance. In emphasising *Verfremdung*, lighting
became an active agent in the drama, exposing the action on the stage in
order to bring the key concerns of the drama into sharp relief.

Light was an essential component of Brecht's performance space since it
assisted in creating an aesthetic that rejected any semblance of naturalism:

It is more important nowadays for the set to tell the spectator he's in a theatre than
to tell him he's in, say, Aulis. The theatre must acquire ... the same fascinating
reality as a sporting arena during a boxing match. The best thing is to show the
machinery, the ropes and the flies. If the set represents a town it must look like
a town that has been built to last precisely two hours. One must conjure up the
reality of time.

Everything must be provisional yet polite. A place need only have the credibility
of a place glimpsed in a dream. The set needs to spring from the rehearsal of
groupings, so in effect it must be a fellow-actor [...] The materials of the set must
be visible [...] there mustn't be any faking.[23]

(Brecht, in Willett, 1964: 233)

---

[21] The Berliner Ensemble's practice was to document their staging through photographs to
assess its impact.

[22] There are oral accounts from technicians who worked with the Berliner Ensemble when they
visited London in 1956 that in fact Brecht's fabled 'white light' was ironically by this time created by a complex combination of steel blue gels carefully balanced so that the light appeared
uncoloured on stage. An equivalent effect today would be achieved through using colour correction filters to modify warm tungsten sources to create a 'whiter' light with a higher colour
temperature.

[23] Unpublished note from Brecht-Archive 331/173 footnote to Brecht (1951) *Stage Design for the
Epic Theatre*.

Just as lighting made visible the materiality of the stage, so too should the lighting equipment itself be exposed to the audience's view. This scenographic *Verfremdungseffekt* was in direct contrast to Wagner's aim of a synthesis of dramatic elements on the stage. Brecht argued instead that the production elements should not be allowed to blend together. Setting, costume, lighting and music should maintain their autonomy in order to further the common aims of the drama in their individual and different ways – each element was seen as a distinct and discrete agent in the presentation of the drama.[24]

MAKING VISIBLE THE SOURCE OF LIGHT

There is a point in showing the lighting apparatus openly, as it is one of the means of preventing an unwanted element of illusion; it scarcely disturbs the necessary concentration. If we light the actors and their performance in such a way that the lights themselves are within the spectator's field of vision, we destroy part of his illusion of being present at a spontaneous, transitory, authentic, unrehearsed event. He sees that arrangements have been made to show something; something is being repeated here under special conditions, for instance in a very brilliant light. Displaying the actual lights is meant to be a counter to the old-fashioned theatre's efforts to hide them. No one would expect the lighting to be hidden at a sporting event, a boxing match for instance. Whatever the points of difference between the modern theatre's presentations and those of a sporting promoter, they do not include the same concealment of the sources of light as the old theatre found necessary.

(Brecht, *Stage Design for the Epic Theatre* (1951) in Willett, 1964: 141)

But whilst Brecht's stage lighting should be above all else bright, it was seemingly never bright enough.[25] Brecht could spend over five days plotting the lighting for a production, often using stand-in extras on the stage in place of the actors, who would return for extended technical rehearsals that could last between a week and a fortnight.[26] This considerable investment in finessing the overall lighting aesthetic contradicts Brecht's assertion that light is simply a mechanism to assist the audience in thinking through the issues of the drama. Brecht's light is much more than a functional tool. The white 'open light' is, despite what Brecht advocates, a signifier. It signifies modernity through the new theatricality of the sports arena, which is in direct opposition to the bourgeois illusionistic theatre with its subtly lit velvet curtains.

---

[24] See Brecht (1949) *A Short Organum for the Theatre*.

[25] 'Neher ... was patience itself at technical rehearsals with Brecht. Brecht tinkered about with the lights, which were never bright and white enough for him'. Brecht *The Tutor* 1950: 114.

[26] See Willett, 1964: 203.

It is also important to note here that, contrary to established histories and common perceptions, Brecht did not use open white light exclusively. On occasions, coloured light was used to emphasise specific theatrical moments, such as to mark the end of a scene or to separate a song from the dramatic material which preceded it.[27] Pink lighting provides a 'happy' ending to *St Joan* and punctuates the action in *The Good Person of Setzuan* to mark the arrival of the Gods, whilst blue lighting was frequently used in a deliberately primitive way to signal night. In *Mother Courage*, designed by Teo Otto in 1941 and restaged at the Deutsches Theater in Berlin in 1949, a series of electric globe lights provided a purely unrealistic visual element to the setting, which was disarming because they contrasted sharply with the events on stage. The suspended lights accompanied the music and served to lift it above the reality of the action, and provided a visible sign that the drama had shifted to another aesthetic level.

Of greater significance to lighting practice in the second half of the twentieth century was Brecht's insistence that the mechanisms for producing this theatrical illumination should be made evident to the audience. This radical departure from established conventions of masking lighting sources was to have a major impact on the way that lighting was considered in the theatre. Lighting fixtures were now accepted as an integral part of the viewer's experience and the overall design of the performance. Brecht's artistic practice therefore established a new kind of creative freedom for future lighting professionals whose practice until this point had been governed by the necessity to hide stage lighting equipment. With this freedom, post-Brecht, new lighting positions within the vision of the audience gradually became accepted and ultimately allowed the potential for new lighting contributions to performance. Brecht's lighting practice, echoing the Enlightenment ideas of knowing through seeing, foregrounded light as a fundamental element in performance that privileges that which enables visual penetration.

PROJECTED LIGHT AND THE LIGHT STAGE

While Brecht was developing a poetics of non-realist light, his contemporary and one-time collaborator **Erwin Piscator** (1893–1966) was also pursuing a dramaturgy that centred on light. Piscator considered the stage as a 'play machine' and sought to employ all technological and mechanical means necessary to communicate his dramatic vision. Productions such as *Hoppla, wir Leben!* (1927) had developed expressionistic staging techniques and created a world on a scaffolding set that provided a 'simultaneous stage' of multiple rooms that offered a complex montage of light, sound and film:

---

[27] See Weber and Munk, 1967: 104.

> Film projections, the colour organ, the interchange on stage between light
> and 'film light,' complete motorization of the stage–through these, and how
> many other, innovations modern creative science can supplant the ancient
> peep-show.
>
> (Piscator 1941, cited in Bentley, 1997: 472)

Piscator's fascination with the relationship between projected light in the
form of film and theatrical light is evident throughout his work, but in 1953
he developed the *Lichtbühne* (light stage), a glass stage on a much larger scale
than Fuller's (see p. 152) and which could be lit from below as well as from
the top and sides.

The technological innovation of the *Lichtbühne* was actually envisioned
as a force that would replace projection and would 'bring freedom from
technology – since in it technology is brought to its last and ultimate, sub-
tlest expression' (Piscator, cited in Innes, 1972: 164). It was first seen in the
Frankfurt adaptation of Sartre's *L'Engrenage*[28] and created an entirely new
lighting aesthetic. Actors were lit brightly from below and, with little front
light, they then appeared as silhouettes, strangely isolated from their sur-
roundings on an unrepresentational stage: 'When men can walk on light –
they become independent of space. Then there will not be the "placeless"
but also the "spaceless" stage [. . . in which the performer] becomes man in
himself.' (Piscator, ibid.). A contemporary Swedish review observed that

> The bare, diffused, spotted light created an empty space in which all of the figures
> seemed to have the same degree of illumination; it was a rational, unemotional
> light.
>
> (*Dagens Nyheter*, 12 February 1955, cited in Bergman, 1977: 381)

This description suggests that Piscator had discovered an alternative solution
to Brecht's use of light to facilitate a distancing effect, but his egalitarian,
'unemotional' light also seemed to provide a new focus upon the words that
the actors were speaking:

> With the new precision and variation of lighting effects new rhythms of movement
> could be created on stage because words could control, conduct and concert the
> interplay of lights – and as a reflex of speech the 'light-stage' made the spoken
> word a focal point in emphasising the actor.
>
> (Innes, 1972: 164)

---

[28] Staged in September 1953. The *Lichtbühne* also featured in the Berlin production of *War and
Peace* and a production of Faulkner's *Requiem for a Nun*.

PLASTIC LIGHT

This chapter began by looking at playwrights' responses to lighting and its incorporation as a specific element within the play script. These ideas were adopted alongside expressionistic techniques in the USA by dramatists and designers concerned alike with the creation of new theatrical forms. Designers such as Robert Edmond Jones, Donald Oenslager and Lee Simonson introduced ideas of the 'new stagecraft' to North America and embraced the design of lighting as an integral aspect of their scenography. Heavily influenced by the plays of Henrik Ibsen, Eugene O'Neill (1888–1953) used light as a central yet fading force in his autobiographical play *Long Day's Journey Into Night*.[29] This presents a slow yet relentless telescoping of light as the action focuses in on a dysfunctional family, and it leaves us finally with a single character isolated in a sea of darkness by a small pool of light.

Jo Mielziner (1901–1976) made a significant contribution to a new production style and, particularly in collaboration with the director **Elia Kazan** (1909–2003), developed a tradition of creating poetic landscapes defined through light which created a tension between the physical constraints of the setting and the psychological states of the characters. Mielziner and Kazan established an approach to production that created a synthesis between the realistic staging methods of Stanislavski and that of using bodies and light favoured by Reinhardt and other German expressionists. Mielziner's scenography provided a catalyst for the realisation of Appia's plea: 'Let us take the first step; the dramatist will soon join us in our anticipation of a flexible scenic art that is conscious of its flexibility' (Appia, 1908 in Volbach, 1989: 180).

Responding to the scenographic opportunities inherent in the plays of Tennessee Williams (1911–1983) and Arthur Miller (1915–2005), Mielziner employed transparent and translucent staging materials such as gauzes, and used light to define, reveal, create focus and shift both time and place on stage. His impact on the dramaturgy of both writers was implicitly acknowledged in Williams' production notes written following the original staging of *The Glass Menagerie* in 1944 and subsequently included in the published script. In this guidance for future scenographic presentation of the play, Williams echoes Appia's conception of a fluid stage space and advocates the importance of a non-realistic use of light in order to create a new form of 'plastic theatre'. This 'memory play' is set in both the present and the past, and Williams uses light as an essential dramatic component – to create mobility on a static stage, to facilitate the claustrophobic atmosphere and as a central symbol with the vulnerable Laura seen like one of the flickering candles that illuminate the Wingfield apartment. Williams calls for a dark stage illuminated by shafts of light that provide focus, 'sometimes in

---

[29] Written in 1942 but not published until 1956, three years after O'Neill's death.

contradistinction' to what might at first appear to be the centre of attention on stage. Thus whilst Tom and Amanda engage in animated conversation, the lighting foregrounds Laura playing silently with her glass animals. The poignancy of this image is heightened further by its juxtaposition with the outside world, lit by lightning and glimpsed through the fire escape, in which the constant flashing of coloured neon lights offers the promise of sexual fulfilment and freedom.

A Streetcar Named Desire (1947) further developed Williams' wish for theatre to present 'a more penetrating and vivid expression of things as they are', exploring the notion of plasticity through constantly shifting expressionistic light. Mielziner acknowledged that

> The magic of light opened up a fluid and poetic world of storytelling [...] Through-out the play the brooding atmosphere is like an impressionistic X-ray [...] This kind of designing is the most fascinating of all designing for the theatre. It deals in form that is transparent, in space that is limited but has the illusion of infinity, in light that is ever changing in quality and in color.
>
> (Mielziner, 1965: 141)

The play's original title, *The Paper Lantern*, provides a clue to the importance of light and its role within the drama. Light is both a central symbol and a motivating force, woven into the fabric of the play, with Blanche Dubois attempting to avoid its glare, yet like a moth drawn fatally to the flame. Mielziner and Kazan collaborated a year later on Miller's *Death of a Salesman* which, influenced by Williams, also used light and gauzes in combination to create a fluid stage space in which elisions between the present and past, the real and the imaginary, are foregrounded by a symbolic use of light.

The explicit use of light as a symbol and its dramatic potential has of course been recognised by many modern playwrights who have drawn heavily on this tradition and incorporated lighting cues in the script. The presence of 'light' in the work of Samuel Beckett, for example, works on multiple levels and requires significant technical artistry in order to achieve the precise demands of the stage directions. Frequently Beckett demands 'a hellish light' for his protagonists. In *NOT I* (1973), in contrast, he requires the entire stage in darkness except for an illuminated mouth, with the rest of the face in shadow and apparently suspended over two metres above the stage. In *PLAY* (1963), the technical challenge is even greater as the three characters fixed on stage are each interrogated by the light itself, which moves from one impassive face to the next. Beckett emphasises that the lighting for this one-act play should be realised predominantly from a single mobile source positioned close to and below the faces of the 'victims'. Importantly, light needs to be understood as emanating from within the theatrical space rather than beyond as it takes on the role of the inquisitor to which the voices must respond instantaneously.

Besbes has undertaken a detailed semiotic analysis of Beckett's use of light, suggesting that

> In Beckett's drama, the functions that can be assigned to light are innumerable. Light can be functional in terms of information, structure, ostension, deixis, and symbolism. Since light, as a semiotic system is especially designed to fulfil a function that is considered necessary and important for the other sign systems to operate, its purposefulness is unquestionable. The first and immediate purpose of light is to produce the dramatic illusion.
>
> (Besbes, 2007: 95)

We might disagree entirely with this last statement, especially since this chapter alone has demonstrated a variety of approaches that have explored the role of light beyond the simple creation of illusion. However, it is useful to think about the impact of lighting on the audience experience, as Brecht did, for example, and to consider further how it makes meaning on the stage and, equally importantly, its phenomenological impact on both performer and audience. These issues are explored further in the following chapters.

Chapter

7   Light and the Body

The body has been at the centre of lighting for performance, and the need to see the human form, and especially the face, has frequently been the over-riding purpose that has governed the illumination of the stage space. This chapter looks at the interrelationship between theatrical lighting and the human form in terms of its physiological impact and its implications for creativity. In considering how images are received by an audience, it also raises questions about that which is not illuminated on stage and not there-fore offered to the audience's view (this material links therefore with issues discussed in Chapter 4).

There appears to be little written about the experience of light from the performer's perspective, but this chapter considers the impact of light in cre-ating mood for the actor and interactions between light, the body and the setting. It ranges from lighting *for* the body to the incorporation of light *on* the body. In exploring the work of Loïe Fuller, it also traces the beginning of a style of lighting that can be seen as the origin of modern dance lighting.

As we have noted already in earlier chapters, the need to see the performer adequately was the reason for the historical development of footlights, and this singular desire underpinned subsequent attempts to find a more 'sym-pathetic' lighting angle – one that was perceived to be able to light the performer from a more 'natural' angle (i.e. from overhead and approximating to the angle of sunlight), but also from a position that did not draw attention to itself within the view of the spectator.

Illuminating the human form took precedence over the lighting of the scenic space and, increasingly, the need to see the actor's face exerted a tyranny over the design of light for drama. The theatrical mantra that 'if an actor cannot be seen they cannot be heard' has rarely been challenged in Western theatre. This has often resulted in overly lit stage spaces where the need for a general, even wash of light has often taken precedence to the detriment of a more sculptural, creative use of light. This practice emphasises the body as the single most important element on the stage and is inter-twined with the cultural status of the performer and their function, which implies an assumed need to see their bodies, movement and expressions in their entirety.

The darkening of the auditorium allowed the faces of the performers to be seen better from the audience, but the focusing of lights from the front of house positions onto the faces of performers also had a secondary effect. The experience of performing on the stage, blinded by the lights and with a consequent loss of visual contact with the audience, enhanced the feeling of separation between the stage and the auditorium. To the performer the audience now resided in a black void, punctuated by spotlights that dazzled the retina and thereby removed direct visual connection with the audience. This isolation of the performer through light altered their experience fundamentally and may well have been instrumental in the development of new acting styles, which reinforced the convention of the fourth wall (see pp. 123–124). It also altered the experience of the spectator, who became more conscious of 'that brilliantly lit rectangle on which all attention is focussed' (Stokes, cited in Jackson, B., 1991: 15) and of viewing performers through beams of light working on the audience's behalf.

The use of the follow-spot (see p. 185) exacerbated this effect of the isolation of the performer. The light from this instrument focuses on the body of the performer, picking them out from their background and continuing to illuminate them wherever they move on stage. 'Selective visibility' is a term that describes the human eye's natural inclination to focus on the brightest object in any given space, and the use of the follow-spot provides an extreme example of the prioritisation of light and its consequent impact on the direction of the audience's gaze. The experience of this effect led directly to the common use of the term of 'being in the limelight', but this generally refers to the view of someone elevated to prominence rather than the phenomenological experience of the performer, who is literally encircled by the dazzling light of the follow-spot. The narrow beam of bright light that defines the body in this way can provide a space of comfort from surrounding darkness, but its prioritisation of the body also makes it a place of no escape: the moving searchlight and the static, relentless interrogator's light, for example, both aim to bring the hidden into sharp focus.

In contrast, lighting designer Rick Fisher (2007) has spoken about the need to reassure performers who felt that they were insufficiently lit in his productions by inviting them into the auditorium to see for themselves. These actors were used to the physiological impact of high levels of front-light hitting their faces from the front of house positions and were slightly unnerved by the more subtle side-light which he had employed.

Light has both a physiological and psychological impact on the way in which we feel and respond. Its quality and intensity have a direct effect upon our well-being and also our creative response. For rehearsals conducted in blacked-out studio spaces, for example, soft floodlighting is often preferred to the ubiquitous fluorescent working light in order to create an appropriate atmosphere and environment for creative work. Director Katie Mitchell observes:

Some [rehearsal] rooms are lit mainly by glaring strip lights. This makes it difficult for actors to concentrate during long rehearsal days. If the lights are not good, ask if you can rig some simple theatre lights and use them instead.

(Mitchell, 2009: 109)

The body has always been the focus for lighting for dance. The development of techniques for dance lighting eliminated the need for footlights and prioritised the sculptural qualities of the body above the illumination of the face. This introduced a new fluidity and creative freedom which has, in turn, influenced all lighting for performance. (Peter Mumford writes extensively about specific approaches to lighting for dance in Chapter 12; see pp. 248–254).

LIGHT AND THE ACTOR – ADOLPHE APPIA

In this seminal essay, Adolphe Appia revisits the problematics inherent in the staging practices at the beginning of the twentieth century and the contradiction evident between two-dimensional painted scenery and the three-dimensional form of the actor. This was a theme to which he regularly returned with the aim of creating 'a *mise en scène* based no longer on the display of dead pictures on vertical flats but on the plastic and moving presence of the human being' (Appia, 1908 in Volbach, 1989: 179).

In this essay, Appia argues that the performer's body needs to be at the centre of the stage picture and that light, with its inherent qualities of plasticity, should replace the need for the inappropriate illusion created by painted canvas. Using an example from Wagner's opera *Siegfried*, Appia explains how light might provide suggestion rather than two-dimensional pictorial illustration, and thus create a fluid atmosphere that restores the performer's body to a place of prominence on the stage.

Appia held a clear sense of the relative importance of the various theatrical elements on the stage. With light, Appia argued:

we have to find the means to make each part [of the drama] pliable and obedient. For the author this is already so in the printed piece, with or without music; there remains the *mise en scène*, with its elements in hierarchic order: the actor, the arrangement of the settings, the light, the scene painting itself.

Giving the actor the independence necessary for dramatic life and for a personal interpretation, we shall still keep enough authority over him to prevent his departing from this organically-established hierarchy. The three other elements are interdependent, but light has the advantage of being ideally flexible and perfectly controllable; hence it is, directly after the actor, foremost in rank among the means of expression.

(Appia, 1908 in Volbach, 1989: 176)

Appia suggests here that light is as malleable as the ideal performer and operates as an actor in the drama. He believed that the performer was an intermediary between the dramatic or musical score and the physical stage space. The following essay articulates how, with the actor at its centre, light needs to serve the needs of the performer by working sculpturally and allowing the human form to escape from the confines of the painted backdrop. This principle goes beyond the creation of a sympathetic and atmospheric environment for the actor (it is useful here to compare the thinking of Stanislavski who is at the same time exploring ways of using lighting to create mood and atmosphere for the actors of the Moscow Art Theatre – see p. 124). Appia envisaged that the lighting of the space of the stage was to become a harmonious, physical extension of the performer themselves. This theory was to be developed further through his work with Dalcroze at Hellerau, and also anticipates the work of Schlemmer at the Bauhaus.

Ideas linking the use of light to the plasticity of stage space are explored in this influential writing, which critiques the prevailing practices of using painted scenery and places the human form at the centre of the drama. Appia argues that light liberates the actor and, through a famous example from *Siegfried*, advocates the role that light can play in creating atmosphere through the power of suggestion.

APPIA – IDEAS ON A REFORM OF OUR *MISE EN SCÈNE* (1904)[1]

Our present stage scenery is entirely the slave of painting – scene painting – which pretends to create for us the illusion of reality. But this illusion is in itself an illusion, for the presence of the actor contradicts it. In fact, the principle of illusion obtained by painting on flat canvas and that obtained by the plastic and living body of the actor are in contradiction. A homogeneous and artistic production, therefore, cannot be achieved by separately developing the manners of these two illusions – as is done on our stages [...]

The floor, therefore, is not really included in the picture; yet the floor is precisely where the actor moves. Our stage directors have forgotten the actor ... Will they sacrifice a little of the dead painting in favor of the living and moving body? Oh no! They would rather renounce the theatre.

[N]ow let us [...] begin with the actor – the plastic and human body, considered solely from the viewpoint of its effect on the stage – just as we have done with the scenery.

An object appears plastic to our eyes only because of the light that strikes it. Its plasticity cannot be artistically emphasized except through an artistic use of light; this is self-evident. So much for the form! The movement of the human body needs levels to express itself. All artists know that the beauty of bodily movements depends on the variety of support provided by the floor and other objects. Therefore, the mobility of the actor can be artistically realized only in relation to an appropriate structure of objects and floor.

---

[1] Written around 1902.

The two primary conditions for an artistic appearance of the human body on the stage would then be: light that enhances its plasticity, and a setting constructed in three dimensions that enhances the actor's postures and movements. Here we are far away from painting!

Dominated by painting, the *mise en scène* sacrifices the actor and, in addition, as we have seen, a great part of its own pictorial effect-since, contrary to the basis principle of this art, the picture has to be so cut up that the stage floor cannot participate in the illusion created by flats and drops.

What would happen if we subordinated it to the actor?

Above all, the light could be given full freedom. Ruled by painting, light is in fact completely absorbed by the setting. The details shown on the flats must be seen; hence, lights and shadows painted on canvas are illuminated [. . .] and from this kind of lighting, alas, the actor obtains whatever he can. Under such conditions there can be no question of true stage lighting or, consequently, of any plastic effect whatsoever.

Lighting is an element in itself whose effects are limitless; set free, it becomes for us what his palette is for the painter; all combinations of color can be created with it. By means of simple or complex, fixed or moving, projections – by justified obstructions, by diverse degrees of transparency, etc.- we can achieve infinite modulations. Thus by means of light we can in a way materialize colors and forms, which are immobilized on painted canvas, and can bring them alive in space. No longer does the actor walk in front of painted shadows and highlights; he is plunged into an atmosphere that is uniquely his own . . .

Here we are at the crucial point: namely, the plasticity of setting necessary for the beauty of the actor's posture and movement. Painting has in the past taken the upper hand on our stages by providing two-dimensionally whatever could not be realized plastically, and for the sole purpose of creating the illusion of reality [. . .] these images are not alive; they are merely indicated on canvas in a sort of hieroglyphical language, merely signifying the items they purport to represent, all the more so since they cannot make real organic contact with the actor.

Plasticity as required by the actor aims at an entirely different effect, for the human body does not try to create any illusion of reality; it is reality! What it demands of a setting is merely support for this reality. Naturally such a conception completely changes the purpose of the setting; in one case it is the realistic appearance of objects that is sought; in the other, the highest possible degree of actuality for the human body.

These two principles are technically opposed to each other; one or the other must, therefore, be chosen. Are we to choose a mass of dead images and an overly decorated abundance of flat canvas, or the performance of a mobile and plastic human being? [. . .] We go to the theatre to witness a dramatic action, set in motion by the presence of characters on the stage; without them there is no action. The actor is, thus, the essential factor in the production; it is he whom we go to see, he from whom we expect the emotion we seek. It is then imperative to base a production on the presence of the actor, and in order to achieve this, to clear the stage of everything that is in conflict with him. We now have the technical problem clearly stated [...] The question of light will occupy us first of all. This will give us the opportunity to experience the tyranny of painting on vertical flats and will make us understand, not merely theoretically, but very tangibly, the immense injustice still done to the actor and, through him, to the playwright.

The second set of *Siegfried* may serve as an example. How are we to present a forest on the stage? First let us have an understanding on this point: is it a forest with characters or characters in a forest? We are in the theatre to see a dramatic action. In the forest an action takes place which, of course, cannot be expressed through painting ... In order to create our setting we need not try to visualize a forest, but we have to imagine in detail the entire sequence of events that occur in this forest. Thorough knowledge of the score is therefore indispensable. It completely changes the nature of the vision that can inspire a stage director; his eyes must remain fixed on the characters. He will then think of the forest as an atmosphere around and above the performers – an atmosphere that can be realized only in relation to living and loving beings, on whom he must focus. Thus he will never envision the setting as an arrangement of lifeless paintings: on the contrary, it will always remain alive. The *mise en scène* thus becomes the composition of a picture in time. Instead of beginning with a painting, ordered no matter by whom for whom, and afterwards reserving for the actor those pitiful devices with which we are familiar, we commence with the actor. It is his performance that we want to stress; we are ready to sacrifice everything for that. It will be Siegfried here and Siegfried there, but never the tree for Siegfried and the path for Siegfried.

I repeat, we shall no longer try to give the illusion of a forest, but the illusion of a man in the atmosphere of a forest. Man is the reality, and nothing else counts. Whatever this man touches must be intended for him – everything else must contribute to the creation of a suitable atmosphere around him. And if, leaving Siegfried for a moment, we lift our eyes, the scenic picture need not give a complete illusion. It is composed for Siegfried alone. When the forest, gently stirred by a breeze, attracts Siegfried's attention, we – the spectators will see Siegfried bathed in ever-changing lights and shadows but no longer moving among cut-out fragments set in motion by stage tricks.

Scenic illusion is the presence of the living actor.

The scenery for this act as it is now offered to us on all the stages of the world leaves much to be desired! We shall have to simplify it a great deal; give up illuminating painted flats as is now required; almost completely rearrange the stage floor; and, above all, provide a control board for the light – one that is conceived on a large scale and that must be handled with meticulous care. Footlights, those astonishing monstrosities, will hardly ever be used. We may add that the larger part of this reform will have to be done with the performers, and it cannot be achieved without several orchestra rehearsals (a strict requirement which, at present, seems exorbitant but is indeed fundamental).

An attempt of this kind cannot fail to show us how to transform our rigid and conventional staging into an artistic medium, alive, flexible, and suitable for the realization of any dramatic vision. We may even be surprised that we have neglected for so long an important branch of art by leaving it to people who are not artists, because we thought it unworthy of our attention.

The subject is difficult and complex mainly because of the misapprehensions that surround it and of the rigid habits to which modern spectacles have conditioned us. My idea would have to be developed much further in order to convince very many people. It would be necessary to talk about an entirely new duty incumbent on the actor, the influence of expressive and artistic scenery on the dramatist, the power of music to create style in a production, the modifications needed in the building of stages and theatres, etc.

(Appia in *La Revue*, 1(9), 1 June 1904: 342–349)

The fundamental interrelationship of the human form and light on the stage is explored further by Appia in this essay, which echoes his thoughts from his earlier writing but was not published until 1954. A short extract from this document neatly summarises Appia's vision for active light in relation to the living human form:

ACTOR, SPACE, LIGHT, PAINTING (1919)

The art of stage production is the art of projecting into Space what the original author was only able to project in Time. The temporal element is implicit within any text, with or without music [...] The first factor in staging is the interpreter: the actor himself. The actor carries the action. Without him there can be no action and hence no drama [...] The body is alive, mobile and plastic; it exists in three dimensions. Space and the objects used by the body must most carefully take this fact into account. The overall arrangement of the setting comes just after the actor in importance; it is through it that the actor makes contact with and assumes reality within the scenic space.

Thus we already have two essential elements: the actor and the spatial arrangement of the setting, which must conform to his plastic form and his three-dimensionality.

What else is there?

Light!

Light, just like the actor, must become active; and in order to grant to it the status of a medium of dramatic expression it must be placed in the service of [...] the actor who is above it in the production hierarchy, and in the service of the dramatic and plastic expression of the actor.

[...] Light has an almost miraculous flexibility [...] it can create shadows, make them living, and spread the harmony of their vibrations in space just as music does. In light we possess a most powerful means of expression through space, if this space is placed in the service of the actor.

So here we have our normal established hierarchy:

the *actor* presenting the drama;

space in three dimensions, in the service of the actor's plastic form;

light giving life to each.

Our staging practice has reversed the hierarchical order: on the pretext of providing us with elements which are difficult or impossible to realize in solid form, it has developed painted decor to an absurd degree, and disgracefully subordinated the living body of the actor to it. Thus light illuminates the backcloths (which have to be seen), without a care for the actor, who endures the ultimate humiliation of moving between painted flats, standing on a horizontal floor.

All modern attempts at scenic reform touch upon this essential problem; namely, on how to give to light its fullest power, and through it, integral plastic value to the actor and the scenic space.

(*Journal de Genève*, 23 January 1954: 3)

LIGHT AND MOVEMENT – LOÏE FULLER

We have already seen how Stanislavski, like Appia, realised that light was not only instrumental to the evocation of mood on the stage but also had an essential phenomenological impact on the performer. The experience of being in the light also inspired Loïe Fuller (1862–1928), an American dancer who came to prominence in Paris in 1892 through the development of spectacular individual performances that relied upon a combination of dance movements, costume and lighting effects. This section explores how light was employed in conjunction with the body and fabric to create a new form of theatrical presentation arising from experimentation with technology and modes of production at the beginning of the twentieth century. Fuller also writes about her experiences of moving in light, which provide useful reference points in considering the impact of light on the creative process itself.

Fuller developed an innovative performance style as a solo dancer by manipulating fabric in constantly changing light, and the resulting visual effects held her audience spellbound. Her performances evolved through playful experimentation with the fundamental qualities of light – intensity, direction, colour mixing and movement – and manipulating these through a series of transitions over time. This interplay between light, fabric and the movement of the body created a new art form which inspired the Symbolists and Futurists alike, and could be argued as establishing the foundations of modern dance. Fuller's methods of lighting her performance combined existing lighting and projection technology in establishing fundamental principles for lighting the body that were to be a major influence on twentieth-century dance and performance lighting.

LIGHT AND THE DANCING BODY

Fuller's new dance form had been discovered fortuitously when she was performing as a 'hypnotised' skirt dancer in a melodrama in 1891. As she moved around the stage, the swirling shapes of thin, white, Indian silk material appeared to be transformed under the green light from the footlights. The rippling light effect received an enthusiastic response from the audience and encouraged her to think further about the potential of her discovery. She studied the effects of fabric in different lighting conditions to develop an awareness of how the qualities of light were also able to reveal her physical form. These observations of how movement, light, material and the body could work in conjunction were developed in Fuller's performances on the stage under theatrical lighting.

By holding long bamboo and aluminium poles to manipulate the fabric in light, Fuller was able to extend the appearance of her body. The use of much larger volumes of fabric, coupled with a new movement style that was required to manipulate these 'wings', transformed the original ubiquitous skirt dance first into her 'Serpentine Dance' and then into a series of other named dances. No longer was Fuller's performance one that focused on the revelation of legs and undergarments more suited to the variety stage; instead a new abstract imagery had been created, centred on the body, in which the female form mutated and was transformed through the combined use of fabric and light. The body was extended in space and glimpsed periodically, at once both central to the creation of the image and also tantalisingly masked, hidden within the capacious folds of the material or concealed by shadow.

Light was at the heart of these transformations. Fuller realised that the visual effect of her dances could be maximised by harnessing the possibilities of light, particularly through variations in its colour and direction, and by the manipulation of glass lenses and other media by technical operators to achieve live transitions of colour. These effects required precise control and extensive rehearsals but created a subtle interplay between individual light sources and the explicit use of darkness in her performance.

Fuller began her performances in blackout, revealing her body on stage gradually in light. Through constantly changing the balance and colour of light from at least six different directions, she was able to create a range of visual effects which astonished her audience. In dancing 'with' rather than simply 'in' the light, her body seemed to disappear and reappear within her costume like an apparition: 'swirling amid her veils which change shape a thousand times a minute' (Alexandre, 1900: 23–24).

This contemporary newspaper interview with Fuller provides us with an insight into her lighting practice:

> I leave nothing to chance. I drill my light-men, drill them into doing just what I want. I will tell them to throw the light so, or so, and they have to do their business with

the exactitude of clockwork. This one has to throw a yellow light up to here – that man a blue one no further than there – the man with the red lamp has to follow suit and to keep within his circuit also. If you watch the ins and outs of the dance you will see that the colors fall as they do through a prism. How this is done by limelights is my secret. I arrange the colours pretty much as an artist arranges his colors on his palette. You must know about colors, the effect of one color on another, and of their combinations also, just as the painter does, and be able to tell how they will appear at such and such an angle. Theme, style, time, all differ in one dance from another. A dance is not built up in a day [. . .] The magic lantern is part of my effects. People have used it before, but I'll warrant that I use it to the best advantage. I experimented with it five years before I took the public into my confidence about it. We work together, the lantern and I. There is not the least slip by chance in the business. I see the colors just as you see them in a kaleidoscope, know where they will fall, and adopt the movements of the dance to their effects. That's how the living picture is made.

(New York Times, 1896b)

Fuller recognised the importance of experimentation and embraced new technologies and scientific discoveries. She patented techniques for lighting the stage and for the construction of costumes and developed new colour media in her own laboratory. She also collaborated with scientists to investigate chemical compounds that could make the fabric iridescent.[2] Experimentation in theatre spaces took advantage of 'fortuitous mistakes' discovered through playing with light, and Fuller's dances were based directly on her sensitivity to light and these discoveries of visual effects using light and fabric.

In order to create the myriad of hypnotic images on stage, Fuller relied upon her own small army of electricians who operated and controlled the lighting during her performances. This team, usually numbering between 14 and 38 technicians, was led by her brothers, Bert and Frank. They rehearsed extensively but famously without any cue sheets, since Fuller feared that her lighting ideas would be stolen by others in the same manner as her movements had been copied. The electricians therefore had to respond to the dance through a series of visual and aural cues, continually shifting the direction, intensity and colour in a precise choreography of light. Fuller describes how a lengthy technical rehearsal of a sequence of five dances at the Folies Bergère came to an abrupt halt at 4 a.m.:

As a finale I intended to dance with illumination from beneath, the light coming through a square of glass over which I hovered, and this was to be the climax of my dances. After the fourth number my electricians, who were exhausted, left me there unceremoniously.

(Fuller, 1913: 57)

---

[2] *New York Times* 5 February 1911 notes that Fuller developed a 'New Luminous Dance' based on iridescent material and ultraviolet light.

Figure 12 *How the Stage is Lighted.* Loïe Fuller in performance (Louis Gunnis in *The Sketch*, 30 December 1896)

The Gunnis sketch *How the Stage is Lighted* shows Fuller in one of these early performances lit by six separate beams of light, at least two of these being manually operated. This drawing clearly shows the use of a transparent floor to create the underlighting effect, as well as a rather precarious lighting position suspended directly above the stage and providing toplight.

The drawing shows that each lighting source had its own technician operator controlling what look like hand-held carbon-arcs similar to the Duboscq portable arc-light.[3] Effectively these units worked as very bright follow-spots

---

[3] Fuller describes these as 'limelights' but, as we have already noted, there was some conflation of this term which was often used to denote electric arc-light. Given the commercial imperatives, the term may also have been employed in an effort to retain the secrets of her craft.

that were not dimmable unless the light source was manually obscured by the operator. The drawing reveals that each beam of light could also be coloured through the manipulation of a circular disc, allowing different-coloured glasses to be introduced by the operator. This precise level of control was essential to the creation of Fuller's imagery and the resulting beams of light are seen to cut through the dusty air of the theatre, creating a visual impact not dissimilar to that of a contemporary rock concert. The space above and around Fuller is therefore articulated with light, although the primary aim is to highlight the solo dancing body as the single focus of attention.

When Fuller toured her performances, she was preceded by a team of electricians who undertook technical preparations necessary for her act. The wooden stage floor was prepared by sawing floorboards to accommodate the installation of the glass. Cables were required to provide electrical supplies for each of the lighting operators, who were required to be located in positions from where lighting did not usually emanate. This account in the New York *Blade* offers a valuable insight into these preparations:

> While somebody else is doing a song and dance in front of the curtain, a force of men is at work behind getting the setting for Loïe's dances in readiness. Heavy black chenille curtains are hung all around the stage and a jet black carpet laid over the entire floor except over a glass plate which has been sunk in a space about four feet by four cut in the center of the stage. Ten feet below this plate stands Bert Fuller guarding his two lamps. Four step ladders of different heights are arranged in the left and right wings nearest the audience, and on each stands an electrician, with his search light in his hand. Revolving in front of each of these lights is a round piece of pasteboard, from 12 to 16 inches in diameter, with a border of gelatine disks of different colours. Some of these disks are solid, and others show a combination of two, three, four or more colors, and the men work them rapidly and harmoniously. The two principal lights underneath the stage are of great power, and they alone produce more effects than all of the side lights put together.
>
> (*Blade*, 11 April 1896, cited in Sommer)

FIRE DANCE – A CHOREOGRAPHY OF LIGHTS

The innovative lighting from directly below the stage was inspired by the new techniques of lighting fountains and their statues from beneath the water. Fuller had noted the Parisian fountains and adapted these ideas through experimentation with a choreography of lights. The play of light on the rippling water of the fountains provided a beautiful effect that was very popular in the *fontaines lumineuses* of the city.[4] Fuller transposed the effect

---

[4] Duboscq had developed similar (if not identical) units for the underwater illumination of *fontaines lumineuses*, which were also lit with lanterns fitted with circular discs so that the colours could change. This effect was used to great acclaim at the famous 1900 Chateau d'Eau in Paris.

of light on a moving surface from the water of the fountain to the shifting folds of her costume. When one of the light sources was a projector such as a magic lantern, striking moving images could be created in tandem with coloured stage lighting.

Lighting the female body from beneath, upwards under the skirt, not only highlighted what was usually concealed but also created unnatural shadows and served to isolate Fuller within her blacked-out stage space. The use of dominant lighting through the glass floor and from beneath the body was primarily responsible for creating moments where her body was engulfed by light and appeared to be literally suspended in space (see Figure 12).

In *Fire Dance*, first performed in 1896, underlighting was used for an extreme effect as Fuller played with light and darkness to achieve maximum dramatic potential:

> Sometimes she would step over the light to reveal the whole of her face bathed in red; at others she would play at the edge of the light, allowing only a sliver of her body or costume to catch the light.
>
> (Allbright, 2007: 70)

Henri Lyonnet recalled how the impression of this dance still endured nearly 30 years after it had first been performed:

> The *Fire Dance* she believed was one of her spectacles that made the strongest impressions on the public. After securing total darkness in the theatre, there suddenly appeared in the background of the stage a vague and uncertain gleam, a sort of phosphorescence, gradually streaking the shadows with its pallid light, then little by little, this light gains a growing intensity, draws outlines, a human shape appears and seems to flutter in the air, made of immeasurable wings with iridescent colorations, made of ruby, sapphire and turquoise.
>
> (Lyonnet, 1928: 757–758)

Contemporary accounts also reflect the visual impact of the combination of light, movement and fabric in her most spectacular dance. The *New York Theatre Review* observed in 1896 that

> In the *Fire Dance*, the two principal lights are used almost exclusively. The dress worn in this dance is a simple full slip made of plain white thin material ... But no sooner does she rest on the glass plate then the hem seems to catch fire. Up the flames creep ... The more she fans the gauze ... the higher the flames leap and the redder they glow, until finally she snatches a gauze scarf from her neck ... beats at her draperies until the scarf too catches the glowing color, and in an instant nothing, but inky blackness is left to tell the tale.

One of the most detailed accounts of a typical sequence of dances that constituted a Fuller performance is provided by a sceptical newspaper reporter who reviews her show on her return to New York on 24 February 1896 at

Koster and Bial's Music Hall. The performance began at 10.30 p.m. to a full house with standing room only. This account provides a very good idea of what it was like to have witnessed a Loïe Fuller performance, and the description of the use of lighting underlines her innovative use of side-light. Without illuminating the floor, the light is able to cross the stage with the shadows lost within the depths of the wings. The light can only be perceived when a body enters the focused beam of light, and the body is therefore invisible until it does so – the use of this technique by Fuller can therefore be seen as the beginning of modern dance lighting:

When the curtain rose on a perfectly dark stage, every one stared into the blackness, with all his eyes, and when a heavily draped form gradually became visible there was a preparatory round of applause . . . The rays of light converging on the veiled figure grew slightly brighter and soon the drapery began to move. Then everybody said, half aloud, 'It is just the old serpentine dance!' Which it was – and wasn't. In the first ten minutes it became evident that 'La Loie' is more skilful than Loie Fuller was, that her movements have become, if not graceful, yet much more pleasing than they used to be, and most especially of all, that she has secured the services of an exceedingly clever electrician.

In the first dance she wore a dress of black gauze, sprinkled with brilliant spangles. She represented 'Night,' or, as the bill said 'La Nuit,' which undoubtedly means about the same thing. The interminable skirt and its luminous border were moved in the old billowing curves, and as the dance moved from side to side of the stage, lights of rich and constantly varying colors played upon her. They touched nothing else, apparently, neither the background of black nor the boards on which she walked. The effect was admirable; it was not novel and the applause that followed was not very prolonged. One could hear, from many parts of the house, 'Is that all?' asked in tones expressing something near to disappointment.

This feeling disappeared during the next dance, of which the name was 'La Feu.' There is no doubt that it was a really and marvellously beautiful spectacle. The woman seemed to be wrapped in towering flames, now vivid scarlet, now streaked with green and purple. Whoever has seen a great configration [sic] late at night could recognize the exact, almost startling, verity of the imitation. Beside it the ordinary 'fire scene,' pales into insignificance.

The applause that ensued was loud, long, and enthusiastic. People said: 'That's great!' and the phrase was hardly an exaggeration. 'La Danse Blanche' and 'Le Firmament' were more like the first, and had no notable features. The second, indeed, contained some stereoptican effects – flowers, faces, moons, stars, and the like, thrown on the waving skirts-that had an unpleasant cheapness and were in questionable congruity with the other effects. They could all be very well spared.

The last production, however, called 'Le Lys de Nile,' was another marvellously beautiful. In this the gauzy clouds were of vastly increased size, and they were tossed in novel and ingenious forms. A huge lily was imitated with singular accuracy, and at moments the dancer seemed to be a gigantic butterfly with jewelled wings flying swiftly through an atmosphere of ever-changing colors.

The exhibition lasted about half an hour. There were many recalls, but no more dancing, and the usual absurd bouquets were handed over the footlights. There is no doubt that Miss Fuller made a popular success.

(*New York Times*, 25 February 1896a)

Although many of Fuller's solo dances had cyclical structures based on the natural world,[5] she was not primarily intending to imitate nature (like other contemporary dancers) but to create abstract imagery through expressive light and movement. Her artistic aims therefore brought her close to the intentions of the symbolists whose stage spaces were also typically required to shift mood and change colour from one scene to another, and to artists who were beginning to experiment with colour music (see pp. 162–164).

Contemporary journalist Arsène Alexandre recognised Fuller's innovative rhythmic use of coloured light and the fact that she was able to adapt technologies to serve this new expressive art form:

Before Loïe Fuller, there was lighting, but no one understood how to use it. A harsh and uniform projection, that was all. She brought us this marvellous discovery: the art of modulation, the ability to shift across the spectrum of color tones, just as we do in sound. The richness of modulations is a distinctive element in modern music and painting, but the theatre never dreamed of these possibilities until Loïe Fuller's innovations.

(cited in Allbright, 2007: 58–59)

Although Appia had certainly both dreamed and written of modulated lighting changes in relation to Wagner's music, Fuller provides the first evidence of the actual realisation of these ideals on stage in performances that clearly influenced symbolist theatre forms, but also the ideas of Craig and the Futurists.[6] She went on to experiment further with light using projected scenery to develop her 'Ballets of Light' in the USA – a series of choreographies with multiple performers that involved sequences of film-based moving images and large-scale shadow plays projected onto the backdrop.

THE EXPERIENCE OF DANCING IN LIGHT

For Fuller, the contribution of light to the performance went beyond the visual aesthetic. In a 1907 interview with Mauclair, she reveals her heightened sensory response to light that borders on synaesthesia. She speaks of the ethereal nature of light and its transformative potential upon the human psyche:

[5] '1, the serpentine; 2, the violet; 3, the butterfly' (Fuller, 1913: 57).
[6] E.g. Craig's 1906 production of *Rosmersholm* (with Eleanor Duse).

If I use light, it is not just for the pleasure of making a fairyland. Yes, it is pretty to see, but, for me, light has a much deeper meaning. Light: it is the deployment of the soul around a human being, it is a language just as music is a language. There are living lights and dead lights. My art derives from a sense of joy, and here I mean that it has the capacity to instant oblivion, soaring it into another world. Colors in painting are opaque and link it, sometimes to the point of absurdity, to the representation of real objects. But I use live colors, colored scents aroused by a ray of light, and, then, why shouldn't I render into the visible realm that which we dream of?

(cited in Allbright, 2007: 141)

Fuller's heightened perception of light and the experience of dancing in light is illustrated well in this excerpt by Ann Cooper Allbright, whose experiments with Jen Groseth in reconstructing the staging environment and the kinaesthetic implications of Fuller's work reveal the intense physicality of the experience for the performer:

One of the most important aspects [...] for me, was a new appreciation of the experience of moving in strongly defined lights. Unlike lighting whose sole purpose is to illuminate the dancers, the lighting we created was an equal partner in the dance. Sometimes the light obscured me, sometimes it revealed my dancing, and sometimes I was simply a screen onto which a variety of moving lights were projected. At various times I felt sheltered and enclosed, inspired, even disoriented (especially when dancing on clear glass with lights shining from underneath). The palpable presence of these lights reminded me of otherworldly spirits [...] I began to understand more concretely the spiritual role that light played for Loïe Fuller. I believe that Fuller experienced a certain kind of euphoria when dancing that was intensified by her dramatic approach to lighting. Her dances generally followed a classic creation narrative. They began in a total blackout (highly unusual for that time), with the first strands of music calling forth a dim illumination of the small motions of her hands and fabric. The lights, movements and music would generally crescendo into a final frenzy of color and motion that faded abruptly back into primordial darkness.

(Allbright, 2007: 9)

THE BODY AS LIGHT

The following excerpt focuses on the use of light as an adornment of the body at the end of the nineteenth century. It provides a fascinating account of the experiments that incorporated electric light onto the (almost exclusively) female body and how this technology was used on the stage.

The fascination with the 'new' force of electricity was exemplified in productions such as *Faust* (1894), in which Irving famously wired up his duellists and used electricity to punctuate the scene with flashes in the air every time their swords clashed. Electricity created a cult of light (Bergman, 1977: 295; Schivelbusch, 1995) and enabled increased volumes of light not only on the stage but also in public and domestic environments. Electric lighting was installed to beautify buildings and to illuminate fountains, and this worship of light can be seen to have culminated in the advent of *bijoux électriques*, where electric light was employed to beautify the body. Electric jewellery was first seen in Paris around 1881, and was adapted for use in the staging of 'fairy operas'. When these portable light sources were secreted about a performer's body or incorporated into costumes, they could create animated, star-like effects. They were employed in a wide range of fairy performances, pantomimes and operettas, such as *Iolanthe* (1882) at the Savoy Theatre, which itself was celebrated as the first public building to be lit throughout entirely by electricity. The performing body was presented as being able to emit its own light since, through the use of batteries, performers could move relatively freely without being permanently connected by electrical cables to an external supply.

However, the equipment needed to create these effects was both cumbersome and dangerous. As Gooday argues in this excerpt, these technological developments, and the use of the female body in particular, were part of a wider agenda – a systematic process aimed at promoting the safety of the new electrical energy source to the general public and, through this demonstration, to supplant gas as the new transformative power of the future.

ELECTRIC FAIRIES – LIGHT AND THE FEMALE BODY

In *Domesticating Electricity: Technology, Uncertainty and Gender 1880–1914*, Graeme Gooday explores the technical, economic and cultural issues behind the sudden phenomenon of the use of electric light as an adornment of the female body in the 1880s. This gendered use of light (both on- and offstage) was in stark contrast with the experience of men who wore extensive protective clothing when working with electricity. In this writing, Gooday traces the use of miniature fairy lights on the performing body in the 1880s:

> [The] technique of naturalizing the electric light within quasi-organic displays of artificial flora was central both to upper class women's elaborate ballroom fashions of electrical jewellery in the 1880s, and to the aesthetic trend for domestic beautification later epitomized in Mrs Gordon's *Decorative Electricity* of 1891. More strikingly, these tiny electric lights were deployed on the bodies of female theatrical performers, perhaps first used in French ballet in 1881 to adorn the breastpiece, necklace and headwear of dancers, as shown in the French periodical *L'Illustration*.
>
> Given the potential harm to the women involved from electric shock, heat burns and burns from battery acid – especially to the fast-moving dancers – these were not just arbitrary whimsical uses of electric light. I argue that

this usage had a special significance in attempts to promote the notion that electricity was not intrinsically dangerous. Since the theatre had been the site of so many horrific deaths of actresses catching their dresses on naked gas footlights and since the female body had become the most characteristic site of cultural anxiety about the danger of domestic illumination, the persistent non-injury of female performers wearing electric lights on their bodies was a powerful piece of visual rhetoric for promoters of both the theatre and of electricity.

In order to perform wearing such lights, these dancers were typically obliged to wear either primary or secondary batteries hidden under their costumes. According to the editor of French journal *L'Electricien*, Edouard Hospitalier, the production of miniature batteries for electric 'jewellery' and theatrical body lights had been a specialism of the French makers Trouvé, Scrivanow and Aboilard; all produced much lower voltages and lower currents than used for room-lighting to minimize the risk.

Having been the first to electrify a theatre with a spectacle of 1,200 Swan incandescent lamps in November 1881, the impresario and electrophile Richard D'Oyly Carte was the first to employ female performers wearing electric ornamentation in his Savoy theatre exactly a year later. [...] [including] these lights in the final scene of 'Iolanthe', Gilbert & Sullivan's new 'fairy' opera. Here, the association between the magical technology of electrical light and the supernatural power of fairies was forcefully illustrated. As the London *Morning Advertiser* reported of the opening night, Monday 27 November 1882, the dramatic *ennui* of the last scene was rescued by a startling innovation:

'In the last scene a very brilliant and original effect is introduced. The Fairy Queen and her three chief attendants wear each an electric star in their hair. The effect of this brilliant spark of electricity is wonderful.'[7]

The absence of any injuries to dancers or infelicitous failures of the lighting paved the way for further daring expansion of this risk-laden enterprise. By mid February 1883 D'Oyly Carte increased the number of electrically-lit fairies involved in the final scene to around thirty. As a reviewer for *The Times* noted this innovation was entirely successful: the ladies' 'flowing drapery' effectively concealing the accumulators carried on their backs to 'maintain the incandescence of the tiny lamps on their foreheads'. [...]

Such was the success of this thespian practice that it was rapidly taken up by other dramatic enterprises. One commentator suggested that, by the mid to late 1880s, few theatres in either London or the provinces would be without them, especially for the Christmas pantomime. In New York, the Edison Company supplied similar miniature forehead lights and [...] a cohort of so-called 'electric girls' was employed by Edison at the Philadelphia Exhibition in 1884, and the 'Electric Girl Lighting Company' hired out their services for respectable social purposes.

---

7 *Crystal Palace International Electrical Exhibition Catalogue* (London, 1882: 117, 146).

Figure 13   Electric Fairy – a ballerina with electric jewels (from *L'Illustration*, 1881)

By 1892, large-scale displays of women adorned in electric light were characteristic features of Edison publicity. Whereas the Edison displays were stage-managed to display apparent safety, Wosk suggests that some female performers in the US were employed in musical hall electrical displays deliberately designed to convey a sense of danger, although the electrical press could always treat such performances sceptically.[8]

(Gooday, 2008: 105–109)

---

[8] Gooday presents a number of examples of the dangers inherent in the practice of wearing early electrical lighting.

The concept of light as an adornment of the human form has been revisited as technological developments have improved safety and enabled the miniaturisation of light sources and their power supplies. Portable light units that are designed to be worn have also made it easier to adapt light sources to the body. In an experimental theatre performance in 2007 of *Forest Floor*,[9] headtorches were worn by the cast and also fitted to each member of the audience who shared the same performance space. The beams from the head-torches became visible in the haze and made clearly apparent what each person was concentrating on – in effect, everyone had their own follow-spot which highlighted whatever they were looking at. When the point of focus became the same, an impressive image was created through the convergence of multiple beams of light in the air.

In the fashion industry, designers such as Hussain Chalayan have also taken advantage of recent technical developments in lighting such as lasers and light-emitting diodes (LEDs) to incorporate light sources in clothing. A Chalayan mini dress created in 2010, for example, incorporates 15,000 LEDs and is able to project video imagery, while his work in collaboration with jewellery designers has created contemporary versions of the *bijoux électriques* for the fashion industry.

---

[9] Created by Joslin McKinney at the University of Leeds.

Chapter

8 Light as Material

This chapter looks at the ways that light, and in particular coloured light, has been used in the arts and explores key twentieth-century practitioners who used light as a material element in performance. It also introduces ways in which light has been at the heart of investigations in human perception in theatre and art, and suggests links between the work of Fuller (see pp. 149–157) and the Futurists to modern multi-media presentations, and from their performances to the works of Beckett, for example. A lineage can also be traced from the work with light and colour at the Bauhaus to the stage lighting of practitioners such as Robert Wilson and Archim Freyer. We have already noted how Adolphe Appia's contribution to lighting in the theatre was inspired by Wagner's music, and analogies between the wavelengths of light and sound became a part of late nineteenth-century aesthetic and physiological discourse that resulted in the flourishing movement concerned with colour music and synaesthesia.

COLOUR MUSIC

The link between sound and light had been identified from the classical period, and comparisons between these two forms were debated by a wide range of scholars.[1] Stimulated by the writings and work with magic lanterns of **Athanasius Kircher** (1601–1680), the mathematician Louis-Bertrand Castel (1688–1757) was the first to propose a performance of colour music through the *clavecin oculaire* or 'harpsichord for eyes'. Erasmus Darwin (1731–1802) suggested that the technical innovation of the Argand oil lamp might be used to create visible music through coloured glasses, while Frederick Kastner (1852–82) developed the pyrophone (1869–1873), a musical instrument in which gas jets appeared within crystal tubes when played from a keyboard.[2] In 1877, Bainbridge Bishop created a light-producing apparatus that was fixed to a conventional organ and allowed for coloured electric arc-light to

---

[1] John Locke, Isaac Newton, Mme de Stael and Goethe are amongst those who explored this connection.
[2] See Dunant (1875: 444).

be mixed on a screen. Although this apparatus didn't create sound it aimed to paint music with light.[3]

Alexander Wallace Rimington (1854–1918) was an artist who became fascinated by the potential of photography and the links between light, colour and sound, which he believed were interlinked aspects of the same reality. In *Colour Music: The Art of Mobile Colour* (1911), he argued that light could act as a bridge between the everyday and an enhanced sense of awareness of the world, and he described the experiments that he had undertaken. Rimington argued that coloured light and sound were both received through vibrations that stimulated the optic and aural nerve endings and that, by creating coloured light at the same time as performing music, the resultant effect would be a harmonious composition on the same wavelengths.

Rimington, like Loutherbourg many years earlier, devoted his London residence to an experimental performance space in which he built his 'colour organ'. Although this installation didn't actually create music, it was the first of many instruments given the same title which were devised for creating colour music throughout the twentieth century. The 'colour organ' was over three metres in height and contained 14 electric arc-lights that projected coloured light onto a screen behind the performer. The five-octave keyboard and stops enabled the three variables of colour perception – colour hue, luminosity and chroma – to be controlled by an operator who witnessed the lighting changes through a rear-view mirror. Rimington's performances staged to orchestral accompaniment inspired Scriabin's colour symphony *Prometheus, the Poem of Fire* (1911), which included a part for coloured lighting: *Testiera per luce* was detailed at the top of the musical score.[4] In this section of his book, Rimington attempts to describe how the light works alongside the music:

It was found after the first experiments that the beauty of colour compositions could be felt and appreciated without any musical accompaniment, but, that in some cases, it added greatly to their interest.

We will suppose for the moment an orchestral composition as being accompanied by colour. Let us assume that the composition opens with a Wagnerian trumpet-blast. The screen is at the same moment flooded by an intense orange which palpitates with the harmonic colours corresponding to a subordinate passage upon some of the other orchestral instruments. The blast ceases, there is a faint echo of it upon the violins while the screen pulsates with pale lemon and saffron, hardly discernible. Again comes the blare of the trumpets, and once more the screen flames with orange modulations.

This is the opening, let us say, of a passage of pathetic character in which accidentals often intervene and the key tends to become minor. The colour scheme,

---

[3] See Peacock (1988: 397–398).

[4] For a detailed account of performances of *Prometheus* and the development of controls for coloured lighting, see Peacock (1988: 397–406).

without being a direct translation, sympathizes with this – it is low in tone and shows slight discords, and then gradually in consonance with the sound – music develops a more joyous character. At last a modified form of the opening phrase is again reached both in sound and colour. This leads to fresh departures, and so the dual composition proceeds.

(Rimington, 1911: 59–60)

ELECTRIC-ART AND THE ILLUMINATING STAGE

Wassisily Kandinsky explored ideas of colour theory and synaesthesia in four experimental theatre pieces that examined the expressive potential of light and sound. The first of these, created in 1909 but prevented from being staged by the outbreak of war, was *Der Gelbe Klang* (The Yellow Sound) – a one-act opera without dialogue consisting of six stage images with figures costumed in single colours.

In the same year, influenced in part by the contemporary writings of Craig and his experiments with light at the Arena Goldoni, Filippo Tommaso Marinetti (1876–1944) issued a *Foundation and Manifesto of Futurism* and inspired a group of artists to create work and explore ideas which sought a coalescence of the arts. Experiments with light and colour were an important aspect of the Futurist movement, which acknowledged the dynamic potential of light as a major element of abstract expression and as a tool to defeat romanticism: to 'murder the moonlight' by the light of the modern electric lamp. The playwright Marinetti was partly responsible for placing performance at the heart of the Futurist movement that, pre-dating Artaud's *Theatre of Cruelty*, advocated a violent reaction to the stagnation of society. The Futurists's radical response to the modern era embraced the use of new tools, technologies, machines and inventions. Electric light was an essential element of expression that would facilitate a transformation of the theatre form, and its potential role is envisioned in Prampolini's *Manifesto for Futurist Scenography*:

Manifesto for Futurist Scenography (April-May, 1915)

Let's reform the stage. [...] It is not only a question of reforming the conception of the *mise-en-scène*; one must create an abstract entity that identifies itself with the scenic action of the play. [...] These two forces that have been diverging (playwright and scenographer) must converge so that a comprehensive synthesis of the play will result.

The stage must live the theatrical action in its dynamic synthesis; it must express the soul of the character conceived by the author just as the actor directly expresses and lives it within himself.

Therefore, in order to reform the stage it is necessary to:

1. Refuse the exact reconstruction of what the playwright has conceived, thus definitely abandoning every real relationship, every comparison between

object and subject and vice versa; all these relationships weaken direct emotion through indirect sensations.

2. Substitute for scenic action an emotional order that awakens all sensations necessary to the development of the work; the resulting atmosphere will provide the interior milieu.
3. Have *absolute synthesis* in material expression of the stage, that is to say, not the pictorial synthesis of all the elements, but synthesis excluding those elements of scenic architecture that are incapable of producing new sensations.
4. Make the scenic architecture be a connection for the audience's intuition rather than a picturesque and elaborate collaboration.
5. Have the colours and the stage arouse in the spectator those emotional values that neither the poet's words nor the actor's gestures can evoke. [...]

Let's renovate the stage. The absolutely new character that our innovation will give the theatre is *the abolition of the painted stage.* The stage will no longer be a coloured backdrop but a *colourless electromechanical architecture, powerfully vitalized by chromatic emanations from a luminous source,* produced by electric reflectors with multicolored panes of glass, arranged, coordinated analogically with the psyche of each scenic action.

With the luminous irradiations of these beams, of these planes of coloured lights, the dynamic combinations will give marvellous results of mutual permeation, of intersection of lights and shadows. From these will arise vacant abandonments, exultant, luminous corporealities.

These assemblages, these unreal shocks, this exuberance of sensations combined with dynamic stage architecture that will move, unleashing metallic arms, knocking over plastic planes, amidst an essentially new modern noise, will augment the vital intensity of the scenic action.

On a stage illuminated in such a way, the actors will gain unexpected dynamic effects that are neglected or very seldom employed in today's theatres, mostly because of the ancient prejudice that one must imitate, represent reality.

And with what purpose?

Perhaps scenographers believe it is absolutely necessary to represent this reality? Idiots! Don't you understand that your efforts, your useless realistic preoccupations have no effect other than that of diminishing the intensity and emotional content, which can be attained precisely through the interpretive equivalents of these realities, i.e., abstractions?

Let's create the stage. In the above lines we have upheld the idea of a dynamic stage as opposed to the static stage of another time; with the fundamental principles that we shall set forth, we intend not only to carry the stage to its most advanced expression but also to attribute to it the essential values that belong to it and that no one has thought of giving it until now.

Let's reverse the roles. Instead of the illuminated stage, let's create the illuminating stage: luminous expression that will irradiate the colours demanded by the theatrical action with all its emotional power.

The material means of expressing this illuminating stage consist in the use of electrochemical colours, fluorescent mixtures that have the chemical property of being susceptible to electric current and diffusing luminous colorations of all tonalities according to the combinations of fluorine and other mixtures of gases. The desired effects of exciting luminosity will be obtained with electric neon (ultraviolet) tubes, systematically arranging these mixtures according to an agreed-upon design in this immense scenodynamic architecture. But the Futurist scenographic and choreographic evolution must not stop there. In the final synthesis, human actors will no longer be tolerated, like children's marionettes or today's super-marionettes recommended by recent reformers; neither one nor the other can sufficiently express the multiple aspects conceived by the playwright.

In the totally realizable epoch of Futurism we shall see the luminous dynamic architectures of the stage emanate from chromatic incandescences that, climbing tragically or showing themselves voluptuously, will inevitably arouse new sensations and emotional values in the spectator.

Vibrations, luminous forms (produced by electric currents and coloured gases) will wriggle and writhe dynamically, and these authentic actor-gases of an unknown theatre will have to replace living actors. By shrill whistles and strange noises these actor-gases will be able to give the unusual significations of theatrical interpretations quite well; they will be able to express these multiform emotive tonalities with much more effectiveness than some celebrated actor or other can with his displays. These exhilarant, explosive gases will fill the audience with joy or terror, and the audience will perhaps become an actor itself as well.

Achille Ricciardi's (1884–1923) *Il teatro del colore* (1919) written in 1913 had inspired Prampolini and informed this manifesto. Ricciardi saw coloured light as able to liberate the stage and orchestrate a mysterious atmosphere for the spectator – a chromatic 'psychic-space' where colour would act as a leitmotif to 'express the unspoken dialogues of the protagonists' and 'reveal their state of mind' (Berghaus, 1998: 39). He worked with Prampolini to create a *Theatre of Colour* at Rome's Teatro Argentina (1919–1920), where he developed detailed lighting scores for the abstract performances that were staged there.

LIGHT AS ACTOR

The potential role of light as a performer was exemplified in **Giacomo Balla**'s (1871–1958) futuristic staging of Stravinsky's *Feu d'Artifice* (*Fuochi d'artificio* or Fireworks) for Diaghilev's Ballet Russe in Rome in 1917.[5] This was a performance that eliminated the actor and had no characters or storyline but instead explored the dynamic role of light, and its potential as a source of

---

[5] Staged at the Constanzi Theatre (now Teatro dell'Opera), Rome, on 12 April 1917. See Berghaus (1998: 253–261) for an account of the technical difficulties in realising this performance.

energy was correlated to movement, form and composition alongside the musical composition.

The staging consisted of a large sculptural wooden form with angular prismatic shapes covered in translucent material and painted with coloured zig-zags and lines. This structure could be illuminated from within to create a dazzling and pulsating light form that was the centre of the theatrical action. Kirby provides us with a description of this fascinating event that pre-dates Bentham by several years (see pp. 232–240):

> Balla built a 'keyboard' of switches in the prompter's box so that he could watch and listen to the performance while he 'played' the lights. His notes for the operation of the lights indicate forty-nine different settings, but, since some passages were repeated, there were actually more than that number of changes in the illumination. The performance [...] lasted five minutes. Thus coordinated with the music, there was a change in the lighting about every five seconds, on the average. Lighting possibilities included various combinations of external illumination on the solid forms, internal illumination of the translucent shapes, and illumination of the black backdrop, which once was colored with rays of red light. Shadows also played a part in Balla's lighting design, and two of the cues on his plot indicate shadow projectors. It was not merely the stage that was lit, however: the auditorium itself was illuminated and darkened during the piece, relating the spectators to the actorless presentation on stage. In *Fireworks*, sound, light, and color were orchestrated into a single, entirely non-representational work.
>
> (Kirby, 1971: 83–86)

Mauro Montalti's manifesto of 1920 also prioritised light, and suggested how its vibrations might impact on the body to create a response that was similar to synaesthesia:

FOR A NEW THEATRE – 'ELECTRIC-VIBRATING-LUMINOUS' (1920)

Brief, elementary hints and a small practical example of Electric-Vibrating-Luminous Theatre will serve to give to youth a concept of what the new form of art wishes to be and what it proposes to do.

It does not wish to throwaway completely the other innovating schools, but it searches only to *translate* and *simplify*, in coloured and luminous vibrations, concepts of art that have already been treated by other techniques (theatre-music-painting-poetry-etc.).

Not all men, in fact, have their own sensitivity equitably distributed in the five senses, so that they indifferently perceive a work of art that the artist created according to his own ability. For example, since not all men completely perceive a dramatic-auditory action with characters on stage, the Electric-Vibrating-Luminous Theatre *translates* the same dramatic conception, with its equivalent emotional power, in such a way that the deaf can also perceive the different cerebral vibrations that gave rise to the dramatic concept. [...] for this new form of ultradynamic art [...] if well felt by the artist, will offer him a new way to express his own sensibility and his own thoughts, by means of luminous, aesthetic, and clear vibrations.

The stage looks like an enormous dark chamber of a camera [...] the backcloth, which constitutes the scenery and which we shall call "sensitive darkness," is formed from myriads of electric' lamps of every colour and tonality. The studied distribution of colours and the studied distribution of electrical currents comprise the subject and treatment of the work. Behind the backcloth an electrical cylinder switch works, which, acting like a phonograph cylinder, lights up now one, now another, zone of the sensitive darkness.

It is well to bear in mind that the Electric Theatre, being eminently dynamic and based on colour and movement, does not allow its luminous vibrations to be geometric expressions like triangles, squares, trapezoids, etc., etc. Instead, they are light-points, nebulas, straight segments, curves, parabolas, hyperbolas, helicoids, ellipses, ellipsoids, spirals, circles, concentrics, eccentrics, ovals, etc.

Montalti outlined how this new electric art form might be realised through a condensed version of Act III of Leonid Andreyev's *The Life of Man* as an example. Montalti's lighting scenario includes directions such as 'The ball lights up. It is formed by swift spirals of every colour that turn in all directions. Several lights move automatically between the dancing couples'; and later in the drama 'From the right a deep orange splash expands and distends itself until it totally covers the surface of the sensitive darkness'; and elsewhere a 'Whisper of lights. Comments of colour' are called for.[6]

Fortunato Depero (1892–1960), in a response to Kandinsky's call for abstract stage compositions, published his play *Colori* (Colours) in 1916. Subtitled 'an abstract theatrical synthesis', it presented an interplay of coloured light, four 'chromo-plastic figures' and sound in a synaesthetic composition without a plot. **Francesco Cangiullo** (1884–1977) devised a Futurist play, *Lights!/Luce!* (1919), that was based entirely on the notion of light, with performers and audience joining in the action. The numerals indicate the number of people who should be speaking the lines:

Lights!/Luce!

Raised curtain. - Neutral stage. - Stage and auditorium completely in DARKNESS for 3 BLACK minutes.

Voices of the PUBLIC

1. - Lights!

2. - Lights!

4. - Lights!

20. - Lights!! Lights!!

---

[6] See Kirby (1971: 222–224) for a full description of lighting effects for *The Life of Man*.

50. - Lights!! Lights!! Lights!! Lights!!

(*Contagious*)

THE ENTIRE THEATRE

L I G H T S!!!!!

(The obsession for light must be provoked – so that it becomes wild, crazy – by various actors scattered in the auditorium, who excite the spectators and encourage their shouting.)

The stage and auditorium are illuminated in an EXAGGERATED *way.*

At the same moment, the curtain slowly falls.

An alternative script for *Lights* was published in *Teatro della Sorpresa* (1922) and provides us with a fuller understanding of how this performance was staged:

Lights/Luce

The curtain rises. The apron, stage, and auditorium of the theatre are in darkness. Dark pause. Until someone shouts LIGHTS! *(Still darkness.) Then two spectators shout* LIGHTS! LIGHTS! *(Still darkness.) Then four, then the impatient shout becomes magnified, contagious, and half the theatre shouts:* LIGHTS LIGHTS LIIIGHTSSS! *The entire theatre:* LIIIIGHTSSSS!!! *Suddenly, the lights come up everywhere on the apron, stage, and in the auditorium. Four minutes of blazing fear.* CURTAIN. *And everything is clear.*

(trans. V.N. Kirby in Kirby,1971: 254–255)

LIGHT PLAYS AT THE BAUHAUS

The tradition of experimenting with light and colour in performance was continued at the Bauhaus in the 1920s as an integral aspect of classes for stage design. **Kurt Schwerdfeger** (1897–1966) pioneered a play with projected light, *Reflektorische Farblichtspiele* (Reflecting Colour-Light-Play), in 1922. His contemporary, **Ludwig Hirschfeld-Mack** (1893–1965), developed work that responded to an accidental discovery witnessed during the presentation of a shadow play. When changing an acetylene lamp, Hirschfeld-Mack observed that double shadows of different colour hues were created. Inspired by this chance observation he developed the *Farblichtmusiken*[7] (1922–1924), a multimedia machine to create colour light plays in response to music, which he described as

a play of yellow, red, green and blue fields of light, developing in organically defined units from darkness to maximum intensity [...] combined with the

---

[7] Colour-light-music.

interactions, combinations and overlayering of the colours and forms, are the musical elements to which they give rise and from which they become insepera-ble.

(Schweitzer and Bohm, 2000)

Oskar Schlemmer (1888–1943) used light as a material to shape stage space, create visual illusion and assist in transforming performers into 'moving architecture'. In a photograph of *Light Play* (1927), which used projection and translucent effects, a large shadow of a hand is seen to dominate the stage and shift the audience's perception of scale. In a 1927 public lecture-demonstration, Schlemmer explained the ongoing experiments with light, colour and space at the Bauhaus:

we have constructed simple flats of wood and white canvas which can be slid back and forth on a series of parallel tracks and can be used as screens for light projection. By back-lighting we can also make them into translucent curtains or wall areas and thereby achieve an illusion of a higher order, created directly from readily available means. We do not want to imitate sunlight and moonlight, noon, evening, and night with our lighting. Rather we let the light function by itself, for what it is: yellow, blue, red, green, violet, and so on. [...] Why should we embellish these simple phenomena with such preconceived equations as: red stands for madness, violet for the mystical, orange for evening, and so on? Let us rather open our eyes and expose our minds to the pure power of color and light. If we can do this, we shall be surprised at how well the laws of color and its mutations can be demonstrated by the use of colored light in the physical and chemical laboratory of the theater stage. With nothing more than simple stage lighting, we can begin to appreciate the many possibilities for the imaginative use of color play.

(Schlemmer in Gropius, 1961: 96–97)

LIGHT AS OBJECT

Laszlo Moholy-Nagy's (1895–1946) work at the Bauhaus also investigated the potential of the stage which, just like a painting, should exhibit the 'mul-tiplicity of colour and surface inter-relationships' (ibid.: 60). His ambition for the theatre and for integrating the human into a living, creative system of stage production meant that all 'means of stage production must be given positions of effectiveness equal to man's' (ibid.):

[This] theater of Totality with its multifarious complexities of light, space, plane, form, motion, sound, man – and with all the possibilities for varying and combining these elements – must be an ORGANISM.

(ibid.: 60)

Moholy-Nagy's *Light Prop for an Electric Stage* responded to this call and envisioned light as performance art. It was an extraordinary kinetic sculp-ture for the theatre composed of colour, light and movement. Constructed in glass and polished metal within a cube that was designed to stand alone on a darkened stage, the machine responded to a two-minute illumination sequence created by 116 coloured light bulbs that flashed on and off whilst the audience watched through a peephole in the box. The object itself became the protagonist of Moholy-Nagy's 1930 abstract film *Light Play: Black-White-Grey*, which captured the Light Prop as it went through it's movements and in turn was projected onto a wall beside it.

The contemporary Norwegian collective Verdensteatret also create kinetic performance machines with objects, sound and light. *The Telling Orchestra* (2008) presents a beguiling choreography of robotically controlled objects and their shadows, which are projected continually onto screens surrounding the space. Complex momentary images and multiple narratives are suggested through light and movement. Twisting mirrors reflect distorted projections and dazzling light changes instantly transform the multitude of shadows, whilst the gradual and repeated darkening and brightening of the space presents the audience with an orchestrated but apparently endless quotidian cycle.[8]

LIGHT AS ART

There is insufficient space in this volume to address the multiple ways in which light has been used as a material in contemporary art, but it is worth concluding this chapter by noting some examples that have built on the traditions established earlier in the twentieth century.

Dan Flavin (1933–1996) used the light object itself in the form of the fluorescent electric tube to create light sculptures. Rosalie (1954–) has used contemporary technologies such as fibre optic lighting to create both performative sculptures of light such as *Helios* (2007) and responsive stage settings for musical events (e.g. *Verklärte Nacht* and *Hyperion* (2006)). Waltraut Cooper (1936–) explores relationships between light and space, often in relation to architecture, environment and urban space. James Turrell (1943–) has used light as sculpture, creating poetic light installations in which his audience are enclosed and their perception of light tightly controlled. Turrell describes these environments as 'spaces that in some way form light, [and] apprehend it to be something that's physically present' (Turrell, online). Frequently these spaces provide an experience in which light, whether emanating from a natural source in his Skyspaces or manipulated at very low levels, is framed in an overtly theatrical way (e.g. *Ganzfeld: Tight End* (2005)):

> I look at the eye as the most exposed part of the brain, as something that is already forming perception. I make these rooms that are these camera-like spaces that

---

[8] See www.verdensteatret.com.

in some way form light, apprehend it to be something that's physically present [...] [which] results in an art that is not about my seeing, it's about your direct perception of the work. I'm interested in having a light that inhabits space, so that you feel light to be physically present. I mean, light is a substance that is, in fact, a thing, but we don't attribute thing-ness to it. We use light to illuminate other things, something we read, sculpture, paintings. And it gladly does this. But the most interesting thing to find is that light is aware that we are looking at it, so that it behaves differently when we are watching it and when we're not, which imbues it with consciousness.[9] Often people say that they want to touch some of the work I do. Well, that feeling is actually coming from the fact that the eyes are touching, the eyes are feeling. And this happens because the eyes are quite sensitive only in low light, for which we were made. We're actually made for this light of Plato's cave, the light of twilight. [...] Through light, space can be formed without physical material like concrete or steel. We can actually stop vision and the penetration of vision with where light is and where it isn't.

(ibid.)

Olafur Eliasson (1967–) has also embraced the theatrical potential of light. *The Weather Project* (2003) filled the turbine hall of the Tate Modern in London with an illusion of the sun, created through light reflected in ceiling mirrors and made tangible through haze. The quality of the light generated by mono-frequency lamps influenced the behaviour of the audience, who became conscious spectators and participants in this strangely illuminated environment. Eliasson is interested in how light affects our perceptions and can dematerialise objects, and the narrow wavelength of light emanating from his artificial sun allowed only the colours yellow and black to be visible. Light in this monochrome world is rendered as both a physiological and a psychological entity directly affecting the responses of the viewers, many of whom felt able to lie down on the floor in a public space and to engage in playful social interactions in the mirrored ceiling.

---

[9] Turrell is referring here to Heisenberg's *Uncertainty Principle*.

9 Gas and Electricity – New Tools and Techniques

This chapter concentrates on key developments in lighting practice which took place from the introduction of gas lighting to the stage (c. 1816) through the advent of electricity (1881) until the early part of the twentieth century.[1] This period of rapid technological change also heralded the introduction of both the limelight and the electric carbon-arc. Together, these important technical innovations and their associated inventions heralded a shift in theatre practice in which the visual aspects of staging became prioritised and lighting offered new creative possibilities. Increased levels of light and the ability to be able to control it much more precisely resulted in dramatists including lighting effects in their plays and producer-directors seeking to create striking visual images on stage with light. Staging practices adapted to accommodate the impact of these new technologies, which are exemplified in this review of a revival of Irving's *Henry VIII* on 5 January 1892:

> It would tax the imagination to believe what can be done on the modern stage until this splendid revival has been witnessed. There are fourteen complete scenes, elaborately set, and they change almost without descent of the curtain as if by magic. The lights are turned down; there is momentary darkness, and a gorgeously equipped scene, complete with furniture, is changed to another equally rich, literally in the twinkling of an eye. What would our ancestors not have given for these marvellous mechanical appliances which [...] have enabled a capable manager to add beauty to beauty, and to bring the theatre as near to nature as it is conceivably possible to do.
>
> (*Daily Telegraph* 6 January 1892)

This description reveals a number of significant developments which had taken place on the nineteenth-century stage:

• The gradual mechanisation of the stage space, which exploited engineering ingenuity and the technical developments of the industrial revolution,

---

[1] This period of lighting history is covered in detail by Rees (1978) and Penzel (1978).

allowed elaborate stage transformations to be achieved with relative ease.

- The coordination of the various production elements towards the creation of scenic illusionism had become an essential component of the production (Irving employed as many as 135 stagehands to undertake these scene changes with military precision).

- Stage lighting had become an integral aspect of the theatre experience. Advancements in lighting technology allowed for instant changes on stage, with transformations able to be undertaken for the first time in near darkness. A fade to a near blackout was now achievable without having to extinguish the lights altogether, while the illumination of the auditorium could also be carefully controlled.

Despite the fact that the electric incandescent light had already made its debut on the London stage at the time of this performance, Irving's practice at the Lyceum represented the pinnacle of creative achievement with gas lighting. This was one of the first theatres to have taken advantage of gas technology 75 years previously and its lighting installation, like that of most other theatres, had undergone a continual process of change as the technologies of distribution and operating techniques had developed. Performances such as those staged by Irving became not only displays of the power of the drama with its central 'star' actors but, with innovations in lighting and setting, also demonstrations of a new virtuosity of the theatre itself.

The discovery of the new fuel of gas, and the equipment that was developed to control it, allowed for a complex arrangement of stage lighting which could be altered throughout a performance and controlled for the first time from a single operating position. Such technological developments transformed the role of light and its artistic potential in the nineteenth-century theatre, providing a new fluidity through a series of lighting cues that could be repeatable in time with the performance. Lighting could now not only be more responsive to the needs of the drama but also, when required, offer the most significant creative contribution to the theatrical image.

However, there was a widespread tendency to over-light parts of the stage through the multiple rows of gas battens. These provided an overall improvement of general levels of illumination but often at the expense of the *chiaroscuro* effects of the previous century. It was observed that

In those days [c. 1881] at the Drury Lane such a thing as a hard shadow was unknown partly by the great number of gas burners in the battens and footlights, and partly by the low power of the gas limes and the great distance they were from the object to be illuminated.

(*The Illuminating Engineer* May 1919, cited in *Tabs* 35/2 Summer 1977: 9)

THE ARRIVAL OF GAS LIGHTING

Although the ability to create light from the gases extracted from coal had been demonstrated in 1600,[2] it was Archibald Cochrane, the ninth Earl of Dundonald (1749–1831), who first was granted a patent for the distillation of coal and its by-products. William Murdoch (1754–1839), one of Cochrane's industrial collaborators, was the first to seize upon the potential of gas as a light source and to develop gas lighting as a viable economic and practical proposition. Murdoch experimented by lighting his own home in Cornwall in 1792 by conducting gas along iron and copper tubes, and his famous illumination of the exterior of Boulton and Watt's factory in Soho, Birmingham, in 1802, to celebrate the Peace of Amiens, brought the use of gas into the public consciousness in a spectacular way, as observed by one eyewitness:

> This luminous spectacle was as novel as it was astonishing; and Birmingham poured forth its numerous population to gaze at and to admire this wonderful display of the combined effects of science and art.
>
> (Matthews, 1827: 23)

In 1804 **Frederick Winsor** (1763–1830) promoted the new light source with theatrical lecture-demonstrations and used his apparatus on stage at the Lyceum, London, to show the public how gas might be created and distributed to create light and heat. Public gas lighting was soon established once developments in the manufacture, metering and supply of gas had been introduced. Covent Garden announced on a playbill that its 'Exterior [...] Grand Hall and Staircase will be lighted with Gas' for its new season in September 1815, and *The Times* remarked on its brilliance and magnificence (Hartnoll, 1967: 564). The illumination of the external façade of the building is interesting since, like the Boulton and Watt's example, it had nothing to do with its functionality but rather worked as an advertisement on a monumental scale: a spectacular statement with light that was 'out of the ordinary'.

The first use of gas lighting for the stage was possibly at the East London Theatre in Wellclose Square,[3] which announced proudly in August 1816 that 'the whole of the interior and exterior [was] totally illuminated by gas'. Within a year, by the opening of the 1817–1818 season, the three major playhouses in close proximity in central London – Theatre Royal Covent Garden, Theatre Royal Drury Lane and the Lyceum – had all introduced gas lighting to the auditorium and to illuminate the stage. At first, gas installations supplemented the oil lamps and spermaceti wax candles, but gas was quickly adopted by theatres as a much more convenient way of illuminating both the

---

[2] By Johanna Baptist van Helmont.
[3] Formerly The Royalty, unfortunately little is known of the stage lighting installation as the building was destroyed by fire in 1826 (Penzel, 1978: 36).

stage and the house. A single, large cupola containing several rings of gas burners typically hung over the auditorium to replace the chandeliers, while gas footlights and wing-lights were installed in permanent positions fed by pipes. They could therefore be controlled from a central position through a series of levers, and this was a major development – not only could the stage be lit with higher levels of light and in a more uniform way, but the intensity of that light could be reasonably easily controlled. Flexible tubing also allowed for portable light sources, such as standards and bunch-lights, to be used from the wings to supplement the general lighting from footlights below and battens above the stage. Coloured mediums made of glass or silk could also be controlled remotely, allowing a new creative and flexible use of coloured light.

However, the introduction of gas created an inherent danger with the multitude of burners arranged around the stage, each with a flame as large as 30 cm in height. Coupled with the glare, smell and considerable heat which they generated, gas made for an unpleasant and hazardous environment for the performer. At first, gas lighting supplemented the Argand lamps but soon proved to be much brighter, especially with the introduction of the gas mantle and the development of new types of burner.

Two new sources of light, limelight and the electric carbon arc, added important new dramatic possibilities of using light as a key visual component of the scene, and there was a growing understanding of the impact that such directional light had on the overall stage picture and the creation of atmosphere.

GAS LIGHTING TECHNIQUES

Percy Fitzgerald – *The World Behind the Scenes* (1881: 14–34)

In this extended excerpt from the most comprehensive account of technical practices on the stage of the nineteenth-century theatre, Fitzgerald provides us with a fascinating description of the lighting techniques of the time. He begins with a discussion of the methods of lighting the stage, the historical dominance of the footlights and the use of the new limelight source, noting the difficulties inherent in its use. It is interesting to note that achieving a balance between different light sources with different qualities and colour temperatures is as much a contemporary concern as it was in the late nineteenth century. The physical difficulties of lighting the actor are explored, as well as the 'new' convention of darkening the auditorium. The great heat and dangers from gas lighting are also implied in Fitzgerald's account and are also evident in Stoker's 1911 article (see below):[4]

---

[4] Fitzgerald (1881: 28–34) cites Fölsch's research that documents the large numbers of theatres destroyed by fire worldwide – 426 theatres were lost between 1761 and 1881. From the 1820s, as gas began to replace oil and candles, the number of theatres destroyed had risen from an average of 3 to 10 per annum by the 1870s.

What wonderful things might not be produced by the light, when not dispensed in that equal manner and by degrees, as is now the custom! Were it to be played off with a masterly artifice, distributing it in a strong mass on some parts of the stage, and by depriving others, as it were, at the same time, it is hardly credible what effects might be produced thereby; for instance, a *chiaro-oscuro* for strength and vivacity not inferior to that so much admired in the pictures of Rembrandt. [...]

Few who nowadays look around them in a brilliantly lighted 'house,' its outline all aglow, the stage brilliant with sheen and bathed in effulgence, will be surprised to think that the great stages of about a hundred and twenty years back were simply lit by four great chandeliers hung in a row from the proscenium [...] the stage was professedly lighted up as a large room would be at night; and though the introduction of lamps or candles in a street or forest might seem unreal, it would be less inconsistent, if we thought of it calmly, than the unnatural, fierce light proceeding from the side and foot lights and suffusing everything. The-lamps were merely intended to light the faces and figures of the actors, which were all the public desired. It was enough that the scene was indicated by a moderate light behind. The amount of light is according as we are accustomed to it. The sempstress girl devouring a novel by a 'mould candle,' finds it ample. The wealthy reader finds his moderator and wax candles scarcely sufficient. Even now the gas is being helped out by the limelight, not occasionally, but almost habitually. In a late revival of 'The Good-Natured Man,' it was a surprise to learn that a scene in St. James's Park, which seemed lit up in the average way, had been set off by no less than three limelights. The limelight will soon give way to the more dazzling electric light. Possibly gas itself, found intolerably hot if used profusely, will disappear. This shows that the chandeliers of the old days were sufficient; and we hear no complaint of the theatre being unduly dark [...]

These four chandeliers were always lowered down when the play was over, a signal for the audience to depart akin to that of the attendants coming with cloths to cover up the boxes. In the case of any conflict with the actors, this sign was resorted to. But, as a principle of illumination, it was far more correct than the present system, the light being cast from above instead of from below, and the shadows falling in the right places. The whole principle of lighting the stage is involved in difficulties of the most perplexing kind, which are not likely to be resolved until some genuine scientific man condescends to take the matter up. The main difficulty is, that the stronger the light, the blacker and more marked are the shadows; which can, however, be neutralised by additional light cast in their direction, but at the sacrifice of the first light. The whole is a series of compromises and shifts. When the dancer is performing and the burlesque queen singing her song, we can see the fierce, strong bar of lime projected from the corner-often, too, the lamp and the man that holds it. Nay, before the drop-scene ascends, he has taken his place aloft, and the rays, not to be restrained, stream out fiercely across the curtain. It performs fitful and irregular motions as the operator changes his glasses to a new colour. There is something grotesque and primitive in the position in which the dancer pirouettes and gambols over the expanse of the large stage; the operator strives to pursue and overtake her with this lamp, always succeeding in displaying his illuminative ring upon the boards.

So as early as the beginning of the century, the oil lamps that served as footlights ascended and descended – 'the floats,' as they were called – when the stage was to be darkened or the reverse, – 'a clumsy machinery,' says Charles Lamb.

This question of lighting up the actors and stage has been perplexed and converted into a difficulty by the corruption of art and an abuse of dramatic principles. On a large stage the footlights are often twelve, or as much as twenty feet, from the figures, and perhaps forty or fifty from the scene. At such a distance an ordinary light would have no effect, and in consequence there is a sort of band of blazing furnaces, which glare and flame fiercely between the audience and the actors. We are so accustomed to this phenomenon, that it is accepted as of course, and seems in the natural order of things, though nothing can be more inartistic, unnatural, or destructive of scenic effect. The flames glow, and bathe the curtain and all within its reach in an extravagant and intense blaze. This, if it be sufficient for the distant, will naturally be too much for what is near.

Footlights were long in use among the French before their introduction to England by Garrick about the year 1765, and they were used in a much more sensible fashion than they are now, being disposed with open spaces between each sconce, thus not obscuring the view, and at the same time distributing the light across. A long board or screen is now run along lined with reflectors, which interfere with the view; to meet which objection the stage is made inclined, appearing even more inclined from the perspective. This inclination, indeed, always gives an unnatural air. When Mr. Fechter became a manager here, he introduced another French device, that of sinking the footlights below the stage in a sort of trench, and 'bevelling' off the boards in front. This seems to be now adopted in nearly all theatres. Yet the result is that the light plays upwards, and that the lower half of the actors is in shadow. In short, the object is to light the stage and actors, and any compromise of the kind is attended by a failure of illumination. Better, then, the old lamps apart, and honestly doing their work. [. . .]

Gas- a revolution- was introduced on the stage almost as soon as it was in the street [. . .] These lamps are furnished with 'chimneys' of white and green glass, which, by an ingenious system of levers commanded by the prompter, ascend or descend as required, and produce moonlight or other optical effects. In some theatres, notably one at Birmingham, a series of coloured glass screens can be shifted in front by a lever, but *with* a loud clatter. It is a curious sight to see the elaborate system of locks and regulators at the prompter's side, some dozen in number, and directing every department in the house. All this depends on the mode in which these are controlled, and many experiments are made, combinations of footlights and others. It may be added that there is a great art even in the management of the limelights, and by crossing the rays of different lamps and of different tints, strange twilight and soft moonlight effects may be produced.

In the French Opera-House there are no less than twenty-eight miles of gas-piping, while the controlling *'jeu d'orgue,'* as it is called, comprises no less than eighty-eight 'stops' or cocks, all collected in one screen, as it were, controlling nine hundred and sixty gas jets, &c. The body of the house should be kept dark while the play is going on, and then suddenly 'start into light, and make the lighter start.' That almost Cimmerian gloom which certain theatres affect is an excess, as is also the bright gay glare which is found in the French theatres. A theatre should be lit soberly enough to see faces and features and to read a play, but that utter darkness is unnatural, and in a measure destroys the illusion and intensifies the glare on the stage. At the Lyceum the happy idea is adopted, which is truly conducive to stage illusion, of lowering all lights as the scene changes. The result-is a kind of charming, pleasing mystery and surprise as a new vision opens, and the violent separatings [sic] and shiftings become invisible, being performed in secrecy.

But this question of lighting is in truth intimately connected with another. [...] The stage should not project beyond the arch; as now, owing to the distance at which the footlights are compelled to be placed, they must be of excessive power to reach the scenes and figures. Were the stage kept within the arch, the lights need only be placed in the same plane of the arch, and would require to be only of moderate strength. But here, again, it is to be feared that a false principle is at work, viz., the eagerness of the performers to be set off by this strong light, and the glittering costume it requires, with a wish to be brought more in contact with the audience. [...]

With the system of lighting the scenes in theatres, it speaks well for the constant care exercised that more conflagrations do not occur. A row of jets, some thirty or forty long, and two or three hundred in number, are hoisted aloft, protected behind by a sort of curved metal screen, and in front by a very open wire net. The amount of heat and flame may be conceived. The lighting even of these jets, which is done from below with a light rod of enormous length, is a matter of danger, as a mere contact with the canvas might set all in a blaze, for the lighter has to carry his rod along every jet. A system lately introduced at the Lyceum happily guards against these dangers. A second row of jets, 'needle points,' which almost touch each other, runs along close beside the more scattered jets; a single light being applied, the flame flies along from jet to jet, until all, in both lines, are lighted. The first row having thus discharged its duty, is extinguished, and the other remains lighted. These rakes and 'battens' can be raised or lowered to any height.

By the 1880s, groups of expert technicians had evolved: limelight operators, gas engineers and electricians who were employed together in their respective teams to realise lighting effects on the stage. The emerging techniques established ways of working, cueing and lighting conventions that still remain in use today.

Technical and lighting rehearsals were established where levels between individual lights and large banks of lights were balanced relative to each other. The increasing complexity of the lighting meant that scenes now needed to be planned in advance and cue sheets developed so that the lighting could be repeated accurately in each performance.

Levels of light on the stage were modulated in response to dramatic moments and were plotted on cue sheets using terms such as 'quarter', 'half', 'three-quarters' and 'full', which were particularly important where colour mixing between banks of lights was required. Both the stage and the auditorium could be dimmed, achieving the first theatrical 'blackout' of the modern era. Individual units could be placed around the stage to create directional and point light sources in any convenient location, whilst standard lights were used on booms hidden in the wings, and battens were arranged and struck from the stage behind scenic units during scene changes.

The brighter light sources of the carbon-arc and limelight could be made visible above the general illumination of the stage and, when focused and carefully controlled, allowed a new flexibility as well as a movable light source. These powerful beams of light could be used to motivate the scene and could also be coloured, just like the gas lighting.

Bright, saturated coloured light on the stage was a significant development with the advent of gas, and the central control of the lighting enabled

Figure 14 A nineteenth-century gas-lit stage as seen from the wings

the colour of the lighting to be changed almost instantaneously in blackout or for the first time as part of a live cross-fade. Colour conventions for the stage were also established at this time as pink and yellow combinations were employed for sunlight, blue for night-time scenes and green/blue for moonlight effects.

NEW SOURCES OF LIGHT – LIMELIGHT AND THE ELECTRIC CARBON-ARC

Limelight

In 1822, Sir **Goldsworthy Gurney** (1793–1875), a brilliant Cornish inventor, demonstrated a new intense light source in a series of lectures in London. He had developed a blowpipe which used a mixture of oxygen and hydrogen to produce a very hot flame. When he added lime to the flame it produced a soft but blindingly white light. The properties of limelight were harnessed by Captain **Thomas Drummond** (1797–1840) for geographical surveying, and in 1826 he built and used a working version with a lens and reflector – the Drummond Light. A ball of lime was heated until it became incandescent and produced an intense beam over 30 times brighter than an Argand lamp. Drummond's Light was adopted widely by operators of magic lanterns in a modified form known as the 'oxy-calcium' lamp, and in the theatre, limelight became an important creative tool – the brightest light source introduced to the stage since daylight had been excluded.

Limelight was used in the theatre as a special effect, probably first on 30 November 1837 at Drury Lane in the premiere of Balfe's opera *Joan of Arc*.[5] Publicity material announced that the production had 'new and extensive scenery' painted by the Grieves, 'and to heighten some of the effects, a new and extraordinary Light will be introduced, called PHOSHELIOULAMPROTERON'.[6]

A review of the performance describes the visual climax on a stage defined by light:

> The scene of the horrid sacrifice is the last in the piece – it is well managed; the light streaming through the windows of an adjoining church, and the pale moonlight thrown on the distant multitude who are waiting the execution, produce a capital effect.
>
> (*Sunday Times* 12 December 1837)

Frederick Gye junior (1810–1878) developed a version of the limelight for theatrical use around the same time, and this appears to have been the type

---

[5] See Rees (1978: 45).

[6] *The Theatrical Observer and Daily Bills of the Play No 4978* Friday 1 December 1837, printed every morning by E. & J. Thomas, 6 Exeter Street, Exeter Hall, Strand.

hired by William Macready (1793–1873) for scenic effect during the 1837–1838 season at Covent Garden. The use of this limelight to create a moonlight effect for the pantomime *Harlequin and Peeping Tom of Coventry*[7] is often erroneously cited as the first use of limelight technology in performance. What is certain is that these experiments in the two rival 'patent theatres' were the early theatrical explorations of the creative possibilities of this new technology with its blinding white light tinged with green luminescence.

While limelight was clearly a significant technological development, it was at first expensive and cumbersome and held a considerable element of danger. Macready considered the expense of hiring the effect at £1 10 shillings per night to be too great and quickly suspended its use at Covent Garden, despite the detrimental impact which this had on the presentation of the scenic effects (Saxe-Wyndham, 1906: 133).[8]

Although the new technology used relatively cheap but caustic lime blocks or cylinders as its raw material, limelight also required the costly manufacture of oxygen and hydrogen, which needed to be kept apart in two separate gas bags and fed to the flame under controlled conditions. Pressure boards, resembling large bellows, were used by the operators of the limes to dispense these gases, but the control of the gases was both dangerous and difficult in practice.

Although as we have already seen there were aesthetic issues with the use of limelight, the new light source became an integral and ubiquitous aspect of theatrical production and its popularity can be gauged by Fitzgerald's account of London's streets:

> In an evening walk through the Strand, one is certain to encounter men carrying on their shoulders enormously inflated bags, much as the 'sandwich men' carry their boards. These are now found necessary at every theatre, and contain the gases for supplying the fiercely-glowing limelight lanterns. They are on the ground between hinged boards, on which weights are laid, thus causing the high pressure necessary.
>
> (Fitzgerald, 1881: 210 footnote)

The Electric Carbon-arc

Most of the contemporary accounts of stage lighting in the second half of the nineteenth century refer to limelight, but in fact many of these effects were actually achieved by an alternative but equally powerful light source which had nothing to do with the heating of lime. The carbon-arc light was the first lighting instrument to harness the new power source of electricity, and created a flickering, blue/white beam that was used on stage in an identical way to the limelight. This intense light was created by causing

---

[7] First performance 26 December 1837.
[8] Lawrence (1889a: 225–226) suggests that it was dispensed with after a week's use.

the electric current to arc between two carbon rods. It too was difficult to operate as it involved a constant tending of the carbon amidst nitric acid fumes from the batteries, and working with the inherent dangers of sulphuric acid and imperfectly insulated electrical equipment. The carbon-arc was introduced to the stage in 1848 at the Princess's Theatre, London, where it was used as a floodlight in a pantomime which a contemporary critic described as

> illuminated by the 'new electric light' so-called, and which makes gigantic shadows and gives a sickly glare to surrounding objects, which is quite peculiar.
>
> (*The Times* 27 December 1848: 5)

CHANGES IN LIGHTING TECHNIQUES

Improvements and modifications to both the carbon-arc and the limelight during the latter part of the nineteenth century led to the rise of lighting consultants who specialised in the design and operation of these specialist theatre luminaires, as well as in the creation of a wide range of other lighting and scenic effects. In Paris, **Louis Jules Duboscq** (1817–1886) was brought into the theatre because of his expertise in projection and photography and, from 1849, created optical effects at the Opéra which were soon copied at other theatres. The new intense light sources had revolutionised what could be achieved by 'magic lantern' slide projectors, and this opened up a whole new series of possibilities for the projection of images. The magic lantern powered by limelight or electric carbon-arc light was used to create elaborate new effects and, because of the strength of the new light sources, adopted widely for entertainments beyond the stage. Arc lights in particular were used for the first time to illuminate areas of the city at night, and on construction sites to allow work to continue after nightfall.[9]

The use of mechanical devices in tandem with the newly discovered light sources allowed complex front and rear scenic projections, transformation scenes and the creation of effects such as moving clouds, sunrises and magical fairy settings. Newly established businesses such as The Electric Light and Colour Company, Delaporte of Paris and Duboscq supplied a range of lighting equipment including arc-light and limelight effects specifically for theatrical use.

As creative lighting tools, limelight and arc-light were at first essentially used as floodlight in relatively close proximity to the stage, either from the wings or as top-side lighting from the fly floors above. Some theatres, such as the Leeds Grand Theatre and Opera House (1878), even had special balconies constructed below the fly floor for limelight operators to work from, while

---

[9] see Schivelbusch (1995: 114–134).

carbon-arc lights offered considerable flexibility and new creative possibilities but their glare lacked subtlety and could disrupt the stage picture. Fitzgerald's aesthetic concerns in the use of the follow-spot and many of the practical difficulties he identifies would be recognisable to technicians in the modern theatre. Indeed, the archaic term 'limes' remains in use to describe both the operators and their equipment, even though limelight ceased to be used as a source for the follow-spot in the early twentieth century as it became replaced by newer variants of the carbon-arc.

NEW STAGING PRACTICES – LIGHT, PAINT AND GAUZE

The new methods of lighting the stage with gas, limelight and the carbon-arc demanded a radically different approach to scenic design. Scenic artists had to adapt to the new technology which, because of the increasing levels of illumination, began to expose the painted scenes as simply paint on canvas.

The scenic painters' craft developed a new sophistication because of the new light source and needed to adapt again with the advent of electricity. By then, however, it was understood that scenic effects such as William Beverley's fairy landscapes and transformation scenes would have been impossible to achieve without the aid of light:

> To excel nowadays [...] [it is necessary to] unite pictorial and constructive talents with mechanical ingenuity, and to possess a perfect knowledge of the possibilities of lighting.
>
> (Lawrence, 1889b: 41–45)

Charles Kean (1811–1868) was instrumental in the development of the new staging techniques of light and scenic effect in his productions staged at the Princess's Theatre between 1851 and 1859. He saw the stage as a canvas in which all of the theatrical elements should contribute to create a unified composition. His productions were characterised by spectacular scenery based on historical research and pictorial techniques in which light was both an essential compositional element and used for specific scenic effect.

His production of *Macbeth* opened with a dimly lit scene of the three 'witches' behind gauze curtains. It was based on historical research into eleventh-century Scandinavian culture and required 19 different settings that emphasised the wildness, roughness and cold desolation of this world. Lighting played an important role in creating the overall atmosphere, and in representing the supernatural elements of the drama. The *Illustrated London News* commented:

> In treating the supernatural scenes, an abundant use has been made of gauze, so that the witches are continually presented enveloped in a thick mist [...] and many

of the scenes besides are so enveloped that the change from one to the other is managed almost with the effect of a dissolving view.

(19 February 1853)

The Times also acknowledged the impact of the lighting on the presentation of the 'witches' and for Banquo's ghostly re-appearance:

The witches speak and sing through thick gauzes, that render them but half real; and, when these artificial fogs disperse, their gaunt figures stand out awfully against the morning sky. Their cave is no common cave, but the 'Pit of Acheron' – a hollow cone, lighted from the top, with a reddish lustre, in the midst of which they perform effective orgies. [...] Banquo hitherto has been but slightly distinguishable from the rest of the party into which he intruded, but here he also becomes a means of producing new effects. Now he rises behind the table, and a strong light thrown on his pallid countenance makes him the focus to the entire picture; now a pillar becomes transparent in order to show his menacing form within.

(15 February 1853)

Frederick Lloyds, one of Kean's scene painters for *Macbeth*, later described how many visual illusions were created on the nineteenth-century stage. To create sparkling water, for example,

a spangle cloth [should be] used in moonlight scenes [...] when the effects caused by a sunset have to be shown. But in this case the spangle cloth must be lighted either with the aid of red glasses on the gas row, or with limelight shining through an amber or red glass. For the sun, use fine Persian amber silk, and let both sun and moon be lighted by a limelight, or if that is not convenient, by a ring of glass and a reflector.

(Lloyds, 1875: 75–79)

Lloyds writes extensively about the techniques required to achieve these scenic effects through the combinations of light and paint. Lloyds advocated dreamy 'indefinite scenery' like a Turner painting for any transformation or fairy scene and techniques of distemper painting, applied quickly and then dried, which allowed layers of painted effects to be applied to materials including silk, cotton, canvas, wood and paper. These painted layers could be transformed by light:

Paint the face of your cloth with very thin size colour [...] and very lightly as it will be lighted from the front only with all the blue mediums over the gas battens, the wings or side lights down, green glass on the footlights, and gas lengths at the sides with green glasses on them. With this amount of light the slightest stain of colour on the sky will be sufficient.

(Lloyds in Finkel, 1996: 167)

The application of subtle layers of paint with their own 'lights' (highlights) was designed specifically to respond under changes in stage lighting. Gauzes

BRAM STOKER – 'IRVING AND STAGE LIGHTING'

in *The Nineteenth Century and After – A Monthly Review* (1911: 903–912)

STAGE lighting, as we understand it now, is the growth of a comparatively few years. The one person to whom the modern cult is due is the late Sir Henry Irving. When he took into his own hands in 1878 the management of the Lyceum Theatre, the lighting or stage scenes was crude and only partially effective. But the possibilities or this branch of art had been for a long time in the actor's mind, and when he became sole master of a playhouse of his own, with undisputed sovereignty, he began to apply to it his theories and his experience, with results which dominate the whole artistic mysteries or the stage to this day. As a matter of fact, the history of the Lyceum Theatre during Henry Irving's management – from 1878 to 1898 – is the history of modern stage lighting.

[...] When the reconstruction of 1878 was in hand special care was taken to bring up to date the mechanical appliances for lighting the stage. In those days gas was the only available means of theatre lighting – except, of course, 'limelights,' which were movable and the appurtenances of which had to be arranged afresh for every play done. But for ordinary lighting purposes gas was used; and, in order to ensure safety, certain precautions were, by Irving's direction, adopted. Instead of having all the gas to be used in the theatre - both for the stage and auditorium – supplied from one main, as had been theretofore done, he had supplies taken from two separate mains. Thus, in case of explosion, or any other cause of interruption outside the theatre, it was possible to minimise the risk of continued darkness. To this end a by-pass was made connecting within the theatre the two supplies. Of course, an explosion in a gas main, no matter where occurring, is apt to put out all the lights fed from it – if lit. This used in those days to be the great source of danger from fire, for with the enormous number of burners in use in a theatre all turned on, and the gas escaping, the introduction of a naked light was an immediate source of danger. Thus, Irving's first care was to minimise such risk by having an immediate supply of gas available from quite another main. In the Lyceum Theatre a large number of men were employed to look after the gas, to light and turn it off as required. The rules regarding this work were very strict. Each gas-man had to carry (and use for his work) a spirit torch. Under no circumstances was he allowed to strike a match except in places suited for the purpose. After all, it was not a very difficult job to light up a scene, so far as the carrying out of the appointed way was concerned. To make this apparent to a reader not well versed in stage appliances it may be as well to explain the various mechanical appliances for lighting used on the stage:

(1) Footlights, or 'floats,' as they were called in the old days of oil-lamps, the name being retained when the special applicability for it had passed away; (2) battens; (3) standards; (4) lengths; (5) ground rows; (6) all sorts of special form and size, made to suit particular pieces of built scenery.

Of these lights, the only kind directly observable by the public are the footlights. That is, they are in front of the stage, but it is essential that they be not themselves seen; otherwise their glare would entirely destroy all distinctions of light. What the public sees are the backs of the reflectors which hide the glare from the audience and send it back upon the stage. These lights are of great power. In the present time, when electric light is used for the purpose, these lamps vary from twenty to a hundred candle-power. To realise this blaze of light it must be remembered that an ordinary domestic light of the 'Swan' or 'Edison' pattern is of some eight candle-power. In Irving's time-at the close of his personal management of the Lyceum the footlight lamps were of sixty candle-power, modified occasionally for artistic purposes, as I shall show further on.

Battens are long frames that run across the top of the stage from side to side. These contain a large number of lamps, placed side by side so as to show a very strong line of light. The battens are hung with such fittings as allow them to be raised or lowered at will. In the gas days the batten was a wooden frame to which was attached, in such a position that the light could not come into contact with anything inflammable, an iron gas-pipe, in which were fixed at regular intervals a multitude of burners. The special burners used for this purpose were what were known as 'fish-tail' burners, which allowed the flame to spread laterally, and so were, by securing good combustion, effective for lighting purposes. This gas-pipe was connected with the main by flexible leather tubes, so that provision could be made for altering the height above the stage without interfering with the supply of gas. At one end of the pipe was a burner fed by quite another tube, so that it would keep alight when the main supply of that pipe was turned off. This jet was known as the 'pilot,' and was specially lit in readiness before the beginning of the play. When the supply of gas was turned on to the batten pipe, the pressure sent the flame along; for as the burners began to be fed all along the line the spreading flame of one burner caught the escaping gas from the next orifice, and in a few seconds the whole line would be alight. To ensure readiness, alterability, and safety in these and other lights, all along the stage from front to back, behind the line of the 'wings' which mask in the scene, were special water-taps connected with the gas mains of the theatre, so as to ensure a constant supply up to these points. The flexible tubes had metal ends which fell easily into place in the taps and left no leakage. Then the gas-man with his key turned on the tap so as to make lighting possible. All these taps were so arranged that the supply at each batten could be turned on or off at the 'Prompt,' where the 'gas-table' was fixed vertically. There was a batten for each portion of the stage, from front to back. For a stage is divided for working purposes by measured distances which are the continuance of the old 'grooves' by which the 'flats' in old days used to be pushed out or drawn off. All stage hands understand No.1, No.2, No.3, and so on.

The standard is a vertical pipe, set on a strong, heavy base, so as to be secure from accident of lateral pressure. The gas supply enters through a flexible tube at base, arranged with the taps in the same manner as are the battens. The top of each is a cluster of very powerful burners; thus, each standard is in itself a source of intense light, which can be moved when required.

Lengths are battens of convenient size, and are 'made adaptable for almost any use. As the purpose of lighting is to throw the light from front and back of the stage, these are often arranged to be hung on the back of the scenic piece in front. Hooks are provided for the purpose. Lengths can be placed in any position or shape; and, so long as their direct light is concealed from the audience, can be made to enhance or supplement any volume of light.

The ground rows are a length applied to special purpose. Stage perspective differs somewhat from the perspective of nature, inasmuch as it is much stronger; and it is therefore necessary at times to even-up this extra strength to eyes accustomed in ordinary to a different perspective focus. In fact, in proper stage lighting – that which produces what seems to be the ordinary appearance of natural forces – it is not sufficient to have all the lighting from one point. The light of nature is so infinitely stronger than any artificial light, and so much better distributed, that science and art have to be requisitioned to produce somewhat similar effect.

As to special lighting pieces for 'built' scenery, these have on each occasion to be made to serve their present purpose. In 'built' scenery it is sometimes difficult to avoid throwing objectionable shadows. The lights are so strong, and the space available is so small, that there is hardly room at times for simple effects. So, when there is a shadow which cannot be avoided, it is generally possible to build in some piece of seemingly solid work, behind which a light can be so placed as to destroy the shadow.

Now, in 1878, all this had practically to be done by gas. Of course, what are known as 'limelights' were in use. These are exceedingly powerful lights, produced by playing burning gas heavily charged with oxygen and hydrogen on a fragment of lime. This light is so concentrated that it is easily adaptable to the localising of strong light. The appliance for producing the light being small, it can be easily placed in a specially-made box, whose face is a lens of strength suitable to the work to be done. The effect is, of course, proportionate to the amount of concentration. In fact, the general scientific law applies that what is gained by direction is lost in force, and *vice versa*. In a well-equipped theatre many different kinds of limelights are now in use, the lenses being in such variety that a skilful operator can select that best adapted to the special occasion: 'open limes,' 'spot lights' of varying focus and intensity, lights so constructed as to cover a certain amount of space, and so on. The moon, the lights from the windows of the 'old home,' the convenient ray which follows the hero about the stage, so that the audience may never forget that he is present, and nearly all such aids to the imagination of the spectator are produced in this way. In '78 these appliances were comparatively rare, but the example set by Henry Irving encouraged other managers to use them, and an industry sprang into existence. New firms undertook work which had hitherto been almost a monopoly. Fresh men in ever-increasing numbers became trained to the work, and nowadays it is hard to imagine that not many years ago it was almost necessary to train workmen for this minor art.

Now as these two methods of lighting-gas and limelight were already in existence when Henry Irving managed a theatre for himself, his part in the general advance was primarily to see that both these means were perfected. To effect this he spared no expense. The equipment of the Lyceum Theatre so as to be able to use gas-light most readily and to the best advantage was a costly job. It would have been almost impossible for a layman to understand why pipes of such calibre were required for the gas of one place of business. The by-pass between the two intakes of gas – only to be used in emergency – was more than twelve inches in diameter, and the piping, fixed and flexible, throughout the building ran into many thousands of feet. But the final result was excellent. When the mechanism was complete it was possible to regulate from the 'Prompt' every lamp of the many thousands used throughout the theatre. This made in itself a new era in theatrical lighting. By it Irving was able to carry out a long thought-of scheme: that the auditorium should be darkened during the play. Up to this time such had not been the custom. Indeed, it was a general aim of management to have the auditorium as bright as possible. The new order of things was a revelation to the public. Of course, when the curtain came down the lights went up, and vice versa. In the practical working of the scheme it was found possible to open new ways of effect. In fact, darkness was found to be, when under control as important a factor in effects as light. With experience it was found that time could be saved in the changing of scenes. It used to be necessary, when one 'full' scene followed another, to drop a curtain temporarily so that the stage could be lit sufficiently for the workmen to see what they were doing. But later on, when the workmen had been trained to do the work as Irving required it to be done, darkness itself became the curtain. The workmen were provided with silent shoes and dark clothing, all of which were kept in the house and put on before each performance. Then, in obedience to preconcerted signals, they carried out in the dark the prearranged and rehearsed work without the audience being able to distinguish what was going on. Later on, when electric power came to be harnessed for stage purposes, this, with different coloured lights, was used with excellent effect.

Irving was always anxious to have the benefit of new discoveries applied to stage effects. In 1885, when he produced *Faust*, electricity was used for effect the first time.

Colonel Gouraud (Edison's partner) kindly arranged an installation for the fight between Faust and Valentine. Two metal plates were screwed on the stage, to either of which the current of one pole was applied. One of the combatants had a metal plate screwed to the sole of the right shoe. From this a wire was carried through the clothing and brought into the palm of the right hand, where, on the rubber glove, was fixed a piece of metal. This being in contact with the metal handle of the sword – and a similar contrivance being arranged for Mephistopheles -a direct communication was established so soon as the demon's sword struck up the weapons of the combatants, and sparks were emitted.

It was not till about 1891 that electric-light was, even in a crude condition, forward enough to be used for general lighting purposes in British theatres. Irving had it then put in by degrees, beginning with the footlights, which formed a test of suitability. Electric-light differs from other lights in that when it is lowered in degree it changes colour. This is perhaps due to the fact that it is not in the ordinary sense a light at all, but a heat visible *in vacuo*. In order to allow the footlights to be turned down it was necessary in those days to have a liquid resistance, which was a wasteful as well as an expensive mechanism. In addition, the light even then afforded was an unpleasing one for the stage, unless the vacuum lamps were tinted. Therefore considerable consideration and experience were necessary before a satisfactory result could be achieved. The purpose of lowering footlights is to create a scenic atmosphere of night or mystery or gloom. Now in nature night and mystery and gloom are shown in tints of blue; but as electric light is produced by red-hot carbon the atmosphere was warm instead of cold, cheerful instead of gloomy. In those days coloured lights on the stage were in their infancy, and the best device which we were able at first to adopt was to cover the lamps of the footlights with bags of thin blue paper. This was effective, though wasteful; for, of course, in getting the colour a portion of the illuminating power was lost. In addition, though the heat of an ordinary electric globe is not very great, when the light within is of sixty or a hundred candle-power a certain amount of heat is created; and if this, or a portion of it, be retained in a paper bag there is a certain amount of danger of combustion. Of this the licensing authorities could not approve, and the device was abandoned in time to avoid trouble. [...] It may hereafter be interesting to remember that even in America, where electric lighting was in those days far ahead of what it was in England, we thought it advisable to bring – and actually to use them – a supply of blue paper bags for the footlights.

It may also be well to remember that though America has gone very fast and very far in her theatrical lighting, it only reached any considerable excellence when Henry Irving showed the stage producers what could be done. When we first visited America, in 1883, there was only one theatre there – the Boston Theatre – had really good appliances for stage lighting. I speak here merely of the mechanism of lighting, not of the art of it. In the Boston Theatre there was a thoroughly well-thought-out scheme for the gas-lighting then in vogue. Its perfection was to be seen in the 'gas-table' in the 'Prompt,' which was then far in advance of that of any other theatre that we played in. I only quote this fact as evidence of the extraordinary rapidity with which in that marvellous land of industry and mechanism a good idea is seized on and developed to the full. At the present time a vast number of the lighting appliances for the theatre are patents of the United States, and the goods are there manufactured.

The installation of electric light in the Lyceum Theatre brought with it one somewhat cumbrous and expensive addition. Up to then the large amount of gas consumed for lighting purposes all over the house created a sufficient heat for the comfort of the audience; but so soon as electricity was used instead of gas as the main lighting, we noticed that the men of the audience began to turn up their coat-collars and the ladies to wear their cloaks. So we had to have an elaborate system of hot-water heating installed. [...]

All that I have said of lighting in the theatre is merely with reference to the mechanism. The part most noteworthy, and which came from Henry Irving's incomparable brain and imagination, was the production of effect. In the 'seventies, as I have said, there was very little attempt to produce fine gradations of light and shade or of colour. Henry Irving practically invented the *milieu*. When he became a manager the only appliances used were what were called 'mediums,' which were woven films of cotton or wool or silk drawn between the lights and the stage or scenery which they lit. The finest stuff we then used was 'scrim,' a thin silk which gave certain colour without destroying or suppressing an undue amount of the illuminating quality. This stuff, dyed only in a few rudimentary colours, could be used to go beneath the battens and encompass the standards, wire guards being affixed everywhere to prevent the possibility of conflagration. It was also used occasionally to cover the bull's-eyes of the limelight boxes. But it was impracticable to produce colour effects, except generally. The stage could be fairly well reduced to one dominating colour, but that was all.

Accordingly Irving set himself to work in his own quiet way, and, with the help of his employés [sic], had various mechanical processes devised. He had transparent lacquers applied to the glasses of the limelights, and, when electric light came in, to the bulbs of the electric lights, and thus produced effects of colour both of intensity and delicacy up to then unknown. Instead of rudimentary colours being mentioned on the lighting 'plots' – by which the operators work – 'blue,' 'red,' &c., the plots began to direct the use of certain fine distinctions of colour, so that before long the men themselves became educated to finer work and would no more think of using 'dark blue' instead of 'light blue,' or, 'steel blue' instead of 'pale blue,' than they would insert a slide of any form of red instead of any form of blue.

Then came quite a number of colours new to this use, as the possibilities of lacquer for the purpose became known and enlarged. Shades began to take the place of colours in matters of choice, and soon even the audience became trained to the enjoyment of fine distinctions of colour.

The artists who worked for the stage and who were always great admirers of the 'Chief' – or the 'Governor' as everybody called him – were very loyal to him and very willing to carry out his wishes, using for the purpose their natural abilities and the skill which they had evolved by labour and experience. Indeed, so far as I could judge, the very men who painted the scenes, and did it in so masterly a way, were glad to have him 'light' them and gave all their understanding to his assistance in the work. He in turn was loyal to his fellow artists and workers; I never knew him to fail in giving all the credit and all the honour to those by whom he was assisted.

Then, having put the matter of degree of light and its colours in good shape for use, he began to make further improvements in the artistic use of it. For instance, it was formerly usual to have the footlights extending in unbroken line from side to side of the proscenium arch. Now he had this line – which contained several rows of lamps of different colours – broken up into sections. Thus any combination of colour could be easily made by use of the lighting table in the 'Prompt.' By this means Irving was able to carry out a class of effects which had long been in his mind. He had noticed that nature seldom shows broad effect with an equality of light. There are shadows here and there, or places where, through occasional aerial density, the light is unevenly distributed. This makes great variety of effect, and such, of course, he wanted to reproduce. An audience – or the bulk of it at any rate – always notices effect, though the notice is not always conscious; it is influenced without knowing the reason. With, then, a properly organised series of sections – both with regard to amount of light and colour of it at disposal – a greater variety of' light was given to a scene. Also, as it is advisable to centre effects on a stage, it became an easy matter to throw any special part of the stage into greater prominence – in fact, to 'vignette' that part of the stage picture which at the moment was of the larger importance.

Irving also began to produce and alter effects of the combinations of coloured lights – to use the media of coloured lights as a painter uses his palette.

within a gas-filled glass bulb created stage lighting that was significantly brighter than anything that had preceded electricity. Electrical dimming had improved by the early 1920s and, with the advent of much more powerful 3kW lamps, even brighter and bolder controlled lighting was suddenly possible.

With the growing influence of visionaries such as Appia and Craig, light began to be considered as a creative tool that went beyond the need simply to illuminate the setting and the actors within it. Practitioners such as David Belasco in the USA (see Chapter 10) used the new technologies to create atmosphere and mood, while the emerging expressionist dramas in Germany embraced the new potential through experimentation with the psychological effects of light, and the intensity, shape and colour of the new electric light became integral aspects of the production style (see Chapter 6).

With the development of electrical lighting, the theatre space itself needed to adapt once again to accommodate the new equipment. To enable the use of spotlights away from the stage, rigging positions needed to be created on the walls outside the proscenium and along balcony and circle fronts. Often this was an uneasy compromise, due to the bulkiness of the early electric lanterns and the available angles for lighting, which were often too shallow from the dress circle and too steep from the balconies.

New theatres, in contrast, were able to incorporate rigging positions within the fabric of the building through the provision of lighting bridges, slots within the ceiling and specifically created positions, such as 'drums' and 'ladders'.[14]

Morgan provides a neat summary of lighting in the inter-war years and argues that the most innovative lighting work could be found in the newly built theatres (Morgan, 2005: 228), although the time-consuming nature of the process of lighting the stage often mitigated against creativity:

> Lamp filaments in early focus spots needed to be re-centred every time they were refocused, a time-consuming and tedious job that was not overcome until the arrival of the pre-focus cap in 1951. Rigs hardwired to the dimmers meant it was difficult to add more equipment or move it around. Resistance dimmers had limited load variation which afforded little flexibility. Plugs and sockets had not been standardised, so moving equipment often meant time-consuming changes to the plugs. Also there were many local variations in voltage supply to complicate matters further.
>
> (ibid.: 228–229)

---

[14] Reinhardt installed hidden positions for his lighting in chandeliers and 'hoods' while a lighting drum was created at the Tribüne (see Patterson, 1981: 101–102). The remodelled Shakespeare Memorial Theatre included lighting bridges within the ceiling, while post-war British theatres such as Nottingham Playhouse also included a drum above the auditorium to enable the downstage area to be lit. Special front-of-house lighting ladders were employed to resolve front-lighting issues at the National's Olivier Theatre. However, lighting positions were not always planned fully (see Pilbrow's account of the Chichester Festival Theatre, 1997: 259–262).

It is important to foreground at this point the introduction of a small but significant piece of engineering by Strand Electric in 1959, which had a significant impact on lighting practice in Britain. The new 'G' clamp was a hook designed to secure each lantern to a lighting bar and to facilitate the speedy movement of lanterns between lighting positions. Until this point, lanterns had been fixed in semi-permanent positions by a traditional and cumbersome 'L' clamp which had dual nuts and bolts. In practice, this method of attaching lanterns to the rig prevented them from being moved frequently to adapt to the needs of individual productions. The 'G' clamp therefore facilitated a much more creative approach to lighting the stage since it allowed a flexible use of all lanterns in a theatre's stock. This engineering solution, in combination with new production methods that allowed the mass production of theatre lights for the first time, finally enabled Appia's vision of 'mobile' light sources to become a practical reality. Specific effects could now be created much more easily, and concerns relating to sufficient illumination of the stage were balanced by the new creative potential of adaptable rigs.

The way in which this creative contribution of light in the electrical era might be organised became the subject of a number of textbooks reflecting existing practices and advocating new technical approaches to lighting the stage, and this is the focus of the next chapter.

A Method of Lighting the Stage (1932), which, in advocating a structural approach to lighting drama, became as influential to lighting designers as Stanislavski's *An Actor Prepares* on the acting profession. Although critics argued that the textbook simply recorded the existing lighting techniques in American theatres, the McCandless 'method' proposed a clear systematic framework for approaching the design of lighting for a dramatic scene for the first time.

It was predicated on four key principles:

> Visibility, naturalism, composition, and atmosphere are the objectives for lighting no matter what the form of theatre or type of production.
>
> (McCandless, 1958: 8)

Although one might well argue about the selection and detail of these objectives, these four functions provided firm foundations for the 'method', which offered practical solutions to the problems of lighting the stage with the equipment of the period. As McCandless himself notes in a foreword to his 1958 (4th) edition,

> Much has happened in the field of stage lighting since this little book first made its appearance. The ellipsoidal reflector spot had not been developed; the fresnel spot was just appearing in 1932. The electronic dimmer had only been thought of [...]
>
> This plan prepares the palette, as it were, of the lighting designer, and suggests a practical method of using the tools that are available, but it does not pretend to guarantee the final results of balance and composition in dramatic pictures. The final result depends upon the eye and taste of the designer. Moreover the method does not solve all the problems of lighting; it is in fact simply an effort to clear the ground for actual expression and experimentation. Following it saves a great deal of time, energy and expense; and it has stood the practical test of varied types of production practice.
>
> (ibid.: 7–11)

McCandless argues that the primary function of lighting is to provide 'controlled visibility' (ibid.: 14), and to this end he advocates an approach to designing lighting that involves four key steps:

- lighting the acting area;
- blending and toning the acting areas;
- lighting background surfaces;
- creating special effects.

The approach drew upon McCandless' experience as an architect, and his system is based on an imaginary grid of squares, each lit by overlapping sources of elliptically shaped light beams. The designer should therefore

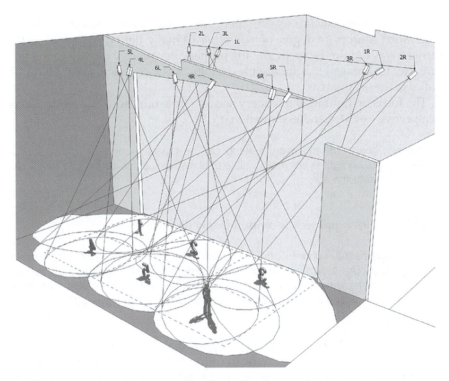

Figure 16 Diagrammatic representation by Christopher Megginson of McCandless' overlapping acting area lights. Downstage areas 1–3 are lit from six lanterns in the auditorium. Upstage areas 4–6 are lit in a similar way from the lighting bridge within the proscenium

first divide the acting area up into separate segments or acting areas and plan to light each of these imaginary 'cubes' from two lanterns: (see Figure 15).

> **Plasticity** is best achieved when the direction of light is at 45 degrees in plan and elevation along a diagonal drawn between the extreme corners of a cube
>
> (ibid.: 55)

The lights needed to be carefully focused so that transitions from one segment or cube to the next were not noticeable to the audience. These areas in turn needed to be complemented by frontal fill lighting to create an even and blended acting area light.

To achieve the maximum revelation of form, McCandless advocated that the lanterns should be coloured in complementary colours, warm from one side and cool from the other. In theory, this arrangement allows a variety of lighting states to be achieved, and both warm sunlight and cool moonlight can be created by balancing the intensity of each colour.

Once an even *visibility* was assured, the McCandless method addressed motivating sources ('a degree of *naturalism*'). Finally, light distribution on the scenery was required to provide 'the proper *compositional* quality to the picture, [which creates] that intangible dramatic essence called *mood*' (ibid.: 19, italics in the original).

The focus on lighting the scenery seems a little odd from our modern-day perspective but McCandless noted that

> Scenery, costumes and even makeup can be called secondary lighting instruments because light is not really visible until it strikes some surface so that it can be reflected to the eye.
>
> (ibid.: 16)

The McCandless approach is centred firmly on the text:

> The fundamental lighting of a production is outlined by the playwright's manuscript. The indications of place and the time of day, demanding specific details such as lamp-light, sunlight, moonlight, etc. (which are called motivating sources), are unconsciously or consciously dictated by the playwright.
>
> (ibid.: 17)

McCandless saw light as fulfilling a supporting role to the requirements of the production, invariably resulting in compromises and acknowledging that 'Lighting a production is, however, not an individual expression, but rather a co-ordinate part of the whole' (ibid.: 16).

The McCandless method did much to improve the overall quality of stage lighting, since it provided a standard technical solution for the staging conditions of the time. It was widely adopted and formed the basis of teaching lighting design, particularly in the United States, where courses in the universities were emerging that inspired the first generation of lighting designers. The method established itself as central to this training and McCandless' ideas remained the basis of much theatrical lighting practice until the latter part of the twentieth century, when technological developments in lamp, lantern and lighting control systems allowed the evolution of a more flexible approach to stage lighting.

Critics of McCandless argue that the method is formulaic and requires a relatively large number of circuits across the theatre, and can result in a characteristic look and style not always appropriate to the needs of the production. The designer Howard Bay was particularly vehement in his critique of the way in which the colour tints were still being used 40 years later, and he neatly summarises why there was dissatisfaction with the widespread adoption and continual dominance of the McCandless style:

> Divide the stage into a grid of twelve circular Areas, all neatly labeled [sic] with large numerals. The spot covering any given Area from one side must be in a warm color and its mate from the other side must be in a cool color [...]

The holes between the Areas must be plugged up with added units, it all ending in an arbitrary patchwork. The static, symmetrical inflexibility of the superimposed Area grid cannot accommodate the varying demands of assorted scripts. Why should an actor be blue when he faces left stage, pink when he faces right stage, and pied when he turns front?

(Bay, 1974: 135)

However, it is important to note that Bay was working with very different lighting equipment in the 1970s and his own proposed alternative approach reflected these technological developments and changing performance conditions (see below). The McCandless approach attempted to solve the practical difficulties of lighting the stage with the equipment available during a particular period in time, but Bay was right to question its dominance as the basis for professional practice and the teaching of lighting design.

Composition and Control

A key aspect of McCandless' thinking about the role of light in the theatre was the importance placed on the composition and control of the overall stage picture from the 'switchboard'. The control of light's 'intensity, distribution, colour and changes' (McCandless, 1958: 61) demanded increasing sophistication in plotting and pre-setting, especially as the ideal McCandless system meant that each lantern needed its own dimmer. The balancing of the individual intensities was recorded on a set-up (or 'pre-set') sheet which recorded the position of each switch together with a reading of the dimmer level for each scene. A separate cue sheet was then used to record the lighting changes that needed to be made during the performance. These notations marked any alterations to the main scenic states, and this process was key to the evolution of the design:

Giving form to all the visual elements on the stage is part of the procedure for a lighting rehearsal (arranged before the dress rehearsal), where everything except the actor should be present.

(ibid.: 61)

While the idea of the lighting plot undoubtedly pre-dates McCandless (certainly Reinhardt and Belasco were both using detailed written cue sheets), this formulation in print of the practice of presetting promoted a standardised way of working that was the basis of lighting control and operation until the computer-controlled lighting board had established itself as a reliable alternative to the paper plot.[3]

---

[3] Morgan (2005: 165–166) suggests that Peter Godfrey was probably the first to detail the procedures for plotting in his 1933 publication *Backstage*.

McCandless' concern with the way in which the lighting design was cre-ated, plotted and operated during performances ensured that his influence and legacy extended beyond his teaching and textbooks.

He is credited with influencing the design of the first all-electronic lighting control board, which marked a significant technological advance in theatre lighting practice. The 314-circuit, five-pre-set lighting control used the thyra-tron dimmer and allowed a new flexibility in both creating lighting states and in their operation. This sophisticated technology was manufactured by General Electric in 1933 and installed in the orchestra pit at New York's Radio City Music Hall.

The shift of location from the wings of the theatre to a front of house posi-tion marked an important departure from existing practices.[4] It recognised that the lighting operator needed to see the stage from the audience's per-spective and signalled the growing importance of the contribution of lighting to the production.

The potential of multiple electric lighting circuits and the growing sophis-tication of control afforded to the operator by the electrical 'switchboard' offered a new flexibility to lighting the stage. The complex shifts of light now possible throughout a performance created a detail and a fluidity which suggested that the aspirations of Appia might be achievable technically for the first time. The movement of light through a performance was becoming considered in the same terms as a musical score:

> Movement is possible with lighting to a limited degree. Abstractly, changes of light can be perceived more readily than changes in sound, but our knowledge of instruments and light, and our light sense, are not yet developed to the point of establishing lighting as an art form in the same terms as music.
>
> (McCandless, 1958: 63)

C. HAROLD RIDGE – *STAGE LIGHTING PRINCIPLES AND PRACTICE* (1936)

> Hitherto lighting was merely utilitarian; it was used solely to illuminate the actors on the stage. Nowadays, in addition to its essential uses as an illuminative, it is an intricate art in itself, and as yet we are only on the fringe of its vast potentialities. You cannot neglect it – [...] it is fundamental.
>
> (Herbert Prince's Introduction in Ridge and Aldred, 1936: xi)

---

[4] In 1924, Bel Geddes notes that the first FOH operator was observed in Reinhardt's production of *The Miracle* when it was staged in New York. Larson notes that the New York Paramount theatre in the early 1930s was the first to install a FOH lighting operator who was required to wear a tuxedo! (see Morgan, 2005: 127 fn). Also, before 1930 Hartmann at the Metropolitan Opera in New York had created a FOH operating position out of the audience's line of sight under the stage hood.

A direct contemporary of McCandless, **Harold Ridge** (1890–1957), has been considered by some to be UK's first specialist lighting designer (Reid, 2005: 21). In a short but key period he worked with Terence Gray (1895–1987) at the Festival Theatre in Cambridge and published several texts on stage lighting. A guide for the lighting of amateur and 'little' theatres in 1925 and his texts *Stage Lighting* (1928) and *Stage Lighting Principles and Practice* (1936) (with Aldred) were important milestones in explaining both the artistry and the practical techniques of contemporary lighting for the stage in the UK. Ridge's volumes contain a wide range of advice, from detailing the planning of whole lighting installations to precise technical instructions on how to construct a liquid dimmer. However, his approach to lighting the stage differs markedly from McCandless in its intent and, for this reason, it is necessary here to understand his practice.

As co-founder of the Festival Theatre, Ridge was responsible for the design of the lighting installation and the lighting designs for Gray's first season of productions in 1926–1927. This season was noted for the presentation of a new stagecraft, inspired by Craig and Appia and in direct opposition to the overt realism of contemporary producers such as Beerbohm Tree, which focused on the creation of theatrical illusion. The performances at the Festival Theatre were characterised by an experimental approach that drew on significant continental influences, such as Lugné-Poë, Jacques Copeau, Louis Jouvet at the Vieux Colombier theatre in Paris and Leopold Jessner's work with scenographer Emil Pircha at the Berlin Staatstheater.

A THEATRE OF LIGHT, COLOUR AND SPACE

Heavily influenced by both Appia and Craig's writings, Ridge and Gray removed the proscenium arch from the Georgian theatre building in Cambridge and added steps down into the auditorium to dissolve the physical barrier between performers and audience. In doing so they created the first modern open-stage theatre in Britain in which an expressive use of light and space would replace painted scenery. In radical contrast with other theatre spaces in the UK, Gray and Ridge did away with standard arrangements of borders and wings and instead used reflected light onto scenic surfaces to create impressions of sky and non-naturalistic atmospheres of spatial infinity.

To achieve the aim of a theatre of light and space, Ridge followed Reinhardt's example in altering the theatre and in 1926 installed a permanent cyclorama. This continental innovation became the key element of the Festival Theatre stage and was lit with a Schwabe lighting system which used glass filters in seven colours to fill the visible stage space with flexible and apparently shadow-free light. Mixing between these mechanically controlled instruments positioned on the lighting bridge above the stage allowed a sophisticated and subtle colour mixing, which became the dominant characteristic of Gray's productions.

Ridge's non-naturalistic approach to lighting the stage was centred on expression through colour:

> A few years ago there was a general belief that players could (or should) not perform in vividly coloured light. It is now realized that with the exception of one or two colours, such as green, the acting-area can be lit with any colour suitable to the spirit of the scene. In presentational productions the producer can proceed boldly and unhesitatingly, and his "motivating" light will be psychological.
>
> (Ridge and Aldred, 1936: 107)

although he also warned:

> I condemn the use of coloured light merely to gain a pretty effect. Coloured light should be used for two purposes:-
>
> (i) To represent the light of nature, and, or,
> (ii) To aid the atmosphere of a play.
>
> In both cases the light should be used to do away with painted scenery as far as possible.
>
> (Ridge, 1928: 77–78)

Ridge advocated a new role for light in the theatre and cited the influence of the hard, concentrated beams of white light which, when seen against a dark background in expressionistic performances, created such dramatic images (Ridge and Aldred, 1936: 105). Ridge embraced European lighting methods and equipment to implement the new aesthetic, and his bold compositions used contrasting coloured light to define abstract qualities of character and action and to focus attention on specific moments. In the 1926 production *The Eumenides*, for example, a collection of screens and boxes provided a sculptural setting against a dark blue cyclorama whilst a bright green light was used to suggest the throne. The main acting area was lit by violets, blues and greens, while the furies on the forestage were lit in a contrasting red.

Ridge's writing and practice demonstrated the potential to move beyond the naturalistic approach of 'motivating light' to performances where light might communicate on a deeper level and where there was 'a chance for the lighting to be subtly altered to assist what is felt rather than seen by the onlooker. This is verging upon purely psychological lighting...' (ibid.: 105).

Ridge provides an interesting summary in *Stage Lighting* of the five main sources of light that were available to the lighting designer in 1928:

1. LIME-LIGHT (Which he notes: 'has been superseded by the electric arc-lamp and gas filled lamp, but it is still very useful in the provinces where neither gas nor electricity are available.')

2. ARC-LAMPS. Are seen as a necessity in large auditoria and for all projected effects: 'They give a very intense light, but have many disadvantages' amongst which Ridge lists; the current consumption; the amount of flicker and the 'loud hissing noise, disturbing both audience and actors.'

3. GAS-FILLED LAMPS (half-watt lamps) which in comparison to the older vacuum lamps give a whiter light which 'approximates to daylight.' They provide 'more light for the same current consumption than the vacuum lamps' and are used in 'flood-lamps, spots and projectors'.

4. VACUUM LAMPS – the older and more fragile type of fitment: 'It is not possible to run the filament at so high a temperature as the gas-filled lamp, and consequently the light is more orange in colour. Where the lamps are visible to the eye this is an advantage.'

5. SPECIAL LAMPS – a catch-all category which covers all non-standard lamps: 'used for spot lights and projectors which are supplied with the apparatus'.

(Summary from Ridge, 1928: 5–7)

In establishing his own rationale and techniques for lighting the stage, Ridge acknowledges how his method differs from that of McCandless. Given the bold approach that placed the expressive use of light and space at the centre of Ridge's practice, it is perhaps surprising that the focus on the performer is seen as paramount and that 'No player should be lit from both sides at once by focused beams that are strong enough to throw double shadows' (Ridge and Aldred, 1936: 106).

Ridge's volume displays an ambition for the role of light that was in stark contrast to practice in the UK, which he regarded as mediocre:

Until stage directors and producers are trained in the technicalities of lighting, and until they can visualize what the effect of it will be, they will continue to pursue the safe, but uninspiring, course; they will use their battens and footlights to fill up the gaps between the important areas picked out by focus-lanterns, and to light the set.

(ibid.: 111)

Colour Mixing

Coloured light, as one might expect, is a significant focus of Ridge's writing and his 1936 publication reveals the methods, costs and practicalities of colour media at the time:

The production of coloured light by *selective reflection* is used in the Fortuny system. White light is directed on to an opaque surface of coloured silk, which reflects those components of similar colour and absorbs the others [...] whilst producing beautiful soft lighting tones, the loss of efficiency renders its use impossible on the large scale required for stage lighting when running costs have to be considered.

For smaller areas, it can be good, particularly for indirect footlights using coloured reflectors.

(Ridge and Aldred 1936: 87)

The most practical method, Ridge argues, is *selective transmission* through the use of transparent media such as gelatine coloured filters, but he notes that for 'any lantern using over 200 watts, glass is the only satisfactory medium' (1936: 90). Based on the Schwabe system which was used for the lighting of the cyclorama, coloured glass filters were the preferred method for all of the additive mixing effects that were characteristic of Gray and Ridge's productions in Cambridge.

Ridge was well acquainted with the coloured light trickery of the 'Samoiloff effect', which was introduced to London audiences in 1921 and named after the Russian émigré who made it famous in the 1922 Hippodrome revue *Round in Fifty*. This technique relied upon the use of saturated coloured light to create mysterious transformations of costume and setting through chromatic adaptation known as the Helson–Judd effect.[5]

Ridge strongly advocated the value of models in planning lighting – particularly in terms of the effect of colour on scenic items (ibid.: 111). The use of colour and the way in which lighting was operated were key concerns for him, as they were for Frederick Bentham. Ridge promoted a new way of controlling light through Bentham's Light Console (ibid.: 79) and dedicated the concluding chapter to the operation of lighting:

Is the lighting plot to be a purely mechanical affair or is the electrician to be treated as an artist and ranked as a performer? The Authors prefer the latter.

(Ridge and Aldred, 1936: 119–120)

ROLLO GILLESPIE WILLIAMS – *THE TECHNIQUE OF STAGE LIGHTING* (1947)

'Applied stage illumination is both a science and an art', **Rollo Gillespie Williams** (1903–1982) states in his Preface to his textbook on lighting practice. He worked for the Holophane company and had considerable experience in the design of colour-changing light effects which were in great demand in cinema auditoria. This expertise extended to surfaces, materials and paint effects upon which coloured light could be played. Colour is therefore a major focus of this text and, in addition to dealing with the equipment and tools of the time, a significant section of the book is concerned with 'The art of stage lighting' and how it is experienced:

---

[5] The tendency of lighter, achromatic surfaces to take on the hue of the light under which they are viewed. Darker achromatic surfaces tend to take on the complementary hue. Samoiloff was therefore able to use camouflage and paint techniques to transform scenery and costume through light changes alone. See Helson (1938: 439–476).

> Line, plane, mass, or volume, contour, texture, light and shade, and colour are the main elements of visual composition [...] perceived by the eye only as elements of light.
>
> (Williams, 1947: 117)

Williams offers a British equivalent of McCandless' practical techniques for the composition of stage lighting and concentrates on the variety of lighting directions:

> This procedure may be likened to constructing the first bones of a body (Dominant Lighting), then covering with flesh (Secondary Lighting), finally, adding charm to its appearance (Rim Lighting and Fill-in Lighting).
>
> (ibid.: 123)

Williams' four-stage process begins with the 'Dominant Lighting' to set the dramatic key to the scene (e.g. moonlight) through the choice of angle, colour and intensity. We know this as a directional or key light. The secondary lighting is complementary and provides a balance and counterpoint to the dominant light – moderating the extent of contrast and shadows from the dominant light – and equates to the McCandless acting area lighting. 'Rim-lighting' enhances the composition by providing backlight of a greater intensity to highlight the performer in an 'attractive "edge" effect' (ibid.: 127). 'Fill-in Lighting' represents soft, blending floodlighting to soften the shadows created by the 'Directional' and 'Secondary' lighting: 'The footlights are excellent for this purpose' (ibid.) but should be used at a low level since

> The art of stage lighting depends on the clever use of shadow and of contrasting areas of brightness and colour. There is all the difference in the world between controlled shadow and unwanted shadow.
>
> (ibid.: 128)

Williams also dedicates several chapters to exploring colour composition on the stage, focusing on 'the three great principles of harmony, contrasts and discord' (ibid.: 138). He explains how to achieve a variety of effects using Samoiloff-style colour change effects and observes that

> A new art of animated colour is now unfolding, and it is difficult to foresee the final effect it is likely to have on stage décor and presentation.
>
> (ibid.: 154)

FREDERICK BENTHAM – *STAGE LIGHTING* (1950) AND *THE ART OF STAGE LIGHTING* (1968)

Frederick Bentham (1911–2001) was undoubtedly one of the most important practitioners in the history of British stage lighting. As an employee of

both in his 1957 revised text and in the much-expanded *The Art of Stage Lighting* (1968), by which time computer-controlled lighting boards had evolved.

The 'Key to lighting is in the Control', Bentham notes (1950: 13), and he advocates the benefits of the Light Console – his own revolutionary innovation in lighting control based upon the keyboard of an organ (see p. 234). The Light Console offered a new subtlety in achieving complex lighting changes over existing stage switchboards, and Bentham uses this publication to promote its economic value, noting that nine switchboard operators had been replaced by one console operator operating the new installation at the London Coliseum. (ibid.: 14–15)

In emphasising the importance of the finished look of a lighting design, Bentham asks performers to be responsive and more aware of lighting since they

> are inclined to move their heads out of the glare of the spotlight. Consequently the body may be beautifully lit while the all-important face is not. Actors must be encouraged to seek the limelight for then, after some practice, we can be sure that even when a spotlight is accidentally knocked slightly out of position they will be able to make the best of the situation.
>
> (ibid.: 272)

It is important to note two other practical guides that were published in Britain in 1954: Percy Corry's *Lighting the Stage* by and Geoffrey Ost's *Stage Lighting*, which tapped into the growing interest in creating lighting for the stage at both professional and amateur level, at a time when the range and quality of equipment was beginning to improve. The introduction of the profile or 'ellipsoidal' spotlight allowed a more precise control of light from a distance away from the stage, and new approaches to the design of light reflected both changing staging conditions and opportunities afforded through modern technological developments. Bentham's 1968 volume *The Art of Stage Lighting* and its major revision of 1976 reflect the major technological changes that had occurred within the theatre industry. The content builds on the earlier book but represents a significant shift in the author's tone and approach. Reading less like a marketing opportunity for Strand (although still foregrounding this manufacturer's equipment), these volumes provide a comprehensive and well-illustrated overview of modern stage lighting and its techniques. The change in title is significant since it represents a shift away from detailing equipment to a more comprehensive account of professional lighting processes and procedures, drawing upon extensive contemporary professional experience. For many in Britain this textbook became the most important educational guide to theatre lighting equipment and practice, whilst in the USA the work of Jean Rosenthal offered an alternative inspiration to a generation of lighting professionals.

JEAN ROSENTHAL – *THE MAGIC OF LIGHT* (1972)

Jean Rosenthal (1912–1969) was the first commercial designer in the USA to concentrate solely on lighting for the stage (Palmer, 1985: 1), and her work and writing has been a significant inspiration to many lighting designers, especially in North America.[6] Her book, which is a combination of autobiography and inspirational advice on how to approach lighting performance, was drafted in the late 1960s and published posthumously. From 1939 she worked closely with Martha Graham and is therefore credited as the creator of contemporary dance lighting.

This section from Chapter 5 of *The Magic of Light* focuses on the lighting designer's process and thinking. It underpins Rosenthal's philosophy on lighting for the stage and represents perhaps the best example of a manifesto for lighting in the latter half of the twentieth century. In contrast to most previous publications that concentrated overwhelmingly on the technical processes involved in lighting design, Rosenthal's book focuses on the artistry of light. This section explains her own creative process from the initial design idea to final realisation on stage. Her feelings and experiences through the fit-up, focusing and the lighting session will strike a familiar chord with those who have experienced the uncertainties and pressures of this environment in which the lighting designer suddenly has to perform. There are some clear parallels here with the thoughts of contemporary designers, such as Fisher (see Chapter 12).

It is interesting to note both the care and the detail that Rosenthal takes to establish the precise nature of the contribution of light to a performance, as well as the perceived hierarchies within the creative team at this period of time. It should be remembered that she was working prior to the introduction of computer-based lighting control boards, which enabled slow and complex changes of light to be realised relatively easily. The importance of the need to ensure that the technical crew are working with you, towards the same artistic goals, underpins the final section here and is also emphasised in the excerpt on collaboration.

Lighting the Play (Rosenthal and Wertenbaker, 1972: 59–64)

> YOU begin by holding a play in your hand. [...] Even if the play is a classic with which I am thoroughly familiar, it becomes a new play for me. I am older than I was, things have happened, the world has changed, and I shall be working with certain people.

> Let us assume, for the purpose of considering the lighting of plays, a single production under a standard set of circumstances.

> You know that the dramatic theatre is a system of communication. Its enormous ability to communicate on many levels has three major elements [...]

---

[6] Because it has been out of print it is less well known in the UK.

- The playwright, who is anxious to communicate what he has to say as he sees it
- The director, who has chosen this play and who is theoretically responsible – *in toto*- for the results
- Us others, who will place the communication on the stage: actors and designers, all of whom are helpless without stage crews, carpenters, electricians.

[...]

The lighting designer does best, I think, to begin with the play – any play – by forgetting the technical aspects which are his responsibility. Otherwise, his lighting ideas are apt to be, as they once were, purely for illumination. Read it as a whole; read quickly, all at once, without care for details: If it is a familiar play, try to read it as if for the first time. Look for the "central image" – the "flash" Professor A. Deal talked about years ago at Yale. If and when it comes, hang on to it and never lose it. It will be your constant guidepost all along the way for what lighting can do within its vital function, which is to fulfill the need of all drama for unhurried concentration and full communication.

Light provides important shortcuts to comprehension. It can instantly establish time of day and cover lapses of time. It accents or establishes place and change of place. And light may also uncover and elaborate undercurrents which there is no time to expose in words; or it can express what cannot be expressed in action or revealed by the actors – the unspoken and the taken for granted. In the conflicts of the drama the final and most important role of lighting is to expose the nature of the struggle, to set the atmosphere for its development, and to underscore its resolution.

But first you must have the "flash", the image, the central thread, the idea [...] You keep this central image clear but fluid. Add in no details at this time. You are obligated first to share this image with the director, your superior authority.

By the time you talk to him, you should have plowed through the script many more times, as many as it requires for understanding it (for *hearing* it). You must have enough background to understand what the director has to say, have a language ready with which to respond to his thoughts and concepts. The theatre is a very autocratic place and can only function autocratically. Within the matrix of collaboration the clear line of authority is based on the degree of responsibility. At the present time the director is responsible and in charge. Even if you have done many more plays than has the director you are working for, which you may well have, you are obliged by the courtesies of relative authority to go to him first without prejudice in your own favor. And to *listen* to him, rather than help him. You do not proffer your ideas at this time. You listen and hear what he has to say.

People are quite curious about listening and often hear only what they want to hear, what suits them [...] For collaboration you need a much greater willingness to hear – not in order to agree, but in order that all ideas may go into one pot and be blended into one whole. There is great pleasure in this.

When you have listened to the director, you find to your astonishment that he does not want to do the play as you have seen it. You do not say anything yet – you just listen.

Next, you see your real friend, the set designer. You are again committed to greater authority. This probably came about because scene design was an entity before lighting design was, but there is less of an authoritative gap than there used to be. In recent years lighting is being used more and more as scenery or instead of scenery or to make minimal scenery possible. You may find that the set designer – who has presumably gone through the same process you have – agrees neither with the director nor with you. He may think the show should be very abstract, for instance, while the director visualizes it realistically. Take it easy. It usually proves to be all a matter of degree. Later you can take the director's realism and the designer's abstraction and relate them to your own image.

If all of you think the play means the same thing, it will begin to come together. Now you take your ideas back to the director and back to the scene designer and say how you see it. Three people can be honest, honorable and truthful and still be part of a unit, which let us assume for the sake of the play they are. If so, you quickly reach the satisfactory point where you can start really doing your part. You become specific, a specific person.

Before I continue with this happy theory, I must admit that a lighting designer leads a most curious life. For one thing he, unlike a scene designer, rarely can draw very well. Besides, it is hard to draw light – I have tried – as well as difficult to describe something as intangible as air. References to paintings help, not because the lighting is supposed to look like Rembrandt or Constable or Hals, but as clues to atmosphere, color, and the kind of focus the director and you have in mind. The common vocabulary which has grown up for communicating about light – those useful terms such as quality of light, pattern, color washes, downlight and backlight, do help us all.

To the area of agreement you should have reached at this point with your "bosses" you set up the boundaries within which you must work.

Boundary 1 is the degree of reality the director wants to suggest.

Boundary 2 is the placement of important scenes within the set.

Boundary 3 is the restrictions under which the performance will take place: what theatre or theatres it will be in, whether the play will have a long tryout run out of town or will open in New York, and what commercial standards it is expected to meet. Economic restrictions must be respected without slighting the aesthetic respect you pay the script.

You then go back to the play. You study it, examining its surface over and over until it is as familiar as a road you drive daily or the blocks you walk to work. You look for images to print as the frames of a cinema are printed, looking for them within your own habits, relating them to your lifetime store of images.

I was lucky enough to be born with visual recall, retaining images rather than words. When anyone talks to me, I see what they say rather than taking it in on the verbal level. My memory bank is in pictures, but before printing, as it were, the ones that apply to *this* play I remind myself of the distinction Georgine Oeri, the art critic, makes when she looks at painting or sculpture.

'Is it an *image* or an *arrangement*?' she asks herself.

An *image*, unlike an arrangement, however effective, has an organic base. For the stage, an *image* blends into the beauty of the whole, contributing to communication.

By now you are living in the familiar terrain of the play, immersed in its implications and in what lies beneath the surface of stage directions, action and dialogue. You identify with the characters in time, place and situation, with their humor, uproar, conflict or tragedies. The look of the play, the scenes, the places, colored by the emotional intentions of the author, becomes clearly visible. At this point your mind begins to organize the use of light into specific shapes.

Light *has* shape – dimension, edges, entity and quality. When I start to develop a light plot – my parallel shadow-script – I think with the tools of my trade. There are many of them and they will do a marvelous variety of things. I no longer have to ask myself what a lekolite or a fresnel [. . .] can do. I know as a matter of habit, at forty feet, at sixty, focused from flood to sharp. It is important that a new lighting designer learn [sic] to know his tools so that he can think easily, without translating, in terms of equipment. If you play with light, are ignorant about it, you are likely to make arrangements rather than create images. Using harsh colors and moving light so fast that you take the eyes of the audience off the actors distract from the whole and may become the style of the production. If it is unsuitable, as it usually is, the result is disastrous.

I have been called "modest" because I insist on lighting unobtrusively, but it is not from modesty. A play's lighting is most successful when it achieves its purposes without obtruding, without adding its demand for the audience's attention to the other demands for attention, when the audience is unconscious of it, when it is at once seen and not seen.

You, the lighting designer, are ready now to listen to the words you already know by heart read by the actors, probably, under stark work light on the stage of that echoing, lonely barn which is any theatre without an audience. You will be lighting, as well as their bodies and faces, the voices of the actors. Proper light is also to hear by.

Since it takes two or three weeks to process and prepare the equipment for installation in the theatre, you are now pressed to plan your layouts and hookups, supply the plots for their exact placement, and specify the kinds of light you need to achieve your patterns and your colors. This work is detailed and demanding, and must be accurately completed before you turn over the mechanics to the electrician. It then becomes the electrician's responsibility to check all your equipment through the shop, to estimate cable lengths, to take over effects [. . .] Should there be a projected effect, he shepherds it through the shop to the balcony or bridge from which it works.

If, while all this is going on, there is mutual understanding between designer and technician, the team makes for the extra magic of performance conjured by the particular respect that keeps each job as cleanly independent as it is interdependent. I remember well when electricians wanted to murder me for using so much slow indiscernible movement of light within scenes, but when they saw what happened they liked it and often were proud of it.

The lighting designer continues to watch rehearsals. You begin to diagram the movements of the actors, continuing all the while to absorb the play. Like music, it yields more and more with each hearing. Light, above all, has the capacity to tie together disjointed moments so that they accumulate into a lasting and significant impression; you are now working out how to manage this sort of unification.

When the lights are hung and the scenery is ready, the time of focusing comes for you. This would seem to be no more than pointing lights where you want them to shine, and the hours it takes are consistently maligned while everyone else clamors for the stage. In fact, focusing is the heart of the mechanical installation of the show. With present-day equipment light can be controlled and shaped into forms and patterns that convey the dramatic intention. Molding light in this way is the hidden part of focusing, with hardly anyone except the designer and the electrician aware of it.

Some shows are easy to focus because they play on an open stage. Musicals I have worked on, like *West Side Story* and *Redhead*, although heavy electrically can be focused much more quickly than dramas like *Winesburg, Ohio* or *Becket*, where as much time is spent in getting to the lights as in focusing them. We use the term 'jockeying' to describe what goes on when stagehands maneuver a thirty- to forty-foot 'A' ladder with a six- or seven-foot base in and around the units that make up the set.

The first time you focus a show is the thorniest, because this is the moment when theory, ideas, thought and pencil lines become patterns of light – reality on the stage. It is the outcome of all that has gone before, the months of reading, think-ing and talking about paintings and degrees of reality and all the rest of it. I have learned to keep a scrupulous record on legal-size paper with columns headed *Circuits*, *Color* and *Focus*, and in that last one I leave room for minute notations of the lens focus (flood to sharp) and the position of the shutters if the lights are ellipsoidal, and the locations of the hot spot in every case. To increase accuracy, designers have devised a grid scheme to subdivide the stage so the area focused on always remains the same. If the focusing is clean, you have done half your lighting.

During the final days of rehearsal, when at the beginning and end of each work-ing day the play is taken through from start to finish without breaks, the lighting designer works out the cues for the various operations of the lights. Some cues are mechanical: fadeouts and blackouts that mark the ends of scenes, presets, fixtures turned on and off, shades lifted so sun streams through windows, and so on. Others are spaced through scenes to reflect the ideas and emotions contained in the scene, which is usually best done by moving light so imperceptibly that the viewer is unaware of any change. These are the ones that try the patience of the electricians, who must take the long, slow counts.

With focusing and cue placements finished, lighting rehearsal begins. These ses-sions are without doubt the most public exhibitions of creative thinking in the world. There you sit in a dark auditorium, usually with the set designer and director as well as those assorted people who are always somehow there. At this time the theoretical design is stated in intensities. It is the time when, if one has absorbed and analyzed the play truly, the ideas and impressions that could not be articulated practitioners and helped this publication to become *the* essential lighting reference book.

When the writing was updated in 1997 and incorporated within a considerably expanded publication entitled *The Art of Stage Lighting – The Art, The Craft, The Life*, the first section was dedicated entirely to 'Design' and 'How to Do It' and it incorporated the Pilbrow methodology espoused in 1970. An overview of the history of stage lighting was included and a new section entitled 'The Life' was devoted to exploring the experience of the lighting designer through accounts of Pilbrow's own career and significant interviews with 14 contemporary lighting designers. 'Mechanics' – the final section of the book – again provided the valuable technical data sheets of the original, updated and expanded to incorporate the many technological developments that had taken place in the intervening period – not least that of lighting software, control and the advent of the 'intelligent' moving light.

ALTERNATIVE APPROACHES

Building on Rosenthal's assertion that performers should appear 'jewel-like', scenographer **Howard Bay** (1912–86) proposed an alternative method of lighting the stage which he termed 'Jewel lighting' and involved lighting the actor from as many positions and angles as possible. Colour and intensity were then adjusted to fill in any shadows and to create an effect of brilliance – as if lighting a diamond in a shop window display. It solved the problems of the paucity of front of house lighting positions in most Broadway theatres by using high-wattage lanterns to create a 'lucid pattern of paths of strong backlight, paths of strong side-light, the necessary fill illumination from the front, plus specials as needed' (Bay,1974: 136).

Similarly the development of the modern thrust and arena stages had required new approaches to lighting the actor. This had not been understood in the design for the Festival Theatre in Chichester, for example, where useable lighting positions had not been provided.[7] Director **Stephen Joseph** (1921–67) also felt the need to advocate alternative methods for lighting the island stage, for which he was a pioneer. 'Stage Lighting for Theatre in the Round' was first published as an article in Strand Electric's *Tabs* magazine[8] and became a dedicated chapter in his seminal *Theatre in the Round* (1967).

STAGE LIGHTING PUBLICATIONS AROUND THE MILLENNIUM

As the interest in stage lighting practice and the number of educational courses in technical theatre has increased, numerous books have been published on the subject in the recent past. Valuable contributions to the field

[7] See Pilbrow (1997: 259–262).
[8] *Tabs* vol. 22/3, September 1964: 25.

include texts by Francis Reid, Nigel Morgan and Nick Moran in Britain, Max Keller in Germany, and Willard Bellman, Michael Gillette and Linda Essig in North America. There are two volumes, however, that are worth commenting on in more detail as they offer unique approaches to other publications in the field.

RICHARD H. PALMER – *THE LIGHTING ART – THE AESTHETICS OF STAGE LIGHTING DESIGN* (1985) (1994, 2ND EDITION)

Palmer notes in his Preface that 'In stage lighting, aesthetic sensibility seems harder to learn than technology' (1994: xv) and, in addressing this issue, his book has become the most important contribution to lighting education in

Figure 17 An example of Svoboda's contralighting for *Oedipus*, Prague, 1963

As the earliest lighting operators, candlesnuffers were a constant presence in the auditorium throughout each performance. Fitzgerald reminds us that their task was not regarded highly: 'the favourite comparison of depreciation was "not fit to be a candlesnuffer", though it was possible to excel or be deficient even in this humble walk' (Fitzgerald, 1881: 17). In some theatres the scenic artists performed the task perhaps as a natural consequence of their vested interest in ensuring the scene was sufficiently illuminated so that their handiwork could be appreciated fully. Larger theatres had at least two candlesnuffers, with one taking responsibility for the house candles and a separate snuffer for the lights on and around the stage. Indeed the act of lighting the footlights along the front of the stage was often the signal to the audience that the performance was about to begin.

During the performance itself, candlesnuffers were an integral and very visible aspect of the play-going experience, and they needed to attend to each individual light source regardless of the dramatic action on stage. Without this constant attention, the candles would go out:

> When the stagelights began to flare or flicker out, the gods commonly set up a cry of 'Snuffers! Snuffers!' forseeing a happy opportunity of indulging in some facetiousness at that worthy's expense – badinage, however, which, as he went about his work, was generally received by him with the utmost aplomb.
>
> (Lawrence, 1935: 130)

THE ADVENT OF THE LIGHTING TECHNICIAN

As candle and oil lamps began to be replaced by gas technology (beginning around 1816), the role of the lighting operator changed dramatically. The advent of the gas table, or *jeu d'orgue*, meant that for the first time all of the lighting of the stage was possible under the central control of a single operator.

However, in addition to the operators of the levers and gas taps that controlled circuits or banks of gas-lights, lighting technicians were also required at the side of the stage for changing silks and gelatines, and operating movable light sources such as standards or bunch-lights. Furthermore, specialist technicians were employed to operate the limelight and carbon-arc follow-spots and these roles as 'follow-spot operator' remain today as regular members of the theatre's technical team.

The gasman's duties involved the precarious lighting of the main chandelier suspended above the orchestra pit, through the use of a long pole with one end soaked in flammable liquid and known as a spirit torch. The chandelier's initial illumination was then followed by all of the other fittings around the stage. The American actor Otis Skinner recounted the practice he observed in 1878:

when the gas man had lighted all the 'borders' at seven-thirty p.m. with torch and
long pole, and his 'floats' in front of the curtain, and turned them 'down to the
blue' all illumination was ready, except for the calcium lights of blended gas from
the red and black cylinders.

(Skinner, 1924: 59)

With the advent of the brighter light of the gas fixtures, the lighting technician suddenly had the potential to sabotage any subtleties inherent in the
stage picture by over-lighting the scene. A report on American theatre practice in 1880 highlights this issue and the need for the levels of light to be set
carefully:

The 'gas-man' of a theatre is the [scenic] artist's mainstay. It lies in his power to
ruin the finest scene that was ever painted. Ground lights turned too high upon
a moonlight scene, calciums with glass not properly tinted, or the shadow of a
straight-edged border-drop thrown across a delicate sky – all those things are
ruin to an artist's most careful work. The proper lighting of a scene is therefore
a matter that requires the most careful study. The artist sits in the centre of the
auditorium and minutely observes every nook and corner of his scene under the
glare of gas. Here a light is turned up and there one is lowered until the proper
effect is secured. The gas-man takes careful note of his directions, and the stage
manager oversees everything.

(*New York Tribune* 27 December 1880)

Henry Irving also championed the specialist skills and detail of care required
to light a production and, in describing the production techniques of a play
for the American Journal *The Spirit of the Times*, suggested that technical operators needed to learn their cues in a similar way to the onstage performers:

The lighting of the scenes is a special department, for on this depends, in a great
measure, the picturesqueness of the play. The change from night to morning,
or from daylight to darkness, is often an essential element of the illusion. The
resources of various systems of lighting has to be in a measure experimental, so
as to benefit by accidental combinations, the labour of lighting an elaborate play
can be guessed at [. . .] The flyman may be said to carry some of the destiny of
the performance in the hollow of his hand, for the movement of a wrong rope, or
neglect to move the right one, might derange the whole performance. Scarcely
less onerous is the duty of the gasmen, who control all the gas above, below, and
around the stage, and who regulate the lights in the auditorium according to the
tone of the scene; while each of the lime-lights, placed in an almost inaccessible
position, requires the attendance of a skilled subordinate who must keep clearly
in his head all the various effects of light to be produced at the right time.

(cited in Richards, 1994: 114)

Lighting, in theory at least, could be controlled by one person, although
there were still practical issues when complex shifts of light were required.
The operation of the gas table from the wings was also problematic as the

view from the side of the stage was significantly different from that of the audience. Operators therefore began to follow and rely upon sequences of cues recorded on paper in order to reproduce the correct lighting on stage. The increasingly ambitious sequences and effects required a formalisation of nomenclature. Shorthand abbreviations for frequent states and actions, such as DBO and FUF, marked the extremes of 'dead blackout' and 'full-up finish', for example. More detailed and precise shifts of light were recorded in a series of lighting cues, and these notations created formal light plots enabling the operator to recreate the design accurately for each performance (see Appendix).

At the Lyceum in London, Irving's investment in gas lighting technology and the centralisation of the control had a far-reaching practical and aesthetic impact on performance practice. As we have already noted, the overall control of illumination and levels of darkness both within the auditorium and on the stage became a key innovation in Irving's work.

The technological innovations of the gas table required a reappraisal of where the operator should be located. At the New York Metropolitan, Kliegl relocated their control system and for the first time the operator was placed under the stage, below the footlights alongside the musical director. The New Theatre (Century) in New York followed suit, but the technological advancement did not necessarily result in better lighting:

> The illumination of the stage was the direct system under perfect control of an operator located under the stage. [However] The combined use of all the illumination provided did not light the scenes and characters properly.
>
> (Hagen, C.L. in Grau, 1912: xxiv)

Sophisticated lighting effects could be achieved by a team of lighting technicians working together and rehearsed carefully (see Fuller, pp. 151–153). Irving was the acknowledged master of gas lighting and rehearsed a small army of technical operators to achieve his staging effects (see Stoker, p. 196). He plotted his lighting late at night after the play of the evening was over and continued technical experimentation into the early morning, working with the technicians to refine each lighting state and dramatic moment. This was exceptional practice, however, and the coordination of technical operators was a major challenge to the artistry of light on the stage. Reid notes that in contrast to the innovations by directors such as Irving and Beerbohm Tree, lighting at the turn of the twentieth century was still rather limited:

> The average lighting standard in the great bulk of theatre was [...] frequently rough. Most theatre was, after all, based on weekly touring, and light control was based on the integrated operations of a local theatre crew of casual employees who had other occupations by day. They faced every Monday night as a first night without rehearsals and without the benefit of the modern communication system by which such crews can now be talked through a performance.
>
> (Reid, 2005: 19)

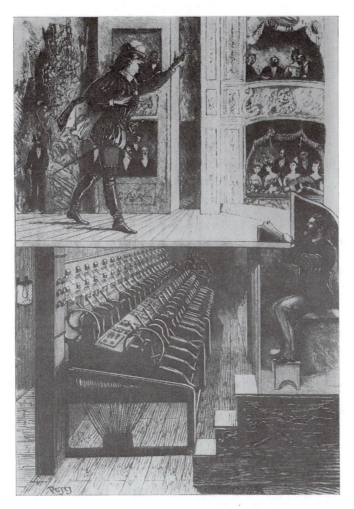

Figure 18 Early electric switchboard under the stage of the Paris Opéra, *L'Illustration*, 1887

The arrival of electricity led to the advent of similar control systems for lighting that were no less unwieldy than the gas tables but allowed a more sophisticated control of levels of light and the possibility of a new lighting dramaturgy:

Electricity with its wide adaptability lends itself to forms of portrayal totally new in their variety and beauty. Through this medium have been evolved many of the elaborate and complicated displays which characterize numerous modern productions, with their wide diversity of effects obtained, rapid changes of settings and furnishings, and vivid depiction brought out by swiftly changing color schemes. With a simplicity that hides the intricacy of mechanical detail, natural phenomena are simulated in the reproduction of scenery, sound and light by means of electrical apparatus with a remarkable accuracy of form, color and motion, illusion of relief, and verisimilitude. American Electric Art, if it may be so termed, is surely exemplified in its highest development as the servant of the Drama.

(Grau, 1912: 344–345)

Grau acknowledges the role of scientific and engineering experiments by companies such as the General Electric Company, which had been a catalyst to the transformation in US theatre during the first years of the twentieth century, but this technological development also relied upon the technician's ability:

The make or break of a scene often depends on the distribution of the stage lighting. [...] Usually they [electric lights] have independent control at the switchboard, so that any angle of the stage may be instantly lighted or obscured. Often the scenic value of many of the best plays is so enhanced by the skillful manipulation of such lights that the striking effects secured play no small part in meriting the enthusiastic approval of the public and the critics.

(ibid.: 345–346)

The control of electric light was not quite as straightforward as Grau suggests. Complex changes of light were still problematic and required extensive rehearsal, but new possibilities for the manipulation of light in the theatre were beginning to emerge, facilitated through new control technology and a new stagecraft. Ivor Brown's experience of Basil Dean's 1939 production of *Johnson over Jordan*[1] prompted him to 'imagine plays in which the "lighting plot" may be as important as the verbal plot' (cited in Rebellato, 1999: 72).

THE OPERATOR AND THE LIGHTING PLOT

The American director **David Belasco** (1853–1931) built a reputation upon the visual quality of his settings, which introduced a new form of naturalism to the stage. His chief lighting engineer, Louis Hartmann, records the practical efforts that Belasco made in order to achieve the lighting that he envisaged. Belasco's practice is reminiscent of Irving, and many of the techniques and plotting methods that were employed had been developed directly from the techniques of gas control.

---

[1] This production at London's New Theatre and subsequent transfer to the Saville was influenced by Craig and lit by Craig's son, Edward Carrick. It employed lanterns specifically designed by Louis Hartmann and manufactured especially for the production by Strand.

Belasco's last production, *Mima* (1928), was the epitome of his craft and was acknowledged for the ingenuity and complexity of the lighting. Hartmann records that the light plot for the play consisted of 50 typewritten pages, comprising the general light plot that gave an overview for each act, a detailed working lighting plot (cue sheets for the board operator), front spotlight cue sheets and a separate plot for the house switchboard (see Appendix for examples). Forty-two dimmers were used in total:

> ranging in capacity from one thousand to five thousand watts. Yet, even with this number of controls, we had to switch dimmers to other circuits during the action of the play. If they had been connected to all the circuits permanently, there would not have been room enough on the stage for the switchboards. As it was, they took up half of one side of the stage.
>
> (Hartmann, 1930: 65–66)

Three men were kept busy operating the switchboard whilst a host of other operators also controlled the follow-spots and lights on lamp stands situated offstage in the wings.

The dedication of such a significant portion of the wing space to lighting instruments and control apparatus underlines Belasco's understanding of the importance of light in creating verisimilitude. It also suggests that a key shift was taking place, where the domination of actors over offstage space was being challenged. The importance of the contribution of the technical staff, coupled with the physical need for space for the equipment, denotes a crucial historical moment where the whole feeling – the phenomenology of ownership of theatre space – was fundamentally altered.

The importance of the lighting operator and their location within the theatre space became an ongoing issue as technological developments in the middle of the twentieth century led to the separation of the bulky electrical dimming equipment from the control board itself. This important advance meant that the operation of the lighting could, for the first time, be undertaken at a distance and remotely from the electrical apparatus that physically controlled the levels of light of each lantern. Newer control boards replaced systems such as the Grand Master that had occupied substantial parts of the wing space in theatres. Lighting controls could now be situated within the auditorium, in side boxes or located in specially constructed control rooms at the rear of the house that allowed a view of the stage which was consistent with that of the audience. Although operators were still following detailed cue sheets, with a clear line of sight there was now the potential for them to exert some autonomy and to respond to changing circumstances in performance with greater confidence.

The developments in control technology led to a reappraisal of the role of the operator:

It is necessary for the lighting installation, even if assembled for a particular production only, to form an instrument under the control of one man. [sic] This man
should be an artist and not necessarily the electrician, in the same way that the
scene designer is not the stage carpenter.

(Bentham in Applebee, 1946: 563)

Bentham's significant contribution to this debate is outlined below, but
Rebellato argues persuasively that Bentham's new control mechanism, the
Light Console, offered radical possibilities both for the role of the operator
and for the contribution of light to performance:

The Light Console existed at the crux of a complex negotiation of power between
writers, designers, directors and lighting technicians. [. . .] Crucially the conception
of this operating system seems to entail the lighting designer's autonomy from the
director and the writer. It even opens up the possibility that lighting itself may one
day 'play the principal role in the theatre'.

(Rebellato 1999: 92)

Nick Hunt, a British lighting designer, educator and researcher, is concerned
with the methodologies inherent in the operation of lighting for performance.
In this essay he explores the contemporary position of the lighting operator in
relation to the historical development of the lighting control board in Britain,
drawing particularly on the theories of the technologist, lighting practitioner
and writer **Frederick Bentham** (1911–2001). This essay provides an account
of the issues inherent in operating lighting in performance with early electrical systems. It charts the key technological developments of the period and
explores Bentham's proposal for the operator to 'play' light in performance
in the same way as a musician plays an instrument.

THE VIRTUOSITY OF THE LIGHTING ARTIST – DESIGNER OR PERFORMER?[2]

Visit the lighting control room of a theatre during a performance, and watch the
lighting operator at work: what you will mostly see is the operator responding to
cues called by a stage manager over the headset intercom by pressing the lighting
console's 'go' button, before the operator returns her or his attention to book,
magazine, television or – more recently – computer game or social networking
website.

Compared with other performance personnel such as actors, musicians and stage
managers, the contemporary theatre lighting operator gives little attention to the

---

[2] This essay draws on research towards Hunt's doctoral thesis, 'Repositioning the Role of the
Lighting Artist in Live Theatre Performance', which seeks to establish a basis for the theatre
lighting artist as a performer through both theory and practice.

activity of the stage or the audience's experience of it. However, it has not always been so.

In order to understand how we have arrived at the present role of the lighting operator, we must trace the history of theatre lighting in terms of three interwoven threads: the thread of advancing lighting control technologies, that have both limited but also suggested ways that lighting on stage can be controlled; the thread of the developing roles of lighting operator and lighting designer, and their respective areas of responsibility; and the thread of the changing lighting process, both during preparation and rehearsal, and during performance. Whilst considering these historical threads, we should also remember that the aims and ambitions for stage lighting on the part of directors[3], lighting professionals, audiences and others have also changed over time, and provide a dynamic context against which a history of lighting operation must be seen.

A Radical Proposal: Fred Bentham's Light Console
Frederick Bentham, widely known in the lighting industry during his lifetime simply as 'Fred', was born in 1911, and in 1932 began working for Strand Electric (later Rank Strand Electric and then Strand Lighting), the company that was the dominant manufacturer of stage lighting equipment in the UK from the 1930s until the 1970s. Soon after joining Strand until his retirement in 1973 some four decades later, Bentham was a significant influence on the development of stage lighting technology in the UK as well as (to a lesser extent) internationally, and this influence was perhaps strongest in the area of lighting control. When Bentham joined Strand, the dimmers in use in the UK to control the intensity of the stage lighting were essentially mechanical affairs, controlled from levers or wheels and mechanically linked to each other in order to provide 'mastering' for the control of several dimmers at once – for example to achieve a general fade of the stage lighting. In the early 1930s the most sophisticated control system produced by Strand Electric was the 'Grand Master', named for its facility to lock any combinations of dimmers onto a single master wheel using a series of shafts, chain drives and clutches.

The Grand Master was so large and heavy that it had to be positioned backstage, typically on a 'perch' position above one of the wings. For lighting of any complexity, several operators were required, who could see little – if anything – of the stage itself from their control position. A well-practiced team of operators could reproduce with some accuracy a lighting plot given to them, synchronised to the performance by cues from the stage manager; however, this was a process of rote reproduction, since the operators had no way of seeing the effect of the lighting or its relationship with the other activities of the stage. There was therefore no expectation that the lighting operator(s) would take responsibility for the artistic contribution of the lighting to the audience's experience of the performance. To the extent that the operators of a Grand Master or similar controls might be said

---

[3] In the early part of the period that I am considering (the 1930s to the present day), the role that we now refer to as the *director* was more often known as the *producer*; however, for the sake of clarity I use the term *director* throughout.

to exhibit *virtuosity*,[4] that virtuosity was one of procedural technique, the quality of which could be measured precisely in terms of the accuracy of replay of the director's lighting plot.[5] There was no opportunity for the lighting operator to make a creative contribution to the making of the performance, and – with some notable exceptions – little interest on the part of directors and other theatre creatives in them doing so. Looking back to the early 1930s, Bentham wrote that 'Good and complicated lighting was done in those days, but only by using several operators both on the house board and the supplementary portables. Personally I have never held Grand Master controls in anything but contempt as a contribution to lighting and, in consequence, as soon as I became active in this field, set about providing an alternative' (Bentham 1976: 50). Within three years of starting work at Strand, Bentham had created his alternative lighting control: the Light Console.

The Light Console was in two key respects a radical departure from the lighting controls of the time. Firstly it separated the control interface from the dimmers themselves, freeing the design of the interface from the constraints of the mechanical dimmers. The Light Console achieved this separation by exploiting the electro-magnetic clutch (invented by Moss Mansell in 1929 but largely neglected until taken up by Bentham), linking controls to dimmers with an *electrical* connection, rather than the previous mechanical rods or tracker wires. The ability to separate the interface from the dimmers meant that the control interface and hence the operator could be placed front-of-house where they could see the activity of the stage and (potentially) take a creative part in its making. The second respect in which the Light Console was a radical departure from the control systems of the time was – to adopt a term Bentham used repeatedly – the Light Console's 'playability'. Bentham adopted cinema organ technology as the basis for the Light Console, for a combination of pragmatic and philosophical reasons. Pragmatically, cinema organ technology had received considerable investment and development during the cinema building boom of the 1920s and 30s, and provided a ready made control interface and sophisticated control logic based on relays that would have been prohibitively expensive and time consuming to develop from scratch. Philosophically, Bentham was drawn to the organ console for its *instrumental* rather than *engineering* approach (Ibid.): he wished to be able to *play* light as a musician plays music. Bentham had, since childhood, constructed a series of large model theatres complete with lighting installations, and had a passion for what he termed 'colour music' – a lighting performance to accompany recorded music. While the Light Console was ostensibly developed as Strand's premier theatre lighting control, its creation and design were driven largely by Bentham's desire to play colour music; all stage lighting was brought under the control of a single, comfortably seated operator, who could select any light or combination of lights for immediate control. Whilst it was still *de rigueur* for

---

[4] Not all lighting operators of the period were professionals in the sense we would mean today; stage crew – including lighting operators – were often employed on a casual basis, and they would typically have non-theatre jobs during the day. Michael Northen (1997: 51) relates that in the 1940s the stage crew at the New Theatre in Hull were mostly firemen from the adjacent fire station, and prioritised emergency call-outs over theatre performances.

[5] The director was responsible for lighting productions; the role of lighting designer, as a named professional specialism, did not begin to appear until the 1950s.

theatrical performances to work out the lighting plot on the console in advance of the performance (as with the Grand Master), the Light Console also made it possible for a practiced operator working with a known lighting rig to improvise lighting *in the moment* in response to stage action or – in the case of Bentham's colour music – to music. The Light Console was the first theatre lighting control to offer such *playability*, and it proposed a virtuosity of the lighting operator that was of a different order to that implied by the Grand Master.

The innovations of playability, and the significant change to the positioning of the operator, came about because of Bentham's central proposal: that lighting should be performed or played in the way that a musician plays music. From this insight sprang Bentham's choice of the cinema organ as the preferred technology platform. When this innovation was coupled with his insistence that the lighting control should be placed front-of-house so that the stage could be seen clearly, the technological barriers to the lighting operator taking a creative role in the making of the performance had been removed.

A Rival Proposal: The Preset Electronic

The Light Console had little immediate impact on the professional practices of the time; the first console made was installed in Strand's demonstration theatre in London in 1935, but the first installation in a public theatre did not take place until 1940. In total only seventeen were made, the last in 1955. The Light Console was well-suited to light entertainment and musicals, because it enabled rapid, complex lighting changes in time with the music, to be sustained throughout the duration of the performance – something that was impossible or at least extremely difficult with a Grand Master where the operators could not see the stage and where timing depended on complex coordination of several operators.

However, for drama, the Light Console had a critical technological limitation: it could not accurately and repeatedly set specific dimmer levels, and so specific light intensities could not be replayed exactly. On activating a lighting change the dimmers kept moving, and so the light intensities kept changing, until the operator released the relevant master-key on the keyboard. If a dimmer reached its desired intensity before others had completed their travel, the operator could 'drop off' that dimmer by releasing its individual stop-key, but to do this for a large number of dimmers with precision of timing (and therefore precision of final light intensities) required of the operator an impossible manual dexterity. In the immediate post-war period, with technological improvements to luminaires[6] and the emergence of the lighting designer as a distinct professional role, the emphasis began to shift away from the earlier techniques of floodlighting and towards new methods of spotlighting, building up the stage picture from an increasingly large number of carefully controlled beams of light rather than broad, ambient washes supplemented by occasional beams for emphasis – a technique that required accurate control of dimmer levels.

---

[6] The Strand Pattern 23 spotlight was a key innovation: introduced in 1953, Strand manufactured the Pattern 23 in batches of 5000 using aluminium die-casting technologies to replace the previous sheet-metal designs, which were hand-made and produced only in small amounts. This approach shifted luminaire manufacture into a high-volume and comparatively low-cost business, and made high-quality spotlighting much more widely available (see *The Strand Archive*).

Bentham was not alone in wishing to promote the role of the operator: for example the theatre manager and director George Devine argued that the operator's 'ability to see the stage should allow more precision and subtlety in operation as well as accuracy of timing' and that the then present 'crude methods of control reduce what should be an orchestration to the level of driving an Underground train' (Devine cited in Morgan 2005: 83 fn). However, for drama, opera and ballet the Light Console's inability to set balanced levels accurately and repeatedly, was a significant drawback. Bentham's proposition through the Light Console that the lighting operator might become a lighting *artist*, deploying a creative virtuosity in addition to a technical skill – was, for the most part, blocked by its technological limitations.

In the late 1940s a new dimming technology was developed in the USA using a type of vacuum tube known as a thyratron. The result was a dimmer with no moving parts that could be remotely controlled by a small fader at the control position; this in turn made *presetting* possible. A delicately balanced lighting state, with any dimmer at any level, could be set by the operator in advance of that state being required, and faded onto the stage on cue 'fully formed'. This required no special dexterity from the operator, and therefore fulfilled the need in drama, opera and ballet for accurate and repeatable setting of levels. The operator could focus on the timing of the transition, rather than ensuring that dimmers arrive at their required intensities as with the Light Console. Strand was to develop its own control based on a thyratron dimmer known as the Preset Electronic,[7] so that by 1950 Strand offered two distinct top-of-the-range controls – the Light Console and the Preset Electronic – representing two very different operating philosophies. The Light Console promoted the operator as a creative interpreter of the director's (and later the lighting designer's) artistic requirements, live in performance; the Preset Electronic prioritised the precise reproduction of the director's or lighting designer's plot, with minimal creative contribution on the part of the operator (the timing of lighting changes was still controlled manually with the Electronic). The two systems proposed differing *virtuosities* on the part of the operator: both required a technical craft skill, but the Light Console additionally promoted a virtuoso *creative* engagement with the performance.

Professional Practices, Professional Status
What both the Preset Electronic and the Light Console had in common was the potential to position the operator so as to have a clear view of the stage. However, while these two control systems established the idea of the operator as someone who could be visually engaged with the performance by virtue of her/his newfound position in the auditorium, there were other factors that resisted the wholesale handing over of creative responsibility for lighting to the operator. The role of the lighting designer as a professional specialist was beginning to emerge in the early 1950s, partly owing to the increasing complexity of the lighting system and processes that in turn were brought about by the greater emphasis on spotlighting

---

[7] Also known as the Wood Electronic, or simply the Electronic. J.T. 'Woody' Wood joined Strand in 1948, bringing with him experience of radar (and so electronics) that he had worked on during the Second World War. He developed Strand's version of the thyratron dimmer; the management of Strand had become aware of the commercial importance of having such a system, following the adoption of thyratron dimming in the USA (Bentham,1992: 149).

rather than floodlighting. Directors began to have greater artistic aspirations for lighting and as a consequence faced greater technical and logistical complexity. Directors began to be receptive to the idea of a lighting specialist to take over some of the creative, technical and logistical responsibility for the lighting, whilst still remaining subordinate. However, the lighting operator was not seen to be the person in whom to invest such responsibility, regardless of the emerging tendencies to shift control to a front-of-house operating position. The role of the operator was well established as a 'back-stage' function – someone involved in the running of the show, not the making of it. Despite the general post-war political shift to the left, and a national sense of the weakening of the structures of class and social and professional boundaries, theatre was still very hierarchical, and lighting operators were strictly 'manual labour': the new lighting specialists were not ex-operators, but ex-stage managers and ex-theatre engineers and master electricians. The early lighting designers came from backgrounds where their status and relationship with the producer was already established: they were already undertaking lighting tasks (stage managers often relit touring productions for each venue, in the absence of the director) and crucially – unlike lighting operators – they were already *managers*.

The emerging specialist lighting designers were for the most part freelance, moving from production to production, and they modelled their role on the established role of the set and costume designer: Michael Northen, from the outset of his career as a lighting designer in the early 1950s, contractually required his credit in programmes and on posters (a sure sign of professional status) to be 'in the same size as the designer's credit and immediately next to or below it.' (Northen 1997: 180). Making the claim for that professional status by aligning lighting artistry as a specialism with the established roles of the set and costume designer constructed a professional persona that other practitioners (crucially, those who controlled who was to be employed) could readily understand and work with, and also proposed lighting as an equal contributor with the other design disciplines to the artistry of the theatre. On the other hand, had those emerging lighting artists instead pursued the notion of the lighting *performer* and aligned themselves with the existing role of the lighting operator, they would have lost the advantage of a pre-defined relationship with other creative personnel (particularly the director), as well as assigning themselves the lower status of 'back-stage' staff.

Modelling the lighting specialist's role on that of the designer implied a lighting design process of: making creative decisions – in response to factors such as the text, the director's approach to the production, the stage action as seen in rehearsal, and so on – in *advance* of performance; testing and refining those decisions through a process of rehearsal; and then reproducing (we might even say *manufacturing*[8]) the lighting for each performance. For such a conception

---

[8] Today, the precise reproduction of lighting is, perhaps unsurprisingly, particularly associated with the most commodified forms of theatre, exemplified by the products of the West End and Broadway that are also toured and replicated on an international circuit across the USA, Europe, Australia and Japan. The lighting design is meticulously documented in plans, lists, photographs and data files so that it can be accurately reproduced for every performance at each and any venue.

of lighting design – design as artefact – the Preset Electronic was perceived as a far more suitable control than the Light Console, prioritising as it did the precise replay of the designer's previously worked-out intentions with minimal intervention by a third party in the shape of the operator. The Light Console's proposition, on the other hand, emphasised design as *process* – an in-the-moment act of creation, based on (but not a mechanical reproduction of) previous rehearsal.

In the mid 1960s the commercial availability of the thyristor (a dependable solid-state equivalent to the unreliable thyratron) made all-electronic dimming relatively cheap and almost completely reliable. With such dimming came the possibility of inexpensive 'manual' controls based on the presetting principle. The subsequent development of lighting control through the 1960s and 1970s came to be a process of increasing automation of the principles of the manual pre-set controls: firstly, 'memory' functions turned two- or three-preset controls into infinite-preset, saving the operator the chore (and arguably the excitement, on a busy show with many cues in close succession) of having to manually set faders to the dimmer levels required for each upcoming lighting change; later, the previously manual operation of the transition became automated, so that the operator set a time in seconds for the change and the lighting control faded down the outgoing state and faded up the incoming state in the allocated time, at the press of the 'go' button. In 1969 the lighting designer Francis Reid argued that:

the future outlook for operators is rosy [...] Except for the declining world of the West End and the expanding world of TV stars at the seaside, the roles of operator and lighting designer will be combined. The future pattern of our theatre will be based on out-of-London repertoire where the productions will be lit and operated by the lighting designers.

(Reid 1969: 44)

However, Reid's optimism for the role of lighting artist as combined designer and operator proved to be misplaced: the repertoire pattern of production was not adopted by more than a handful of theatres, the professional model of lighting artist as freelance *designer* increasingly dominated, and the virtuosity of the operator – both in terms of technical skill and creative artistry – diminished. Today, almost all lighting for the professional theatre stage is created by freelance designers whose role is to predetermine as far as possible a lighting plot that can be mechanically replayed in performance by the operator pressing the 'go' button when instructed by a stage manager. The design of lighting controls and the professional practices of the lighting operator during the performance are mutually reinforcing: for a lighting control to be commercially successful it must conform to the perceived need to operate in the conventional way, and it is very difficult for a lighting designer to request a different way of operating because both the perceived role and responsibility of the operator and the interface design of the control system resist such a departure from convention. In consequence, lighting professionals are locked into their present working practices by a complex network of interdependent factors, variously technological, contractual, organisational and historical.

To Move Forward, First Look Back

I have argued that the present role of the theatre lighting artist as *designer* has been shaped by the professional, social and technological circumstances at the time of its emergence in the mid twentieth-century, but that at that time an alternative role of the lighting artist as *performer* was proposed by at least one practitioner: Fred Bentham. I have presented this history not only because of its value *as history* but also in the spirit of Francis Reid's oft-repeated mantra, 'to move forward, first look back'[9]: the history is, I would suggest, also instructive in that it can help us better to understand the present, and perhaps even to shape the future.

To begin with, the history serves to point out the often-overlooked connections that exist between technologies, working practices and artistic outcomes. At a time of rapid technological development, it is easy to see technology as the driver of change in theatre practices – particularly in the practices of theatre lighting, which is such a technologically dependent field. However, the history of Bentham's Light Console points us to a more complex understanding of the forces at work: the Light Console was made possible by Bentham's ingenious reworking of one of the new technologies of the day – the cinema organ – but his proposal that the lighting operator should be a lighting *artist* was in the end stymied not by the Light Console's technological limitations but by the social and professional forces that shaped the emerging role of the lighting *designer*. While the opportunities and limitations presented by the available technology were influential, they did not in themselves determine the outcome, and on the same basis we might usefully remind ourselves that the technologies of the present, and those to come, will not exclusively determine how theatre performances are lit in the future. Similarly, the history serves to remind us that the professional roles of lighting designer and lighting operator – defined in terms of working practices and responsibilities, staffing hierarchies and reporting lines, contractual arrangements, and indeed the very conception of what a lighting design *is* and how it is made – are neither accidental nor inevitable. These roles are defined by their historical origins and are at least in part shaped by the perceived needs and professional environment of earlier times, and can legitimately (and perhaps profitably) be called into question.

The professional role of the lighting designer continues to be aligned with the more established role of the set and costume designer, and this alignment is a powerful but largely unrecognised factor in shaping the professional practices of lighting artists. Lighting designers, in common with other theatre designers, are represented by the trades union Equity, and are included in Equity's standard contractual agreements with employer representatives the Society of London Theatres, the Theatrical Management Association, and the Independent Theatre Council. In these standard contracts lighting designers are scarcely mentioned as such, so completely has the role become aligned – in contractual terms – with that of other designers. One of the central principles of these contracts is that designers are creators of intellectual property, and that they are paid for the use of that intellectual property while retaining ownership of it. The contract specifies

---

[9] Reid (2005: 216), but the phrase also appears on numerous occasions elsewhere.

certain duties that the designer will perform, deadlines to meet, and so on, but these obligations on the designer follow on from the central concept of intellectual property, and are in place to ensure that the theatre producer can make the required use of the intellectual property that is being paid for. Constructing the designer's role as one in which the primary responsibility is to produce intellectual property sets up – in epistemological terms – the idea of *design-as-(abstract)-object*, as opposed to *design-as-process*. In contrast, performers, technicians, managers and other personnel involved in the making of the performance are paid for their time and labour (for their *process*); they are not paid royalties, and they retain no rights over the artistic work that they help to create.

It is this distinction between design as object – a *thing* that can be made, and reproduced on demand at the press of a button – and design as process – inextricably bound up with the lighting artist's presence at, and engagement with, the performance event – that I want to conclude with. The distinction is encapsulated in the operating philosophies of Strand's two premier lighting controls of the 1950s, the Light Console and the Preset Electronic, and the subsequent history of lighting control development charts how the theatre lighting profession came to reject Bentham's vision of the lighting artist as *performer* and instead adopted the ready-made role of *designer*. A full analysis of what has been gained, and what has been lost, by this choice is beyond the scope of this essay, but such an analysis might first look to the concert stage and its lighting, where often the lighting designer and operator are one person, or at least form a partnership working closely together and allowing the operator significant creative freedom in the moment of performance. The analysis might go on to consider that, in an age in which cultural artefacts – including performances – are subject to extensive transmission and mediation, the theatre distinctively offers audiences the opportunity to witness a performance in the time and place of its making. A conception of lighting design not as object, pre-made for reproduction, but as process – a continuous creative act up to and through the moment of performance – might prove to be a better fit with the immediacy with which theatre is made and experienced.

THE CREATIVE TECHNICIAN

In 1967, the performance practitioner and academic Richard Schechner made some observations and radical suggestions about the creative role of technicians as performers. Schechner advocated a collaborative way of making theatre, termed 'Environmental Theatre, where all of the space within the theatre is used and the audience becomes immersed within the performance. Inspired by Svoboda's scenography, Schechner realised that although production elements such as lighting are generally seen as secondary aspects in performance, they had the potential to become foregrounded. In *Six Axioms for Environmental Theatre*, he argued that 'production elements need no longer "support" a performance. These elements are more important than the performers' (Schechner, 1995: xxiv–v). Schechner's vision for a new form of theatre and way of working led him to reconsider the role of technology and the way in which its operators were involved in the creative process:

> ...the key to making technical elements part of the creative process is not simply to apply the latest research to theatrical productions. The technicians themselves must become an active part of the performance. This does not necessarily mean the use of more sophisticated equipment, but rather the more sophisticated use of the human beings who run whatever equipment is available. The technicians' role is not limited to perfecting during rehearsals the use of their machines. During all phases of workshop and rehearsals the technicians should participate. And during performances the technicians should be as free to improvise as the performers, modulating the uses of their equipment night-to-night. Light boards locked into pre-sets do not foster the kind of experimentation I'm talking about. The experience of discos is instructive. The rhythm and content of some light-shows are modulated to accompany and sometimes lead or dominate the activity of the spectator-dancers. During many intermedia performances, the technicians are free to chose [sic] where they will project images, how they will organize sound contexts. There is nothing sacred about setting technical elements. If human performance is variable (as it most certainly is) then a unified whole – if one is looking for that – will become better assured by a nightly variation of technical means.

> Thus, possibilities exist for 'performing technicians' whose language is the film-strip or the electronic sound, and whose range of action includes significant variations in where and what is to be done. The same goes for other technical elements. The separation between performers and technicians is erodable because the new accompany can be used not only to completely program all the material [...] but also to permit the nearly total flexibility of bits that can be organized on the spot, during the performance. The performing group is expanding to include technicians as well as actors and dancers.

> Once this is granted, the creative technician will demand fuller participation in performances and in the workshops and rehearsals that generate performances. At many times during a performance actors and dancers will support the technician, whose activated equipment will be 'center stage.' A wide-ranging mix is possible where the complexity of images and sounds – with or without the participation of 'unarmed' performers – is all but endless.

> To achieve this mix of technical and live performers nothing less than the whole space is needed. The kind of work I'm talking about can't happen if one territory belongs to the audience and another to the performers. The bifurcation of space must be ended. The final exchange between performers and audience is the exchange of space, spectators as scene-makers as well as scene-watchers. This will not result in chaos: rules are not done away with, they are simply changed.

> (ibid.: xxvi–vii)

Other contemporary commentators have also sought to address the prevalent ways of working and attitudes to the role and status of those who work with technology in performance. Although the role of the lighting

designer has been well established for 50 years, the artistic contribution is not always readily acknowledged. In the UK the Association of
Lighting Designers is a professional organisation that represents lighting designers working in the live performance industry, and has sought
to further the art of lighting design and to raise the professional status
of the lighting designer within the creative team. The OISTAT[10] Lighting
Design Working Group (LDWG) has also evolved to examine contemporary practices throughout the world, to advocate the contribution of lighting as a separate and distinct element of theatre and to seek ways to
enhance the collaborative relationships between all members of the creative
team.

Academic commentators such as Michael Ramsaur, Professor of Lighting
Design at Stanford University, and Markku Uimonen, Professor of Lighting Design at Helsinki Theatre Academy, Finland, have advocated the need
to challenge existing working practices and spoken passionately about the
quality of training for lighting designers and operators. Henk van der Geest
has established a training centre in the Netherlands specifically to address
these issues,[11] while Chris van Goethem, an experienced theatre practitioner,
technical consultant and lecturer at RITS, Erasmus Hogeschool in Brussels,
argues that the lighting operator is a 'hidden actor' out of sight of the audience and that instead of discrete technical training they need to be educated
alongside all other theatre-makers.[12]

DESIGN AND THE OPERATOR – CONTROLLING LIGHT

There are many contemporary examples where technology is foregrounded
and the operators are not 'hidden' but an integral part of the performance
aesthetic. Robert Lepage's *Elsinore* (1996) – a retelling of *Hamlet* – for example, consciously placed stage technologies at the centre of his dramatic vision
and the mechanised revolving stage, lighting, sound and projection were
clearly co-performers in this production. The lighting designer/operators
were visible throughout, placed downstage of the proscenium and responding in the moment to the changing performance conditions. In contemporary
dance performance, operators of sound, light and computing technology
are frequently located on stage with the dancers. We have moved from a
contestation of backstage space to a very visible onstage presence.

The offstage operators of bunch-lights of the nineteenth century have
also at times moved from the wings to centre stage. Kneehigh Theatre, for
example, have used onstage performers to manipulate light as an integral
part of the dramatic action. This apparently low-tech approach, where the

---

[10] International Organisation of Scenographers, Theatre Architects and Technicians.
[11] See ILO, the International Lighting Designers' Organisation, www.lichtontwerpen.
[12] Paper given at OISTAT International Symposium, Nottingham Trent University (2005).

source of light and its human controller are deliberately visible as a part of the stage picture, represents a logical development of Brecht's lighting practice as well as creating a flexible and truly intelligent moving light source! The live manipulation of the light source as a transparent element of the dramaturgy offers the audience both the image it is working to create and also the mechanics being employed to create it. Katie Mitchell has employed similar techniques with onstage technology to create stunning images as a central element of the dramatic narrative. Using a range of materials and projected light in *Waves* (2006), for example,[13] scenographic images were carefully created by the company through the foregrounding of the very mechanics of their creation. The audience witnessed the resulting images that were captured by live video cameras from within the scene and re-projected cinematically within the stage space. The images were lit by anglepoise lamps and focused by the performers to create the desired keylight for each image observed on the screen. The fragmentary nature of Woolf's novel was captured through these moments, but the audience also experienced the spectacle of their creation on stage – the performers working as both actor and technician to manipulate light sources, materials, objects, sound and bodies to craft a succession of beautifully framed filmic images.

The ability to rehearse lighting alongside the performers with access to the full range of lighting technology is a distant dream for many working in this field. However, contemporary dance and experimental performance companies increasingly appear to value the opportunities and creative benefits of experimenting with light at an earlier stage of the rehearsal process rather than as a necessary theatrical element that is added to the performance at the last moment.

PROJECTING PERFORMANCE – THE EXPERIENCE OF THE OPERATOR

Research at the University of Leeds investigating the role of the light operator as a performer has concentrated on the experience and nature of the performer-operator. In contrast to van Goethem's notion of 'hidden actors', *Projecting Performance*[14] operators were visible both physically alongside the audience and through their embodied presence in the stage space through their expressive control of the projected light.

The live manipulation of this light, created digitally and projected into the stage space, was facilitated through an operator using a pen and graphics tablet. This interface, in contrast to the conventional lighting board with 'go'

[13] A dramatisation of Virginia Woolf's novel *The Waves*, designed by Vicki Mortimer with lighting design by Paule Constable.
[14] *Projecting Performance* was funded by AHRC in collaboration with digital artists KMA Creative Technology. See Popat, S.; Palmer, S. (2005, 2008).

Figure 19 Light is drawn live into the stage space to gradually create Titania's bower in *A Midsummer Night's Dream*, part of the *Projecting Performance* research project, 2007

buttons or faders, freed the operator to use a wider palette of gestural control from broad, sweeping motions to precise, fine-motor movements, enabling a more intuitive and expressive operation of the light and promoting a playful experience of working between technology and performance.

By literally drawing light in the stage space, even first-time operators were able to achieve complex interactions and to experience themselves as performer-operators alongside the on-stage performers. The intuitive interface allowed for expressive improvisation and, when working along-side dancers, many performer-operators commented that they felt as if they were dancing as equal partners in a lighting duet with the on-stage performer, despite having little prior experience or skills in dancing with their whole bodies. The research sought to explain feelings of dislocation or translocation reported during this experience of operating, which is in marked contrast to the operation of light in more conventional theatre environments.

Projecting Performance raised a number of issues relating to the perception and role of the operator as a performer, and it raises further questions around how operators might be trained or rehearsed to create performance work in this way. Bentham's view that lighting operation should be memorised, rather than replayed by pre-established cue sheets and pre-sets, seems to have a contemporary relevance. If we wish lighting operators to take a more creative role in performance then the act of lighting operation might be considered more like choreography that needs to be learnt and felt through the body before it can be expressed on stage.

NEW WAYS OF CONTROLLING LIGHT

The development of moving lights during the 1980s and 1990s saw the evolution of the lighting programmer as a distinct role in large-scale events. A new generation of lighting control equipment was necessary to coordinate the complex range of parameters of each sophisticated lighting fixture. These allowed the operator a significant amount of autonomy and the ability to play the lighting in relation, for example, to live music once it had been programmed. This was much closer in philosophy to Bentham's Light Console than the conventional computerised lighting boards that had been designed for the theatre and which were based on the sequential recall and replaying of memories. Their architecture did not easily accommodate the new automated fixtures and did not tend to allow the live flexibility that was now required. New computerised lighting controls evolved, therefore, to allow a range of operator preferences to be set and complex lighting moments with moving lights to be created and amended more easily.

Lighting could therefore be designed alongside the music and explored in real time through the rehearsal process with the musicians. With the development of visualisation software such as CAST Lighting's *WYSIWYG* in the late 1990s, lighting could be created off-line on computer before the lights were rigged in the venue. This innovation has had a significant impact on the live event industry, and large-scale events such as Olympic Games ceremonies are all pre-programmed in this way. For music events, lighting is often designed and tested on-screen in advance before further refinement in rehearsal. Crucially, though, the operator/programmer usually retains some autonomy and creative licence to interact with the music and respond in real time to the conditions of the performance and the atmosphere in the venue.

Designers Peggy Eisenhauer and Jules Fisher have spoken about the new language, techniques and thinking required to plot and operate moving lights.[15] Designers and operators both now need to think through the complexity inherent in determining parameters for each fixture (intensity, speed, shape, time, orientation, etc.). For the first time they are also required to consider cues that are invisible to the audience but which allow each lantern to 'move whilst dark'.

Christine White has critiqued the tendency to locate the theatre lighting operator behind glass in a control room outside the actual space of performance, in contrast to the practice of lighting for rock and roll events which is

---

[15] Presentation at *Showlight*, Edinburgh, 22 May 2001.

operated from amidst the audience. White argues that, in mainstream theatre, lighting operators (unlike sound operators) are divorced from the creative act of performance both by their location and by the advent of computer-based control systems that often require little human interaction. She argues that the architecture of the control interface alters the very nature of lighting practice:

> The advent of computer control systems started a revolution in lighting design of far greater significance than that of the thyristor dimmer. Although the mechanics of theatre lighting, as in the specific method of dimming, did ultimately affect the technology of control, it is the structure and operation of access to particular lighting systems, which has the greatest impact on the final look of a piece of theatre, in that, the control equipment is responsible for the level of performance. It is not just the hardware of the control but the layout of the control board and the organisation of the lantern stock, which changes the nature of the lighting design, and the role of the lighting designer.
>
> (White, 1999)

White is critical of the way in which the lighting controls are designed and argues for a more intuitive interface that might allow a greater creative engagement between technician operator and lighting designer:

> Even though designer's palettes have been in operation for many years now few shows are plotted on them by the lighting designer experimenting during a lighting session. Still rarer is the use of the palette as an instructional tool to the operator by which the lighting designer could show the kind of feel and mood to a cue as an expression of what the operator should try to achieve. This would be closest to the transposed idea of the operator as the instrument player, and the lighting designer as the composer.
>
> (ibid.)

There are further complexities associated with the role and status of the lighting designer and the amount of time allocated to the preparation of light for theatrical performance that also impact upon the relationship which White critiques. However, the musical analogy is important and echoes the thoughts of Bentham in potentially providing a legitimating discourse for the operator-artist and designer. Appia developed his lighting score in musical terms, and the temporal aspect of the lighting has been acknowledged to be as important to the performance as the lighting states themselves:

> Light, in fact, is no longer about unity but about transition. How we get from one place or moment to the next has become more important than what it looks like when we are there.
>
> (Aronson, 2005: 35)

Rebellato argues persuasively that the emergence of the role of the lighting designer and operator was irrevocably altered through the campaign against

Bentham's Light Console. Instead of the evolution of a creative lighting artist who 'played' the lighting, the responsibility was handed to the technician to replay light to a fixed series of pre-set cues. In explaining the advent of Pilbrow's Lightboard in 1957, Rebellato argues that

> This new board had much of the flexibility of the Light Console but crucially included presets. Although they were capable of being overridden in an emergency, the preset states represent the triumph of the director who could once again dictate the operation of the lights in the lighting plot; the actions of the operator were easily distributed into correct and mistaken actions, a division under the control of director, and cemented by the development of the computer memory board.
>
> (Rebellato, 1999: 93–94)

The advent of the computer lighting control board had far-reaching effects, finally putting an end to the need for a creative individual, a designer-operator who Bentham envisaged would memorise and play a continual lighting track, and instead legitimising the role of the lighting designer as a member of the creative production team:

> The lighting designer achieved certain things, a national association, a job title, but at the cost of any further creative development and autonomy.
>
> (ibid.: 94)

Chapter

12   The Lighting Designer

In this final chapter we examine some of the current issues facing lighting designers in contemporary performance through the thoughts and writings of professional designers. We examine the processes involved in creating lighting designs and their observations on the key issues that impact on their work. There are some fascinating insights underlining the difficulties inherent in the process of shaping the ephemeral material of light in modern performance practice.

The role of the lighting designer emerged, as we have seen, during the first part of the twentieth century when equipment became more complex and the possibilities for the creative role of light on the stage became acknowledged. Morgan documents this evolution in detail in *Stage Lighting Design in Britain: The Emergence of the Lighting Designer, 1881–1950*. Rebellato summarises the situation in British theatre pre-1940 and observes that although the professionalism of the role was acknowledged in the post-war period, this was at the expense of creative autonomy within the artistic team (1999: 94).

The next article, written in 1985 by Peter Mumford, advocates an alternative view of the position of the lighting designer as a creative collaborator. Like Jean Rosenthal and Jennifer Tipton who developed their art primarily through an engagement with dance, Mumford explored the mixed media of setting, lighting and projection with Moving Being and Siobhan Davies' Second Stride dance company during the 1980s.

Although this article was written at a time when the first remote-controlled, movable 'intelligent' light had just been introduced (specifically referred to here as the 'Vari-lite'), the writing retains a contemporary relevance and provides a wide-ranging and valuable insight into the role of light within choreography. Echoing concerns articulated elsewhere in this volume, Mumford examines how light gives shape and structure to a performance, how colour can be used and introduces the notion of lighting as 'scenery of the air'. It is an article that deserves to be more widely known and raises a number of issues and ideas that remain pertinent today in thinking about how light contributes to performance in general and to dance in particular.

LIGHTING DANCE – PETER MUMFORD

It is not the intention of this article to attempt a definitive, comprehensive description of how to light dance: there are quite enough procedural manuals in existence already, and anyway there are no real rules, only technical limitations within which one must learn to work. However, it is useful to examine various approaches to lighting and to reach a critical understanding of the medium. The dialogue about the role of lighting design as an art form within the theatre certainly needs sharpening, particularly as it concerns dance. In spite of popular notions of lighting as a 'glitzy' framing for dance [...] lighting is not just a decorative facility: it is essentially an illustrative medium, which is certainly not the same thing. Lighting is a scenic art concerned not only with the evoking of atmosphere and ideas, but also with the definition of space and 'body form' in relationship to space. Its relationship to pigment and structure is crucial; and in the case of lighting for dance or for opera there is an equally important relationship to musical interpretation. Unlike music, dance must be seen before it can be appreciated. Those who agree that it is sufficient simply to illuminate a space to an acceptable level of visibility, maintain that 'the dance is the thing' and all else mere periphery. Although they may be right in certain circumstances, the very decision to work in a hall, lit by fluorescent tubes or using a plain cover of 'white' light on stage, is, for instance, a design decision that will affect and control responses to a performance [...] The process of conceiving, producing and performing a dance work entails decisions about its visual presentation: there is, properly, no such thing as working without costume, set or lighting.

The New Lighting

In the relatively short history of lighting design, there has been a wide variety of approaches to lighting ranging from naturalism and hyper realism to abstraction. And yet the question needs to be posed, is lighting design an art or is it the domain of the technocrat?

The controlling of light in the theatre is still largely regarded as a technical facility, a craft rather than an art: the subject literature is dominated by manuals rather than critiques, and it's only when a painter or sculptor is directly involved in a lighting project that critical discussion includes aesthetic criteria. One of the main reasons for this is that the lighting designer's emergence as a member of the production team has coincided with a major advance in lighting technology that began in the fifties; [...] the new breed, 'the lighting designers', emerged through the industry that produced and developed the improved equipment.

A whole new world of effects and visualisations now opened up, a new kind of theatrical magic, a world of illusion, to match the technology of film and television. [...] The growth in importance of lighting within new and radical forms of theatre is such that few productions now fail to give importance to lighting. The lighting designer's 'palette' is now vast, and still developing: and it makes possible a visual language as fluid as the painter's, almost unlimited in its scope, and most importantly, capable of communicating ideas through the use of colour, form, surface and space. Even so this new art still lacks critical appraisal and well structured training programmes, and its relationship to other art areas remains unexamined. The relationship between the choreographer and the lighting designer is not properly understood or defined and its importance often underestimated.

I have always believed in 'User Technology': that is, a practical, mastery of the use of tools and instruments that enables the user to work with them imaginatively and creatively but which requires no perfect knowledge of how they work. There exists a tendency for its exponents to wrap stage lighting in mystery by emphasising the need for a technical understanding of the associated electronic, engineering and computer technologies. The current accessibility of video and computers represents a shift in public attitudes to and familiarity with technology: we no longer expect a 'good driver' to be an 'ace mechanic'. The new technologies must not control ideas, but must be a means of producing new thoughts. [...]

[T]he emergence of the lighting designer was based on an expanding technology, and depended in the early days upon individuals with the capacity to comprehend technology. The accelerating inventions of technology increasingly extend the lighting designer's range, and if the lighting designer is to innovate, he or she must learn to exploit the new creative possibilities in conjunction with the technologists. While innovative technicians have an important place and the lighting designer's work requires a consistently practical approach to creativity, it is important that we do not get so fascinated by equipment for its own sake, that creative thinking is sacrificed. For lighting is a creative medium, the candle is as essential as the 'Vari-Light', the switch as important a control as the most complicated computerised memory system. It should be remembered that what we are dealing with is light itself; and the fact that light sources and controls are being improved and extended simply means that there is an ever present opportunity to extend the visual vocabulary.

The Scenery of the Air

The use of lighting in the theatre as 'scenery' is an important development. Theatrical lighting was originally used functionally to illuminate the surfaces and structures before which the piece was acted or danced, and this illumination of landscape backdrops and interiors demands considerable skill, as also does the clear lighting of actors and dancers. However, when the medium of light itself is used to express landscapes and rooms, cloudy skies and prison cells or more emotional and intellectual concepts such as isolation, hope, coolness, heat and time passing, then it is clear that a new visual language is in use, and that the designer's role has become a creative one. In several respects, lighting for contemporary dance has led the way in the development of lighting as a visual language, and the progress made in this area is now reflected in drama, musical theatre and television. One of the main reasons for this is the spatial demands that dance makes on its performing area. In the majority of dance works, the entire floor space is required; and this leads to special design limitations, forcing the designer to work with the edges of the stage area. In such a space, in which solid scenery cannot exist, a shaft of light can assume the function of a three-dimensional object. Lighting is therefore used to build walls and linear structures, to change background and floor colours, to redefine areas, to contract and expand the stage space, and even to clothe the performers. Dance, in making all these visual requirements (and taking up all or most of the stage), has become the natural culture for the growth of 'scenic' lighting. Lighting can express time, space and mood, and can be orchestrated rhythmically in relation to, or in juxtaposition with the musical score; it is like painting the air, and its effect is much more than the mere 'wall-papering' of a production. Indeed, lighting for dance is central to the process of visual communication, the link between movement and its perception, and the balance between the body and surface design. At the same time, lighting is there to support, amplify and reinforce the objectives and ideas of the dance work, and not to overpower it or distract from it.

Colour

Although colour does not really exist apart from light, we tend to connect colour with paint, inks or dyes and yet we can only establish constant colour values when we have 'constants' in light [. . .] [C]hanges of colour and lighting conditions are commonplace experiences and pass generally unnoticed yet they contribute significantly to our emotional, psychological and physical perception of people, objects and events. If we are to start painting with light and making creative decisions about the controlled use of light, it is important properly to understand and observe the way in which colour and light relate. When we enter the dark world of the theatre it is possible with the 'blank black canvas' offered there and the constant light qualities available, to control and adjust perception in a consistent way. As with any art form, what is created is an interpretation: a mirror of real life, adjusted to bring attention to aspects of that 'reality' that might otherwise go unnoticed. The lighting designer also has a major responsibility in controlling what the audience sees both of the dances and of the set; and in this he must remain faithful to the idea of the piece and unify the total impression conveyed to the audience.

When the electric light bulb was introduced to the stage all shades of colour were at first mixed from varying proportions of the three primary colours of light (red, green and blue). An even distribution of these primary colours around the stage produces 'white light'. 'Primary mixing', however, is not an efficient means of achieving either brightness or subtlety of hue, and the system tends to issue in warm toned 'white' general light and a gaudy use of separate colours.

Somewhat surprisingly, the red, green and blue system is still sometimes used, although the 'straight out of the tube' range of intermediate shades available to the modern lighting designer includes approximately one hundred hues; and the colour range can be further increased by mixing these hues themselves so the colour 'palette' is extensive and subtle. The availability of different kinds of lamp sources (such as tungsten, quartz, iodine and fluorescent) extends the range further, because each has a different white light colour temperature: this offers us a change of quality as much as of identifiable colours. 'Colour correction filters' such as 'no colour blue' and 'no colour straw' which are currently in general use, simply 'warm' or 'cool' a white light source.

In visual interpretation, the brain accommodates a complex combination of superimposed and 'collaged' images. Somehow the brain organises everything so that one can rapidly look from one thing to another without confusion. The brain's processing of what we see can naturally control perception in general, and perception of colour in particular. The intense, pure colours of a sunny day are transformed if one closes one's eyes or blocks out light with one's hand: this does not produce darkness; rather, a plethora of mixed images floods the vision of the brain. Often the impression is no less vibrant than the 'open eyed' view, but it is different: shapes remain but the colours have altered (it is a kind of multiple-colour negative of the view through open eyes). It is a series of 'after-images' and colours finding their natural opposites or complementary colours. (Complementary colours are opposite in the spectral circle so reds become greens, yellows become purples, blues become oranges and so on.)

So perception of colour is relative not only to the quality of light, but also to the colours which have been perceived immediately before. Since the audience's perception of colour is tempered by what it has most recently experienced, it is possible for the same colour to be perceived differently by means of technical adjustments: blues may appear greenish or mauvish, depending on what has been seen before, or adjacent to the surface; a strongly lit red stage will produce a green 'after image' in the mind which will then mix visually until the eyes re-adjust with the first sight of a blue-lit stage cover. This is a control principle which operates on a more complex and subtle basis than the 'primary mix' principle; though the natural scientific laws are the same.

The use and understanding of colour is therefore aesthetically central to lighting for dance; in dance, perception of colour not only fulfils a decorative function, it informs the action, emotion and 'placement' of the dance. Colour helps to direct an audience how to perceive movement relative to the space in which it is performed, as well as modulating the quality of that space, and thereby the dance within it.

Structure

Dance demands, in the most part, large areas of flat space, thus ruling out the kind of physical structures that might be used in opera or drama. Lighting can therefore assume the structural role of a set design, replacing solid materials with areas and shapes defined by light. The shaping of the stage from lighting source to stage surface is now being used more widely as a scenic device within the dance space. Beams of light can be 'coloured' in a variety of subtle ways to achieve a three-dimensional physical existence, creating walls and pillars where no solid object could exist. The close relationship between contemporary dance and lighting that has been established over the last twenty years has exerted a considerable stylistic influence upon theatrical lighting generally. The technological developments that have been created by the commercial popular music industry (that is largely dependent on lighting effects in live performances) have resulted in the development of new forms of equipment like laser generators and powerful beam sources to exploit the structural uses of light to considerable advantage.

The lighting designer must tread warily, however; the technology can encourage spectacular 'effect' for its own sake, and circumscribe invention by the limited aesthetic vision of the technocrat. It is easy to end up with just a rather spectacular electronic 'firework display'.

It is important to find ways of ensuring that new technological equipment enhances the creative range of the lighting designer. If I am unable to 'draw' or 'paint', with some new invention, then it is of no use to me: a brush that paints the same picture over and over again is only usable once. In fact the basic tools often provide the widest range of possibilities and the shaping and structuring of light can be achieved in the simplest of visual statements.

Just as the role that lighting plays within dance has been extended in recent years, so its visual language is more understood by those who watch. We are all familiar with the editing techniques used in film and television, and this extension of our visual language is helpful when lighting is used to express structure and special definition on the stage. The modern audience can read and understand such techniques as cutting from a restricted area of light to an open space, and presenting a wall of light as a physical barrier. This relatively new visual understanding also makes it possible to undertake a rapid scene change in view of the audience who will see it rather like a 'cut' from one camera to another on television; and it has naturally extended the range of communicable ideas for dance and its audiences: a hard-edged beam will indicate a complete space with walls (that are not physically there) while a soft, out of focus edge implies a larger space of which we only see a part. Such innovations have become part of the usable scenic language of the lighting designer, and, significantly, have extended the vocabulary of the stage for the choreographer.

Content and Form in the Creative Process

The importance of the lighting designer's contribution has created changes in the relationship with the choreographer, and in the approach to new works. The notion of a piece of choreography as being developed in isolation from its visual presentation is changing, and in many instances has already changed. The lighting designer's ideas are now integral to the creation of many new dances; very often these ideas are developed even before rehearsal has begun, and they can influence the making of the choreography. While the starting point and central idea for a new work is likely to come from the choreographer, the end result is a creative collaboration in which both the content and the form of the piece have been agreed. Choreographer, composer and designers, work together to 'make theatre', for theatre is a mixed media art form operating at multi-faceted levels of communication and expression. When the starting-point for the dance and design is musical (as it often is) lighting can play a major role in expressing musical rhythms and in illuminating the dance. Even if there is no composed musical accompaniment the rhythm of the dance itself becomes a 'seed' to work from. Music naturally evokes images, and the lighting designer who cannot respond creatively to music cannot hope to play a useful part in expressing the work. The 'cue structure' of lighting design is rather like a musical score; and the rhythmical way in which one lighting state changes to another is as important as the 'look' of the lighting itself. The 'music to light' function is crucial to the balance of every dance piece, involving as it does a musical implementation of lighting design.

Lighting for dance demands a close working relationship with the choreographer from the rehearsal stage. When the lighting ideas developed from this cooperation are brought to the stage it falls to the lighting designer to incorporate and express the fruits of that collaboration.

Creating a lighting design is not like designing costumes or sets when it is possible to illustrate designs before they are made. A model of a set or a costume drawing can be discussed with the choreographer and composer before it is made, and everybody has a fairly clear idea of what is expected. But a lighting design cannot be represented through a drawing or model. The lighting designer prepares technical instructions for the lighting technicians and prepares a colour filtering scheme, but in describing what the stage and dancers will actually look like the designer has to fall back on verbal descriptions, and such aids as sketches indicating the direction of light. So it is essential that the lighting designer has the confidence of the other collaborators. Before mounting the new dance in the theatre, the designer will have a fairly accurate picture of his collaborators' work, but they will have a less precise idea of his or her work. The lighting designer must possess an aesthetic and intellectual understanding of the terms of reference of the work in progress, for the expressive and creative role of lighting in dance is to support and illustrate the ideas and movement of the piece through the structure, shape and separation of colour of light: this constitutes a visual language mingling with and modulating the expressive, physical movements of the dance. The currency and range of ideas used in lighting design, have their root in natural human responses and an intuitive understanding of images and symbols.

Conclusion

The major development of contemporary dance in this country over the last twenty years has coincided with the development of lighting design as an expressive medium. The two forms have served each other well over the years, and an inseparable link now exists between dance and the light in which it is perceived. The reasons for this are simple enough: contemporary dance constantly involves the creation of new works: and it is a visual medium, and therefore does not have the limitations that a script might impose on the actors in a theatre.

New forms of dance expression have found a perfect scenic counterpart in newly creative designs for lighting; and concurrent technological developments have constantly fed and supported this mutual growth. The spatial requirements of dance are perfectly met by the 'scenic' quality of light, both controlling space and offering no physical barriers within the space. Lighting is able to develop more creatively and freely within dance than in any other aspect of theatre. This apparent 'freedom' however must be handled with care and an integral understanding of dance must be a basic part of the lighting designer's sensitivity or the relationship may be abused.

This alliance between contemporary dance and lighting design has stylistically influenced lighting everywhere. Through dance lighting an understandable 'language of light' has emerged, from which all sorts of other performance areas in theatre and music have benefited.

(First published in *Dance Research: The Journal of the Society for Dance Research*, 3(2) Summer 1985: 46–55)

AN INSPECTOR CALLS – A CASE STUDY

Rick Fisher is an award-winning lighting designer and, until recently, Chair of the Association of Lighting Designers – an organisation dedicated to representing lighting designers, furthering the art of lighting and raising the professional status of the lighting designer as a member of the creative team. This section examines Fisher's particular approach to the lighting process and his notion of 'post-design rationalisation' – a reflection that comes about after the work has been staged when the role of the lighting can be analysed from a more objective standpoint. In the first part of this conversation, Fisher explains how the term evolved in relation to the lighting design for the award-winning production of *An Inspector Calls*.[1]

Stephen Daldry's production was a radical reinterpretation of Priestley's play that transposed it in time and space from the traditional Edwardian interior to a 1944 desolate wasteland. MacNeil's setting and Fisher's lighting gave the production an immediacy that brought the key issues of the production into sharp focus. The lighting relied heavily on side-light, more common to dance productions than word-based drama, and, in the conversation

Figure 20   Rick Fisher's lighting for *An Inspector Calls*, National Theatre, 2009

---

[1] The production was first created in York (1989), was reworked at the National Theatre (1992) and has been performed almost continually since.

below, Fisher explains in detail how this came about. Overhead rigging positions were not available because the angle of MacNeil's false proscenium
frame created a major obstruction. However, the creative response to this
limitation worked towards the evolution of the expressionistic dreamscape
and, underpinned by Stephen Warbeck's musical score, ultimately defined
the world of this play and led to its critical success.

The working process between director and designers on this production
has been documented previously, although insufficient credit has been given
to the impact of the visual and aural elements of the staging.[2] Fisher notes:

> If you were to ask the creative team whose idea many of the things were, I think
> none of us could tell. We know that we came to a lot of the ideas together and then
> we just fed off each other, tried different things out and made it better. [...] The
> opening images are still the best five minutes you are going to have in a theatre
> anywhere. And I think that makes you sit up and listen to what people say in a
> very fresh and exciting way.
>
> (Fisher in Greengrass,1999: 26–30)

Lighting takes a prominent role in the way in which the production is
received and understood by the audience. The reliance on side-lighting
meant that Fisher was able to

> light the people very brightly but still keep the dark, foreboding atmosphere, which
> is one of the things which is central to the whole interrogation style of the piece.
>
> (ibid.: 28)

At the end of the second act of Priestley's play, the lighting suddenly illuminates the audience when the Inspector shouts 'Stop!' This is a significant
theatrical moment when Fisher feels

> it is as if God has peeled off the roof of the theatre and switched a big searchlight
> on to look at these people. We drain all the theatricality out of the event and it is
> as if someone has just turned the work lights on in the theatre. This is a moment
> out of time [...] a satisfying and a jarring moment.
>
> (ibid.: 22)

RICK FISHER – IN CONVERSATION

In this honest and open discussion with the academic Nick Hunt, Fisher
provides a unique insight into his working practice and explores a range
of issues that are pertinent to our thinking about the contemporary lighting design process. The conversation ranges from examining how Fisher is

---

[2] See Wendy Lesser's *A Director Calls: Stephen Daldry and the Theatre* (1997), which although
rather reverential was inspired by her experience of witnessing this production.

able to analyse the contribution of light in performance to the way in which the lighting design idea originates and comes together in the production process. Fisher's reflection on the feelings experienced when first faced with a blank plan on the drawing board, and at the moment when the first light is turned on prior to the lighting session, will be recognised by most designers who have engaged in this process. It is reassuring that these feelings are also experienced by someone of Fisher's stature and experience. His modest analysis of his instinctive process of creating light in the theatre space during the production period hints at the technical ability, artistic sensitivity and subtlety that is inherent in his work.

Hunt: Can you explain how the term 'post-design rationalisation' came about?

Fisher: I hit on the phrase when I was preparing one of my *Showlight*[3] talks and it occurred to me that once I had completed a show, particularly one that I had done many times such as *An Inspector Calls* or *Swan Lake*,[4] I was able to analyse the contribution of the lighting in an objective way. These are two of the shows I find easiest to talk about, because there are key moments in them that differ both in their lighting style and the way in which I've come to realise them. I began to understand why they worked in the way that they do and how to keep on reproducing them despite the need to make changes every time you restage them or put them into a different theatre. I began to question what I needed in order to make what I thought actually work on stage. Also in presenting to student groups and fellow theatre professionals – I felt, as I often do, and maybe most of us lighting designers do, somewhat of a fraud, thinking that they must have thought that my process was that I sat down at the drawing board, had these particular ideas and goals and then figured out how to achieve them, and then put them into practice, tweaked them, refined them, and – you know – that was it! That somehow the 'Eureka!' moment of lighting design was somewhere at the drawing board, or even before you got to the drawing board – and the truth of the matter for me is that it is almost never that way.

I still panic at the drawing board: an empty piece of paper is my greatest enemy, I will do anything but sit down and make those first few marks on the paper and I still do it by hand – I don't visualise light on the computer or anything like that – and even with a show that I have done before I still find the blank piece of paper frightening – but I kind of know a little bit more about what I want to achieve, and I know that I know how to make certain things work and when I can get away with them. I hit upon this idea that actually I was able to theorise the lighting once I had completed the design, as opposed to starting with the theory and putting it into practice in a design. This sort of understanding of what I had done became much easier to talk about once the process was finished, the performance had been staged and I could look at it again and analyse the lighting objectively. So to make it sound more honest to me, the design was rationalised after I had completed it, as opposed to before I had done it.

---

[3] A quadrennial symposium for professional lighting designers.

[4] Matthew Bourne's provocative reworking of the classical ballet premiered at Sadler's Wells in 1995.

So, instead of saying: 'Oh, I decided when we did *An Inspector Calls* at the National Theatre 15 years ago, that I wasn't going to use the overhead rig in the Lyttelton, but gradually began to use their side ladders and their slots front of house, low angle side-light to wash across the stage in a version of the McCandless method but from a different angle ...' this would be completely untrue! In fact the designer had drawn a piece of scenery through the number one bar, so that wasn't going to work for me, and because the number one bar wasn't there to set up those 'rep'[5] systems, the number two and the number three and the number six bar didn't really make much sense either.

And when you turned on those lights which are the meat and drink for most of us in the theatre, the floor looked like it was made of plastic – because it was! Whereas when you skimmed it with a little bit of light or you kept light off it, it reflected light in a way like you used to light old-fashioned scenery, in that you actually didn't at all, since the flare out of old lighting equipment was good enough to take care of the magic of the scenery, which was largely painted detail.

So, I found that I was not lighting the floor directly, but lighting the people. And then as I realised that every time we turned on that cue that had that element in it, we liked it more than the cues that didn't, and slowly but surely we began cutting the overhead rig. This was apart from a couple of lamps that just happened to hit a couple of pieces of scenery in a nicely accidental way because it was the National's 'rep focus' and the piece of scenery shouldn't have been there but it was!

Slowly as I recreated that design over and over again for different theatres, and improved on it, and solved the new problems that this kind of lighting had created – I found that I could talk about it and have this so-called system, which was not by any means a unique personal discovery, but it was rationalised or it was explainable *after* I had done it, rather than pretending that it was something I was going to try and do in advance.

I think as a lighting designer, every time you are starting with a blank piece of paper or a blank canvas on stage, you just start to respond to what works. The good designers feel confident that they can respond at that moment and deal with it. Some designers start out with a theory, and then encounter problems if the theory isn't working, they don't then know where to go.

I still have moments like that, where I think that I can use my usual tricks, and they don't work, and I feel a little bit lost until the show begins to tell me how to do it, and hopefully you find an answer – it can just be a moment when you think: 'Oh that looks good! Now I just need to make the rest of the show look a little bit more like that.' And so I have become very aware of the fact that I don't always bring a theory or even a style to my work – but by the end of the process the theory and the style may be there, but it's not something that (I hope!) I've imposed on it, but that it's grown organically out of the creative process itself.

---

[5] The lighting for a performance within a repertoire season often relies heavily upon using or reusing a generic rig already employed on other shows using the same stage. In this instance the lighting bars above the stage were unavailable. Numbered from downstage, they are usually crucial angles for the lighting inside the proscenium.

Hunt: At what point does this rationalisation tend to occur?

Fisher: Lighting designers don't have to explain our work very often. There is nothing worse than sitting at a 'tech table'[6] and having a lighting designer start to tell the director and designer about why they are doing something or how they do something, or why they shouldn't do something. Sometimes I find myself doing that as I get older and more experienced, and probably a little bit more dogmatic – but I'd like to hope I don't do this!

I think the rationalisation part of the process only perhaps comes during previews or even afterwards when someone says that they really like what you did, and you think: 'Oh what *have* I done?' and then you look at it again. Generally I think I just try to live in the moment and respond. I suppose I do have my rules and my concepts and when I get asked to do something at the 'tech table', I might think: 'Ooh I don't want to do that' or 'Oh that's wrong, that doesn't feel right'. Sometimes I do it and sometimes I don't. Sometimes it's more useful to show your colleagues what they have asked for and let them decide that it's not actually a very good idea. Because I have lots of bad ideas and only by showing some bad ideas do you actually begin to get the common language of what's working. So the rationalisation is really very much after the process rather than during it. And actually when I'm aware of it during a design process then I sometimes think I'm not producing my most honest and most immediate work because I'm making it conform to how I think I do things as opposed to how that particular piece should be done.

I think that sometimes lighting designers all end up developing a shorthand and there's certain things I wouldn't leave home without. It's been jokingly told to me once, when I phoned up a colour call and the person on the other end at the hire company kind of offered to do it for me before I told them – and they were 75% right! Now that's not to say those colours were particularly unique to me but they basically had me down for what I was likely to be using. And certainly I feel more confident at thinking that I'm going to be able to get something I like, if I can get certain lighting angles and positions in. When I can't get them I begin to really worry that I don't know what I'm going to do.

Indeed in two of the last operas I just did in America, there were side walls to the set and so I wasn't able to get most of my usual side-light positions in that I rely upon to cover the stage and to light people's faces. We ended up having to do some modified side-light that was coming from just in front of where the walls were, and that still worked enough for me.

But there are certainly things that when I do finally get around to putting something on the drawing board and on to the plan, there's certain stuff I suppose I always try and use up first, which are the larger instruments or the side-light positions that I know are going to pick people out from the scenery in a good way that I feel confident of doing, whether they are lighting booms or pipe ends or whatever positions you get around the proscenium. Those are the areas where I put my bare bones of what I know I'm going to need and I can almost always just colour it up in one, two or three of the colours that I like to use

---

6 A temporary workstation used by technical and design staff during the final stages of a production and often set up in the stalls of a theatre. Lighting is plotted here with the director.

for that sort of lighting and then feel relatively confident that's a starting point for me.

Hunt: How does the lighting design evolve through the production week? How do you know whether the lighting is actually working as you intended?

Fisher: Sometimes it's when you just kind of feel: 'Oh that's working ... that's a moment ... I can see people the way I want to see them' or: 'Oh there's the right atmosphere'. It can be when a colour comes up. It can be when an angle of light hits somebody or something that people get excited about. You feel it among your colleagues or sometimes you just feel it yourself, you think: 'Oh that feels right for this moment'. And if you get two or three moments – and they don't have to necessarily be next to each other initially – then you start to define and develop a language of what's going to work. You get even one good moment and then it's a little bit like doing Sudoku I think, you get so many numbers in a line and all of a sudden the rest of the numbers become a little bit more obvious and what is required next.

And so I have certain moments in a plotting session or a technical session where I'm lighting over,[7] and I hear a director or designer say: 'Oh I like that' and if it's one of my favourite moments, I relax and think: 'Oh good, we've a shared aesthetic here'. It can be just in the use of one of my strange colours that I happen to like, or for example it can be when I'm lighting performers and even though it's a somewhat naturalistic moment I might turn on a shin light if I happen to have one, and the response is immediately positive. They don't mind the fact that it may be casting a larger shadow on a side wall or on a piece of scenery or into the wing, and if they say: 'Oh yes they look really good!' I think: 'OK, that's something I know I like to do and I know how to use'. Sometimes I even censure myself and think: 'I can't light this show that way because that's how I light all my shows' and yet if it's dramatically useful maybe that's why people have asked me to do it in the first place – although I'm never really sure how much people assess someone's style and make a casting decision based upon that.

These moments happen on almost every show, that you start to think: 'Great, we've reached a little bit of a moment of agreement' where I can see, even if a director hasn't said anything that they are starting to reshape things in the way the technical rehearsal is going, based around the lighting state that we were working on. So if I hear them tell the performer: 'That's really good, but if you stand here you will cast a shadow', I know that they're starting to alter things because they like the look, even though they've not told me that specifically. I think: 'OK we're beginning to work together here' and it takes a while sometimes to develop that language, it doesn't always happen first time. It doesn't even happen second time sometimes, and sometimes you get to the end of the show and you haven't done it and it only slowly starts to come.

I'm specifically thinking about light throughout the process. But, you know, you watch a rehearsal and it's that old moment when the hairs on the back of your neck start to raise, you think: 'Oh this is going to be good' – that the moment is so strong that you've forgotten where you're going to have lunch or about all the things you still have to do. These moments still excite me when you see them

---

[7] Creating or re-plotting the lighting at the same time as the technical or dress rehearsals are in progress onstage.

in a rehearsal room or when you have a design meeting and you are looking at a model and not just taking your Maglight and putting it through a hole in the set, you're playing around because you've just experienced a frisson of something. But I suppose it's my job to be obsessed about the lighting so that's what I try and do – after all no-one else is going to!

Hunt: How do these less tangible aspects of the performance process become absorbed in the creative process and translated into a lighting design?

Fisher: Sometimes it can be in the patterns that people are making when they're standing. It can be in the angle of where they're looking at. It can be somehow in the mood a good performance creates. One of the things I think I am rather good at, without sounding too big-headed, is I can sit and watch a run-through even if I don't know very much about the piece that I'm doing, and I can sit down and I can write a list of cues while I'm watching it. This is almost from instinct now. And it can be dictated by music – I've recently been doing operas. Usually it's just done by staging and what they're saying. I can just watch an absolutely bare bones rehearsal and sort of know where there might possibly be a lighting change, or where there's a moment that maybe needs holding in a special way. And so I can sit down and literally just write 'cue point' 'cue point' 'cue point' in a notebook.

Hunt: Do you have a picture of that cue point or just an awareness that something needs to change?

Fisher: I don't necessarily have a picture of that cue point, I just know that something's going to happen. There's a change – and it can be based on a piece of blocking, it can be based on dialogue, it can be based on an atmosphere. And sometimes I just write 'concentrate', meaning that I just want to make sure that this moment is held differently than the moment before it because the discussion's getting into a more intense vein. Sometimes it's based on more obvious things like music or a scenic change. Sometimes it's based on a mood – a suggestion that the stage should brighten or that the lighting should relax as the tension's gone out of the scene. My note doesn't usually mean that I know exactly what I'm going to do; I just know that something has got to happen.

And often I don't even know what I do. I find when I prepare a design nowadays, because I'm an experienced old hack, I basically prepare different sorts of brush strokes and types of brush strokes, without necessarily knowing how I'm going to be applying them. And then the design just sort of happens in the lighting session.

If I find that I'm not using 20 things that I put up in the air, or had someone else put up in the air for me, I don't actually feel that badly about it because I think: 'Great, I'm glad I didn't need that!' And I do believe that good design is not what you turn on, it's what you turn off. And so finding what things work.

I've just been working in a repertory situation much like the National Theatre where you get given a rig where there's basically a light almost anywhere you want to put a light, but you still manage to squeeze a few extras in, in places where you wouldn't normally want to put a light. Slowly but surely I find that I'm breaking those systems apart and I'm using one lamp because it happens to work and re-focusing them as specials. But I'm not using those good 'rep' covers because I don't need them very often. And I'm letting them not even bother to focus some of them because they just don't work for that particular piece. It's trying to make the lighting look as specific as it needs to do. Sometimes you do need those covers and they're absolutely useful but increasingly, a lot of times, I'm finding that they're not. This doesn't mean that I don't want to have them to start with, I like the security of them being there.

That's also in a way how I try and use moving lights. If there's a really good lighting position and I feel that I could use 20 different things in that one place that's where you start to begin to believe that is where a more intelligent light or a more versatile light might be very useful to me. But if they don't earn their keep I'm the first one to get rid of them.

Hunt: How do you visualise light during the pre-production process?

Fisher: I don't draw. If I drew I don't think I'd be a lighting designer. Occasionally when I'm watching rehearsals, I might start to doodle and do a little bit of very bad drawing to see if I can get better at it. Sometimes I find that useful, but usually I don't. I don't do storyboards, although I do think that students should. I don't use pre-visualisation software, almost never spent time on those and never spent time on a CAD suite either, partly because it's never been cost effective. One of the things I love about the theatre is that it's there, strangely enough – it's real even though it's the most artificial thing in the world. You're in the room with it and so that's where you can react to it and get excited by it.

Often I will walk into a first focus session, I won't really know exactly what I'm doing and then slowly I start to turn one or two lights on and I see the way they take the space, and the space takes them and I think: 'Oh that's what it's for', or: 'Oh I'll do that with it', or perhaps: 'I didn't think I would do that with it but that looks nice'. Occasionally I'll have a very strong view from watching a rehearsal that it needs to have this sort of shape or that sort of angle to it, but often I don't anymore.

Hunt: Do you have a different approach to envisaging the lighting when you are working in more open processes such as with a devised performance?

Fisher: I think then I mostly just respond to the space. And I think probably I still mostly respond to the space even when it's a more scripted piece. It's the space that the designer has given me that gets me going and how I can prepare to get light into that space and on to the performers in a way that I find interesting and that allows me to see their faces. I'm unfortunately very old fashioned and I really crave visibility in the theatre, and making people visible in dark spaces is the pleasure and the challenge of lighting design. Making people visible in scenes that wouldn't naturalistically have any light in them is also a challenge, and I think it's one that I've been able to deal with successfully at times, for example learning how sometimes by making a scene brighter it looks darker, or whether you decide to make it more theatrical and bump up a deep colour to give more of a night-time feeling or maybe you choose to pick people out in different ways.

I don't really treat pieces differently, I think in a way I treat all pieces like dance pieces, because what's interesting about dance lighting as it was traditionally taught, was that it was all about picking out the performer in space. And I can't figure out why lighting should be anything other than that. You pick out the performer in space and then you light the space as you need to, and that should give you everything you need. So I suppose when I'm happiest at work I know that I'm picking out the performer and lighting the environment in a way that conveys the atmosphere. Then as a separate element I'm hopefully making the floor receive the light that it accrues from all the light that's lighting the performer and the space so that the design conveys the right atmosphere but yet looks kind of clean and simple as opposed to endless blobs of light in places that you don't need it. If I can accomplish those three strands yet still tie it all together to make a good picture, I'm happy. And I don't think this changes too much whether I'm doing a devised piece or a big Broadway-style musical.

Sometimes though I just don't know where I'm going, the thing about devised work or newer work is you just don't know. The rig is already ordered up, focused, everything, and that's just the way it is, so you plan for the flexibility and the kind of light that you know you think might be useful.

Hunt: Do you wish that you had more of an opportunity to light in the rehearsal room or to have more time on stage while the piece is still developing?

Fisher: Working on *Sweeney Todd* for the Gate Theatre, Dublin which has a low ceiling, no moving lights, no wings or wing space really and so we planned to do the show in a more minimal way. The director had managed to negotiate a week of on-stage rehearsals prior to the tech but some of that time was going to be taken up with the building of the scenery. So I knew that this onstage rehearsal time was going to be very important for me because of the limited amount of tech time and so I said: 'I think what I'll do is I'll just light over your rehearsals' but I didn't want it to become a week extra of lighting sessions. So I decided very quickly to leave the work lights on, so there were about four or five 1K[8] floods shining at the stage the entire time. And as much as I was desperate to turn them off at certain moments when I thought that I had lit a scene, I thought: 'No, that's going to start to turn into a tech and I don't think that's fair to either the director, the performers, or myself'. So I learned, in a way, in my mind, how to mentally subtract the light. Of course it was coming from overhead and it was coming from out front, so I could tell from the direction and quality of light and that experience was really useful because nobody looked at the light at all until the technical rehearsal. And I had a cue structure of 350 cues in place for the show that never would have been made in that amount of time. Because the director was repeatedly going back over things, in a way that you don't even do in a tech. I was able to refine them and if I didn't catch up with something I just left a few blank cues and had my own little mental cue list there.

I love lighting over the real performance as opposed to a lighting session where I think you make a lot of artificial and 'arty' choices that aren't actually often appropriate to where you're going. Also the performers don't just stand looking the way somebody else walking for you will[9] . They have a funny tendency of turning to the side and talking to whoever else is on stage. I think that as we expect more naturalistic acting from our performers, due to television and film, the idea that everyone should stand at 45 degree angles and have a conversation with each other so that you are half to the audience and half to who you are talking to, has gone. Now people stand opposite each other so that their faces are pointing towards the wings as opposed to facing the audience. Therefore you want your face light to be coming from the wings, or at least in the same direction

---

[8] This is shorthand to denote lanterns that are 1 kW (1000 watts).

[9] The practice in a lighting plotting session where performers are substituted by stage management or technical staff to 'walk' across the stage to check that there is sufficient light.

as the wings, rather than that nice 45 degree angle from a front of house position, in three colours if you're lucky!

Sometimes we just have to work much faster. On *Billy Elliot*[10] we had a month of techs and it was very hard keeping fresh and not over fussing about something. Some bits still didn't get done in a month of technical rehearsal. I think you always want more time but sometimes you can have too much time and you just make more mistakes! The danger signs are when you start to be too aware of what you're doing, so you mainly make things over-fussy. Some designers are very confident at making 12 cues on a page of dialogue – so if someone moves over there a light comes up 10% and a light goes down 10%, and I've done shows where that has happened. On the whole I think you've got to feel that the change of light is justified dramatically. I don't necessarily see the point of doing 100 invisible cues. I'd rather try and have 2 or 3 or 12 states that can get you through until I feel a change is dramatically justified. I think you notice when something's changing all the time. Other designers don't feel that way and are very adept at not making you notice when things are changing. I know because I've followed those shows into the theatre and the stage manager says: 'That's so different than when so-and-so was here, we had 600 lighting cues in that play!'

Hunt: How much do you want the lighting design to be visible to the audience or for them to be aware that there is some kind of structure or idea that underpins the design?

Fisher: That's a good question and I think that really changes and that's hopefully a matter of collaboration. It's a difficult conversation sometimes to have and know how to form. I find increasingly at the moment some of the directors who I work with never really talk to me about the lighting at all. I mean we have a couple of vague conversations, or we may talk about a quality of light, but usually they say: 'What did you think of the run-through?' and I tell them and they say: 'Do you have any questions?' and I say: 'No, I think it just needs to be lit now' and a conversation like this suggests that I know that they're probably not after big, bold moments and so you begin to take for granted that someone's going to be working along the same lines as you, and I think that it's bad that we don't have detailed conversations more often. Ironically the further you go up the tree the less likely you are to have those conversations.

I think that it's part of the collaborative process when you start to realise that actually you're not there to draw attention to yourself. You still might be doing rather beautiful work with any luck but it should be a little bit more in the background. And that's just feeling what is right. Some shows, very early on you find out that they need that element where the lighting really adds to the language of it and sometimes the lighting just has to support the language of the piece and be seamlessly part of it without calling any attention to itself. It varies with each piece and sometimes collaborators have different aspirations for what the lighting should do, and you don't always reach agreement either. It's our job as lighting designers to listen and to be sensitive to what the needs are for that particular performance.

---

[10] Also with Daldry and MacNeill, see www.billyelliotthemusical.com.

There are some people who I work with who really want the lighting to be full blooded and very noticed. There are a lot of people who I work with who are very happy if the lighting isn't really noticed and admire it when it's just good at what it does without calling attention to it. And that can change if there are certain moments which are lighting moments. I think most lighting designers will be very familiar with the horrendous moment when you sit down at the beginning of a lighting session and you argue for the first hour over the pre-set, which can be a defining lighting moment. My heart sinks then and I'd just as soon not even set one! I'd rather start from the blackout that follows the pre-set because you often hopefully learn what that pre-set should be once you've gone on a little bit.

And there are just certain moments where people tell you: 'No I don't want that'. I think I'm actually a harsher critic of the lighting than hopefully my director and designers are – not always true but sometimes true! Like all of us, we don't see the full effect of what we do. We will look at a certain aspect of it that might be pleasing. For example, I may love the way side-light sculpts a face and allows people to see into their eyes, and kind of ignore the fact that it casts two to three shadows of a person on a side wall – it may drive the designer absolutely nutty, or the director. I recently had a designer who I have worked with for years and after I'd done the show said: 'I'm not really happy with the way the scenery looks' and I wanted to say: 'How do you feel about how the actors look?' Well that obviously wasn't a worry for him but I realised the effect of the side-light on the scenery and had that wall been in a different position on the stage I would never have dreamed of lighting it with that angle of light, so the wall did end up losing much of its definition because the side-light was just flattening it – as perceived by the audience. Actually I'm about to re-do that particular show in another incarnation and unusually for me, I've rigged certain lights which I'm sort of dedicating to not light people at all but to perhaps reclaim the scenery a little bit – which I had just lost sight of.

I wish my collaborators worried about the same things that I did but I know that they don't. Eventually you find certain people that you think: 'Actually we're not on the same page, we don't want the same things from lighting'. There are certain directors whose work I admire and like to go and see, who like very bright, flat, open white, lighting which to me is really boring. It sort of works for their shows but I think: 'I wouldn't have minded had he given me a bit of atmo-sphere or a bit of modelling or a bit of shape [...] I think I might have enjoyed this performance more'. However, that's clearly not what they want from light-ing, they just want it to give them the freedom to see what they see. I try not to work with those directors because I don't think we're going to be very happy together.

You just have to keep being really critical of your own work and judge how prominent it feels and whether the lighting is helping the rhythm of the piece, or the mood of the piece. Yes, lighting gives you the atmosphere but if you sometimes think that the rhythm, the way that scenes flow together, the way that moments are picked out, if they're not somehow working for the audi-ence, it may be that the lighting can help deliver them more. And that can mean the speed of cue or the type of light. That I think is an important part of the job.

THE ROLE AND POTENTIAL OF LIGHT

Paule Constable's design process, in contrast, often involves planning the lighting in considerable detail at a relatively early stage of the process and developing both conceptual structures for the lighting alongside a detailed rig and cue structure. Nevertheless, this elaborate planning is also viewed as 'provisional' because it has yet to be tested within the theatre space itself. Constable has described her own lighting design process as a structuring of ideas towards the creation of a landscape, which

> starts at the moment you accept the work and continues all the way through. I plan very, very carefully, and that's not because I've got a fixed idea of what I want, but it's the more carefully I plan and the clearer my structure is, the more I have room to allow myself a creative process, because I'm not worrying about the managing of a rig. All that I do beforehand, so that if I get it wrong, at least I am wrong within a structure I can then change – rather than wrong within a structure that is elliptical and unformed. [The structure] is absolutely an aid [...] You have your intellectual responses to a text and a rehearsal space and a model; you have your intuitive responses to them. You have the bizarre thing of trying to articulate [those responses] into a form that is essentially abstract and you can't test, so all of that I try to tie down into some form – in the shape of a rig plan and a cue structure. But then once I get into the space, even though I might stick to that to start with, what that then gives me is more room to manoeuvre beyond that. I like to work really quickly [...] to paint and paint and paint, and once you've got something to look at, even if it's wrong it is something to rage against, something actual in front of you to respond to, and [...] that's the point where I think I start to get creative. You know, it's that terrible thing about lighting design, where you have a sense of what a show feels like, what it smells like, what it tastes like. If you articulate that into a rig, you have no way of knowing if that's going to smell right when you start. I just do it in order to give myself more room to manoeuvre and get it wrong.[11]

Echoing Fisher in describing the pressures and uncertainties of the environment in which the lighting designer operates, Mark Henderson also recognises the need for the lighting designer to be able to improvise and respond quickly to changing circumstances during the production period. This flexibility and ability to respond creatively and sensitively might be seen as the most important of all of the contemporary lighting designer's attributes:[12]

> I think I'm a little bit more flexible to be able to react to what works and what doesn't work at the time, rather than going in with a very clear and specific idea

---

11 Nick Hunt, interview with Paule Constable, 28 May 2008.
12 Scott Palmer, interview with Mark Henderson, 19 July 2000.

of what's going to work. It's just being able to have enough things to be able to manipulate to get the best from what you're creating as you go along.

You always live in fear that the next show you do is 'half a pile of crock' and you're going to get kicked off it – every show I go into you're always wondering. You develop ways to get out of trouble and make the most of what's there although I'm not sure it's necessarily the best way of doing this. Sometimes, well a lot of the time, I go into a show and I don't actually know what it's going to turn out like and you're just trusting your training and your instinct that the kit you've put up there is going to do the job and that you're going to pull something out, because very rarely does a show turn out like you thought it would. It is quite frightening in some ways. It's really scary I think because you don't know how it is going to turn out!

[...] You often find that if you do have a picture in your head of what it is going to be, that isn't actually what works best or doesn't work at all and so you have to be able to manipulate that. [...] You sort of get to learn those little tricks about those happy accidents. I think possibly I try and put things in 'happy accident' places now, because you know that that weird angle might work well there, [...] it is very often those quirky things that work best. But you've still got to have the basics there.

Trust is a key component in successful collaborative processes and is critical to the way in which the lighting designer is able to work. Henderson notes:

The notion of trust is essential [...] because in a technical you can say: 'I'll look at that later' [...] and people have then got to be able to trust you that you're going to do that. Often because the technical is so pressured you're very blinkered towards the picture that you're looking at and it's only really after a dress rehearsal or even maybe after the first preview when you're able to stand back, look at it and think: 'Oh my God it's appalling' or: 'That's rather good, I'll work on that a bit more' and you can then work the process from there.

Despite these observations, there are clearly still issues inherent in the creative process of lighting performance work. Director Katie Mitchell provides advice about how to work with a lighting designer and outlines the process of lighting a play in straightforward terms. There are, however, some interesting assumptions about the creative process that leads up to the final realisation of the lighting, which underlines the tendency, in British theatre at least, for lighting to be seen as something that is only added to the production at the last minute:

The lighting plotting session is the moment at which you look at the lighting designer's proposals for the lighting states for the first time. [...] [although] You will already have discussed the lighting design in detail with the lighting designer *during the last week of rehearsals*.

(Mitchell, 2009: 205, my italics)

In fairness, Mitchell is also clear elsewhere that the lighting designer should be involved early on in discussions with the set designer and in three-way conversations with the designer and director. Her remarkable work in collaboration with Paule Constable would certainly bear this out but, as we have seen, the constraints under which lighting designers work means that often there is relatively little time to engage in dialogue through the rehearsal process or to execute the design in the production week. These production practices (in mainstream theatre at least), coupled with the disparate levels of fees for lighting designers, suggest that often lighting is still seen as a necessary but subsidiary element of the theatrical event.

The debate about the role and potential of light continues, even amongst lighting technicians and designers:

> Lighting is there [...] to assist the performer, actor or variety act in their performance. You assist in the best way you can, without drawing attention to yourself. I hate to say it, but if you notice the lighting, then it's lousy because it shouldn't draw attention to itself.
>
> (Brian Legge, lighting technician[13])

The outdated and conservative view that the best lighting is that which is not noticed is frequently replicated in print by theatre critics. If the contribution of the lighting designer is noted at all, critics rarely understand the language of light or seem to have the ability to articulate its impact in written form. Little seems to have changed since Herbert Prentice, director of Birmingham Repertory Theatre, observed:

> I have often read dramatic criticisms, written by prominent critics, in which there has been a merciless and wholesale condemnation of the lighting. Often it is justified, but occasionally one finds a glimmer of hope and enlightenment, which is generally criticized through lack of understanding. Many critics have not attempted to understand modern stage lighting, so the line of least resistance is to condemn it. This does not mean that the lighting is wrong: the critics need to be severely criticized. Lighting is a new medium of expression, and must be approached from that point of view.
>
> (Ridge and Aldred, 1936: xi)

The advent of new lighting sources, including LEDs, offers new technical possibilities and potential creative solutions. LED 'projection' screens have become significant light sources that are employed widely in the television and events industries, both as scenic backdrops and also, as their output has improved, as light sources in their own right.

---

[13] British Library *Theatre Archive Project* (www.bl.uk/theatrearchive).

Economic and environmental factors have also come into play – from the overall power consumption of lighting rigs to the European theatre industry's fight to keep quartz halogen lamps from becoming outlawed due to their energy inefficiency. This recent development has seen the loss of the conventional domestic light bulb with its tungsten filament (which alone causes issues with historical accuracy in plays set in the twentieth century), but there are far-reaching implications of the loss of the specialised tungsten theatre lamp with its particular quality of warm, white light. Our experience of performance may well be about to change radically, through political decisions that will alter the colour temperature of the light in which we are able to observe it.

Lights that use different lamps and which operate at higher colour temperatures are already widely used in tandem with the conventional theatre lantern. They offer a number of design options since, like the historic lime-light and carbon-arc, they are able to be perceived above an existing lighting state. The development of moving lights since the late 1980s, and their widespread adoption, has been the greatest change in lighting practice since the advent of electricity. The convergence of this technology with that of the video projector controlled with computers is now beginning to offer sophisticated lighting instruments of which Appia and Craig could only have dreamed. Projected light has been beyond the immediate scope of this book but the potential that any light might be controlled remotely and capable of projecting complex combinations of animated, textured images opens up fascinating new possibilities for the creative use of light in performance.

Fabrizzio Cristafulli, an Italian lighting designer who uses projection as a key element in his work, advocates an active role for light on the stage. In his book *Luce Attiva*, he counters those who believe that light should not consciously draw attention to itself in performance. This concluding comment, with an echo of Appia, brings us back to the aspirations of the Swiss pioneer in providing a reminder of the essential and dynamic role that light brings to performance and also of its future potential:

In my theatre work, I seek to entrust light with a role similar to that which it occupies in the natural world. Not by imitating it, but by considering light as a vital substance – an essential, primal and emergent element – and thereby liberating it from its secondary role as a tool for effect or staging to which it is often relegated. I believe that light does not belong only to the technical or visual domain. Its fundamental functions are to shape time and space, to become a dramatic structure, and serve as a means of unfolding or producing 'actions'. [...] This process is crucial for determining the role of light, which, even though it differs from production to production, remains an integral and evolving element within the entire set of relations. In other words, light is not a technical element 'projected' onto the production, but becomes a component of the relational place itself: woven into the actions, time, spaces, forms, sounds and words that define themselves through their relationship with each other. In relation to these elements, light is both origin and consequence. From the beginning it is considered an active and formative factor.

(Cristafulli, in Hannah and Harsløf, 2008: 93)

Appendix: *Mima* (1928): Excerpts from Operator Cue Sheets

Belasco Theatre, New York
12 December 1928 – 16 May 1929

These cue sheets were created by Belasco and Hartmann for the various operators of the lighting for *Mima* and they reveal how the lighting was plotted and operated. The production was over two years in the planning and the final rehearsals lasted four weeks, ensuring that 'every phase of illumination was under perfect control' (Hartmann, 1930: 120).

The General Plot provided a condensed summary of how the lighting should be realised throughout the whole play.

General Plot for Act I

As music of overture starts, house lights go down. Pull house switches from top to bottom separately, leaving blue dome and boxes on.

Stereopticon effects are thrown on both sides of proscenium arch at definite music cue during overture.

Whirligigs on either side of stage come up together slowly on second music cue.

Cave (Icebox-green) lights follow whirligigs.

Whirligigs die down on music cue; also stereopticons.

Pull house lights at roll of drums, so that auditorium will be totally dark before last note of overture is sounded.

Red lens is thrown on Malacoda after he has entered and stands in place. The lens should be thrown simultaneously with the last note of the overture.

When Magister enters: Throw red spot on him.

'Then let us begin our search.' Bring blue reflectors on Right to one half. Dim white and amber pockets to low mark.

'... of his home life.' Bring drapery strip to four mark. The curtains on the School-master's Scene have been opened and blue lights in Schoolmaster's vision begin to develop. Pink and amber lenses come up, the amber lights working up as the vision descends.

'... plate of appetiz...''Pull lights to flash out Schoolmaster's Scene. Drapery strip goes out.

When curtains close: Bring drapery strip to mark.

The House Switchboard Plot contains the instructions for the board operator who controlled the auditorium lights and front lighting for the stage. These cues are for the very first moments of Act I.

House Switchboard Plot

No front lights, this act.
Music cue: Pull house switches from top to bottom separately leaving blue dome and boxes on.
Music cue: Front switch. Fire effect, Dim up full.
Music cue: Dim fire. Dim to out. Pull switch.
Workers repeat: 'Turning, bobbing, throbbing': Front switch and dim two reflectors up about one-half. Drapery strip to four mark.
Court enters pit: Drapery strip to high mark and dim out reflectors. Fronts while Court stands. After song put front dimmer to full for spotlight.

The Working Plot provided a detailed scene-by-scene cue sheet for the main lighting board operator indicating which circuits are to be used. It is interesting to note the lack of detailed timing information. This excerpt covers the beginning of the play only.

Working Plot

Music cue: No. 1 up slow.
Music cue: No. 1 down and out. No. 9 Cave up to first mark.
Last note of music: No. 14 flashed in (Dimmer set one-third) Lens. No. 13 flashed in (Dimmer full) Ref.
'Thank you, Sir.' No. 14 up full. No. 13 down and out.
'See what it is-it is the Adjutant.' No. 12 Aisle up full.
'. . . to your electric bridge.' No. 6 Switchboard up one-third mark.
At Devil's Hymn: No. 12 down and out.

The Front Spotlight Cue Sheets provided information for each of the follow-spot operators, detailing who they should pick up and the size and colour of the beam. These examples are from the first scene of Act II.

FRONT SPOTLIGHT NUMBER ONE

Magister's entrance, first entrance Right: Throw red pin spot on him.
'. . . schedule': Increase spot at Center of stage.
When Workers enter: Cover all.
Follow Magister throughout act.

FRONT SPOTLIGHT NUMBER TWO

'Bring on the Manikins!' Green spot as cave door opens. Stay till last Manikin is up to top of steps and out slowly.

'Bring on Mima!' Green spot on cave door as it opens, and follows Mima to Left of stage. Blind off slowly as she starts to Center of stage.

'She will awaken!' Violet spot large on Mima as Mima light comes on. Violet spot small.

'My darling! My darling!' Blind off.

This operator then has to concentrate mainly on following Mima and undertaking a series of colour change cues, which alternate between red, pink, green, violet and blue spots on specific cue lines.

(Hartmann 1930: 119–131)

References

Alexandre, Arsène (1900) 'Le Théâtre de la Loïe Fuller' in *Le Théâtre* 40, 11/8/1900 23–25.

Algarotti, Francesco (1773 [1755]) *Saggio sopra l'opera in musica*, Venice published in *Mercure de France* May 1757 (trans. Chevalier de Chastelleux as *Essai sur l'opéra* Paris 1773 and in English as *An Essay on the Opera*, Davis & Reymers 1767.

Allbright, Ann Cooper (2007) *Traces of Light Absence and Presence in the Work of Loïe Fuller* (Middletown, CT: Wesleyan University Press).

Allen, David (2000) *Performing Chekhov* (London, New York: Routledge).

Alma-Tadema, Lawrence (1901) 'Rome in the Theatre: A talk with Sir Lawrence Alma-Tadema' *Daily News* 16/4/1901.

Anon (1936) 'Der Schwur unter dem Lichtdom' Der Parteitag der Ehre vom 8. bis 14. September 1936. *Offizieller Bericht über den Verlauf des Reichsparteitages mit sämtlichen Kongreßreden*, Munich: Zentralverlag der NSDAP.1936, 170–177 translated Bytwerk, R L as 'The Oath under the Cathedral of Light at the 1936 Nuremberg Party Rally' [online] http://www.calvin.edu/academic/cas/gpa/pt36dom.htm (accessed 10/5/2010).

Antoine, André (1903) 'Causerie sur la mise en scène' in *La revue de Paris*, 1 April, 596–612.

Appia, Adolphe (1895) *The Staging of Wagnerian Drama. (La mise en scène du drame wagnérien)* (Paris: Léon Chailley).

Appia, Adolphe (1904) 'Ideas on a Reform of Our *Mise en Scène*' *La Revue des revues* 1(9), June, 342–349.

Appia, Adolphe (1908) 'Comments on the Theatre' *La Vie Musicale* 1(15) 1, April, 233–238 and 1(16) 8 April, 253–256.

Appia, Adolphe (1954a [1919]) 'Actor, Space, Light, Painting (1919)' *Journal de Genève* 19, January, 23–24 (originally written in 1919 as 'L'avenir du drame et de la mise en scène').

Appia, Adolphe (1954b) 'Comments on the Staging of *The Ring of the Nibelungs*' in *Revue d'histoire du théâtre*, 1–2 1954.

Appia, Adolphe (1983) *Oeuvres Complètes* Vol. 1, Bablet-Hahn, M L (ed.) (Lausanne: l'Age d'homme: Société Suisse du théâtre) 1880–1894.

Appia, Adolphe (1983–1992) *Oeuvres Complètes* Vol. 1–4, Bablet-Hahn, M L (ed.) (Lausanne: l'Age d'homme: Société Suisse du théâtre).

Appia, Adolphe (1986) *Oeuvres Complètes* Vol. 2 Bablet-Hahn, M L (ed.) (Lausanne: l'Age d'homme: Société Suisse du théâtre) 1895–1905.

Applebee, L G (1946) 'The Evolution of Stage Lighting' Lecture given at the Nineteenth Ordinary Meeting 15/4/1946 published in *Journal of the Royal Society of Arts* Volume XCIV 2/8/1946 (London: G Bell & Sons) 550–563.

Aristotle (c.350 BC) *Poetics* trans. S H Butcher, MIT Classics [online] http://classics.mit.edu/Aristotle/poetics.1.1.html (accessed 15/7/2010).

Aronson, Arnold (2005) *Looking into the Abyss: Essays on Scenography* (Ann Arbor: University of Michigan Press).

Artaud, Antonin (1964) *Le Théatre et son Double (sic) in Oeuvres Completes d'Antonin Artaud*, Vol. IV (Paris: Gallimard).

Artaud, Antonin (1976) *Selected Writings trans. Helen Weaver* (Farrar, Straus & Giroux: New York).

Bab, Julius (1928) *Das Theater der Gegenwart: Geschichte der dramatischen Bühne seit 1870* (Leipzig: J J Weber).

Bablet, Denis (1966) *Edward Gordon Craig* trans. Woodward, D (London: Heinemann).

Bablet, Denis (1982) *Appia and Theatrical Space: From Revolt to Utopia in Adolphe Appia 1862–1928, Actor-Space-Light Exhibition Catalogue* (London: John Calder Ltd).

Bablet-Hahn, Marie-Louise (1992) *Notes to Oeuvres Complètes Volume 4, 1921–28* (Lausanne, l'Age d'homme: Société Suisse du théâtre).

Balukhaty, S D (ed.) (1952) *The Seagull produced by Stanislavsky. Production Score for the Moscow Art Theatre by K.S. Stanislavsky* trans. D Magarshack (London: Dennis Dobson Ltd).

Banham, Martin (1995) *Cambridge Guide to Theatre* (Cambridge: Cambridge University Press).

Baugh, Christopher (1987) 'Phillipe James de Loutherbourg and the Early Pictorial Theatre: Some Aspects of its Cultural Context' in Redmond, James (ed.) *The Theatrical Space (Themes in Drama series)* (Cambridge: Cambridge University Press).

Baugh, Christopher (1994) 'Brecht and Stage Design: The Bühnenbildner and the Bühnenbauer' in Thomson, P and Sacks, G (eds.) *The Cambridge Companion to Brecht* (Cambridge: Cambridge University Press).

Baugh, Christopher (2005) *Theatre, Performance and Technology: The Development of Scenography in the Twentieth Century* (Basingstoke: Palgrave Macmillan).

Baugh, Christopher (2007) 'Scenography and Technology' in Moody, J and O'Quinn, D (eds.) *The Cambridge Companion to British Theatre, 1730–1830* (Cambridge: Cambridge University Press) 43–56.

Bay, Howard (1974) *Stage Design* (New York: Drama Book Specialists).

Beacham, Richard (1993) *Adolphe Appia: Texts on Theatre* (London: Routledge).

Beacham, Richard (1994) *Adolphe Appia: Artist and Visionary of the Modern Theatre* (Amsterdam: Harwood Academic).

Belasco, David (1919) *The Theatre Through its Stage Door* (New York and London: Harper & Bros).

Bennett, Susan (1997) *Theatre Audiences: A Theory of Production and Reception* 2nd edition (London, New York: Routledge).

Bentham, Frederick (1950) *Stage Lighting* (London: Sir Isaac Pitman & Son).

Bentham, Frederick (1957) *Stage Lighting* revised 2nd edition (London: Sir Isaac Pitman & Sons).

Bentham, Frederick (1968) *The Art of Stage Lighting* (London: Pitman Publishing).

Bentham, Frederick (1976) *The Art of Stage Lighting* 2nd edition (London: Pitman Publishing Ltd.).

Bentham, Frederick (1992) *Sixty Years of Light Work* (Isleworth: Strand Lighting Ltd).

Bentley, Eric (1955) 'Review of performance of Tennessee Williams's *Cat on a Hot Tin Roof*' in *The New Republic*, 4/4/1955.

Bentley, Eric (ed.) (1997) *The Theory of the Modern Stage* (New York: Applause).

Berghaus, Günter (1998) *Italian Futurist Theatre, 1909–1944* (Oxford: Clarendon Press).

Berghaus, Günter (2005) *Theatre, Performance and the Historical Avant-garde* (New York, Basingstoke: Palgrave Macmillan).

Bergman, Gösta M (1977) *Lighting in the Theatre* (Stockholm: Almqvist & Wiksell International; Totowa, NJ: Rowman & Littlefield).

Besbes, Khaled (2007) *The Semiotics of Beckett's Theatre: A Semiotic Study of the Complete Dramatic Works of Samuel Beckett* (Boca Raton, Fla: Universal Publishers).

Bibliothèque de la Comédie Française (1719) 'Dépense des Chandelles orders et des Lampions et Chandelles extraordres à commencer aujord'huy samedy 22e avril 1719' in *Dépenses pour l'année 1719* (Paris).

Bolt, Barbara (2004) *Art beyond Representation: The Performative Power of the Image* (London and New York: I B Tauris & Co).

Booth, Michael R (1981) *Victorian Spectacular Theatre* (London: Routledge & Kegan Paul).

Braun, Edward (1982) *The Director and the Stage: From Naturalism to Grotowski* (London: Methuen).

Brecht, Bertolt (1951 [1940]) Appendix to 'Kurze Beschreibung einer neuen Technik der Schauspielkunst, die einen Verfremdungseffekt hervorbringt', in *Versuche 11* (Frankfurt: Suhrkamp).

Brecht, Bertolt (1952) *Theaterarbeit, 6 Aufführungen des Berliner Ensembles* (Dresden: Dresdner Verlag).

Brecht, Bertolt (1959) 'Über experimentelles Theater' from *Theater der Zeit*, 4 East Berlin ('On Experimental Theatre' trans. J Willett 1964).

Brecht, Bertolt (1962) 'Notizen über die Züricher Erstaufführung' (1948) in *Herr Puntila und sein Knecht Matti*, trans. Alan Clarke (Leipzig: Verlag Philipp Reklam Jr.) 109–111.

Brecht, Bertolt (1965) *The Messingkauf Dialogues* (c.1942), trans. J Willett (London: Eyre Methuen).

Brecht, Bertolt (1966) *Über Theater* (Leipzig: Verlag Philipp Reklam Jr).

Brecht, Bertolt (1987) *Poems 1913–1956* 2nd revised edition, Willett, J. and Manheim, R. (eds) (London and New York: Methuen).

Brockett, Oscar G (1991) *History of the Theatre* 6th edition (Boston, London: Allyn & Bacon).

Burian, Jarka M (1970) 'Josef Svoboda: Theatre Artist in an Age of Science' in *Educational Theatre Journal*, 22(2) (May 1970), 123–145 (John Hopkins University Press) [online] http://www.jstor.org/stable/3205717 (accessed 20/10/2010).

Butterworth, Philip (1998) *Theatre of Fire: Special Effects in Early English and Scottish Theatre* (London: The Society for Theatre Research).

Carter, Huntley (1914) *The Theatre of Max Reinhardt* (London: F & C Palmer).

Catel, Louis (1802) *Vorchläge zur Verbesserung der Schauspielhäuser* (Berlin: Gottlieb August Lange).

Cheney, Sheldon (1914) *The New Movement in the Theatre* (New York: Mitchell Kennelly).

Clegg, Brian (2001) *Light Years: An Exploration of Mankind's Enduring Fascination with Light* (London: Piatkus).

Cole, Toby and Krich Chinoy, Helen (eds.) (1953) *Directing the Play: A Sourcebook of Stagecraft* (Indianapolis and New York: Bobbs-Merrill).

Cole, Toby and Krich Chinoy, Helen (eds.) (1963) *Directors on Directing: A Sourcebook of the Modern Theatre* (Indianapolis and New York: Bobbs-Merrill).

Corneilson, Paul (1997) 'Reconstructing the Mannheim court theatre' in *Early Music* February 1997 (Oxford) 63–81.

Corry, Percy (1954) *Lighting the Stage* (London: Pitman).

Cowell, Joseph (1844) *Thirty Years Passed Among the Players of England and America* (New York: Harper & Bros).

Craig, E G (1913) *Towards a New Theatre* (London and Toronto: J M Dent & Sons).

Craig, E G (1915) *The Mask* VII(2) May, 159–160.

Craig, E G (1923) *Scene* (London: Humphrey Milford, Oxford University Press).

Craig, E (1968) *Gordon Craig: The Story of his Life* (London: Victor Gollancz Ltd).

Cristafulli, Fabrizio (2007) *Luce Attiva: Questioni della luce nel teatro contemporaneo* (Pisa: Titivillus Edizioni).

Current, Richard Nelson and Current, Marcia Ewing (1997) *Loïe Fuller, Goddess of Light* (Boston: Northeastern University Press).

Davis, Charles (2002) 'Architecture and Light: Vincenzo Scamozzi's Statuary installation in the Chiesetta of the Palazzo Ducale in Venice' *Annali di architettura*, 14/2002 (Rivista del Centro internazionale di Studi di Architettura Andrea Palladio di Vicenza: Vicenza).

Dekker, Thomas (1606) *Seven Deadly Sins of London* printed by E.A. for Nathaniel Butter, and are to bee sold at his shop neere Saint Austens gate (London).

Delgado, Maria M and Heritage, Paul (eds.) (1996) *In Contact with the Gods? Directors Talk Theatre* (Manchester and New York: Manchester University Press).

Di Benedetto, Stephen (2010) *The Provocation of the Senses in Contemporary Theatre* (London and New York: Routledge).

Diderot, D (1875) *Oeuvres complétes* Vol. vii (Paris: Garner).

Dobson, Austin (1912) *At Prior Park and Other Papers* (London: Chatto & Windus)

Dorn, Dieter (1999) *'Making Light – A Forward'* in Max Keller, *Light Fantastic* (Munich: Prestel).

Dunant, Henry (1875) 'The Pyrophone' *Popular Science Monthly* 7, August 444–454.

Eco, Umberto (1986) *'The Aesthetics of Light'* in *Art and Beauty in the Middle Ages* trans. Hugh Bredin (New Haven and London: Yale University Press) 43–51.

Esslin, Martin (1977) 'Max Reinhardt – High Priest of Theatricality' *TDR* 21(2), 3–24.

Esslin, M (1987) *The Field of Drama: How the Signs of Drama Create Meaning on Stage and Screen* (London and New York: Methuen).

Finkel, Alicia (1996) *Romantic Stages: Set and Costume Design in Victorian England* (Jefferson, North Carolina, and London: McFarland & Company, Inc.).

Fischer-Lichte, Erika (1992) *The Semiotics of Theater* trans. Jeremy Gaines and Doris L Jones (Bloomington and Indianapolis: Indiana University Press).

Fisher, Rick (2007) Conversation with Nick Hunt at National Theatre, 6th August 2007 edited by Palmer, S.

Fitzgerald, Percy (1881) *The World Behind the Scenes* (London: Chatto & Windus).

Flecknoe, Richard (1908 [1664]) 'A Short Discourse of the English Stage' in Spingarn, J E (ed.) *Critical Essays of Seventeenth Century* (Oxford: Clarendon Press).

Foulkes, Richard (ed.) (2008) *Henry Irving: A Re-evaluation of the Pre-eminent Victorian Actor-Manager* (Aldershot: Ashgate Publishing Ltd).

Fuchs, Theodore (1929) *Stage Lighting* (Boston: Little, Brown & Co).

Fuller, Loïe (1913) *Fifteen Years of a Dancer's Life, With Some Account of Her Distinguished Friends* (Boston: Small, Maynard & Co).

Furttenbach, J (1628) *Architectura Civilis* (Ulm: Johann Gaurn) [online] http://books. google.co.uk/books?id=9fJPAAAAcAAJ&printsec=frontcover&source=gbs_ge_ summary_r&cad=0#v=onepage&q&f=false.

Furttenbach, J (1640) *Architectura Recreationis* (Augsburg: Johann Sebastian Medern) [online] http://books.google.co.uk/books?id=8vJPAAAAcAAJ&printsec= frontcover&source=gbs_ge_summary_r&cad=0#v=onepage&q&f=false.

Furttenbach, J (1663) *(The Noble Mirror of Art (Manhafter Kunst-Spiegel)* (Augsburg: Johann Schultes) [online] http://echo.mpiwg-berlin.mpg.de/ECHOdocuView? url=/permanent/library/AWDSR505/pageimg&pn=1&mode=imagepath.

Garelick, Rhonda K (2009) *Electric Salome: Loie Fuller's Performance of Modernism* (Woodstock, NJ: Princeton University Press).

Gassner, J and Allen, R (eds.) (1992) *Theatre and Drama in the Making: Antiquity to the Renaissance* 2nd edition (New York: Applause Theatre Books).

Gibson, J (1983 [1966, 1968]) *The Senses Considered as Perceptual Systems* (Westport, CT: Greenwood Press).

Goffin, Peter (1938) *Stage Lighting for Amateurs* (London: Frederick Muller).

Golub, Spencer (1984) *Evreinov: The Theatre of Paradox and Transformation* (Ann Arbor, Michigan: UMI Research Press).

Gooday, Graeme (2008) *Domesticating Electricity: Technology, Uncertainty and Gender*, 1880–1914 (London: Pickering & Chatto) 105–109.

Grau, Robert (1912) *The Stage in the 20th Century*, Vol. 3 (New York: Broadway Publishing Co).

Graves, R B (1980) 'Shakespeare's Outdoor Stage Lighting' *Shakespeare Studies* (Cranbery: Associated University Presses) 13, 235–250.

Graves, R B (1999) *Lighting the Shakespearean Stage* (Carbondale: Southern Illinois University Press).

Greengrass, Kim (1999) *An Inspector Calls – Teacher's Resource Pack*, written for the Magenta Partnership, Royal National Theatre.

Gropius, Walter (ed.) (1961) *The Theater of the Bauhaes: Oskar Schlemmer, Laszlo Moholy-Nagy, Farkas Molnár*, trans. Arthur S Wensinger (Middletown, CT: Wesleyan University Press).

Gualterotti, Rafaello (1579) *Feste nelle nozze del Serenissimo Don Francesco Medici Gran Duca di Toscana, e della Sereniss. sua Consorte la Sig. Bianca Cappello . . .* (Florence: Nuovamente Ristampate).

Hannah, D and Harsløf, O (eds.) (2008) *Performance Design* (Copenhagen: Museum Tusculanum Press, University of Copenhagen).

Hartmann, Louis (1930) *Theatre Lighting – A Manual of the Stage Switchboard* (New York, London: D. Appleton & Co).

Hartnoll, Phyllis (1967) *Oxford Companion to the Theatre* 3rd edition (London: Oxford University Press).

Helson, H (1938) 'Fundamental problems in Colour Vision' *Journal of Experimental Psychology* 23 439–476.

Herald, Heinz (1918) 'Notiz zur Bettler-Aufführung' *Das junge Deutschland* (Berlin: Deutsches Theatre) 1(1) 30.

Hewitt, B (ed.) (1958) *The Renaissance Stage Documents of Serlio, Sabbattini and Furttenbach*. trans. Nicoll (Coral Gables, Fla: University of Miami Press).

Holmburg, Arthur (1996) *The Theatre of Robert Wilson* (Cambridge: Cambridge University Press).

Howard, Pamela (2002) *What is Scenography?* (London: Routledge).

Hughes, Alan (1979) 'Henry Irving's Artistic Use of Stage Lighting' *Theatre Notebook* (The Society for Theatre Research) 33(3) 100–109.

Ihering, H (1920) Review in *Der Tag* Berlin 22/1/1920 reprinted in Rühle, G (ed.) (1967) *Theater für die Reublik 1917–1933 im Spiegel der Kritik* (Frankfurt/Main: S Fischer) 187–188.

Ingegneri, Angelo (1598) *Della Poesia rappresentativa e del modo di rappresentare le favole sceniche*, Ferrara 1598; reprinted in *Delle Opere del Cavalier Battista Guarini*, Verona

1738, iii, 526–527. English translation in Nicholl, A (1957) *Stewart Masques and the Renaissance Stage* (London: Harrap & Co) 133–134.

Innes, Christopher D (1972) *Erwin Piscator's Political Theatre: The Development of Modern German Drama* (Cambridge: Cambridge University Press).

Innes, Christopher D (1998) *Edward Gordon Craig: A Vision of Theatre* (London: Harwood Academic Publishers).

Izenour, G (1988) *Theater Technology* (New York: McGraw-Hill Companies).

Jackson, Barry (1991) 'Diaghilev: Lighting Designer' *Dance Chronicle* 14(1) (Taylor & Francis) 1–35 [online] http://www.jstor.org/stable/1567780 (accessed 18/10/2009).

Jackson, Russell (ed.) (1989) *Victorian Theatre: A New Mermaid Background Book* (London: A & C Black).

Jones, Robert Edmond (1969 [1941]) *The Dramatic Imagination: Reflections and Speculations on the Art of the Theatre* (New York: Theatre Arts Books).

Joseph, Stephen (1967) 'Stage Lighting for Theatre in the Round' in Theatre in the Round (London: Barrie & Rockcliff).

Journal de Genève, 23 January 1954, trans. S. Palmer, 3.

Keller, Max (1999) *Light Fantastic* (Munich: Prestel).

Kernodle, G R (1942) 'The Magic of Light' *Theatre Arts* XXVI, November 1942 717–722.

Kernodle, G R (1944) *From Art and Theatre: Form and Convention in the Renaissance* (Chicago: University of Chicago Press).

Kirby, Michael (1971) *Futurist Performance* (New York: E P Dutton & Co. Inc).

KMA (2006) information from web site [online]: http://www.kma.co.uk/ (accessed 10/12/2006).

Lavoisier, Antoine L (1865) 'Mémoire sur la manière d'éclairer les salles de spectacle', *Oeuvres* Vol. III Paris [online] http://moro.imss.fi.it/lavoisier/main.asp (accessed 22/04/2008).

Lawrence, William J (1889a) 'First use of lime-light on the stage' *Notes & Queries* 8 (London).

Lawrence, William J (1889b) 'Some famous scene painters' Magazine of Art (London: Cassell, Petter, Galpin & Co).

Lawrence, William J (1927) *Pre-Restoration Stage Studies* (London: Oxford University Press).

Lawrence, William J (1935) *Old Theatre Days and Ways* (New York: Benjamin Blom Inc).

Leacroft, R H (1984) *Theatre and Playhouse – An Illustrated Survey of Theatre Building from Ancient Greece to the Present Day* (London: Methuen).

Lehmann, Hans-Thies (2006) *Postdramatic Theatre* trans. Karen Jürs-Munby (London, New York: Routledge).

Lesser Wendy (1997) *A Director Calls: Stephen Daldry and the Theatre* (Berkeley, Los Angeles: University of California Press).

Lloyds, Frederick (1875) *Practical Guide to Scene Painting and Painting in Distemper* (London: G Rowney).

LUCI Association [online] http://www.luciassociation.org (accessed 23/11/2006).

Lyonnet, Henri (1928) 'Loïe Fuller' *Larousse Mensuel Illustré* July1928 757–758.

MacGowan, Kenneth (1921) *The Theatre of Tomorrow* (New York: Boni & Liveright, Inc).

MacGowan, Kenneth and Jones, Robert (1922) *Continental Stagecraft* (New York: Benjamin Blom).

Matthews, William (1827) *A Historical Sketch of the Origin, Progress and Present State of Gas Lighting* (London: Rowland Hunter).

Mauclair, Camille (1907) 'Loïe Fuller as Salomé,' "Actualités" folder on Loïe Fuller, Bibliothèque de la Ville de Paris (cited in Allbright).

McCandless, Stanley Russell (1926) *A Glossary of Stage Lighting* Theatre Arts Monthly,10 (New York: Theatre Arts) 627–642.

McCandless, Stanley, Russell (1931) *A Syllabus of Stage Lighting* (New Haven, CT: Whitlock's).

McCandless, Stanley (1932) *A Method of Lighting the Stage* (New York: Theatre Arts).

McCandless, Stanley (1958) *A Method of Lighting the Stage* 4th edition (New York: Theatre Arts Books).

McKinney, Joslin and Butterworth, Philip (2009) *The Cambridge Introduction to Scenography* (Cambridge: Cambridge University Press).

Meizel, Martin (1983) *Realizations: Narrative, Pictoral and Theatrical Arts in Nineteenth Century England* (New Jersey: Princeton University Press).

Merleau Ponty, Maurice (1964) "Eye and Mind' trans. Dallery in Edie, J M (ed.) *The Primacy of Perception* (Evanston: Northwestern University Press).

Mielziner, Jo (1965) *Designing for the Theatre* (New York: Atheneum).

Mitchell, Katie (2009) *The Director's Craft – A Handbook for the Theatre* (London: Routledge).

Montalti, Mauro (1920) For a *New Theatre: 'Electric-Vibrating-Luminous'* [online] http://www.391.org/manifestos/1920mauromontalti-foranewtheatre.htm (accessed 1/4/2010).

Morgan, Nigel (2005) *Stage Lighting Design in Britain: The Emergence of the Lighting Designer 1881–1950* (Cambridge: Entertainment Technology Press).

Morita, Naoko (2006) 'An American in Paris: Loie Fuller, Dance and Technology' in Holmes, D and Tarr, C (eds.) *A "Belle Epoque"? Women in French Society and Culture, 1890–1914* (Oxford: Berghan Books).

Morton, Hugh (1896) 'Loïe Fuller and Her Strange Art' in *Metropolitan Magazine*, Vol. 3, 4 May, 277–283.

Mukařovský, Jan (1976) 'The Essence of the Visual Arts', a lecture at the institute for National education on 26/1/1944, *Studie z estetiky*, Prague, 1966, 188–195 in Matejka, Ladislav and Titunik, Irwin R. (eds) (1976) *Semiotics of Art: Prague School Contributions* (Cambridge, MA; London: MIT Press).

Mulryne, J R and Shewring, M (eds.) (1991) *Theatre of the English and Italian Renaissance* (Basingstoke: Palgrave Macmillan).

Mumford, Peter (1985) 'Lighting Dance' in *Dance Research: The Journal of the Society for Dance Research*, 3(2) (Summer 1985) 46–55 Edinburgh University Press [online] http://www.jstor.org/stable/1290557 (accessed 15/2/2013).

Nagler, A M (1964) *Theatre Festivals of the Medici, 1539–1637* (New Haven and London: Yale University Press).

Nagler, A M (1952) *A Source Book in Theatrical History* (New York: Dover Publications).

Nelson, Alfred L and Cross, Gilbert B (eds.) (1974) *James Winston, Drury Lane Journal: Selections from James Winston's Diaries 1819–1827* (London: Society For Theatre Research).

New York Theatre Review (1896) Accessed online (9/11/2009) from Theatre Collection, Lincoln Center Library.

New York Tribune (1880) 'Labors of the Scene Painter' 27/12/1880.

New York Times (1896a) 'La Loie and Her Dances'; 25/2/1896 p. 5 Retrieved November 2, 2009 from ProQuest Historical Newspapers *New York Times* (1851–2006).

New York Times (1896b) 'La Loïe Talks of Her Art – Why She Does Not Think Much of Muslin-Twirling and Toe-kicking Imitators – Her Costumes.' article in *New York*

Times March 1st 1896. Retrieved 2/11/2009, from ProQuest Historical Newspapers *New York Times* (1851–2006).

New York Times (1908) 'Loie Fuller Tells of Her Many Adventures with the Serpentine Dance *New York Times* Review, 8/11/1908 p.SM11 (accessed online) 2/11/2009 from ProQuest Historical Newspapers, *The New York Times* (1851–2006).

Nicholl, Allardyce (1948) *The Development of the Theatre* 3rd edition (London: George G Harrap & Co. Ltd).

Nicholl, Allardyce (1957) *Stewart Masques and the Renaissance Stage* (London: Harrap & Co).

Nicholl, Allardyce (1966) *The Development of the Theatre*, 5th edition (London: George G Harrap & Co. Ltd.)

Nicholl, Allardyce (1980) *The Garrick Stage – Theatres and Audience in the Eighteenth Century* (Manchester: Manchester University Press).

Northen, Michael (1997) *Northen Lights: A Life Behind the Scenes* (Chichester: Summersdale Publishers).

Noverre, Jean-Georges (1760) *Lettres sur la danse* (Lyon: Aimé Delaroche) .

Oenslager, Donald (1975) *Stage Design: Four Centuries of Scenic Invention* (New York, London: Thames & Hudson).

Orrell, John (1988) *The Human Stage: English Theatre Design, 1567–1640* (New York, London: Thames & Hudson).

Ost, Geoffrey (1954) *Stage Lighting* (London: Herbert Jenkins).

Palmer, Richard H (1985) *The Lighting Art: The Aesthetics of Stage Lighting Design* (Englewood Cliffs, NJ: Prentice Hall).

Palmer, Richard H (1994) *The Lighting Art: The Aesthetics of Stage Lighting Design* 2nd edition (Englewood Cliffs, NJ: Prentice Hall).

Palmer, S and Popat, S (2006) 'Dancing in the Streets: The Sensuous Manifold as a Concept for Designing Experience' *International Journal of Performance Arts and Digital Media* 2(3) 297–314.

Patte, Pierre (1782) 'Essai sur l'architecture théâtrale' in Paul Corneilson 'Reconstructing the Mannheim court theatre' in *Early Music* February 1997, 63–81 (Oxford Journal Press).

Patterson, Michael (1981) *The Revolution in German Theatre 1900–1933* (London: Routledge & Kegan Paul).

Pavis, Patrice (2003) *Analysing Performance: Theater, Dance, and Film* trans. David Williams (Ann Arbor: University of Michigan Press).

Peacock, Kenneth (1988) 'Instruments to Perform Color-Music: Two Centuries of Technological Experimentation' *Leonardo, Journal of the International Society for the Arts, Sciences and Technology* 21(4), 397–406 [online] http://www.paulj.myzen.co.uk/blog/teaching/voices/files/2008/08/instrumentstoperformcolor.pdf.

Penzel, Frederick, I (1978) *Theatre Lighting before Electricity* (Middletown, CT: Wesleyan University Press).

Pichel, Irving (1925) *Modern Theatres* (New York: Harcourt, Brace & Company).

Pilbrow, Richard (1970) *Stage Lighting (1979)* 2nd edition (London: Cassell & Co).

Pilbrow, Richard (1997) *Stage Lighting Design: The Art, The Craft, The Life* (London: Nick Hern Books Ltd).

Piscator, Erwin (1941) 'The Theatre Can Belong to Our Century' in Bentley, Eric (ed.) *The Theory of the Modern Stage. (1997)* (New York: Applause) 471–473.

Popat, S and Palmer, S (2005) 'Creating Common Ground: Dialogues between Performance and Digital Technologies' *International Journal of Performance Arts and Digital Media* 1(1) 47–65.

Popat, S and Palmer, S (2008) 'Embodied Interfaces: Dancing with Digital Sprites' *Digital Creativity* 19(2) 125–137.

Pyne, W H (1823) *Wine and Walnuts* Vol. 1 (London: Longman, Hurst, Rees, Orme & Brown).

Rebellato, Dan (1999) *1956 and All That: Making of Modern British Drama* (London: Routledge).

Rees, Terence (1978) *Theatre Lighting in the Age of Gas* (London: The Society for Theatre Research).

Reid, Francis (1969) *Tabs* 27/3 (September) (London: Rank Strand Electric).

Reid, Francis (2005) *Yesterday's Lights: A Revolution Reported* (Cambridge: Entertainment Technology Press).

Richards, Jeffrey (ed.) (1994) *Sir Henry Irving – Theatre, Culture and Society – Essays, Addresses and Lectures* (Keele: Ryburn Publishing).

Ridge, Harold (1928) *Stage Lighting* (Cambridge: Heffer & Sons).

Ridge, Harold C and Aldred, F S (1936) *Stage Lighting Principles and Practice* (London: Sir Isaac Pitman & Sons Ltd).

Rimington, Wallace, A (1911) *Colour-Music, The Art of Mobile Colour* (London: Hutchinson & Co).

Rosenfield, S (1964) 'The Eidophusikon illustrated', in *Theatre Notebook* October 1963–July 1964 (The Society for Theatre Research).

Rosenfeld, Sybil (1974) *Alma-Tadema's Designs for Henry Irving's Coriolanus* (Heidelberg: Quelle & Myer).

Rosenthal, Jean and Wertenbaker, Lael (1972) *The Magic of Light: The Craft and Career of Jean Rosenthal, Pioneer in Lighting for the Modern Stage* (Boston: Little, Brown & Company).

Sabbattini, Nicoló (1637–1638) '*Manual for Constructing Theatrical Scenes and Machines* (Pratica di Fabricar Scene e Machine ne' Teatri) Ravenna, trans. McDowell, J (1958)' in Hewitt, B (ed.) *The Renaissance Stage* (Coral Gables, Fla: University of Miami Press).

Saxe-Wyndham, Henry (1906) *Annals of Covent Garden Theatre from 1732 to 1897* Vol II (London: Chatto & Windus).

Scamozzi, Vincenzo (1615) *Idea dell'architecttura universale* (Venice: Presso Lavtore) [online] http://books.google.co.uk/books?id=rUBPAAAAcAAJ &printsec=frontcover&dq=Scamozzi+Idea+dell'architettura+universale+ 1615&hl=en&sa=X&ei=X-0bUeWtJ-nJ0QX5koHgCw&ved=0CE8Q6AEwBQ #v=onepage&q&f=false.

Schechner, Richard (1995) *Environmental Theater* 2nd edition (New York: Applause).

Schechner, Richard (2002) *Performance Studies: An Introduction* (London and New York: Routledge).

Schivelbusch, Wolfgang (1995) *Disenchanted Night: The Industrialization of Light in the Nineteenth Century* trans. Angela Davies (Berkeley, Los Angeles: The University of California Press).

Schlemmer, Oskar, Moholy-Nagy, Laszlo and Molnár, Farkas (1961) *The Theatre of the Bauhaus* trans. Arthur S Wensinger (Middletown, CT: Wesleyan University Press).

Schweitzer, Corinne and Böhm (2000) 'A Gesamtkunstwerk in the Bauhaus style – The coloured lightplays of Ludwig Hirschfeld-Mack' Accompanying notes to film *Farben, Licht, Spiele by Ludwig Hirschfeld-Mack Reconstruction 2000* [online] http://www.mlab.at/falisp/farbenlichtspiele_aboutthemovie.html/ (accessed 20/10/2010).

Senelick, Lawrence (1997) *The Chekhov Theatre: A Century of the Plays in Performance* (Cambridge: Cambridge University Press).

Serlio, Sebastiano (1657 [1545]) *The Second Book Treating of Perspective* This second book of architecture made by Sebastian Serly, entreating of perspective, touching the superficies, translated out of Itallian into Dutch, and out of Dutch into English, London: printed by M[ary]. S[immons]. for Thomas Jenner at the south-entrance of the Royall Exchange, 1657.

Serlio, Sebastiano (1958 [1545]) "The Stage' in *The Second Book of Architecture'* in Hewitt, Barnard (ed.) *The Renaissance Stage: Documents of Serlio, Sabbattini and Furttenbach* (Coral Gables, Fla: University of Miami Press) 24–33.

Shevtsova, M (2001) 'Meditations on Space, the Theatre of Robert Wilson' accompanying programme for *A Dream Play* by August Strindberg, Barbican Theatre, London.

Skaftymov, A (1967) 'Principles of Structure in Chekhov's Plays' in Jackson, R L (ed.) *Chekhov: A Collection of Critical Essays* (Englewood Cliffs, NJ: Prentice Hall).

Skinner, Otis (1924) *Footlights and Spotlights: Recollections of My Life on the Stage* (Indianapolis: The Bobbs-Merrill Co).

Sokel, Walter H (1959) *The Writer in Extremis: Expressionism in Twentieth-Century German Literature* (Palo Alto, CA: Stanford University Press).

Sokel, Walter H (ed.) (1963) *An Anthology of German Expressionist Drama: A Prelude to the Absurd* (New York: Anchor Books).

Somi, di Leone (1565) *The Development of the Theatre* 5th edition, trans. in Nicholl, A (1966) (London: Harrap).

Sommer, Sally (1975) 'Loïe Fuller' *The Drama Review* 19(1) 53–67 (March) (MIT Press).

Stanislavski, Konstantin S (1967) *My Life in Art* trans. J J Robbins (London: Harmondsworth).

Stanislavski, K S (1983) *Rezhisserskie ekzemplyary K.S. Stanislavskogo* Vol. 3 (Moscow: Iskusstvo) trans. Allan.

Stanislavski, K S (1988) *Sobranie sochinemi v devyati tomakh* (Collected work in 9 volumes) (Moscow: Iskusstvo) 1988–1995.

States, Bert O (1985) *Great Reckonings in Little Rooms: On the Phenomenology of Theatre* (London, Berkeley and Los Angeles CA: University of California Press).

Stern, Ernst and Herald, Heinz (1919) *Reinhardt und seine Bühne: Bilder von der Arbeit des Deutschen Theaters* (Berlin: Verlag Dr. Eysler & Co).

Stern, Ernest (1951) *My Life, My Stage* trans. Edward Fitzgerald (London: Victor Gollancz Ltd).

Stoker, Bram (1911) 'Irving and Stage Lighting' *The Nineteenth Century and After – A Monthly Review* 69(CCCXI) 903–912 (London: Spottiswoode & Co. Ltd.) May, 1911.

Stone, George (ed.) (1962) *The London Stage, 1660–1800: A Calendar of Plays, Entertainments & Afterpieces, Together with Casts, Box-Receipts and Contemporary Comment*, 4(1) (Winchester Carbondale: Southern Illinois University Press).

The Strand Archive, http://www.strandarchive.co.uk/ (accessed 02/02/2010).

Strindberg 1888 (1980) 'Introduction to Miss Julie' in *Strindberg Plays 1* trans. Michael Meyer (London: Methuen).

Styan, J L (1981) *Modern Drama in Theory and Practice Volume 3: Expressionism and Epic Theatre* (Cambridge: Cambridge University Press).

Styan, J L (1982) *Max Reinhardt – Directors in Perspective Series* (Cambridge: Cambridge University Press).

The Sunday Record-Herald (1908) 'Memoirs of Loïe Fuller', Chicago 29/11/1908.

Svoboda, Josef (1993) *The Secret of Theatrical Space: The Memoirs of Josef Svoboda* (Edited and trans. J.M.Burian) (New York, Tonbridge: Applause Theatre Books).

Tabs (1937–1985) Strand Electric Ltd (London: The Rank Strand Organisation).

Terry, Ellen (1908) *The Story of My Life* (London: Hutchinson & Co).

Thomas, Russell (1944) 'Contemporary Taste in the Stage Decorations of London Theaters, 1770–1800' *Modern Philology* 42, 65–78.

Thomson, Peter and Sacks, Glendyr (eds.) (1994) *The Cambridge Companion to Brecht* (Cambridge: Cambridge University Press).

Trimingham, Melissa (2004) 'Oskar Schlemmer's Research Practice at the Dessau Bauhaus' *Theatre Research International* 29(2) 128–142.

Trimingham, Melissa (2009) *The Theatre of the Bauhaus: The Modern and Postmodern Stage of Oskar Schlemmer* (London, New York: Routledge).

Tufnell, Miranda and Crickmay, Chris (1990) *Body. Space, Image: Notes towards improvisation and performance* (London: Virago Press).

Turrell, James [online] interview with Egg: the arts show http://www.pbs.org/wnet/egg/flash/2152/2152.html (accessed 21/1/2010).

Ursic, Giorgio Ursini (ed.) (1998) *Josef Svoboda, Scenographer* (Paris: Union of the Theatres of Europe).

Vasari, Giorgio (1912 [1550]) *Vite de' più eccellenti architettori, pittori e scultori italiani Lives of the most eminent painters, sculptors and architects* trans. Gaston du C. de Vere (London: Macmillan and the Medici Society) 1912–1915.

Veltruský, Jiří (1964 [1940]) 'Man and Object in the Theater' in Garvin, Paul (ed.) *A Prague School Reader on Esthetics, Literary Structure and Style* (Washington: Georgetown University Press) 83–91.

Volbach, Walter Richard (1989) *Adolphe Appia: Essays, Scenarios, and Designs* (edited and with notes and commentary by Richard C. Beacham) (Ann Arbor, Michigan and London: UMI Research Press).

Wagner, Manfred (1999) *'The Nature of Light in the Theatre'*, in Max Keller, *Light Fantastic* (Munich: Prestel).

Wearing, J P (1976–1993) *The London Stage: A Calendar of Plays and Players 1890–1959*, (London and NJ: Methuen).

Weber, Carl and Munk, Erika (1967) *Brecht as Director TDR* 12(1) (Autumn) (MIT Press) 101–107.

Webster, John (1612) *The White Diuel, or, The Tragedy of Paulo Giordano Vrsini, Duke of Brachiano with the Life and Death of Vittoria Corombona the Famous Venetian Curtizan. Acted by the Queenes Maiesties Seruants*, London, Printed by N O for Thomas Archer, and are to be sold at his Shop in Popes head Pallace, neere the Royall Exchange.

Wickham, Glynne (1992) *A History of the Theatre* 2nd edition (London: Phaidon).

Willett, John (ed and trans.) (1964) *Brecht on Theatre: The Development of an Aesthetic* (London: Eyre Methuen).

Williams, Rollo Gillespie (1947) *The Technique of Stage Lighting* (London: Sir Isaac Pitman & Sons).

White, Christine (1999) 'The Changing Scenographic Aesthetic' *Scenography International* Issue 1, 7/10/1999 (University of Loughborough, online).

White, Martin (1998) *Renaissance Drama in Action: An Introduction to Aspects of Theatre Practice and Performance* (London, New York: Routledge).

Yeats, W B (1910) 'The Tragic Theatre' *The Mask* III (4–6).

Yeats, W B (1911) Letter to editor of *Evening Telegraph*, Dublin, 9/1/1911.

Zornitzer, Amy (1998) 'Loïe Fuller and the Futurists: Two Views: II. Revolutionaries of the Theatrical Experience: Fuller and the Futurists' *Dance Chronicle – Studies in Dance and the Related Arts* 21(1) 93–105.

Zorzi, E G and Sperenzi, M (2001) *Teatro e Spettacolo nella Firenze dei Medici* (Firenze: L S Olschkl).

Index